Who's Buying Food & Drink

Who's Buying Food & Drink

1st EDITION

Who spends how much
on food and alcohol,
at and away from home

BY MARCIA MOGELONSKY

New Strategist Publications, Inc.
P.O. Box 242, Ithaca, NY 14851
607 / 273-0913

ISBN 1-885070-04-7

Printed in the United States of America

For Sylvie and Michael

Contents

Chapter 4: Spending by Household Type

Chapter 5: Spending by Region

Chapter 6: Spending by Race and Hispanic Origin

Chapter 7: Spending by Education

Chapter 8: Spending by Number of Earners

Chapter 9: Spending by Occupation

Appendix: History and Description of the Consumer Expenditure Survey

Introduction

Food is both a necessity and an obsession. Americans are constantly on the look-out for food that will keep them healthy and make them slim. We want food with bold taste and a timid fat content. We want food that is safe and comforting. We are willing to try just about anything—from alligator to zhou (Asian rice porridge); at the same time, few are willing to give up the basics, whether white bread, hamburgers, chitterlings, or tortillas.

As the 20th century comes to a close, Americans are more interested in the food they eat than ever before. But information overload and nutritional confusion are influencing the way we prepare and eat food. For each food we are told to eat, there is a corresponding item we are urged to shun. First, butter was bad and margarine was better. Then margarine was bad and butter was better. Eggs have endured a similar rise and fall and just about every ethnic cuisine, in its transition from margins to mainstream, has been scrutinized, analyzed, and examined for health-worthiness. The food we consume at breakfast, lunch, and dinner, as well as the food we snack on and the food we eat on the run, are all subject to intense examination and banner headlines. Sorting through food myths has become a chore for many food shoppers, whether they read nutrition labels or not.

Food safety is another issue facing consumers. Product tampering was the major concern in the 1980s; in the 1990s, it's bacteria and germs we're obsessed with avoiding. A rash of deaths associated with food-borne pathogens has made people suspicious of the food they buy, both in restaurants and in supermarkets. Shoppers are no longer afraid to ask if a product is fresh, and they will look with suspicion at a food service worker who is not garbed in the requisite protective gear. Most of us can remember when the diner cook flipped hamburgers with a cigarette hanging out of his mouth and a dirty apron tucked into his waistband. The food back then may have had character, but in the 1990s we'd rather have cleanliness.

Food safety and nutrition are not the only factors governing food spending patterns. Since food is such an elemental component of daily life, the way people buy food—and the foods they buy—reveal the changing times. A growing dependence on fast foods, and a shift toward buying finished products rather than ingredients illustrates our need for convenience—one of the food industry's most popular buzzwords. The search for convenience—foods that will allow busy parents to throw a meal together fast enough for a family to actually eat together—lies behind increased spending on packaged and frozen prepared meals, pre-made salads, and oven-ready breads and desserts. Convenience is also important to singles, for whom cooking may be a necessary evil. And convenience is important to working single parents, who, like dual-income parents, must feed a family without the time to cook every dish themselves.

Personal tastes, ethnic traditions, and regional and seasonal availability of foods can influence food spending, as can age, economic status, or family composition. The tables that follow look at food spending from a variety of perspectives. Thus, it is possible to look at indexed per-capita food spending by race, average food spending in dollars by income, or total food spending by age. It is important to remember, however, that while each set of tables provides exhaustive information about one demographic segment—race, income, or age, for example—the people behind the numbers do not exist only in that universe. It may be necessary to look at more than one segment to get the best understanding of the numbers. Looking at food spending by age and region may give a clearer picture of spending patterns than looking at age or region alone, for example.

Eating Patterns

American households spent more than $450 billion on food in 1994. On a per capita basis, that's about $1,764 for every man, woman, and child in the country. Of that amount, the greatest share went to food at home—approximately $1,085 per capita. Spending on alcohol averaged $111 per capita, and spending on food away from home amounted to $679 per capita.

What do we spend the most on? On a per capita basis, for all households, spending is highest on "other foods consumed at home." This category includes sugar, fats and oils, packaged and prepared foods, candy, snack foods, and non-alcoholic beverages. Each person in this country spent $330 on "other foods" in 1994. We also spent a lot of money on meats, poultry, fish, and eggs—about $293 per person. We spent $175 per person on fruits and vegetables, both fresh and canned, and $171 per person on cereals and bakery products, including bread, rice, and pasta. Spending on dairy products, including milk, cheese, and ice cream, amounted to $116 per person in 1994.

Although the United States Department of Agriculture's (USDA) food pyramid encourages healthy eating, the typical American spends more each year on candy and chewing gum ($25) than on apples ($10). We spend more on potato chips, nuts, and other snacks ($30) than on lettuce and tomatoes ($14). And we spend more on beer ($55) than on milk ($48).

But all is not lost. The average American spends more on fresh vegetables ($54 per year) than on sugar and other sweets ($42) and more on fresh fruit ($53) than on cola ($36). America isn't just about averages, however, and the usefulness of the tables presented here lies in their ability to reveal how old and young, college graduates and high school drop-outs, retired and self-employed, high income and low income, singles and families, spend on food.

As an example, consider the following: on a per capita basis, the typical consumer (or "average American") spends $36 a year on ground beef. But spending on ground beef ranges from $29 per capita in households headed by a college graduate to $40 in single-person households with no earners. Spending on alcoholic beverages consumed at home is highest for single-person, one-earner households ($200) and lowest in single-parent households ($22). The average consumer spends $66 a year on alcoholic beverages consumed at home.

The Food Industry

The food industry is a multi-billion dollar enterprise. Like so many other industries today, it is experiencing structural changes at all points in the food chain, from the production of raw materials to the distribution of finished products. But the food industry is different from many others, because its output will only continue to grow. While it is possible for a food manufacturer or distributor to go out of business, it is impossible for people to stop eating. Nonetheless, there is little room for complacency in the food industry. Everyone may eat, but what they eat, where they eat, and where they buy food are important hot-button issues changing the face of food manufacturing and retailing.

In the battle for the American stomach, food industry analysts track how much Americans spend on food at home versus away from home. They argue about whether restaurants are taking business away from supermarkets, or whether supermarkets are regaining market share. One current industry statistic—that spending on food away from home approaches 50 percent of all food spending in the country—is a myth if one looks at households overall, according to Kenneth Partch, editor-in-chief of the major trade magazine, *Supermarket Business*. Partch claims food away from home accounts for a 38 percent share of food spending for most households, with the exceptions being those in the highest income brackets and those in the Northeast and West.

Those in the food service business tend to differ with Partch's analysis. Experts at Technomic, Inc., a Chicago-based food service consulting firm, have gone so far as to predict that in 1995 spending for food away from home will eclipse that for food at home. It is not surprising that agreement on this issue is difficult to find. There are many gray areas that can tilt the balance one way or the other. A chicken purchased raw in a supermarket and cooked at home, for example, is obviously "food at home," just as a cooked chicken purchased and consumed at a restaurant is "food away from home." But is a cooked chicken purchased at a supermarket and eaten on the run "food at home?" Is a precooked take-out bird purchased at a fast-food restaurant and eaten at home "food away from home?" The boundaries are not always clear.

The supermarket and food service industries are keeping a careful eye on this trend because the numbers—even if they don't agree to the decimal point—have been tilting toward a more equal distribution of market share since the end of the 1980s. In 1989, food at home accounted for 55.1 percent of total food spending; by 1994, that figure was 53.1 percent, according to the USDA. The Department of Commerce puts at-home spending at 52.6 percent in 1989 and 48.8 in 1994. Other sources, both governmental and private, divvy up the pie in different ways.

The Consumer Expenditure Survey data in this book can be used to determine market shares for food at home and away from home. They reveal spending patterns for any category of food at home as well as for breakfast, lunch, and dinner away from home.

About the Numbers

Who's Buying Food & Drink is based on data from the Bureau of Labor Statistics' Consumer Expenditure Survey, an ongoing, nationwide survey of household spending. The Consumer Expenditure Survey is an exhaustive compilation of household expenditures, including everything from big-ticket items such as homes and cars, to small purchases like laundry detergent and film. The survey collects more than 35,000 spending records from 25,000 U.S. households each year. It does not include expenditures by government, business, or institutions. Between data collection and publication, there is about a two-year lag. The data in this book are from the 1994 Consumer Expenditure Survey, unless otherwise noted.

The Consumer Expenditure Survey uses consumer units as its sampling unit. A "consumer unit" is defined by the Bureau of Labor Statistics as "a single person or group of persons in a sample household related by blood, marriage, adoption or other legal arrangement or who share responsibility for at least two out of three major types of expenses—food, housing, and other expenses." For convenience, consumer units are referred to as households in the text of this book. For more information about the Consumer Expenditure Survey and consumer units, see the appendix.

Chapter 1 of *Who's Buying Food & Drink* is devoted to summary food spending statistics for cross-tabulated consumer segments: age by income, age by region, region by income, and single-person consumer units by age. Chapters 2 through 9 present detailed food spending statistics organized by demographic segment (age, income, household type, and so on). For each demographic segment, tables show average spending, indexed spending, average per capita spending, indexed per capita spending, total (or aggregate) spending, and share of spending. The chapter on age also includes projections of total spending and spending shares to the year 2000 based on the shifting age structure of the population.

How to Use This Book

The data in this book reveal how American households allocate the dollars they spend on food. Average annual spending statistics are the starting point for all calculations in *Who's Buying Food & Drink*. The indexed spending tables reveal whether spending by households in a given segment is above or below the average for all households (or for all households in that segment), and by how much. The per capita spending tables adjust average spending for household size. The indexed per capita spending tables reveal the individual consumers who spend the most on food. The total (or aggregate) spending tables show the overall size of a particular market. The market share tables reveal how much of a market is controlled by a household segment. These four types of tables are described in detail below.

Average Spending Tables

The average spending tables report the average annual spending of households on each food category in 1994. The Consumer Expenditure Survey presents average spending data for all households in a segment; i.e., all households with incomes of $30,000 to $40,000, not just for purchasers of an item. When reviewing the spending data, it is important to remember that by including both purchasers and non-purchasers in the calculation of the average, the average spending amount is diluted for items that are not purchased universally. Married couples, for example, spent an average of $51 on coffee in 1994. Since not all married couples purchased coffee, this figure underestimates the amount spent on coffee by those who bought it. For items purchased by small numbers of consumers, then, the average spending tables are less important than the other types of spending tables in the book. For frequently purchased items—such as milk—the average spending tables give a more accurate account of actual spending.

The average spending tables are good for comparing spending levels among household segments. They can also be used to determine the market potential of any item in a sales area. For example, by multiplying the average amount families with children spend on restaurant dinners by the number of such families in an area, the potential market for kid-friendly, family-style restaurants can be estimated.

Indexed Spending Tables

The indexed spending tables compare the spending of each household segment with that of the average U.S. household. On some of the summary tables, such as age by income, the comparison is with the average within a household segment. An index of 100 is the average for all households. An index of 132 means that average spending for a household segment is 32 percent above the all-household average. An index of 68 indicates spending that is 32 percent below the average for all households. Indexed spending figures identify the best customers for a food category. Households with an index of 178 for sweet rolls, for example, are a strong market for this product. Those with an index below 100 are either a weaker or an underserved market.

The spending indexes can reveal hidden markets—household segments that have a high propensity to buy a particular product or service but which are overshadowed by larger household segments that account for a bigger share of the total market. For example, householders aged 55 to 64 spend much more than 35-to-44-year-olds on instant coffee, with spending indexes of 148 and 83, respectively. But the spending of the older age group has been overshadowed by the spending of the larger 35-to-44 age group. These younger adults accounted for 19 percent of total household spending on instant coffee in 1994, versus the 17 percent accounted for by 55-to-64-year-olds. Using the indexed spending tables, marketers can determine that older households are actually the biggest spenders on instant coffee and adjust their business strategy accordingly.

Per Capita Spending Tables

The per capita spending tables show how much households spend on each food category after dividing average spending by the number of people in the household segment. While average spending tables show which households are the big spenders, the per capita spending tables show which people spend the most.

Households that include the largest number of people (the middle-aged and married couples with children) typically spend more on food simply because there are more people to feed. By dividing average spending by the number of people in a household, larger households often turn out to spend less than average on a per capita basis. For example, households headed by 45-to-54-year-olds spend more than those younger or older on restaurant dinners ($817 per household in 1994). But after dividing this figure by the 2.8 people in households headed by 45-to-54-year-olds, the spending of this age group on restaurant dinners drops to $292 per capita, less than the $328 per capita spent on restaurant dinners by householders aged 55 to 64.

Indexed Per Capita Spending Tables

The indexed per capita spending tables compare the spending of each household segment with the spending of the average household, after adjusting for household size. An index of 100 is the per capita average for all households. An index of 125 means that per capita spending by households in the segment is 25 percent greater than per capita spending of the average household. An index of 75 means that per capita spending by the segment is 25 percent below the per capita spending of the average household.

The per capita spending indexes reveal who the best customers are for products and services. For example, while householders aged 35 to 44 are the biggest spenders on ice cream—spending 23 percent more than the average household—after dividing the spending of these households by the 3.2 people in them, their per capita spending on ice cream has an index of just 96—or 4 percent below average. In contrast, householders aged 65 to 74 spend 43 percent more per capita than the average household on ice cream, making this age group the best customers for ice cream. They may not account for the largest share of the ice cream market, but they have the greatest propensity to spend on ice cream.

By knowing who the best customers are for products and services, businesses can insure that the household segments most likely to buy their products are not overshadowed by the spending of households with more people in them.

Total Spending Tables

To produce the total spending tables, average spending figures are multiplied by the number of households in a segment. The result is the dollar size of the total household market and of each market segment. All totals are shown in thousands of dollars. To convert the numbers in the total spending tables to dollars, you must append "000" to the number. For example, households headed by people aged 45 to 54 spent approximately $5.3 billion ($5,284,286,000) on nonalcoholic beverages in 1994.

Total spending is projected for age groups to the year 2000. This calculation is done by multiplying the average spending figures of 1994 by the projected number of consumer units by age in 2000. These projections show that householders aged 45 to 54 will spend $6.4 billion on nonalcoholic beverages in 2000, an increase of $1.1 billion.

When comparing these total spending figures with total spending estimates from the Bureau of Economic Analysis or other agencies, keep in mind that the Consumer Expenditure Survey includes only household spending, not spending by businesses or institutions. Sales data may also differ from household spending totals because total sales figures for consumer products include the value of goods sold to industries, government, and foreign markets, which can be a significant proportion of sales.

Market Share Tables

The market share tables are produced by converting the total spending data to percentages. This makes it easier to see which household segments account for most of the spending on a food item. In 1994, for example, householders aged 45 to 54 accounted for 22 percent of total household spending on meals at restaurants. By 2000, householders in this age group will account for 25 percent of this market as the age group expands with aging baby boomers.

Spending by
Age and Income

Spending on food rises with income, regardless of age. In all age groups, the wealthiest households spend the most on food at home, food away from home, and alcoholic beverages.

In most age groups, household size increases with income, which is one reason why spending on food also rises with income. One exception to this rule is among households headed by 25-to-34-year-olds, where the largest households are in the $40,000-to-$49,999 income category. This income group spends above-average on many foods, but it spends less than its more affluent counterparts despite its greater household size.

The picture is different for households headed by people aged 65 or older. Within this age group, the middle-class spent the most on food at home. Perhaps this is because more affluent older households spend so much on food away from home—over $3,700 in 1994.

Age/Income: Under age 25
average spending

(average annual spending on food and alcoholic beverages by consumer units headed by persons under age 25, by before-tax income, 1993-94; complete income reporters only)

	complete income reporters, <25	under $20,000	$20,000 to $29,999	$30,000 to $39,999	$40,000 or more
Number of consumer units (in thousands, add 000's)	6,407	4,490	946	496	475
Average number of persons per cu	1.9	1.7	2.2	2.3	2.8
Average before-tax income of cu	$16,464	$8,607	$24,400	$33,599	$57,031
Average spending of cu, total	18,494	13,963	23,393	29,840	39,955
FOOD	**$2,820**	**$2,469**	**$3,295**	**$3,598**	**$4,438**
Food at home	**1,526**	**1,339**	**1,849**	**1,929**	**2,221**
Cereals and bakery products	236	208	274	297	375
Cereals and cereal products	106	98	115	130	150
Bakery products	129	110	159	166	225
Meats, poultry, fish, and eggs	394	368	442	483	451
Beef	122	117	122	167	135
Pork	87	81	97	119	82
Other meats	47	41	65	65	39
Poultry	69	65	74	69	89
Fish and seafood	49	46	58	39	-
Eggs	19	16	26	25	32
Dairy products	164	136	218	192	280
Fresh milk and cream	75	60	105	97	133
Other dairy products	89	76	113	95	146
Fruits and vegetables	216	187	279	282	281
Fresh fruits	56	47	80	71	77
Fresh vegetables	61	54	73	73	87
Processed fruits	57	47	78	86	63
Processed vegetables	42	40	48	51	54
Other food at home	517	441	636	675	834
Sugar and other sweets	55	48	65	73	78
Fats and oils	45	40	60	49	57
Miscellaneous foods	253	218	281	353	429
Nonalcoholic beverages	143	115	209	176	233
Food prepared by cu on out-of-town trips	21	18	21	-	37
Food away from home	**1,294**	**1,130**	**1,446**	**1,669**	**2,217**
Alcoholic beverages	**300**	**256**	**243**	**333**	**904**

Note: Expenditures listed for items in a given category may not add to the total for that category because the listing is incomplete. (-) means insufficient data.

Age/Income: *Under age 25*

indexed spending

(indexed average annual spending on food and alcoholic beverages by consumer units headed by persons under age 25, by before-tax income, 1993-94; complete income reporters only. Index definition: an index of 100 is the average for all consumer units under age 25; an index of 132 means that spending by consumer units under age 25 in the income group is 32 percent above the average for all consumer units under age 25; an index of 68 indicates that spending by consumer units under age 25 in the income group is 32 percent below the average for all consumer units under age 25)

	complete income reporters, <25	under $20,000	$20,000 to $29,999	$30,000 to $39,999	$40,000 or more
Number of consumer units (in thousands, add 000's)	*6,407*	*4,490*	*946*	*496*	*475*
Average before-tax income of cu	*100*	*52*	*148*	*204*	*346*
Average spending of cu, total	*100*	*76*	*126*	*161*	*216*
FOOD	**100**	**88**	**117**	**128**	**157**
Food at home	**100**	**88**	**121**	**126**	**146**
Cereals and bakery products	100	88	116	126	159
Cereals and cereal products	100	92	108	123	142
Bakery products	100	85	123	129	174
Meats, poultry, fish, and eggs	100	93	112	123	114
Beef	100	96	100	137	111
Pork	100	94	111	137	94
Other meats	100	88	138	138	83
Poultry	100	95	107	100	129
Fish and seafood	100	95	118	80	-
Eggs	100	86	137	132	168
Dairy products	100	83	133	117	171
Fresh milk and cream	100	80	140	129	177
Other dairy products	100	86	127	107	164
Fruits and vegetables	100	87	129	131	130
Fresh fruits	100	84	143	127	138
Fresh vegetables	100	88	120	120	143
Processed fruits	100	83	137	151	111
Processed vegetables	100	94	114	121	129
Other food at home	100	85	123	131	161
Sugar and other sweets	100	88	118	133	142
Fats and oils	100	89	133	109	127
Miscellaneous foods	100	86	111	140	170
Nonalcoholic beverages	100	80	146	123	163
Food prepared by cu on out-of-town trips	100	87	100	-	176
Food away from home	**100**	**87**	**112**	**129**	**171**
Alcoholic beverages	**100**	**85**	**81**	**111**	**301**

Note: (-) means insufficient data.

Age/Income: *Aged 25 to 34*
average spending

(average annual spending on food and alcoholic beverages by consumer units headed by persons aged 25 to 34, by before-tax income, 1993-94; complete income reporters only)

	complete income reporters, 25-34	under $20,000	$20,000 to $29,999	$30,000 to $39,999	$40,000 to $49,999	$50,000 to $69,999	$70,000 or more
Number of consumer units (in thousands, add 000's)	17,673	5,781	3,610	2,953	1,969	2,129	1,230
Average number of persons per cu	2.8	2.6	2.6	2.9	3.0	2.9	2.8
Average before-tax income of cu	$33,508	$11,495	$24,858	$34,435	$44,243	$57,694	$101,075
Average spending of cu, total	30,437	17,350	25,489	31,230	38,616	47,485	59,598
FOOD	**$4,304**	**$3,088**	**$3,732**	**$4,295**	**$4,799**	**$6,035**	**$6,926**
Food at home	**2,562**	**2,198**	**2,310**	**2,369**	**2,703**	**3,302**	**3,620**
Cereals and bakery products	401	328	363	365	463	509	572
Cereals and cereal products	161	142	153	150	172	196	203
Bakery products	240	186	210	215	290	313	368
Meats, poultry, fish, and eggs	653	628	645	576	623	751	838
Beef	212	216	224	180	196	236	231
Pork	130	128	138	100	133	136	161
Other meats	85	71	85	78	99	106	95
Poultry	121	104	106	114	107	175	183
Fish and seafood	76	79	66	71	60	69	136
Eggs	29	30	26	32	27	29	32
Dairy products	284	232	257	263	329	372	370
Fresh milk and cream	130	114	127	118	148	158	151
Other dairy products	153	118	130	145	181	214	220
Fruits and vegetables	395	303	330	372	418	504	715
Fresh fruits	114	90	92	106	118	130	233
Fresh vegetables	121	90	100	113	122	158	237
Processed fruits	89	60	69	90	100	124	166
Processed vegetables	71	63	68	63	78	92	78
Other food at home	829	706	715	794	871	1,166	1,125
Sugar and other sweets	115	143	82	92	99	170	124
Fats and oils	67	67	60	64	62	83	72
Miscellaneous foods	397	293	356	399	430	579	556
Nonalcoholic beverages	213	183	191	197	234	269	289
Food prepared by cu on out-of-town trips	37	19	26	41	45	65	85
Food away from home	**1,743**	**891**	**1,422**	**1,926**	**2,097**	**2,732**	**3,306**
Alcoholic beverages	**350**	**165**	**359**	**396**	**378**	**528**	**628**

Note: Expenditures listed for items in a given category may not add to the total for that category because the listing is incomplete.

indexed spending

(indexed average annual spending on food and alcoholic beverages by consumer units headed by persons aged 25 to 34, by before-tax income, 1993-94; complete income reporters only. Index definition: an index of 100 is the average for all consumer units aged 25 to 34; an index of 132 means that spending by consumer units aged 25 to 34 in the income group is 32 percent above the average for all consumer units aged 25 to 34; an index of 68 indicates that spending by consumer units aged 25 to 34 in the income group is 32 percent below the average for all consumer units aged 25 to 34)

	complete income reporters, 25-34	under $20,000	$20,000 to $29,999	$30,000 to $39,999	$40,000 to $49,999	$50,000 to $69,999	$70,000 or more
Number of consumer units (in thousands, add 000's)	17,673	5,781	3,610	2,953	1,969	2,129	1,230
Average before-tax income of cu	100	34	74	103	132	172	302
Average spending of cu, total	100	57	84	103	127	156	196
FOOD	**100**	**72**	**87**	**100**	**112**	**140**	**161**
Food at home	**100**	**86**	**90**	**92**	**106**	**129**	**141**
Cereals and bakery products	100	82	91	91	115	127	143
Cereals and cereal products	100	89	95	93	107	122	126
Bakery products	100	77	88	90	121	130	153
Meats, poultry, fish, and eggs	100	96	99	88	95	115	128
Beef	100	102	106	85	92	111	109
Pork	100	98	106	77	102	105	124
Other meats	100	83	100	92	116	125	112
Poultry	100	86	88	94	88	145	151
Fish and seafood	100	103	87	93	79	91	179
Eggs	100	104	90	110	93	100	110
Dairy products	100	82	90	93	116	131	130
Fresh milk and cream	100	88	98	91	114	122	116
Other dairy products	100	77	85	95	118	140	144
Fruits and vegetables	100	77	84	94	106	128	181
Fresh fruits	100	79	81	93	104	114	204
Fresh vegetables	100	74	83	93	101	131	196
Processed fruits	100	67	78	101	112	139	187
Processed vegetables	100	88	96	89	110	130	110
Other food at home	100	85	86	96	105	141	136
Sugar and other sweets	100	125	71	80	86	148	108
Fats and oils	100	100	90	96	93	124	107
Miscellaneous foods	100	74	90	101	108	146	140
Nonalcoholic beverages	100	86	90	92	110	126	136
Food prepared by cu on out-of-town trips	100	51	70	111	122	176	230
Food away from home	**100**	**51**	**82**	**110**	**120**	**157**	**190**
Alcoholic beverages	**100**	**47**	**103**	**113**	**108**	**151**	**179**

(average annual spending on food and alcoholic beverages by consumer units headed by persons aged 35 to 44, by before-tax income, 1993-94; complete income reporters only)

	complete income reporters, 35-44	under $20,000	$20,000 to $29,999	$30,000 to $39,999	$40,000 to $49,999	$50,000 to $69,999	$70,000 or more
Number of consumer units (in thousands, add 000's)	19,047	4,316	2,674	2,836	2,535	3,468	3,218
Average number of persons per cu	3.3	2.9	3.1	3.2	3.4	3.5	3.6
Average before-tax income of cu	$45,610	$11,190	$24,453	$34,504	$44,419	$58,340	$106,367
Average spending of cu, total	38,768	19,611	27,173	34,142	40,255	47,221	67,734
FOOD	**$5,578**	**$3,594**	**$4,581**	**$5,141**	**$5,698**	**$6,786**	**$7,984**
Food at home	**3,421**	**2,716**	**3,068**	**3,136**	**3,458**	**4,018**	**4,215**
Cereals and bakery products	555	410	454	498	593	661	731
Cereals and cereal products	216	184	177	185	219	250	277
Bakery products	339	227	277	314	374	411	454
Meats, poultry, fish, and eggs	909	828	955	833	859	1,012	974
Beef	294	249	332	289	272	330	298
Pork	186	191	199	176	171	196	176
Other meats	120	106	116	110	131	133	126
Poultry	171	157	171	139	163	198	194
Fish and seafood	105	87	106	83	91	119	146
Eggs	35	38	32	35	31	37	33
Dairy products	376	290	298	341	382	470	479
Fresh milk and cream	165	145	146	152	179	191	182
Other dairy products	211	145	152	189	203	279	297
Fruits and vegetables	520	420	435	452	537	623	663
Fresh fruits	156	126	135	128	168	185	199
Fresh vegetables	160	143	138	143	146	185	201
Processed fruits	111	83	86	94	120	144	141
Processed vegetables	93	68	76	86	104	108	122
Other food at home	1,061	768	925	1,013	1,087	1,253	1,367
Sugar and other sweets	138	104	132	139	128	157	172
Fats and oils	98	84	88	99	102	99	121
Miscellaneous foods	472	330	396	458	467	587	615
Nonalcoholic beverages	297	235	274	279	324	328	356
Food prepared by cu on out-of-town trips	55	19	34	38	67	82	104
Food away from home	**2,157**	**877**	**1,513**	**2,005**	**2,240**	**2,768**	**3,770**
Alcoholic beverages	**346**	**167**	**234**	**281**	**317**	**471**	**618**

Note: Expenditures listed for items in a given category may not add to the total for that category because the listing is incomplete.

Age/Income: *Aged 35 to 44*
indexed spending

(indexed average annual spending on food and alcoholic beverages by consumer units headed by persons aged 35 to 44, by before-tax income, 1993-94; complete income reporters only. Index definition: an index of 100 is the average for all consumer units aged 35 to 44; an index of 132 means that spending by consumer units aged 35 to 44 in the income group is 32 percent above the average for all consumer units aged 35 to 44; an index of 68 indicates that spending by consumer units aged 35 to 44 in the income group is 32 percent below the average for all consumer units aged 35 to 44)

	complete income reporters, 35-44	under $20,000	$20,000 to $29,999	$30,000 to $39,999	$40,000 to $49,999	$50,000 to $69,999	$70,000 or more
Number of consumer units (in thousands, add 000's)	19,047	4,316	2,674	2,836	2,535	3,468	3,218
Average before-tax income of cu	100	25	54	76	97	128	233
Average spending of cu, total	100	51	70	88	104	122	175
FOOD	100	64	82	92	102	122	143
Food at home	100	79	90	92	101	117	123
Cereals and bakery products	100	74	82	90	107	119	132
Cereals and cereal products	100	85	82	86	101	116	128
Bakery products	100	67	82	93	110	121	134
Meats, poultry, fish, and eggs	100	91	105	92	94	111	107
Beef	100	85	113	98	93	112	101
Pork	100	103	107	95	92	105	95
Other meats	100	89	97	92	109	111	105
Poultry	100	92	100	81	95	116	113
Fish and seafood	100	83	101	79	87	113	139
Eggs	100	107	91	100	89	106	94
Dairy products	100	77	79	91	102	125	127
Fresh milk and cream	100	88	88	92	108	116	110
Other dairy products	100	69	72	90	96	132	141
Fruits and vegetables	100	81	84	87	103	120	128
Fresh fruits	100	81	87	82	108	119	128
Fresh vegetables	100	89	86	89	91	116	126
Processed fruits	100	75	77	85	108	130	127
Processed vegetables	100	74	82	92	112	116	131
Other food at home	100	72	87	95	102	118	129
Sugar and other sweets	100	75	96	101	93	114	125
Fats and oils	100	86	90	101	104	101	123
Miscellaneous foods	100	70	84	97	99	124	130
Nonalcoholic beverages	100	79	92	94	109	110	120
Food prepared by cu on out-of-town trips	100	35	62	69	122	149	189
Food away from home	100	41	70	93	104	128	175
Alcoholic beverages	100	48	68	81	92	136	179

average spending

(average annual spending on food and alcoholic beverages by consumer units headed by persons aged 45 to 54, by before-tax income, 1993-94; complete income reporters only)

	complete income reporters, 45-54	under $20,000	$20,000 to $29,999	$30,000 to $39,999	$40,000 to $49,999	$50,000 to $69,999	$70,000 or more
Number of consumer units							
(in thousands, add 000's)	14,143	3,038	1,996	1,830	1,756	2,545	2,978
Average number of persons per cu	2.8	2.3	2.5	2.7	2.9	3.0	3.1
Average before-tax income of cu	$49,375	$10,737	$24,881	$34,658	$44,759	$58,799	$108,928
Average spending of cu, total	42,799	17,670	28,539	33,078	42,877	49,922	77,574
FOOD	$5,661	$3,061	$4,192	$4,953	$6,261	$6,293	$8,758
Food at home	3,260	2,258	2,706	3,116	3,701	3,623	4,152
Cereals and bakery products	510	338	380	490	573	584	678
Cereals and cereal products	186	133	142	168	230	204	236
Bakery products	324	205	238	322	343	380	442
Meats, poultry, fish, and eggs	878	718	797	863	986	886	1,027
Beef	276	229	256	261	348	259	317
Pork	181	155	173	183	197	191	193
Other meats	117	100	89	111	116	125	150
Poultry	165	124	155	161	192	163	201
Fish and seafood	104	75	86	114	96	118	134
Eggs	34	35	37	33	36	30	33
Dairy products	339	233	291	322	388	365	437
Fresh milk and cream	145	119	150	131	156	152	165
Other dairy products	194	114	141	191	232	213	271
Fruits and vegetables	519	351	416	482	541	615	682
Fresh fruits	164	107	129	144	143	220	221
Fresh vegetables	162	120	127	149	164	175	221
Processed fruits	108	66	79	103	127	126	145
Processed vegetables	85	58	81	86	107	94	94
Other food at home	1,015	618	822	959	1,214	1,174	1,328
Sugar and other sweets	127	85	106	151	158	143	140
Fats and oils	90	65	74	83	105	99	111
Miscellaneous foods	428	254	314	407	501	487	593
Nonalcoholic beverages	297	194	269	282	339	360	355
Food prepared by cu on out-of-town trips	73	32	59	36	110	84	130
Food away from home	2,401	803	1,486	1,837	2,560	2,670	4,606
Alcoholic beverages	314	128	177	269	326	340	581

Note: Expenditures listed for items in a given category may not add to the total for that category because the listing is incomplete.

(indexed average annual spending on food and alcoholic beverages by consumer units headed by persons aged 45 to 54, by before-tax income, 1993-94; complete income reporters only. Index definition: an index of 100 is the average for all consumer units aged 45 to 54; an index of 132 means that spending by consumer units aged 45 to 54 in the income group is 32 percent above the average for all consumer units aged 45 to 54; an index of 68 indicates that spending by consumer units aged 45 to 54 in the income group is 32 percent below the average for all consumer units aged 45 to 54)

	complete income reporters, 45-54	under $20,000	$20,000 to $29,999	$30,000 to $39,999	$40,000 to $49,999	$50,000 to $69,999	$70,000 or more
Number of consumer units							
(in thousands, add 000's)	14,143	3,038	1,996	1,830	1,756	2,545	2,978
Average before-tax income of cu	100	22	50	70	91	119	221
Average spending of cu, total	100	41	67	77	100	117	181
FOOD	**100**	**54**	**74**	**87**	**111**	**111**	**155**
Food at home	**100**	**69**	**83**	**96**	**114**	**111**	**127**
Cereals and bakery products	100	66	75	96	112	115	133
Cereals and cereal products	100	72	76	90	124	110	127
Bakery products	100	63	73	99	106	117	136
Meats, poultry, fish, and eggs	100	82	91	98	112	101	117
Beef	100	83	93	95	126	94	115
Pork	100	86	96	101	109	106	107
Other meats	100	86	76	95	99	107	128
Poultry	100	75	94	98	116	99	122
Fish and seafood	100	72	83	110	92	113	129
Eggs	100	104	109	97	106	88	97
Dairy products	100	69	86	95	114	108	129
Fresh milk and cream	100	82	103	90	108	105	114
Other dairy products	100	59	73	98	120	110	140
Fruits and vegetables	100	68	80	93	104	118	131
Fresh fruits	100	65	79	88	87	134	135
Fresh vegetables	100	74	78	92	101	108	136
Processed fruits	100	61	73	95	118	117	134
Processed vegetables	100	69	95	101	126	111	111
Other food at home	100	61	81	94	120	116	131
Sugar and other sweets	100	67	83	119	124	113	110
Fats and oils	100	73	82	92	117	110	123
Miscellaneous foods	100	59	73	95	117	114	139
Nonalcoholic beverages	100	65	91	95	114	121	120
Food prepared by cu on out-of-town trips	100	44	81	49	151	115	178
Food away from home	**100**	**33**	**62**	**77**	**107**	**111**	**192**
Alcoholic beverages	**100**	**41**	**56**	**86**	**104**	**108**	**185**

Age/Income: Aged 55 to 64
average spending

(average annual spending on food and alcoholic beverages by consumer units headed by persons aged 55 to 64, by before-tax income, 1993-94; complete income reporters only)

	complete income reporters, 55-64	under $20,000	$20,000 to $29,999	$30,000 to $39,999	$40,000 to $49,999	$50,000 to $69,999	$70,000 or more
Number of consumer units							
(in thousands, add 000's)	9,784	3,405	1,457	1,341	916	1,285	1,379
Average number of persons per cu	2.2	1.9	2.3	2.2	2.4	2.5	2.5
Average before-tax income of cu	$39,973	$10,497	$24,757	$34,504	$44,495	$58,788	$113,654
Average spending of cu, total	34,418	19,179	26,054	31,956	37,062	45,740	71,690
FOOD	$4,710	$3,100	$3,694	$4,727	$5,314	$6,130	$8,365
Food at home	2,920	2,229	2,662	2,948	3,080	3,525	4,325
Cereals and bakery products	444	335	383	453	457	556	690
Cereals and cereal products	148	114	149	164	146	136	236
Bakery products	296	220	234	288	312	420	454
Meats, poultry, fish, and eggs	820	652	739	772	885	994	1,188
Beef	253	180	219	263	356	322	336
Pork	182	184	147	148	165	217	236
Other meats	109	79	109	96	116	139	166
Poultry	139	107	139	130	135	156	209
Fish and seafood	105	72	93	100	79	129	208
Eggs	32	29	32	34	35	32	33
Dairy products	304	230	293	367	311	336	406
Fresh milk and cream	127	111	123	150	120	131	149
Other dairy products	177	119	170	218	191	205	257
Fruits and vegetables	480	344	468	486	460	568	773
Fresh fruits	151	96	149	154	146	189	252
Fresh vegetables	149	113	142	151	124	156	260
Processed fruits	93	71	86	98	92	109	140
Processed vegetables	88	62	91	84	99	114	121
Other food at home	872	669	778	870	967	1,071	1,268
Sugar and other sweets	121	97	117	123	119	150	163
Fats and oils	89	73	86	98	79	121	95
Miscellaneous foods	348	256	317	387	361	405	530
Nonalcoholic beverages	251	215	212	186	340	299	359
Food prepared by cu on out-of-town trips	62	33	45	75	67	96	121
Food away from home	1,790	871	1,032	1,780	2,234	2,604	4,039
Alcoholic beverages	302	175	206	292	300	456	612

Note: Expenditures listed for items in a given category may not add to the total for that category because the listing is incomplete.

Age/Income: *Aged 55 to 64*
indexed spending

(indexed average annual spending on food and alcoholic beverages by consumer units headed by persons aged 55 to 64, by before-tax income, 1993-94; complete income reporters only. Index definition: an index of 100 is the average for all consumer units aged 55 to 64; an index of 132 means that spending by consumer units aged 55 to 64 in the income group is 32 percent above the average for all consumer units aged 55 to 64; an index of 68 indicates that spending by consumer units aged 55 to 64 in the income group is 32 percent below the average for all consumer units aged 55 to 64)

	complete income reporters, 55-64	under $20,000	$20,000 to $29,999	$30,000 to $39,999	$40,000 to $49,999	$50,000 to $69,999	$70,000 or more
Number of consumer units (in thousands, add 000's)	9,784	3,405	1,457	1,341	916	1,285	1,379
Average before-tax income of cu	100	26	62	86	111	147	284
Average spending of cu, total	100	56	76	93	108	133	208
FOOD	**100**	**66**	**78**	**100**	**113**	**130**	**178**
Food at home	**100**	**76**	**91**	**101**	**105**	**121**	**148**
Cereals and bakery products	100	75	86	102	103	125	155
Cereals and cereal products	100	77	101	111	99	92	159
Bakery products	100	74	79	97	105	142	153
Meats, poultry, fish, and eggs	100	80	90	94	108	121	145
Beef	100	71	87	104	141	127	133
Pork	100	101	81	81	91	119	130
Other meats	100	72	100	88	106	128	152
Poultry	100	77	100	94	97	112	150
Fish and seafood	100	69	89	95	75	123	198
Eggs	100	91	100	106	109	100	103
Dairy products	100	76	96	121	102	111	134
Fresh milk and cream	100	88	97	118	94	103	117
Other dairy products	100	67	96	123	108	116	145
Fruits and vegetables	100	72	98	101	96	118	161
Fresh fruits	100	64	99	102	97	125	167
Fresh vegetables	100	76	95	101	83	105	174
Processed fruits	100	77	92	105	99	117	151
Processed vegetables	100	71	103	95	113	130	138
Other food at home	100	77	89	100	111	123	145
Sugar and other sweets	100	80	97	102	98	124	135
Fats and oils	100	82	97	110	89	136	107
Miscellaneous foods	100	74	91	111	104	116	152
Nonalcoholic beverages	100	86	84	74	135	119	143
Food prepared by cu on out-of-town trips	100	53	73	121	108	155	195
Food away from home	**100**	**49**	**58**	**99**	**125**	**145**	**226**
Alcoholic beverages	**100**	**58**	**68**	**97**	**99**	**151**	**203**

average spending

(average annual spending on food and alcoholic beverages by consumer units headed by persons aged 65 or older, by before-tax income, 1993-94; complete income reporters only)

	complete income reporters, 65+	under $20,000	$20,000 to $29,999	$30,000 to $39,999	$40,000 to $49,999	$50,000 to $69,999	$70,000 or more
Number of consumer units							
(in thousands, add 000's)	18,836	12,208	3,015	1,346	822	760	686
Average number of persons per cu	1.7	1.5	2.0	2.2	2.3	2.4	2.2
Average before-tax income of cu	$22,494	$10,999	$24,409	$34,379	$44,832	$57,986	$129,110
Average spending of cu, total	22,468	15,945	25,977	32,392	37,934	41,741	64,030
FOOD	$3,368	$2,585	$3,928	$4,633	$5,686	$5,871	$7,080
Food at home	2,361	2,008	2,773	3,003	3,595	3,070	3,370
Cereals and bakery products	386	329	447	499	613	489	508
Cereals and cereal products	131	116	141	177	196	158	151
Bakery products	255	212	306	322	417	330	357
Meats, poultry, fish, and eggs	589	515	698	741	834	643	796
Beef	164	139	202	200	251	172	242
Pork	139	125	181	161	145	131	173
Other meats	81	69	100	97	139	76	112
Poultry	101	91	94	124	162	137	144
Fish and seafood	75	61	92	131	108	94	95
Eggs	29	29	29	28	29	32	30
Dairy products	263	233	287	334	362	345	347
Fresh milk and cream	114	104	128	135	121	159	145
Other dairy products	149	129	158	199	241	186	203
Fruits and vegetables	452	376	531	534	727	715	718
Fresh fruits	147	117	180	191	259	230	236
Fresh vegetables	132	114	150	149	216	158	221
Processed fruits	98	79	123	109	149	185	166
Processed vegetables	74	65	77	86	102	142	95
Other food at home	672	556	810	895	1,060	878	1,001
Sugar and other sweets	100	89	104	126	142	126	154
Fats and oils	75	69	83	84	90	90	84
Miscellaneous foods	278	227	335	356	483	390	422
Nonalcoholic beverages	183	151	242	279	266	195	193
Food prepared by cu on out-of-town trips	36	23	46	51	79	77	148
Food away from home	1,008	577	1,155	1,630	2,091	2,801	3,710
Alcoholic beverages	166	103	223	254	368	359	419

Note: Expenditures listed for items in a given category may not add to the total for that category because the listing is incomplete.

Age and Income: *Aged 65 or older*

indexed spending

(indexed average annual spending on food and alcoholic beverages by consumer units headed by persons aged 65 or older, by before-tax income, 1993-94; complete income reporters only. Index definition: an index of 100 is the average for all consumer units aged 65 or older; an index of 132 means that spending by consumer units aged 65 or older in the income group is 32 percent above the average for all consumer units aged 65 or older; an index of 68 indicates that spending by consumer units aged 65 or older in the income group is 32 percent below the average for all consumer units aged 65 or older)

	complete income reporters, 65+	under $20,000	$20,000 to $29,999	$30,000 to $39,999	$40,000 to $49,999	$50,000 to $69,999	$70,000 or more
Number of consumer units (in thousands, add 000's)	*18,836*	*12,208*	*3,015*	*1,346*	*822*	*760*	*686*
Average before-tax income of cu	*100*	*49*	*109*	*153*	*199*	*258*	*574*
Average spending of cu, total	*100*	*71*	*116*	*144*	*169*	*186*	*285*
FOOD	**100**	**77**	**117**	**138**	**169**	**174**	**210**
Food at home	**100**	**85**	**117**	**127**	**152**	**130**	**143**
Cereals and bakery products	100	85	116	129	159	127	132
Cereals and cereal products	100	89	108	135	150	121	115
Bakery products	100	83	120	126	164	129	140
Meats, poultry, fish, and eggs	100	87	119	126	142	109	135
Beef	100	85	123	122	153	105	148
Pork	100	90	130	116	104	94	124
Other meats	100	85	123	120	172	94	138
Poultry	100	91	93	123	160	136	143
Fish and seafood	100	82	123	175	144	125	127
Eggs	100	101	100	97	100	110	103
Dairy products	100	88	109	127	138	131	132
Fresh milk and cream	100	91	112	118	106	139	127
Other dairy products	100	87	106	134	162	125	136
Fruits and vegetables	100	83	117	118	161	158	159
Fresh fruits	100	80	122	130	176	156	161
Fresh vegetables	100	86	114	113	164	120	167
Processed fruits	100	81	126	111	152	189	169
Processed vegetables	100	88	104	116	138	192	128
Other food at home	100	83	121	133	158	131	149
Sugar and other sweets	100	89	104	126	142	126	154
Fats and oils	100	92	111	112	120	120	112
Miscellaneous foods	100	82	121	128	174	140	152
Nonalcoholic beverages	100	83	132	152	145	107	105
Food prepared by cu on out-of-town trips	100	64	128	142	219	214	411
Food away from home	**100**	**57**	**115**	**162**	**207**	**278**	**368**
Alcoholic beverages	**100**	**62**	**134**	**153**	**222**	**216**	**252**

Spending by
Age and Region

In every age group, there are important regional variations in spending on food. Among households headed by the youngest adults, spending on food at home is highest in the West where, not surprisingly, household size is also the largest.

Among 25-to-34-year-olds, the biggest spenders are in the Northeast and West, where spending on food at home is 9 percent above average. Spending on poultry, fish and seafood, dairy products, and fruits and vegetables is above average for 25-to-34-year-olds in the Northeast, while Westerners spend more on fresh fruits and vegetables. The spending patterns of households headed by 35-to-44-year-olds are similar to those of the younger age group.

Households headed by 45-to-54-year-olds in the Northeast and West spend 7 percent more than average on food at home. But among households headed by 55-to-64-year-olds, spending on food at home is 14 percent above average in the Northeast, but 5 percent below average in the West. Spending on alcohol is 43 percent higher than average for this age group in the West and 38 percent above average in the Northeast.

Among households headed by people aged 65 or older, spending on food at home is highest in the West, at 9 percent above average. Northeasterners do not lag far behind, spending 7 percent above average.

(average annual spending on food and alcoholic beverages by consumer units headed by persons under age 25, by region, 1993-94)

	total consumer units < age 25	Northeast	Midwest	South	West
Number of consumer units (in thousands, add 000's)	7,605	1,354	2,220	2,505	1,527
Average number of persons per cu	1.9	1.7	1.9	2.0	2.1
Average before-tax income of cu	$16,464	$14,404	$14,393	$17,092	$19,889
Average spending of cu, total	17,937	14,780	16,521	18,351	21,972
FOOD	**$2,715**	**$2,357**	**$2,683**	**$2,689**	**$3,048**
Food at home	**1,482**	**1,274**	**1,468**	**1,427**	**1,735**
Cereals and bakery products	229	213	211	224	270
Cereals and cereal products	101	96	92	95	124
Bakery products	128	117	118	130	145
Meats, poultry, fish, and eggs	384	337	377	387	423
Beef	121	111	103	135	131
Pork	86	53	100	88	87
Other meats	46	38	52	42	51
Poultry	66	78	55	63	73
Fish and seafood	46	38	51	40	55
Eggs	19	18	15	18	26
Dairy products	161	133	161	151	200
Fresh milk and cream	74	58	77	68	91
Other dairy products	87	75	84	82	109
Fruits and vegetables	213	166	203	210	263
Fresh fruits	57	45	54	47	83
Fresh vegetables	60	47	58	63	69
Processed fruits	55	40	55	56	66
Processed vegetables	40	33	36	44	45
Other food at home	495	426	517	455	579
Sugar and other sweets	53	47	56	56	50
Fats and oils	43	34	40	45	52
Miscellaneous foods	242	197	254	209	309
Nonalcoholic beverages	137	132	148	129	141
Food prepared by cu on out-of-town trips	19	16	19	17	27
Food away from home	**1,233**	**1,083**	**1,215**	**1,262**	**1,313**
Alcoholic beverages	**275**	**280**	**333**	**243**	**246**

Note: Expenditures listed for items in a given category may not add to the total for that category because the listing is incomplete.

(indexed average annual spending on food and alcoholic beverages by consumer units under age 25, by region, 1993-94; index definition: an index of 100 is the average for all consumer units under age 25; an index of 132 means that spending by consumer units under age 25 in the region is 32 percent above the average for all consumer units under age 25; an index of 68 indicates that spending by consumer units under age 25 in the region is 32 percent below the average for all consumer units under age 25)

	total consumer units < age 25	Northeast	Midwest	South	West
Number of consumer units (in thousands, add 000's)	7,605	1,354	2,220	2,505	1,527
Average before-tax income of cu	100	87	87	104	121
Average spending of cu, total	100	82	92	102	122
FOOD	**100**	**87**	**99**	**99**	**112**
Food at home	**100**	**86**	**99**	**96**	**117**
Cereals and bakery products	100	93	92	98	118
Cereals and cereal products	100	95	91	94	123
Bakery products	100	91	92	102	113
Meats, poultry, fish, and eggs	100	88	98	101	110
Beef	100	92	85	112	108
Pork	100	62	116	102	101
Other meats	100	83	113	91	111
Poultry	100	118	83	95	111
Fish and seafood	100	83	111	87	120
Eggs	100	95	79	95	137
Dairy products	100	83	100	94	124
Fresh milk and cream	100	78	104	92	123
Other dairy products	100	86	97	94	125
Fruits and vegetables	100	78	95	99	123
Fresh fruits	100	79	95	82	146
Fresh vegetables	100	78	97	105	115
Processed fruits	100	73	100	102	120
Processed vegetables	100	83	90	110	113
Other food at home	100	86	104	92	117
Sugar and other sweets	100	89	106	106	94
Fats and oils	100	79	93	105	121
Miscellaneous foods	100	81	105	86	128
Nonalcoholic beverages	100	96	108	94	103
Food prepared by cu on out-of-town trips	100	84	100	89	142
Food away from home	**100**	**88**	**99**	**102**	**106**
Alcoholic beverages	**100**	**102**	**121**	**88**	**89**

(average annual spending on food and alcoholic beverages by consumer units headed by persons aged 25 to 34, by region, 1993-94)

	total consumer units aged 25-34	Northeast	Midwest	South	West
Number of consumer units (in thousands, add 000's)	20,342	3,701	5,009	7,186	4,447
Average number of persons per cu	2.8	2.7	2.8	2.7	2.9
Average before-tax income of cu	$33,508	$38,685	$33,243	$30,950	$33,670
Average spending of cu, total	29,541	30,810	29,147	28,100	31,250
FOOD	**$4,165**	**$4,402**	**$3,962**	**$4,032**	**$4,396**
Food at home	**2,487**	**2,721**	**2,359**	**2,312**	**2,710**
Cereals and bakery products	390	449	368	357	415
Cereals and cereal products	155	175	152	140	167
Bakery products	234	274	216	217	249
Meats, poultry, fish, and eggs	643	728	586	634	646
Beef	209	226	184	218	207
Pork	129	131	127	139	113
Other meats	82	84	93	74	81
Poultry	119	162	107	106	117
Fish and seafood	76	95	55	69	92
Eggs	28	30	19	29	36
Dairy products	272	318	266	240	292
Fresh milk and cream	124	136	129	109	133
Other dairy products	148	181	137	131	159
Fruits and vegetables	385	450	340	341	452
Fresh fruits	112	123	95	99	141
Fresh vegetables	116	141	106	94	141
Processed fruits	88	113	76	74	103
Processed vegetables	69	72	63	74	66
Other food at home	796	777	798	739	904
Sugar and other sweets	107	92	100	91	154
Fats and oils	66	73	57	65	71
Miscellaneous foods	383	375	394	356	422
Nonalcoholic beverages	205	197	213	197	215
Food prepared by cu on out-of-town trips	36	40	35	30	43
Food away from home	**1,678**	**1,681**	**1,602**	**1,721**	**1,686**
Alcoholic beverages	**327**	**382**	**303**	**299**	**351**

Note: Expenditures listed for items in a given category may not add to the total for that category because the listing is incomplete.

(indexed average annual spending on food and alcoholic beverages by consumer units aged 25 to 34, by region, 1993-94; index definition: an index of 100 is the average for all consumer units aged 25 to 34; an index of 132 means that spending by consumer units aged 25 to 34 in the region is 32 percent above the average for all consumer units aged 25 to 34; an index of 68 indicates that spending by consumer units aged 25 to 34 in the region is 32 percent below the average for all consumer units aged 25 to 34)

	total consumer units aged 25-34	Northeast	Midwest	South	West
Number of consumer units (in thousands, add 000's)	20,342	3,701	5,009	7,186	4,447
Average before-tax income of cu	100	115	99	92	100
Average spending of cu, total	100	104	99	95	106
FOOD	**100**	**106**	**95**	**97**	**106**
Food at home	**100**	**109**	**95**	**93**	**109**
Cereals and bakery products	100	115	94	92	106
Cereals and cereal products	100	113	98	90	108
Bakery products	100	117	92	93	106
Meats, poultry, fish, and eggs	100	113	91	99	100
Beef	100	108	88	104	99
Pork	100	102	98	108	88
Other meats	100	102	113	90	99
Poultry	100	136	90	89	98
Fish and seafood	100	125	72	91	121
Eggs	100	107	68	104	129
Dairy products	100	117	98	88	107
Fresh milk and cream	100	110	104	88	107
Other dairy products	100	122	93	89	107
Fruits and vegetables	100	117	88	89	117
Fresh fruits	100	110	85	88	126
Fresh vegetables	100	122	91	81	122
Processed fruits	100	128	86	84	117
Processed vegetables	100	104	91	107	96
Other food at home	100	98	100	93	114
Sugar and other sweets	100	86	93	85	144
Fats and oils	100	111	86	98	108
Miscellaneous foods	100	98	103	93	110
Nonalcoholic beverages	100	96	104	96	105
Food prepared by cu on out-of-town trips	100	111	97	83	119
Food away from home	**100**	**100**	**95**	**103**	**100**
Alcoholic beverages	**100**	**117**	**93**	**91**	**107**

average spending

(average annual spending on food and alcoholic beverages by consumer units headed by persons aged 35 to 44, by region, 1993-94)

	total consumer units aged 35-44	Northeast	Midwest	South	West
Number of consumer units (in thousands, add 000's)	22,242	4,569	5,328	7,402	4,943
Average number of persons per cu	3.3	3.3	3.3	3.2	3.3
Average before-tax income of cu	$45,610	$48,446	$42,919	$44,209	$47,675
Average spending of cu, total	37,510	38,219	35,750	36,285	40,576
FOOD	**$5,364**	**$5,661**	**$5,101**	**$5,174**	**$5,661**
Food at home	**3,336**	**3,519**	**3,178**	**3,116**	**3,669**
Cereals and bakery products	540	597	524	488	581
Cereals and cereal products	208	224	194	189	236
Bakery products	332	372	330	298	345
Meats, poultry, fish, and eggs	906	973	821	920	916
Beef	289	298	265	300	290
Pork	188	186	175	197	190
Other meats	117	128	122	109	114
Poultry	171	210	154	172	152
Fish and seafood	106	118	78	106	130
Eggs	34	33	28	36	40
Dairy products	364	392	362	311	420
Fresh milk and cream	161	158	165	140	189
Other dairy products	204	234	197	171	231
Fruits and vegetables	508	572	451	458	588
Fresh fruits	154	164	140	131	193
Fresh vegetables	155	182	120	142	188
Processed fruits	108	130	99	91	122
Processed vegetables	92	96	91	94	85
Other food at home	1,018	985	1,020	939	1,165
Sugar and other sweets	130	129	136	115	148
Fats and oils	96	97	88	95	106
Miscellaneous foods	455	428	460	410	541
Nonalcoholic beverages	284	281	287	273	300
Food prepared by cu on out-of-town trips	53	51	49	45	69
Food away from home	**2,027**	**2,142**	**1,923**	**2,059**	**1,992**
Alcoholic beverages	**310**	**320**	**292**	**281**	**363**

Note: Expenditures listed for items in a given category may not add to the total for that category because the listing is incomplete.

(indexed average annual spending on food and alcoholic beverages by consumer units aged 35 to 44, by region, 1993-94; index definition: an index of 100 is the average for all consumer units aged 35 to 44; an index of 132 means that spending by consumer units aged 35 to 44 in the region is 32 percent above the average for all consumer units aged 35 to 44; an index of 68 indicates that spending by consumer units aged 35 to 44 in the region is 32 percent below the average for all consumer units aged 35 to 44)

	total consumer units aged 35-44	Northeast	Midwest	South	West
Number of consumer units (in thousands, add 000's)	22,242	4,569	5,328	7,402	4,943
Average before-tax income of cu	100	106	94	97	105
Average spending of cu, total	100	102	95	97	108
FOOD	100	106	95	96	106
Food at home	100	105	95	93	110
Cereals and bakery products	100	111	97	90	108
Cereals and cereal products	100	108	93	91	113
Bakery products	100	112	99	90	104
Meats, poultry, fish, and eggs	100	107	91	102	101
Beef	100	103	92	104	100
Pork	100	99	93	105	101
Other meats	100	109	104	93	97
Poultry	100	123	90	101	89
Fish and seafood	100	111	74	100	123
Eggs	100	97	82	106	118
Dairy products	100	108	99	85	115
Fresh milk and cream	100	98	102	87	117
Other dairy products	100	115	97	84	113
Fruits and vegetables	100	113	89	90	116
Fresh fruits	100	106	91	85	125
Fresh vegetables	100	117	77	92	121
Processed fruits	100	120	92	84	113
Processed vegetables	100	104	99	102	92
Other food at home	100	97	100	92	114
Sugar and other sweets	100	99	105	88	114
Fats and oils	100	101	92	99	110
Miscellaneous foods	100	94	101	90	119
Nonalcoholic beverages	100	99	101	96	106
Food prepared by cu on out-of-town trips	100	96	92	85	130
Food away from home	100	106	95	102	98
Alcoholic beverages	100	103	94	91	117

average spending

(average annual spending on food and alcoholic beverages by consumer units headed by persons aged 45 to 54, by region, 1993-94)

	total consumer units aged 45-54	Northeast	Midwest	South	West
Number of consumer units (in thousands, add 000's)	17,322	3,401	4,400	5,709	3,813
Average number of persons per cu	2.8	2.8	2.8	2.6	2.9
Average before-tax income of cu	$49,375	$54,634	$48,037	$45,489	$51,765
Average spending of cu, total	41,238	42,719	40,567	38,091	45,352
FOOD	**$5,551**	**$6,058**	**$5,326**	**$5,320**	**$5,698**
Food at home	**3,266**	**3,499**	**2,972**	**3,190**	**3,505**
Cereals and bakery products	517	558	480	505	539
Cereals and cereal products	194	197	176	201	202
Bakery products	323	361	304	304	337
Meats, poultry, fish, and eggs	906	1,050	788	933	866
Beef	285	281	276	310	258
Pork	183	189	174	195	168
Other meats	120	141	112	113	119
Poultry	173	239	136	156	181
Fish and seafood	112	167	64	122	99
Eggs	34	34	26	36	41
Dairy products	336	371	314	312	365
Fresh milk and cream	142	140	142	137	152
Other dairy products	194	231	173	175	213
Fruits and vegetables	520	592	461	494	560
Fresh fruits	164	189	153	146	182
Fresh vegetables	161	197	131	153	174
Processed fruits	107	116	104	101	112
Processed vegetables	88	91	72	94	92
Other food at home	988	928	929	945	1,175
Sugar and other sweets	123	109	107	123	153
Fats and oils	91	96	79	92	100
Miscellaneous foods	418	404	397	400	483
Nonalcoholic beverages	289	260	293	283	321
Food prepared by cu on out-of-town trips	67	60	53	48	120
Food away from home	**2,285**	**2,558**	**2,355**	**2,130**	**2,193**
Alcoholic beverages	**292**	**365**	**283**	**240**	**317**

Note: Expenditures listed for items in a given category may not add to the total for that category because the listing is incomplete.

(indexed average annual spending on food and alcoholic beverages by consumer units aged 45 to 54, by region, 1993-94; index definition: an index of 100 is the average for all consumer units aged 45 to 54; an index of 132 means that spending by consumer units aged 45 to 54 in the region is 32 percent above the average for all consumer units aged 45 to 54; an index of 68 indicates that spending by consumer units aged 45 to 54 in the region is 32 percent below the average for all consumer units aged 45 to 54)

	total consumer units aged 45-54	Northeast	Midwest	South	West
Number of consumer units (in thousands, add 000's)	17,322	3,401	4,400	5,709	3,813
Average before-tax income of cu	100	111	97	92	105
Average spending of cu, total	100	104	98	92	110
FOOD	100	109	96	96	103
Food at home	100	107	91	98	107
Cereals and bakery products	100	108	93	98	104
Cereals and cereal products	100	102	91	104	104
Bakery products	100	112	94	94	104
Meats, poultry, fish, and eggs	100	116	87	103	96
Beef	100	99	97	109	91
Pork	100	103	95	107	92
Other meats	100	118	93	94	99
Poultry	100	138	79	90	105
Fish and seafood	100	149	57	109	88
Eggs	100	100	76	106	121
Dairy products	100	110	93	93	109
Fresh milk and cream	100	99	100	96	107
Other dairy products	100	119	89	90	110
Fruits and vegetables	100	114	89	95	108
Fresh fruits	100	115	93	89	111
Fresh vegetables	100	122	81	95	108
Processed fruits	100	108	97	94	105
Processed vegetables	100	103	82	107	105
Other food at home	100	94	94	96	119
Sugar and other sweets	100	89	87	100	124
Fats and oils	100	105	87	101	110
Miscellaneous foods	100	97	95	96	116
Nonalcoholic beverages	100	90	101	98	111
Food prepared by cu on out-of-town trips	100	90	79	72	179
Food away from home	100	112	103	93	96
Alcoholic beverages	100	125	97	82	109

average spending

(average annual spending on food and alcoholic beverages by consumer units headed by persons aged 55 to 64, by region, 1993-94)

	total consumer units aged 55-64	Northeast	Midwest	South	West
Number of consumer units (in thousands, add 000's)	11,938	2,464	2,858	4,166	2,449
Average number of persons per cu	2.2	2.3	2.0	2.3	2.3
Average before-tax income of cu	$39,973	$44,811	$36,817	$36,299	$44,484
Average spending of cu, total	33,339	34,681	30,686	32,239	36,819
FOOD	**$4,596**	**$5,106**	**$4,539**	**$4,389**	**$4,455**
Food at home	**2,819**	**3,221**	**2,777**	**2,670**	**2,671**
Cereals and bakery products	425	508	418	389	398
Cereals and cereal products	140	142	145	138	135
Bakery products	284	366	273	251	264
Meats, poultry, fish, and eggs	810	1,034	778	764	677
Beef	256	292	244	244	249
Pork	178	199	197	186	116
Other meats	105	132	117	86	93
Poultry	138	211	121	125	100
Fish and seafood	103	168	72	90	91
Eggs	31	33	28	32	28
Dairy products	289	328	277	271	291
Fresh milk and cream	120	128	119	121	111
Other dairy products	169	200	158	150	181
Fruits and vegetables	460	541	457	415	445
Fresh fruits	143	167	140	126	146
Fresh vegetables	144	174	134	133	141
Processed fruits	90	107	96	76	87
Processed vegetables	82	93	87	79	70
Other food at home	836	810	847	830	860
Sugar and other sweets	116	112	131	117	99
Fats and oils	84	85	85	89	75
Miscellaneous foods	334	312	320	316	406
Nonalcoholic beverages	243	231	248	252	232
Food prepared by cu on out-of-town trips	59	68	63	56	49
Food away from home	**1,777**	**1,885**	**1,762**	**1,719**	**1,784**
Alcoholic beverages	**292**	**403**	**204**	**211**	**417**

Note: Expenditures listed for items in a given category may not add to the total for that category because the listing is incomplete.

(indexed average annual spending on food and alcoholic beverages by consumer units aged 55 to 64, by region, 1993-94; index definition: an index of 100 is the average for all consumer units aged 55 to 64; an index of 132 means that spending by consumer units aged 55 to 64 in the region is 32 percent above the average for all consumer units aged 55 to 64; an index of 68 indicates that spending by consumer units aged 55 to 64 in the region is 32 percent below the average for all consumer units aged 55 to 64)

	total consumer units aged 55-64	Northeast	Midwest	South	West
Number of consumer units (in thousands, add 000's)	*11,938*	*2,464*	*2,858*	*4,166*	*2,449*
Average before-tax income of cu	*100*	*112*	*92*	*91*	*111*
Average spending of cu, total	*100*	*104*	*92*	*97*	*110*
FOOD	**100**	**111**	**99**	**95**	**97**
Food at home	**100**	**114**	**99**	**95**	**95**
Cereals and bakery products	100	120	98	92	94
Cereals and cereal products	100	101	104	99	96
Bakery products	100	129	96	88	93
Meats, poultry, fish, and eggs	100	128	96	94	84
Beef	100	114	95	95	97
Pork	100	112	111	104	65
Other meats	100	126	111	82	89
Poultry	100	153	88	91	72
Fish and seafood	100	163	70	87	88
Eggs	100	106	90	103	90
Dairy products	100	113	96	94	101
Fresh milk and cream	100	107	99	101	93
Other dairy products	100	118	93	89	107
Fruits and vegetables	100	118	99	90	97
Fresh fruits	100	117	98	88	102
Fresh vegetables	100	121	93	92	98
Processed fruits	100	119	107	84	97
Processed vegetables	100	113	106	96	85
Other food at home	100	97	101	99	103
Sugar and other sweets	100	97	113	101	85
Fats and oils	100	101	101	106	89
Miscellaneous foods	100	93	96	95	122
Nonalcoholic beverages	100	95	102	104	95
Food prepared by cu on out-of-town trips	100	115	107	95	83
Food away from home	**100**	**106**	**99**	**97**	**100**
Alcoholic beverages	**100**	**138**	**70**	**72**	**143**

Age/Region: *Aged 65 or older*
average spending

(average annual spending on food and alcoholic beverages by consumer units headed by persons aged 65 or older, by region, 1993-94)

	total consumer units aged 65 or older	Northeast	Midwest	South	West
Number of consumer units (in thousands, add 000's)	21,680	4,976	5,682	7,234	3,788
Average number of persons per cu	1.7	1.7	1.7	1.7	1.8
Average before-tax income of cu	$22,494	$22,383	$20,920	$19,238	$30,547
Average spending of cu, total	21,931	23,399	20,406	20,364	25,291
FOOD	**$3,247**	**$3,479**	**$3,072**	**$3,076**	**$3,545**
Food at home	**2,292**	**2,518**	**2,084**	**2,275**	**2,357**
Cereals and bakery products	371	412	362	346	383
Cereals and cereal products	126	128	118	127	136
Bakery products	245	284	243	219	248
Meats, poultry, fish, and eggs	590	700	520	607	528
Beef	173	194	166	173	157
Pork	135	130	127	162	105
Other meats	81	116	68	70	76
Poultry	103	126	80	106	99
Fish and seafood	71	107	52	67	62
Eggs	28	27	26	29	29
Dairy products	252	282	217	263	248
Fresh milk and cream	109	111	95	124	99
Other dairy products	143	171	122	138	149
Fruits and vegetables	433	494	393	418	442
Fresh fruits	140	174	123	128	145
Fresh vegetables	128	149	102	127	139
Processed fruits	94	103	100	84	91
Processed vegetables	72	68	67	79	67
Other food at home	646	630	592	641	756
Sugar and other sweets	94	94	87	93	109
Fats and oils	73	73	61	82	77
Miscellaneous foods	269	249	240	269	340
Nonalcoholic beverages	174	180	167	173	180
Food prepared by cu on out-of-town trips	35	35	37	25	50
Food away from home	**955**	**961**	**988**	**801**	**1,188**
Alcoholic beverages	**156**	**173**	**126**	**144**	**204**

Note: Expenditures listed for items in a given category may not add to the total for that category because the listing is incomplete.

Age/Region: *Aged 65 or older*
indexed spending

(indexed average annual spending on food and alcoholic beverages by consumer units aged 65 or older, by region, 1993-94; index definition: an index of 100 is the average for all consumer units aged 65 or older; an index of 132 means that spending by consumer units aged 65 or older in the region is 32 percent above the average for all consumer units aged 65 or older; an index of 68 indicates that spending by consumer units aged 65 or older in the region is 32 percent below the average for all consumer units aged 65 or older)

	total consumer units aged 65 or older	Northeast	Midwest	South	West
Number of consumer units (in thousands, add 000's)	21,680	4,976	5,682	7,234	3,788
Average before-tax income of cu	100	100	93	86	136
Average spending of cu, total	100	107	93	93	115
FOOD	**100**	**107**	**95**	**95**	**109**
Food at home	**100**	**110**	**91**	**99**	**103**
Cereals and bakery products	100	111	98	93	103
Cereals and cereal products	100	102	94	101	108
Bakery products	100	116	99	89	101
Meats, poultry, fish, and eggs	100	119	88	103	89
Beef	100	112	96	100	91
Pork	100	96	94	120	78
Other meats	100	143	84	86	94
Poultry	100	122	78	103	96
Fish and seafood	100	151	73	94	87
Eggs	100	96	93	104	104
Dairy products	100	112	86	104	98
Fresh milk and cream	100	102	87	114	91
Other dairy products	100	120	85	97	104
Fruits and vegetables	100	114	91	97	102
Fresh fruits	100	124	88	91	104
Fresh vegetables	100	116	80	99	109
Processed fruits	100	110	106	89	97
Processed vegetables	100	94	93	110	93
Other food at home	100	98	92	99	117
Sugar and other sweets	100	100	93	99	116
Fats and oils	100	100	84	112	105
Miscellaneous foods	100	93	89	100	126
Nonalcoholic beverages	100	103	96	99	103
Food prepared by cu on out-of-town trips	100	100	106	71	143
Food away from home	**100**	**101**	**103**	**84**	**124**
Alcoholic beverages	**100**	**111**	**81**	**92**	**131**

Spending by
Region and Income

In every region, spending on food rises with income. There are few exceptions to this rule.

In the West, the only categories in which the wealthiest households spend somewhat less than others are beef, pork, eggs, dairy products, sugar and other sweets, fats and oils, and nonalcoholic beverages. In none of these categories do the wealthiest household spend less than average, however.

In the South, the only item on which the wealthiest households spend less than average is eggs (3 percent below average).

In the Midwest, the wealthiest households spend more than average in every category, but spending on dairy products, processed fruits and vegetables, and sugar and other sweets is even higher for households with incomes between $50,000 and $69,999.

Northeasterners with incomes of $40,000 to $49,999 spend 35 percent more than average on processed vegetables, a slightly higher spending level than the most affluent households. Those with incomes between $50,000 and $69,999 spend more than other income groups on beef, pork, and sugar and other sweets. In all other categories, the wealthiest households spend the most.

(average annual spending on food and alcoholic beverages by consumer units in the Northeast, by before-tax income, 1993-94; complete income reporters only)

	Northeast, complete income reporters	under $20,000	$20,000 to $29,999	$30,000 to $39,999	$40,000 to $49,999	$50,000 to $69,999	$70,000 or more
Number of consumer units (in thousands, add 000's)	16,989	6,301	2,646	1,842	1,656	2,212	2,332
Average number of persons per cu	2.5	1.9	2.4	2.7	2.8	3.0	3.2
Average before-tax income of cu	$38,461	$10,838	$24,732	$34,617	$44,657	$58,148	$108,682
Average spending of cu, total	33,496	16,739	25,548	32,461	39,777	46,487	70,329
FOOD	$4,941	$2,945	$3,829	$4,999	$5,817	$6,489	$8,776
Food at home	3,063	2,194	2,589	3,060	3,514	4,017	4,408
Cereals and bakery products	506	366	400	501	570	682	744
Cereals and cereal products	175	144	145	162	182	215	246
Bakery products	331	222	254	339	388	468	498
Meats, poultry, fish, and eggs	846	645	733	822	937	1,125	1,138
Beef	244	182	241	234	268	346	293
Pork	159	134	132	153	178	214	187
Other meats	117	86	109	94	133	160	166
Poultry	176	132	136	178	215	225	245
Fish and seafood	120	83	87	133	113	147	209
Eggs	31	28	27	30	31	33	38
Dairy products	346	245	289	373	419	425	486
Fresh milk and cream	136	110	130	132	153	161	169
Other dairy products	210	135	159	241	266	265	317
Fruits and vegetables	520	379	430	493	609	676	760
Fresh fruits	159	117	140	149	180	198	236
Fresh vegetables	164	119	125	161	180	215	252
Processed fruits	113	81	95	102	135	155	161
Processed vegetables	84	62	70	80	113	108	112
Other food at home	845	559	737	871	979	1,108	1,280
Sugar and other sweets	111	79	87	125	122	159	148
Fats and oils	83	60	74	82	99	100	124
Miscellaneous foods	365	232	311	387	441	482	547
Nonalcoholic beverages	237	167	223	231	269	291	348
Food prepared by cu on out-of-town trips	49	20	43	46	48	75	113
Food away from home	1,878	751	1,240	1,939	2,302	2,473	4,368
Alcoholic beverages	341	159	230	442	321	498	673

Note: Expenditures listed for items in a given category may not add to the total for that category because the listing is incomplete.

Region/Income: *Northeast*
indexed spending

(indexed average annual spending on food and alcoholic beverages by consumer units in the Northeast, by before-tax income, 1993-94; index definition: an index of 100 is the average for all consumer units in the Northeast; an index of 132 means that spending by consumer units in the income group is 32 percent above the average for all consumer units in the Northeast; an index of 68 indicates that spending for that income group is 32 percent below the average for all consumer units in the Northeast)

	Northeast, complete income reporters	under $20,000	$20,000 to $29,999	$30,000 to $39,999	$40,000 to $49,999	$50,000 to $69,999	$70,000 or more
Number of consumer units							
(in thousands, add 000's)	16,989	6,301	2,646	1,842	1,656	2,212	2,332
Average before-tax income of cu	100	28	64	90	116	151	283
Average spending of cu, total	100	50	76	97	119	139	210
FOOD	100	60	77	101	118	131	178
Food at home	100	72	85	100	115	131	144
Cereals and bakery products	100	72	79	99	113	135	147
Cereals and cereal products	100	82	83	93	104	123	141
Bakery products	100	67	77	102	117	141	150
Meats, poultry, fish, and eggs	100	76	87	97	111	133	135
Beef	100	74	99	96	110	142	120
Pork	100	84	83	96	112	135	118
Other meats	100	74	93	80	114	137	142
Poultry	100	75	77	101	122	128	139
Fish and seafood	100	69	73	111	94	123	174
Eggs	100	92	87	97	100	106	123
Dairy products	100	71	84	108	121	123	140
Fresh milk and cream	100	81	96	97	113	118	124
Other dairy products	100	64	76	115	127	126	151
Fruits and vegetables	100	73	83	95	117	130	146
Fresh fruits	100	74	88	94	113	125	148
Fresh vegetables	100	72	76	98	110	131	154
Processed fruits	100	72	84	90	119	137	142
Processed vegetables	100	73	83	95	135	129	133
Other food at home	100	66	87	103	116	131	151
Sugar and other sweets	100	71	78	113	110	143	133
Fats and oils	100	72	89	99	119	120	149
Miscellaneous foods	100	64	85	106	121	132	150
Nonalcoholic beverages	100	71	94	97	114	123	147
Food prepared by cu on out-of-town trips	100	41	88	94	98	153	231
Food away from home	100	40	66	103	123	132	233
Alcoholic beverages	100	46	67	130	94	146	197

Region/Income: *Midwest*

average spending

(average annual spending of consumer units on food and alcoholic beverages by consumer units in the Midwest, by before-tax income, 1993-94; complete income reporters only)

	Midwest, complete income reporters	under $20,000	$20,000 to $29,999	$30,000 to $39,999	$40,000 to $49,999	$50,000 to $69,999	$70,000 or more
Number of consumer units							
(in thousands, add 000's)	21,125	8,428	3,375	2,887	2,008	2,644	1,783
Average number of persons per cu	2.5	1.9	2.4	2.8	3.0	3.2	3.1
Average before-tax income of cu	$33,638	$10,448	$24,558	$34,562	$44,596	$58,538	$109,638
Average spending of cu, total	30,129	16,500	25,881	31,015	38,427	46,885	66,402
FOOD	**$4,307**	**$2,742**	**$3,972**	**$4,280**	**$5,101**	**$6,640**	**$7,848**
Food at home	**2,631**	**1,912**	**2,562**	**2,637**	**3,065**	**3,686**	**4,001**
Cereals and bakery products	424	314	383	428	505	581	664
Cereals and cereal products	157	116	140	144	204	215	257
Bakery products	267	198	243	284	302	367	407
Meats, poultry, fish, and eggs	667	547	695	628	721	803	938
Beef	213	165	216	195	255	269	313
Pork	155	140	154	140	154	167	225
Other meats	98	73	112	109	118	121	117
Poultry	113	92	115	105	117	150	157
Fish and seafood	63	52	76	56	54	65	99
Eggs	25	25	23	24	24	30	26
Dairy products	287	200	274	297	332	436	427
Fresh milk and cream	131	95	132	147	162	180	168
Other dairy products	155	105	141	151	170	256	259
Fruits and vegetables	411	297	384	391	465	622	646
Fresh fruits	124	83	121	110	145	191	209
Fresh vegetables	114	90	106	106	114	145	195
Processed fruits	97	72	82	102	117	151	139
Processed vegetables	76	51	75	73	88	134	103
Other food at home	843	555	826	894	1,041	1,244	1,327
Sugar and other sweets	111	76	108	111	118	173	173
Fats and oils	73	60	65	78	77	94	103
Miscellaneous foods	372	232	380	408	451	564	588
Nonalcoholic beverages	242	166	232	255	313	340	371
Food prepared by cu on out-of-town trips	45	21	42	41	81	72	92
Food away from home	**1,676**	**830**	**1,410**	**1,643**	**2,036**	**2,954**	**3,847**
Alcoholic beverages	**269**	**148**	**250**	**283**	**378**	**409**	**510**

Note: Expenditures listed for items in a given category may not add to the total for that category because the listing is incomplete.

(indexed average annual spending on food and alcoholic beverages by consumer units in the Midwest, by before-tax income, 1993-94; index definition: an index of 100 is the average for all consumer units in the Midwest; an index of 132 means that spending by consumer units in the income group is 32 percent above the average for all consumer units in the Midwest; an index of 68 indicates that spending for that income group is 32 percent below the average for all consumer units in the Midwest)

	Midwest, complete income reporters	under $20,000	$20,000 to $29,999	$30,000 to $39,999	$40,000 to $49,999	$50,000 to $69,999	$70,000 or more
Number of consumer units							
(in thousands, add 000's)	21,125	8,428	3,375	2,887	2,008	2,644	1,783
Average before-tax income of cu	100	31	73	103	133	174	326
Average spending of cu, total	100	55	86	103	128	156	220
FOOD	100	64	92	99	118	154	182
Food at home	100	73	97	100	116	140	152
Cereals and bakery products	100	74	90	101	119	137	157
Cereals and cereal products	100	74	89	92	130	137	164
Bakery products	100	74	91	106	113	137	152
Meats, poultry, fish, and eggs	100	82	104	94	108	120	141
Beef	100	77	101	92	120	126	147
Pork	100	90	99	90	99	108	145
Other meats	100	74	114	111	120	123	119
Poultry	100	82	102	93	104	133	139
Fish and seafood	100	83	121	89	86	103	157
Eggs	100	101	92	96	96	120	104
Dairy products	100	70	95	103	116	152	149
Fresh milk and cream	100	73	101	112	124	137	128
Other dairy products	100	68	91	97	110	165	167
Fruits and vegetables	100	72	93	95	113	151	157
Fresh fruits	100	67	98	89	117	154	169
Fresh vegetables	100	79	93	93	100	127	171
Processed fruits	100	74	85	105	121	156	143
Processed vegetables	100	67	99	96	116	176	136
Other food at home	100	66	98	106	123	148	157
Sugar and other sweets	100	69	97	100	106	156	156
Fats and oils	100	82	89	107	105	129	141
Miscellaneous foods	100	62	102	110	121	152	158
Nonalcoholic beverages	100	68	96	105	129	140	153
Food prepared by cu on out-of-town trips	100	46	93	91	180	160	204
Food away from home	100	50	84	98	121	176	230
Alcoholic beverages	100	55	93	105	141	152	190

Region/Income: *South*
average spending

(average annual spending on food and alcoholic beverages by consumer units in the South, by before-tax income, 1993-94; complete income reporters only)

	South, complete income reporters	under $20,000	$20,000 to $29,999	$30,000 to $39,999	$40,000 to $49,999	$50,000 to $69,999	$70,000 or more
Number of consumer units (in thousands, add 000's)	28,502	11,798	4,870	3,477	2,574	3,011	2,773
Average number of persons per cu	2.5	2.1	2.5	2.7	2.8	2.9	3.0
Average before-tax income of cu	$33,188	$10,421	$24,546	$34,243	$44,408	$58,136	$106,474
Average spending of cu, total	30,438	16,383	26,282	32,604	38,646	46,165	69,803
FOOD	$4,281	$2,824	$3,789	$4,655	$5,335	$5,944	$7,912
Food at home	2,588	2,063	2,479	2,694	2,958	3,228	3,759
Cereals and bakery products	397	304	380	408	485	503	598
Cereals and cereal products	152	123	149	164	177	178	210
Bakery products	245	181	231	244	309	325	388
Meats, poultry, fish, and eggs	723	605	753	762	780	842	934
Beef	233	184	250	265	274	260	304
Pork	164	153	183	155	154	177	180
Other meats	86	71	79	90	102	103	114
Poultry	125	102	124	121	124	168	180
Fish and seafood	84	64	87	93	95	104	126
Eggs	31	30	31	37	31	30	30
Dairy products	269	222	248	275	302	329	392
Fresh milk and cream	123	109	121	125	125	142	160
Other dairy products	146	113	127	150	177	186	231
Fruits and vegetables	409	325	386	414	455	505	638
Fresh fruits	121	95	113	120	126	159	200
Fresh vegetables	125	100	117	130	138	144	200
Processed fruits	83	63	78	85	97	111	132
Processed vegetables	79	68	78	78	93	91	107
Other food at home	790	607	713	836	935	1,049	1,197
Sugar and other sweets	105	87	98	114	115	128	140
Fats and oils	80	76	78	78	75	88	101
Miscellaneous foods	340	250	291	370	402	473	548
Nonalcoholic beverages	225	178	216	229	292	276	309
Food prepared by cu on out-of-town trips	40	15	29	44	52	84	98
Food away from home	1,693	761	1,309	1,961	2,378	2,716	4,153
Alcoholic beverages	254	141	250	256	307	427	497

Note: Expenditures listed for items in a given category may not add to the total for that category because the listing is incomplete.

indexed spending

(indexed average annual spending on food and alcoholic beverages by consumer units in the South, by before-tax income, 1993-94; index definition: an index of 100 is the average for all consumer units in the South; an index of 132 means that spending by consumer units in the income group is 32 percent above the average for all consumer units in the South; an index of 68 indicates that spending for that income group is 32 percent below the average for all consumer units in the South)

	South, complete income reporters	under $20,000	$20,000 to $29,999	$30,000 to $39,999	$40,000 to $49,999	$50,000 to $69,999	$70,000 or more
Number of consumer units (in thousands, add 000's)	28,502	11,798	4,870	3,477	2,574	3,011	2,773
Average before-tax income of cu	100	31	74	103	134	175	321
Average spending of cu, total	100	54	86	107	127	152	229
FOOD	100	66	89	109	125	139	185
Food at home	100	80	96	104	114	125	145
Cereals and bakery products	100	77	96	103	122	127	151
Cereals and cereal products	100	81	98	108	116	117	138
Bakery products	100	74	94	100	126	133	158
Meats, poultry, fish, and eggs	100	84	104	105	108	116	129
Beef	100	79	107	114	118	112	130
Pork	100	94	112	95	94	108	110
Other meats	100	83	92	105	119	120	133
Poultry	100	82	99	97	99	134	144
Fish and seafood	100	76	104	111	113	124	150
Eggs	100	96	100	119	100	97	97
Dairy products	100	82	92	102	112	122	146
Fresh milk and cream	100	88	98	102	102	115	130
Other dairy products	100	78	87	103	121	127	158
Fruits and vegetables	100	79	94	101	111	123	156
Fresh fruits	100	79	93	99	104	131	165
Fresh vegetables	100	80	94	104	110	115	160
Processed fruits	100	75	94	102	117	134	159
Processed vegetables	100	86	99	99	118	115	135
Other food at home	100	77	90	106	118	133	152
Sugar and other sweets	100	83	93	109	110	122	133
Fats and oils	100	95	98	98	94	110	126
Miscellaneous foods	100	73	86	109	118	139	161
Nonalcoholic beverages	100	79	96	102	130	123	137
Food prepared by cu on out-of-town trips	100	38	73	110	130	210	245
Food away from home	100	45	77	116	140	160	245
Alcoholic beverages	100	55	98	101	121	168	196

(average annual spending on food and alcoholic beverages by consumer units in the West, by before-tax income, 1993-94; complete income reporters only)

	West, complete income reporters	under $20,000	$20,000 to $29,999	$30,000 to $39,999	$40,000 to $49,999	$50,000 to $69,999	$70,000 or more
Number of consumer units							
(in thousands, add 000's)	19,275	6,712	2,807	2,595	2,037	2,457	2,668
Average number of persons per cu	2.7	2.1	2.6	2.7	3.1	3.1	3.1
Average before-tax income of cu	$39,929	$11,448	$24,820	$34,500	$44,232	$58,581	$112,270
Average spending of cu, total	35,511	18,303	27,279	33,734	42,413	49,816	71,797
FOOD	$4,760	$3,034	$4,302	$4,841	$5,766	$6,438	$7,684
Food at home	2,959	2,180	2,885	2,962	3,500	3,757	4,084
Cereals and bakery products	465	324	431	463	591	605	678
Cereals and cereal products	183	135	167	196	227	226	252
Bakery products	281	189	263	267	364	379	425
Meats, poultry, fish, and eggs	700	539	726	695	803	845	917
Beef	218	169	226	226	273	255	266
Pork	136	105	157	140	157	161	159
Other meats	92	69	91	91	115	108	132
Poultry	126	90	122	119	154	159	183
Fish and seafood	91	73	89	84	67	123	141
Eggs	36	33	40	35	38	38	36
Dairy products	326	247	316	322	395	423	422
Fresh milk and cream	143	112	147	136	178	184	165
Other dairy products	183	135	168	186	218	239	257
Fruits and vegetables	492	365	494	483	529	602	729
Fresh fruits	160	116	160	161	169	199	238
Fresh vegetables	156	120	158	141	156	193	237
Processed fruits	102	70	105	101	115	124	160
Processed vegetables	74	58	72	80	89	85	94
Other food at home	977	704	920	998	1,182	1,281	1,338
Sugar and other sweets	138	131	116	136	145	162	152
Fats and oils	83	64	86	93	101	111	88
Miscellaneous foods	443	310	406	477	536	587	626
Nonalcoholic beverages	249	174	266	247	297	335	325
Food prepared by cu on out-of-town trips	64	26	47	46	104	88	148
Food away from home	1,801	853	1,416	1,879	2,265	2,681	3,600
Alcoholic beverages	342	182	285	300	457	467	691

Note: Expenditures listed for items in a given category may not add to the total for that category because the listing is incomplete.

(indexed average annual spending on food and alcoholic beverages by consumer units in the West, by before-tax income, 1993-94; index definition: an index of 100 is the average for all consumer units in the West; an index of 132 means that spending by consumer units in the income group is 32 percent above the average for all consumer units in the West; an index of 68 indicates that spending for that income group is 32 percent below the average for all consumer units in the West)

	West, complete income reporters	under $20,000	$20,000 to $29,999	$30,000 to $39,999	$40,000 to $49,999	$50,000 to $69,999	$70,000 or more
Number of consumer units							
(in thousands, add 000's)	19,275	6,712	2,807	2,595	2,037	2,457	2,668
Average before-tax income of cu	100	29	62	86	111	147	281
Average spending of cu, total	100	52	77	95	119	140	202
FOOD	100	64	90	102	121	135	161
Food at home	100	74	97	100	118	127	138
Cereals and bakery products	100	70	93	100	127	130	146
Cereals and cereal products	100	74	91	107	124	123	138
Bakery products	100	67	94	95	130	135	151
Meats, poultry, fish, and eggs	100	77	104	99	115	121	131
Beef	100	77	104	104	125	117	122
Pork	100	77	115	103	115	118	117
Other meats	100	75	99	99	125	117	143
Poultry	100	72	97	94	122	126	145
Fish and seafood	100	80	98	92	74	135	155
Eggs	100	91	111	97	106	106	100
Dairy products	100	76	97	99	121	130	129
Fresh milk and cream	100	78	103	95	124	129	115
Other dairy products	100	74	92	102	119	131	140
Fruits and vegetables	100	74	100	98	108	122	148
Fresh fruits	100	73	100	101	106	124	149
Fresh vegetables	100	77	101	90	100	124	152
Processed fruits	100	69	103	99	113	122	157
Processed vegetables	100	79	97	108	120	115	127
Other food at home	100	72	94	102	121	131	137
Sugar and other sweets	100	95	84	99	105	117	110
Fats and oils	100	77	104	112	122	134	106
Miscellaneous foods	100	70	92	108	121	133	141
Nonalcoholic beverages	100	70	107	99	119	135	131
Food prepared by cu on out-of-town trips	100	40	73	72	163	138	231
Food away from home	100	47	79	104	126	149	200
Alcoholic beverages	100	53	83	88	134	137	202

Spending by
Single Men by Age

Single men aged 25 to 34 spend more than those younger or older on food away from home and alcoholic beverages.

Their spending on food at home, however, is 11 percent below average. Spending on food at home is even lower for single men under age 25, who spend 12 percent less than the average single man on food overall and 35 percent less on food at home.

Single men aged 35 to 54 spend more than the average single man on food overall. Those aged 35 to 44 spend 21 percent more on food at home, while those aged 45 to 54 spend 18 percent more. Categories in which 35-to-44-year-olds spend the most include dairy products, fresh vegetables, fats and oils, miscellaneous foods (including snack foods), and nonalcoholic beverages. This age group spends about an average amount on food away from home, while its spending on alcoholic beverages is 12 percent above average. Single men aged 45 to 54 spend 40 percent more than the average single man on meat, poultry, fish, and eggs.

Single men aged 55 to 64 spend 8 percent more than the average single man on food at home, while those aged 65 and older spend 16 percent more. The oldest singles spend the most on cereals and bakery products, eggs, fresh fruits, and processed fruits and vegetables. Alcohol spending is slightly above average among single men aged 55 to 64 (9 percent), but drops to 47 percent below average among those aged 65 or older.

Single Men/Age
average spending

(average annual spending on food and alcoholic beverages by single-person consumer units headed by men, by age, 1993-94)

	total cu's headed by single men	under 25	25 to 34	35 to 44	45 to 54	55 to 64	65+
Number of consumer units							
(in thousands, add 000's)	12,455	2,147	3,047	2,159	1,634	1,099	2,368
Average before-tax income of cu	$23,525	$11,014	$25,848	$30,295	$33,058	$22,351	$19,580
Average spending of cu, total	20,343	13,764	22,376	24,553	24,540	19,150	17,455
FOOD	$2,670	$2,350	$2,751	$2,991	$2,990	$2,648	$2,356
Food at home	1,210	789	1,078	1,468	1,425	1,306	1,402
Cereals and bakery products	188	117	173	216	209	197	235
Cereals and cereal products	66	47	61	77	69	59	84
Bakery products	122	70	112	139	140	138	151
Meats, poultry, fish, and eggs	309	179	275	374	433	351	329
Beef	97	58	85	125	135	119	92
Pork	58	33	47	69	82	72	69
Other meats	45	24	40	46	56	53	59
Poultry	54	34	52	61	74	51	56
Fish and seafood	41	22	36	56	68	42	35
Eggs	15	9	15	16	17	15	19
Dairy products	127	87	104	170	129	149	149
Fresh milk and cream	58	42	45	74	63	73	66
Other dairy products	69	45	58	97	66	76	82
Fruits and vegetables	204	118	169	232	224	210	306
Fresh fruits	60	31	47	69	69	63	92
Fresh vegetables	55	28	45	74	54	73	70
Processed fruits	55	40	48	48	63	46	84
Processed vegetables	36	19	29	41	38	28	59
Other food at home	382	288	357	476	431	399	383
Sugar and other sweets	43	31	33	49	42	64	54
Fats and oils	30	24	20	41	36	40	34
Miscellaneous foods	167	124	160	213	180	149	176
Nonalcoholic beverages	112	87	115	133	130	119	98
Food prepared by cu on out-of-town trips	29	22	29	39	43	27	20
Food away from home	1,461	1,562	1,672	1,523	1,565	1,342	954
Alcoholic beverages	411	416	496	459	397	447	217

Note: Expenditures listed for items in a given category may not add to the total for that category because the listing is incomplete.

(indexed average annual spending on food and alcoholic beverages by single-person consumer units headed by men, by age, 1993-94; index definition: an index of 100 is the average for all single men; an index of 132 means that spending by single men in the age group is 32 percent above the average for all single men; an index of 68 indicates that spending by single men in the age group is 32 percent below the average for all single men)

	total cu's headed by single men	under 25	25 to 34	35 to 44	45 to 54	55 to 64	65+
Number of consumer units (in thousands, add 000's)	12,455	2,147	3,047	2,159	1,634	1,099	2,368
Average before-tax income of cu	100	47	110	129	141	95	83
Average spending of cu, total	100	68	110	121	121	94	86
FOOD	100	88	103	112	112	99	88
Food at home	100	65	89	121	118	108	116
Cereals and bakery products	100	62	92	115	111	105	125
Cereals and cereal products	100	71	92	117	105	89	127
Bakery products	100	57	92	114	115	113	124
Meats, poultry, fish, and eggs	100	58	89	121	140	114	106
Beef	100	60	88	129	139	123	95
Pork	100	57	81	119	141	124	119
Other meats	100	53	89	102	124	118	131
Poultry	100	63	96	113	137	94	104
Fish and seafood	100	54	88	137	166	102	85
Eggs	100	60	100	107	113	100	127
Dairy products	100	69	82	134	102	117	117
Fresh milk and cream	100	72	78	128	109	126	114
Other dairy products	100	65	84	141	96	110	119
Fruits and vegetables	100	58	83	114	110	103	150
Fresh fruits	100	52	78	115	115	105	153
Fresh vegetables	100	51	82	135	98	133	127
Processed fruits	100	73	87	87	115	84	153
Processed vegetables	100	53	81	114	106	78	164
Other food at home	100	75	93	125	113	104	100
Sugar and other sweets	100	72	77	114	98	149	126
Fats and oils	100	80	67	137	120	133	113
Miscellaneous foods	100	74	96	128	108	89	105
Nonalcoholic beverages	100	78	103	119	116	106	88
Food prepared by cu on out-of-town trips	100	76	100	134	148	93	69
Food away from home	100	107	114	104	107	92	65
Alcoholic beverages	100	101	121	112	97	109	53

Spending by

Single Women by Age

Women under age 25 who live alone spend the least on food at home—30 percent less than the average single woman. But this age group spends 33 percent more than the average single woman on alcoholic beverages.

Single women aged 25 to 34 spend 17 percent more than the average single woman on fresh vegetables. At the same time, they spend 22 percent more on sugar and other sweets, and 24 percent more on miscellaneous foods, which includes frozen meals, chips, and snack foods. These young singles spend 64 percent more than the average single woman on food away from home and 98 percent more on alcoholic beverages.

Single women aged 35 to 44 spend less on food at home than single men of the same age, and less than single women in any other age group except those under age 25. Women in this age group spend 40 percent more than the average single woman dining out. Alcoholic beverage spending is 72 percent above average for this age group.

Single women aged 45 to 54 spend 26 percent more than the average single woman on food, and 16 percent more on food at home. Spending on food at home falls with increasing age after the age of 54. Single women aged 55 to 64 spend 11 percent more than the average single woman on food at home, while those aged 65 or older spend only 7 percent more. Spending on food away from home also falls with age. Single women aged 45 to 54 spend 45 percent more than the average single woman on food away from home, while those aged 55 to 64 spend 6 percent more, and those aged 65 or older spend 41 percent less.

Single Women/Age
average spending

(average annual spending on food and alcoholic beverages by single-person consumer units headed by women, by age, 1993-94)

	total cu's headed by single women	under 25	25 to 34	35 to 44	45 to 54	55 to 64	65+
Number of consumer units							
(in thousands, add 000's)	*16,456*	*1,661*	*2,018*	*1,657*	*1,604*	*1,949*	*7,567*
Average before-tax income of cu	*$17,519*	*$9,351*	*$25,522*	*$29,679*	*$26,829*	*$18,019*	*$12,499*
Average spending of cu, total	*17,415*	*11,805*	*22,921*	*24,483*	*22,011*	*18,621*	*14,325*
FOOD	**$2,203**	**$1,537**	**$2,711**	**$2,393**	**$2,768**	**$2,408**	**$1,999**
Food at home	**1,449**	**716**	**1,475**	**1,338**	**1,674**	**1,611**	**1,552**
Cereals and bakery products	232	135	235	210	263	256	247
Cereals and cereal products	79	55	89	69	94	74	83
Bakery products	153	80	145	141	170	182	163
Meats, poultry, fish, and eggs	345	128	314	271	439	443	375
Beef	93	41	93	79	128	107	97
Pork	75	16	61	45	84	104	90
Other meats	42	14	32	31	68	40	49
Poultry	74	29	77	64	79	102	77
Fish and seafood	45	22	37	40	58	71	44
Eggs	16	7	14	12	23	19	18
Dairy products	160	98	147	157	164	146	184
Fresh milk and cream	65	32	51	55	68	64	80
Other dairy products	95	66	96	101	97	82	104
Fruits and vegetables	271	101	273	241	300	274	312
Fresh fruits	88	28	80	70	101	88	106
Fresh vegetables	86	34	101	71	88	92	95
Processed fruits	55	24	52	48	55	50	66
Processed vegetables	42	15	40	52	56	45	44
Other food at home	441	254	506	460	507	492	435
Sugar and other sweets	64	30	78	57	68	73	68
Fats and oils	45	16	41	37	46	41	55
Miscellaneous foods	189	111	235	205	218	206	181
Nonalcoholic beverages	121	77	123	135	148	146	116
Food prepared by cu on out-of-town trips	21	20	29	27	28	27	15
Food away from home	**754**	**821**	**1,236**	**1,054**	**1,094**	**797**	**447**
Alcoholic beverages	**129**	**172**	**256**	**222**	**137**	**133**	**58**

Note: Expenditures listed for items in a given category may not add to the total for that category because the listing is incomplete.

indexed spending

(indexed average annual spending on food and alcoholic beverages by single-person consumer units headed by women, by age, 1993-94; index definition: an index of 100 is the average for all single women; an index of 132 means that spending by single women in the age group is 32 percent above the average for all single women; an index of 68 indicates that spending by single women in the age group is 32 percent below the average for all single women)

	total cu's headed by single women	under 25	25 to 34	35 to 44	45 to 54	55 to 64	65+
Number of consumer units (in thousands, add 000's)	16,456	1,661	2,018	1,657	1,604	1,949	7,567
Average before-tax income of cu	100	53	146	169	153	103	71
Average spending of cu, total	100	68	132	141	126	107	82
FOOD	100	70	123	109	126	109	91
Food at home	100	49	102	92	116	111	107
Cereals and bakery products	100	58	101	91	113	110	106
Cereals and cereal products	100	70	113	87	119	94	105
Bakery products	100	52	95	92	111	119	107
Meats, poultry, fish, and eggs	100	37	91	79	127	128	109
Beef	100	44	100	85	138	115	104
Pork	100	21	81	60	112	139	120
Other meats	100	33	76	74	162	95	117
Poultry	100	39	104	86	107	138	104
Fish and seafood	100	49	82	89	129	158	98
Eggs	100	44	88	75	144	119	113
Dairy products	100	61	92	98	103	91	115
Fresh milk and cream	100	49	78	85	105	98	123
Other dairy products	100	69	101	106	102	86	109
Fruits and vegetables	100	37	101	89	111	101	115
Fresh fruits	100	32	91	80	115	100	120
Fresh vegetables	100	40	117	83	102	107	110
Processed fruits	100	44	95	87	100	91	120
Processed vegetables	100	36	95	124	133	107	105
Other food at home	100	58	115	104	115	112	99
Sugar and other sweets	100	47	122	89	106	114	106
Fats and oils	100	36	91	82	102	91	122
Miscellaneous foods	100	59	124	108	115	109	96
Nonalcoholic beverages	100	64	102	112	122	121	96
Food prepared by cu on out-of-town trips	100	95	138	129	133	129	71
Food away from home	100	109	164	140	145	106	59
Alcoholic beverages	100	133	198	172	106	103	45

Chapter 2

Spending by
Age

The baby-boom generation accounts for the biggest share of food spending in almost every category, and will continue to do so in the near future.

But older Americans spend more per capita on food in many categories. Households headed by people aged 55 to 64 or older spend the most per capita on all food (17 percent more than average). They also spend the most on alcohol (38 percent more than average) and on food away from home (22 percent above average).

The youngest households spend the least in most food categories. Among households headed by people under age 25, the only categories in which spending is much higher than average are away-from-home snacks and non-alcoholic beverages (35 percent above average and the highest spending among all age groups), meals as pay (178 percent above average, which is not surprising, considering the average age of food-service employment), and beer and ale consumed away from home (96 percent).

Households headed by 25-to-34-year-olds spend a lot more than average on baby food (98 percent more), and at-home beer and ale (41 percent more). The two youngest age groups together account for a 38 percent share of the beer-at-home market and a 40 percent share of the beer-away-from-home market. By 2000, they will account for somewhat less of the beer market, both at home and away from home. Human physiology being what it is, these youngest households will continue to corner the market on baby food.

Baby-boom households do not necessarily spend much more than average on food; it is their sheer number that guarantees their importance to the food industry. Younger boomers—households headed by 35-to-44-year-olds—spend 22 percent more than average on frozen fruit juices, 18 percent more on potato chips and other snacks, 15 percent more on non-carbonated fruit flavored drinks, and 94 percent more on school lunches. Households headed by 45-to-54-year-olds spend significantly more than average on some beef products, poultry, cheese, and snacks. But these two groups together account for an almost 50 percent share of spending on all food products, a 49 percent share of the food-at-home market, and just over 50 percent of food away from home. Their share of the alcoholic beverage market is about 42 percent. By 2000, families headed by 35-to-55 year olds will hold a more than 50 percent share of spending on all food products, both at home and away from home.

Despite the importance of the middle-aged to the food industry, supermarkets and restaurants should keep an eye on older consumers. For most food categories, it is older consumers who are the best customers, spending the most per capita on everything from bread to ice cream.

Age
average spending

(average annual spending of consumer units on food and alcoholic beverages, by age of consumer unit reference person, 1994)

	total consumer units	under 25	25 to 34	35 to 44	45 to 54	55 to 64	65 to 74	75+
Number of consumer units (in thousands, add 000's)	102,210	7,453	20,606	22,825	17,812	12,015	12,038	9,463
Average number of persons per cu	2.5	2.0	2.8	3.2	2.8	2.2	1.8	1.5
Average before-tax income of cu	$36,838.00	$16,407.00	$34,051.00	$46,217.00	$49,627.00	$41,884.00	$26,266.00	$20,736.00
Average spending of cu, total	31,750.63	18,417.73	30,465.86	37,587.69	41,443.60	33,702.18	25,093.18	19,305.61
Food, average spending	4,410.52	2,793.42	4,159.25	5,366.69	5,614.35	4,549.27	3,542.59	2,871.06
Alcoholic beverages, average spending	278.03	246.61	346.96	295.99	291.67	337.55	230.82	77.34
FOOD AT HOME	**$2,712.05**	**$1,616.60**	**$2,453.59**	**$3,336.05**	**$3,319.26**	**$2,733.25**	**$2,346.38**	**$2,111.91**
Cereals and bakery products	**428.68**	**250.28**	**387.40**	**535.66**	**511.68**	**414.08**	**385.25**	**346.39**
Cereals and cereal products	161.74	114.40	157.88	210.32	188.24	137.51	126.81	125.21
Flour	7.60	5.98	8.96	8.07	8.48	5.84	6.71	6.81
Prepared flour mixes	12.79	8.93	11.10	15.87	14.06	11.91	11.83	12.59
Ready-to-eat and cooked cereals	98.27	69.35	93.93	130.51	110.69	82.45	81.04	76.55
Rice	15.43	11.02	16.83	20.41	19.17	12.92	9.07	9.32
Pasta, cornmeal, other cereal products	27.65	19.12	27.05	35.47	35.85	24.39	18.16	19.94
Bakery products	266.93	135.89	229.52	325.34	323.43	276.58	258.44	221.17
Bread	76.22	41.00	67.14	87.07	91.60	80.80	75.52	68.40
White bread	37.65	23.16	35.78	46.07	41.81	37.81	35.34	29.68
Bread, other than white	38.57	17.84	31.37	40.99	49.79	42.99	40.18	38.72
Crackers and cookies	62.56	30.35	51.56	78.94	70.43	65.94	64.21	54.69
Cookies	42.97	20.44	36.41	54.33	48.79	44.07	43.20	37.52
Crackers	19.59	9.91	15.15	24.62	21.64	21.88	21.01	17.17
Frozen/refrigerated bakery products	21.56	12.01	20.72	25.52	28.37	19.89	19.42	15.15
Other bakery products	106.59	52.53	90.09	133.80	133.03	109.95	99.30	82.93
Biscuits and rolls	35.96	17.78	28.50	44.42	48.38	39.35	33.55	24.67
Cakes and cupcakes	31.19	17.77	27.45	41.00	37.04	35.38	27.18	17.28
Bread and cracker products	4.72	2.54	3.52	6.82	5.81	5.11	4.22	2.50
Sweetrolls, coffee cakes, doughnuts	21.92	7.93	18.18	24.61	29.03	17.51	24.30	25.44
Pies, tarts, turnovers	12.80	6.50	12.44	16.94	12.77	12.60	10.05	13.05
Meats, poultry, fish, and eggs	**732.45**	**429.33**	**650.42**	**918.57**	**935.68**	**772.86**	**596.33**	**500.06**
Beef	226.76	132.51	209.60	290.71	296.63	230.45	169.71	140.87
Ground beef	88.45	67.27	90.95	113.80	105.78	79.50	60.44	58.85
Roast	39.41	15.26	28.63	49.00	55.91	43.56	36.80	29.86
Chuck roast	12.26	6.07	9.86	14.33	13.27	15.84	11.49	12.59
Round roast	14.84	4.89	10.51	17.46	22.76	14.56	15.94	11.48
Other roast	12.31	4.30	8.27	17.22	19.88	13.16	9.38	5.79
Steak	84.75	45.11	78.84	104.59	121.02	96.15	58.45	41.26
Round steak	16.00	7.01	13.87	20.98	25.43	16.49	10.62	6.51
Sirloin steak	24.44	13.64	22.57	28.34	33.54	26.56	21.59	13.60
Other steak	44.31	24.46	42.40	55.28	62.05	53.10	26.24	21.14
Other beef	14.15	4.87	11.17	23.32	13.93	11.24	14.02	10.90
Pork	155.74	103.78	128.58	190.72	187.54	175.15	137.81	119.38
Bacon	22.78	15.36	18.27	25.21	26.05	24.36	20.84	27.96
Pork chops	39.32	26.43	38.17	50.44	50.41	41.94	25.16	22.48

	total consumer units	under 25	25 to 34	35 to 44	45 to 54	55 to 64	65 to 74	75+
Ham	$36.88	$20.74	$23.71	$45.31	$42.03	$44.44	$42.32	$33.40
Ham, not canned	34.16	18.67	21.95	41.37	40.79	41.89	39.37	28.45
Canned ham	2.72	2.07	1.76	3.94	1.23	2.55	2.95	4.95
Sausage	22.82	18.45	19.39	30.48	24.24	24.59	20.60	14.03
Other pork	33.93	22.80	29.04	39.27	44.81	39.83	28.90	21.51
Other meats	93.95	51.26	79.89	118.72	119.48	89.74	81.96	78.28
Frankfurters	18.76	14.06	16.59	24.17	21.22	18.45	13.80	17.19
Lunch meats (cold cuts)	65.66	35.23	55.26	82.16	85.10	63.84	58.34	52.78
Bologna, liverwurst, salami	23.73	16.15	20.79	29.74	28.79	22.16	20.81	19.18
Other lunchmeats	41.93	19.08	34.47	52.42	56.31	41.68	37.52	33.60
Lamb, organ meats and others	9.53	1.97	8.05	12.38	13.17	7.45	9.81	8.30
Lamb and organ meats	9.35	1.97	7.41	12.20	13.17	7.45	9.69	8.30
Mutton, goat and game	0.18	-	0.64	0.18	-	-	0.13	-
Poultry	136.58	69.95	124.03	175.35	182.81	141.51	101.27	88.12
Fresh and frozen chickens	107.89	60.44	101.88	139.65	144.05	110.30	72.75	66.14
Fresh and frozen whole chicken	29.56	12.34	25.51	38.08	38.65	34.20	21.40	21.87
Fresh and frozen chicken parts	78.33	48.10	76.38	101.57	105.40	76.10	51.35	44.27
Other poultry	28.69	9.51	22.14	35.70	38.76	31.21	28.52	21.98
Fish and seafood	89.43	49.81	81.07	108.57	114.48	106.88	74.44	50.06
Canned fish and seafood	15.03	6.59	13.09	18.67	15.91	17.63	15.45	12.40
Fresh fish and shellfish	51.26	31.96	46.13	63.08	66.81	67.57	33.92	26.04
Frozen fish and shellfish	23.15	11.27	21.85	26.82	31.76	21.68	25.08	11.61
Eggs	30.00	22.02	27.25	34.50	34.75	29.14	31.14	23.35
Dairy products	**288.92**	**180.36**	**261.01**	**360.38**	**338.21**	**272.43**	**257.43**	**248.04**
Fresh milk and cream	127.13	82.85	123.41	156.85	145.14	112.00	107.72	115.44
Fresh milk, all types	118.94	78.46	116.34	146.88	135.38	104.36	100.86	106.15
Cream	8.19	4.38	7.07	9.97	9.77	7.64	6.86	9.29
Other dairy products	161.79	97.51	137.59	203.54	193.07	160.44	149.71	132.60
Butter	11.65	6.80	10.99	13.66	17.42	10.86	9.14	6.64
Cheese	81.83	49.77	72.30	104.89	93.85	78.45	71.41	71.99
Ice cream and related products	47.64	26.21	37.79	58.47	56.15	52.21	48.98	39.11
Miscellaneous dairy products	20.66	14.73	16.51	26.52	25.64	18.92	20.18	14.87
Fruits and vegetables	**436.57**	**237.56**	**384.08**	**507.28**	**521.56**	**448.04**	**415.04**	**417.13**
Fresh fruits	133.02	66.34	113.77	149.84	163.72	133.90	133.56	135.96
Apples	25.37	12.39	24.55	33.02	30.89	24.94	20.35	17.54
Bananas	29.66	15.92	27.20	30.97	35.82	28.74	30.87	32.38
Oranges	16.36	11.33	16.16	17.00	22.25	16.32	14.68	11.51
Citrus fruits, excl. oranges	10.96	4.79	8.29	11.62	12.44	12.86	12.69	13.21
Other fresh fruits	50.67	21.91	37.57	57.23	62.32	51.04	54.97	61.31
Fresh vegetables	134.89	68.71	119.00	159.77	162.72	144.84	125.43	118.02
Potatoes	28.01	15.45	23.87	32.93	33.86	29.69	24.81	27.88
Lettuce	17.38	8.99	18.03	19.63	21.36	16.83	15.98	13.35
Tomatoes	21.01	11.25	20.03	25.52	24.53	21.83	18.34	17.10
Other fresh vegetables	68.50	33.03	57.07	81.69	82.97	76.49	66.31	59.69

	total consumer units	under 25	25 to 34	35 to 44	45 to 54	55 to 64	65 to 74	75+
Processed fruits	$93.08	$61.55	$83.37	$106.44	$108.73	$88.22	$87.15	$95.74
Frozen fruits and fruit juices	16.28	13.50	14.74	20.76	17.73	14.23	15.75	12.11
Frozen orange juice	9.49	8.92	8.59	11.07	10.47	7.83	9.66	8.31
Frozen fruits	1.60	0.41	1.43	1.58	1.42	2.94	2.12	0.94
Frozen fruit juices	5.19	4.16	4.71	8.11	5.84	3.46	3.97	2.86
Canned fruit	14.23	5.23	11.95	14.03	14.24	16.18	15.10	23.74
Dried fruit	5.89	1.91	3.43	5.59	8.03	6.17	8.20	8.21
Fresh fruit juices	17.90	10.21	16.95	19.81	25.19	17.08	14.71	14.39
Canned and bottled fruit juices	38.78	30.69	36.30	46.24	43.55	34.56	33.40	37.28
Processed vegetables	75.57	40.96	67.95	91.23	86.40	81.08	68.90	67.41
Frozen vegetables	24.83	13.62	21.76	33.87	27.22	27.74	21.24	16.54
Canned and dried vegetables and juices	50.74	27.34	46.19	57.37	59.17	53.34	47.66	50.88
Canned beans	10.44	8.13	8.80	11.85	11.74	10.53	9.78	11.12
Canned corn	6.81	5.06	6.89	8.24	7.89	5.62	4.26	7.69
Other canned and dried vegetables	27.05	11.97	24.53	30.58	31.87	29.80	26.09	26.38
Frozen vegetable juices	0.23	0.21	0.27	0.36	0.31	0.06	0.15	-
Fresh and canned vegetable juices	6.21	1.97	5.70	6.33	7.37	7.33	7.38	5.70
Other food at home	**825.43**	**519.07**	**770.68**	**1,014.15**	**1,012.13**	**825.84**	**692.32**	**600.29**
Sugar and other sweets	105.25	53.86	94.48	127.30	127.28	107.31	100.44	85.30
Candy and chewing gum	62.32	27.26	58.36	74.78	79.89	66.39	58.27	40.78
Sugar	18.31	12.81	17.68	23.26	21.99	15.16	16.23	12.84
Artificial sweeteners	3.39	1.03	1.65	3.42	3.92	2.70	4.97	6.96
Jams, preserves, other sweets	21.23	12.76	16.79	25.84	21.48	23.06	20.98	24.71
Fats and oils	79.25	50.14	66.94	95.56	90.96	75.90	75.50	80.55
Margarine	14.16	7.97	8.75	14.88	14.74	15.11	14.44	26.74
Fats and oils	23.09	14.76	22.56	26.81	27.48	20.74	21.59	19.75
Salad dressings	23.75	14.57	19.65	29.35	29.94	25.45	21.54	17.09
Nondairy cream and imitation milk	6.56	3.80	4.91	8.08	8.24	6.12	7.58	5.15
Peanut butter	11.70	9.04	11.07	16.45	10.57	8.47	10.35	11.83
Miscellaneous foods	361.62	248.13	366.51	462.21	424.56	328.24	281.41	246.75
Frozen prepared foods	66.14	35.12	61.55	77.10	86.77	65.14	51.56	60.89
Frozen meals	21.43	6.79	18.14	22.96	28.56	21.55	18.14	29.09
Other frozen prepared foods	44.71	28.33	43.42	54.14	58.20	43.58	33.43	31.80
Canned and packaged soups	29.55	19.48	26.67	35.14	32.10	30.92	27.64	27.40
Potato chips, nuts, and other snacks	74.07	40.37	66.77	104.04	95.10	66.37	60.08	38.71
Potato chips and other snacks	58.18	33.64	55.35	87.63	73.04	47.90	39.54	26.78
Nuts	15.89	6.73	11.43	16.42	22.06	18.47	20.53	11.93
Condiments and seasonings	79.74	57.16	71.03	104.00	96.50	76.56	66.29	52.67
Salt, spices and other seasonings	19.30	13.27	16.05	23.69	22.02	23.29	17.17	14.14
Olives, pickles, relishes	10.16	5.67	6.55	13.42	12.55	10.40	10.03	9.75
Sauces and gravies	36.43	26.96	36.50	49.39	45.12	31.23	25.84	18.85
Baking needs and misc. products	13.85	11.26	11.92	17.49	16.81	11.64	13.24	9.93
Other canned/packaged prepared foods	112.12	96.01	140.48	141.94	114.10	89.26	75.84	67.08
Prepared salads	10.97	3.83	7.53	14.00	13.80	12.57	13.27	7.34
Prepared desserts	7.99	3.68	6.29	9.14	8.97	7.59	9.21	9.78

	total consumer units	under 25	25 to 34	35 to 44	45 to 54	55 to 64	65 to 74	75+
Baby food	$28.11	$39.88	$62.41	$32.94	$17.32	$10.85	$5.00	$3.74
Miscellaneous prepared foods	65.05	48.61	64.26	85.86	74.01	58.24	48.38	46.21
Nonalcoholic beverages	232.89	148.22	206.56	279.78	296.67	258.80	189.21	164.36
Cola	89.45	65.02	83.04	113.08	117.44	95.20	67.36	41.13
Other carbonated drinks	38.89	30.72	37.82	47.06	44.94	43.58	29.55	24.67
Coffee	43.01	14.65	28.50	41.32	58.19	63.36	43.78	49.51
Roasted coffee	29.13	9.72	19.83	29.82	40.68	42.80	26.93	29.70
Instant and freeze-dried coffee	13.88	4.93	8.67	11.51	17.51	20.56	16.85	19.81
Noncarb. fruit flavored drinks incl. non-frozen lemonade	21.86	14.34	18.83	32.31	27.49	15.94	16.53	14.54
Tea	16.25	6.72	15.51	18.02	23.89	15.29	15.94	9.99
Nonalcoholic beer	0.66	-	0.61	0.63	0.26	1.21	1.18	0.78
Other nonalcoholic beverages	22.77	16.76	22.26	27.35	24.46	24.22	14.88	23.74
Food prepared by cu on out-of-town trips	46.41	18.72	36.19	49.30	72.66	55.58	45.75	23.32
FOOD AWAY FROM HOME	**1,698.46**	**1,176.82**	**1,705.67**	**2,030.64**	**2,295.08**	**1,816.01**	**1,196.21**	**759.14**
Meals at restaurants, carry-outs, other	**1,306.21**	**951.21**	**1,414.98**	**1,589.57**	**1,629.75**	**1,340.52**	**922.97**	**600.55**
Lunch	451.76	304.78	498.87	595.07	563.23	414.03	262.39	237.89
Dinner	651.79	480.17	692.30	746.26	816.60	722.04	521.68	283.17
Snacks and nonalcoholic beverages	101.72	110.23	125.40	135.93	122.75	79.17	51.34	20.17
Breakfast and brunch	100.95	56.03	98.40	112.32	127.16	125.27	87.56	59.32
Board (including at school)	**50.72**	**68.57**	**6.47**	**36.25**	**153.10**	**63.72**	**4.42**	**17.55**
Catered affairs	**56.09**	**10.45**	**41.90**	**38.27**	**139.06**	**82.82**	**26.08**	**14.02**
Food on out-of-town trips	**207.89**	**90.83**	**157.97**	**213.92**	**284.02**	**284.93**	**232.66**	**121.62**
School lunches	**53.76**	**2.76**	**46.56**	**133.68**	**68.90**	**12.19**	**5.16**	**2.96**
Meals as pay	**23.79**	**53.00**	**37.79**	**18.95**	**20.25**	**31.83**	**4.92**	**2.44**
ALCOHOLIC BEVERAGES	**278.03**	**246.61**	**346.96**	**295.99**	**291.67**	**337.55**	**230.82**	**77.34**
At home	**165.13**	**120.33**	**208.87**	**183.64**	**173.89**	**191.19**	**142.74**	**47.28**
Beer and ale	99.68	89.21	157.51	112.23	95.20	87.63	66.78	20.89
Whiskey	13.68	6.18	9.68	9.01	10.85	29.23	25.82	9.36
Wine	36.41	16.80	27.76	45.29	48.20	52.88	34.58	11.96
Other alcoholic beverages	15.35	8.14	13.92	17.10	19.64	21.45	15.56	5.06
Away from home	**112.91**	**126.28**	**138.10**	**112.35**	**117.78**	**146.36**	**88.09**	**30.06**
Beer and ale	38.56	60.55	54.85	36.65	36.17	45.98	21.95	6.07
Wine	15.79	14.68	18.36	16.36	17.09	23.25	11.77	3.55
Other alcoholic beverages	27.96	28.26	31.67	28.57	29.51	43.51	21.13	5.16
Alcoholic beverages purchased on trips	30.61	22.79	33.21	30.76	35.01	33.62	33.24	15.28

Note: Expenditures listed for items in a given category may not add to the total for that category because the listing is incomplete. (-) means insufficient data.

Age
indexed spending

(indexed average annual spending of consumer units on food and alcoholic beverages, by age of consumer unit reference person, 1994; index definition: an index of 100 is the average for all consumer units; an index of 132 means that spending by consumer units in the age group is 32 percent above the average for all consumer units; an index of 68 indicates that spending by the age group is 32 percent below the average for all consumer units)

	total consumer units	under 25	25 to 34	35 to 44	45 to 54	55 to 64	65 to 74	75+
Average spending of cu, total	*$31,750.63*	*$18,417.73*	*$30,465.86*	*$37,587.69*	*$41,443.60*	*$33,702.18*	*$25,093.18*	*$19,305.61*
Average spending of cu, index	*100*	*58*	*96*	*118*	*131*	*106*	*79*	*61*
Food, spending index	*100*	*63*	*94*	*122*	*127*	*103*	*80*	*65*
Alcoholic beverages, spending index	*100*	*89*	*125*	*106*	*105*	*121*	*83*	*28*
FOOD AT HOME	**100**	**60**	**90**	**123**	**122**	**101**	**87**	**78**
Cereals and bakery products	**100**	**58**	**90**	**125**	**119**	**97**	**90**	**81**
Cereals and cereal products	100	71	98	130	116	85	78	77
Flour	100	79	118	106	112	77	88	90
Prepared flour mixes	100	70	87	124	110	93	92	98
Ready-to-eat and cooked cereals	100	71	96	133	113	84	82	78
Rice	100	71	109	132	124	84	59	60
Pasta, cornmeal, and other cereal products	100	69	98	128	130	88	66	72
Bakery products	100	51	86	122	121	104	97	83
Bread	100	54	88	114	120	106	99	90
White bread	100	62	95	122	111	100	94	79
Bread, other than white	100	46	81	106	129	111	104	100
Crackers and cookies	100	49	82	126	113	105	103	87
Cookies	100	48	85	126	114	103	101	87
Crackers	100	51	77	126	110	112	107	88
Frozen/refrigerated bakery products	100	56	96	118	132	92	90	70
Other bakery products	100	49	85	126	125	103	93	78
Biscuits and rolls	100	49	79	124	135	109	93	69
Cakes and cupcakes	100	57	88	131	119	113	87	55
Bread and cracker products	100	54	75	144	123	108	89	53
Sweetrolls, coffee cakes, doughnuts	100	36	83	112	132	80	111	116
Pies, tarts, turnovers	100	51	97	132	100	98	79	102
Meats, poultry, fish, and eggs	**100**	**59**	**89**	**125**	**128**	**106**	**81**	**68**
Beef	100	58	92	128	131	102	75	62
Ground beef	100	76	103	129	120	90	68	67
Roast	100	39	73	124	142	111	93	76
Chuck roast	100	50	80	117	108	129	94	103
Round roast	100	33	71	118	153	98	107	77
Other roast	100	35	67	140	161	107	76	47
Steak	100	53	93	123	143	113	69	49
Round steak	100	44	87	131	159	103	66	41
Sirloin steak	100	56	92	116	137	109	88	56
Other steak	100	55	96	125	140	120	59	48
Other beef	100	34	79	165	98	79	99	77
Pork	100	67	83	122	120	112	88	77
Bacon	100	67	80	111	114	107	91	123
Pork chops	100	67	97	128	128	107	64	57

	total consumer units	under 25	25 to 34	35 to 44	45 to 54	55 to 64	65 to 74	75+
Ham	100	56	64	123	114	120	115	91
Ham, not canned	100	55	64	121	119	123	115	83
Canned ham	100	76	65	145	45	94	108	182
Sausage	100	81	85	134	106	108	90	61
Other pork	100	67	86	116	132	117	85	63
Other meats	100	55	85	126	127	96	87	83
Frankfurters	100	75	88	129	113	98	74	92
Lunch meats (cold cuts)	100	54	84	125	130	97	89	80
Bologna, liverwurst, salami	100	68	88	125	121	93	88	81
Other lunchmeats	100	46	82	125	134	99	89	80
Lamb, organ meats and others	100	21	84	130	138	78	103	87
Lamb and organ meats	100	21	79	130	141	80	104	89
Mutton, goat and game	100	-	356	100	-	-	72	-
Poultry	100	51	91	128	134	104	74	65
Fresh and frozen chickens	100	56	94	129	134	102	67	61
Fresh and frozen whole chicken	100	42	86	129	131	116	72	74
Fresh and frozen chicken parts	100	61	98	130	135	97	66	57
Other poultry	100	33	77	124	135	109	99	77
Fish and seafood	100	56	91	121	128	120	83	56
Canned fish and seafood	100	44	87	124	106	117	103	83
Fresh fish and shellfish	100	62	90	123	130	132	66	51
Frozen fish and shellfish	100	49	94	116	137	94	108	50
Eggs	100	73	91	115	116	97	104	78
Dairy products	**100**	**62**	**90**	**125**	**117**	**94**	**89**	**86**
Fresh milk and cream	100	65	97	123	114	88	85	91
Fresh milk, all types	100	66	98	123	114	88	85	89
Cream	100	53	86	122	119	93	84	113
Other dairy products	100	60	85	126	119	99	93	82
Butter	100	58	94	117	150	93	78	57
Cheese	100	61	88	128	115	96	87	88
Ice cream and related products	100	55	79	123	118	110	103	82
Miscellaneous dairy products	100	71	80	128	124	92	98	72
Fruits and vegetables	**100**	**54**	**88**	**116**	**119**	**103**	**95**	**96**
Fresh fruits	100	50	86	113	123	101	100	102
Apples	100	49	97	130	122	98	80	69
Bananas	100	54	92	104	121	97	104	109
Oranges	100	69	99	104	136	100	90	70
Citrus fruits, excl. oranges	100	44	76	106	114	117	116	121
Other fresh fruits	100	43	74	113	123	101	108	121
Fresh vegetables	100	51	88	118	121	107	93	87
Potatoes	100	55	85	118	121	106	89	100
Lettuce	100	52	104	113	123	97	92	77
Tomatoes	100	54	95	121	117	104	87	81
Other fresh vegetables	100	48	83	119	121	112	97	87

	total consumer units	under 25	25 to 34	35 to 44	45 to 54	55 to 64	65 to 74	75+
Processed fruits	100	66	90	114	117	95	94	103
Frozen fruits and fruit juices	100	83	91	128	109	87	97	74
Frozen orange juice	100	94	91	117	110	83	102	88
Frozen fruits	100	26	89	99	89	184	133	59
Frozen fruit juices	100	80	91	156	113	67	76	55
Canned fruit	100	37	84	99	100	114	106	167
Dried fruit	100	32	58	95	136	105	139	139
Fresh fruit juices	100	57	95	111	141	95	82	80
Canned and bottled fruit juices	100	79	94	119	112	89	86	96
Processed vegetables	100	54	90	121	114	107	91	89
Frozen vegetables	100	55	88	136	110	112	86	67
Canned and dried vegetables and juices	100	54	91	113	117	105	94	100
Canned beans	100	78	84	114	112	101	94	107
Canned corn	100	74	101	121	116	83	63	113
Other canned and dried vegetables	100	44	91	113	118	110	96	98
Frozen vegetable juices	100	91	117	157	135	26	65	-
Fresh and canned vegetable juices	100	32	92	102	119	118	119	92
Other food at home	**100**	**63**	**93**	**123**	**123**	**100**	**84**	**73**
Sugar and other sweets	100	51	90	121	121	102	95	81
Candy and chewing gum	100	44	94	120	128	107	94	65
Sugar	100	70	97	127	120	83	89	70
Artificial sweeteners	100	30	49	101	116	80	147	205
Jams, preserves, other sweets	100	60	79	122	101	109	99	116
Fats and oils	100	63	84	121	115	96	95	102
Margarine	100	56	62	105	104	107	102	189
Fats and oils	100	64	98	116	119	90	94	86
Salad dressings	100	61	83	124	126	107	91	72
Nondairy cream and imitation milk	100	58	75	123	126	93	116	79
Peanut butter	100	77	95	141	90	72	88	101
Miscellaneous foods	100	69	101	128	117	91	78	68
Frozen prepared foods	100	53	93	117	131	98	78	92
Frozen meals	100	32	85	107	133	101	85	136
Other frozen prepared foods	100	63	97	121	130	97	75	71
Canned and packaged soups	100	66	90	119	109	105	94	93
Potato chips, nuts, and other snacks	100	55	90	140	128	90	81	52
Potato chips and other snacks	100	58	95	151	126	82	68	46
Nuts	100	42	72	103	139	116	129	75
Condiments and seasonings	100	72	89	130	121	96	83	66
Salt, spices and other seasonings	100	69	83	123	114	121	89	73
Olives, pickles, relishes	100	56	64	132	124	102	99	96
Sauces and gravies	100	74	100	136	124	86	71	52
Baking needs and misc. products	100	81	86	126	121	84	96	72
Other canned/packaged prepared foods	100	86	125	127	102	80	68	60
Prepared salads	100	35	69	128	126	115	121	67
Prepared desserts	100	46	79	114	112	95	115	122

	total consumer units	under 25	25 to 34	35 to 44	45 to 54	55 to 64	65 to 74	75+
Baby food	100	142	222	117	62	39	18	13
Miscellaneous prepared foods	100	75	99	132	114	90	74	71
Nonalcoholic beverages	100	64	89	120	127	111	81	71
Cola	100	73	93	126	131	106	75	46
Other carbonated drinks	100	79	97	121	116	112	76	63
Coffee	100	34	66	96	135	147	102	115
Roasted coffee	100	33	68	102	140	147	92	102
Instant and freeze-dried coffee	100	36	62	83	126	148	121	143
Noncarb. fruit flavored drinks incl. non-frozen lemonade	100	66	86	148	126	73	76	67
Tea	100	41	95	111	147	94	98	61
Nonalcoholic beer	100	-	92	95	39	183	179	118
Other nonalcoholic beverages	100	74	98	120	107	106	65	104
Food prepared by cu on out-of-town trips	100	40	78	106	157	120	99	50
FOOD AWAY FROM HOME	**100**	**69**	**100**	**120**	**135**	**107**	**70**	**45**
Meals at restaurants, carry-outs, other	**100**	**73**	**108**	**122**	**125**	**103**	**71**	**46**
Lunch	100	67	110	132	125	92	58	53
Dinner	100	74	106	114	125	111	80	43
Snacks and nonalcoholic beverages	100	108	123	134	121	78	50	20
Breakfast and brunch	100	56	97	111	126	124	87	59
Board (including at school)	**100**	**135**	**13**	**71**	**302**	**126**	**9**	**35**
Catered affairs	**100**	**19**	**75**	**68**	**248**	**148**	**46**	**25**
Food on out-of-town trips	**100**	**44**	**76**	**103**	**137**	**137**	**112**	**59**
School lunches	**100**	**5**	**87**	**249**	**128**	**23**	**10**	**6**
Meals as pay	**100**	**223**	**159**	**80**	**85**	**134**	**21**	**10**
ALCOHOLIC BEVERAGES	**100**	**89**	**125**	**106**	**105**	**121**	**83**	**28**
At home	**100**	**73**	**126**	**111**	**105**	**116**	**86**	**29**
Beer and ale	100	89	158	113	96	88	67	21
Whiskey	100	45	71	66	79	214	189	68
Wine	100	46	76	124	132	145	95	33
Other alcoholic beverages	100	53	91	111	128	140	101	33
Away from home	**100**	**112**	**122**	**100**	**104**	**130**	**78**	**27**
Beer and ale	100	157	142	95	94	119	57	16
Wine	100	93	116	104	108	147	75	22
Other alcoholic beverages	100	101	113	102	106	156	76	18
Alcoholic beverages purchased on trips	100	74	108	100	114	110	109	50

Note: (-) means insufficient data.

Age
average per capita spending

(average annual per capita spending of consumer units on food and alcoholic beverages, by age of consumer unit reference person, 1994; per capita figures are calculated by dividing the average spending of consumer units by the average number of persons per consumer unit)

	total consumer units	under 25	25 to 34	35 to 44	45 to 54	55 to 64	65 to 74	75+
Average number of persons per cu	2.5	2.0	2.8	3.2	2.8	2.2	1.8	1.5
Per capita before-tax income of cu	$14,735.20	$8,203.50	$12,161.07	$14,442.81	$17,723.93	$19,038.18	$14,592.22	$13,824.00
Per capita spending of cu, total	12,700.25	9,208.87	10,880.66	11,746.15	14,801.29	15,319.17	13,940.66	12,870.41
Food, per capita spending	1,764.21	1,396.71	1,485.45	1,677.09	2,005.13	2,067.85	1,968.11	1,914.04
Alcoholic beverages, per capita spending	111.21	123.31	123.91	92.50	104.17	153.43	128.23	51.56
FOOD AT HOME	**$1,084.82**	**$808.30**	**$876.28**	**$1,042.52**	**$1,185.45**	**$1,242.39**	**$1,303.54**	**$1,407.94**
Cereals and bakery products	**171.47**	**125.14**	**138.36**	**167.39**	**182.74**	**188.22**	**214.03**	**230.93**
Cereals and cereal products	64.70	57.20	56.39	65.73	67.23	62.50	70.45	83.47
Flour	3.04	2.99	3.20	2.52	3.03	2.65	3.73	4.54
Prepared flour mixes	5.12	4.47	3.96	4.96	5.02	5.41	6.57	8.39
Ready-to-eat and cooked cereals	39.31	34.68	33.55	40.78	39.53	37.48	45.02	51.03
Rice	6.17	5.51	6.01	6.38	6.85	5.87	5.04	6.21
Pasta, cornmeal, other cereal products	11.06	9.56	9.66	11.08	12.80	11.09	10.09	13.29
Bakery products	106.77	67.95	81.97	101.67	115.51	125.72	143.58	147.45
Bread	30.49	20.50	23.98	27.21	32.71	36.73	41.96	45.60
White bread	15.06	11.58	12.78	14.40	14.93	17.19	19.63	19.79
Bread, other than white	15.43	8.92	11.20	12.81	17.78	19.54	22.32	25.81
Crackers and cookies	25.02	15.18	18.41	24.67	25.15	29.97	35.67	36.46
Cookies	17.19	10.22	13.00	16.98	17.43	20.03	24.00	25.01
Crackers	7.84	4.96	5.41	7.69	7.73	9.95	11.67	11.45
Frozen/refrigerated bakery products	8.62	6.01	7.40	7.98	10.13	9.04	10.79	10.10
Other bakery products	42.64	26.27	32.18	41.81	47.51	49.98	55.17	55.29
Biscuits and rolls	14.38	8.89	10.18	13.88	17.28	17.89	18.64	16.45
Cakes and cupcakes	12.48	8.89	9.80	12.81	13.23	16.08	15.10	11.52
Bread and cracker products	1.89	1.27	1.26	2.13	2.08	2.32	2.34	1.67
Sweetrolls, coffee cakes, doughnuts	8.77	3.97	6.49	7.69	10.37	7.96	13.50	16.96
Pies, tarts, turnovers	5.12	3.25	4.44	5.29	4.56	5.73	5.58	8.70
Meats, poultry, fish, and eggs	**292.98**	**214.67**	**232.29**	**287.05**	**334.17**	**351.30**	**331.29**	**333.37**
Beef	90.70	66.26	74.86	90.85	105.94	104.75	94.28	93.91
Ground beef	35.38	33.64	32.48	35.56	37.78	36.14	33.58	39.23
Roast	15.76	7.63	10.23	15.31	19.97	19.80	20.44	19.91
Chuck roast	4.90	3.04	3.52	4.48	4.74	7.20	6.38	8.39
Round roast	5.94	2.45	3.75	5.46	8.13	6.62	8.86	7.65
Other roast	4.92	2.15	2.95	5.38	7.10	5.98	5.21	3.86
Steak	33.90	22.56	28.16	32.68	43.22	43.70	32.47	27.51
Round steak	6.40	3.51	4.95	6.56	9.08	7.50	5.90	4.34
Sirloin steak	9.78	6.82	8.06	8.86	11.98	12.07	11.99	9.07
Other steak	17.72	12.23	15.14	17.28	22.16	24.14	14.58	14.09
Other beef	5.66	2.44	3.99	7.29	4.98	5.11	7.79	7.27
Pork	62.30	51.89	45.92	59.60	66.98	79.61	76.56	79.59
Bacon	9.11	7.68	6.53	7.88	9.30	11.07	11.58	18.64
Pork chops	15.73	13.22	13.63	15.76	18.00	19.06	13.98	14.99

	total consumer units	under 25	25 to 34	35 to 44	45 to 54	55 to 64	65 to 74	75+
Ham	$14.75	$10.37	$8.47	$14.16	$15.01	$20.20	$23.51	$22.27
Ham, not canned	13.66	9.34	7.84	12.93	14.57	19.04	21.87	18.97
Canned ham	1.09	1.04	0.63	1.23	0.44	1.16	1.64	3.30
Sausage	9.13	9.23	6.93	9.53	8.66	11.18	11.44	9.35
Other pork	13.57	11.40	10.37	12.27	16.00	18.10	16.06	14.34
Other meats	37.58	25.63	28.53	37.10	42.67	40.79	45.53	52.19
Frankfurters	7.50	7.03	5.93	7.55	7.58	8.39	7.67	11.46
Lunch meats (cold cuts)	26.26	17.62	19.74	25.68	30.39	29.02	32.41	35.19
Bologna, liverwurst, salami	9.49	8.08	7.43	9.29	10.28	10.07	11.56	12.79
Other lunchmeats	16.77	9.54	12.31	16.38	20.11	18.95	20.84	22.40
Lamb, organ meats and others	3.81	0.99	2.88	3.87	4.70	3.39	5.45	5.53
Lamb and organ meats	3.74	0.99	2.65	3.81	4.70	3.39	5.38	5.53
Mutton, goat and game	0.07	-	0.23	0.06	-	-	0.07	-
Poultry	54.63	34.98	44.30	54.80	65.29	64.32	56.26	58.75
Fresh and frozen chickens	43.16	30.22	36.39	43.64	51.45	50.14	40.42	44.09
Fresh and frozen whole chicken	11.82	6.17	9.11	11.90	13.80	15.55	11.89	14.58
Fresh and frozen chicken parts	31.33	24.05	27.28	31.74	37.64	34.59	28.53	29.51
Other poultry	11.48	4.76	7.91	11.16	13.84	14.19	15.84	14.65
Fish and seafood	35.77	24.91	28.95	33.93	40.89	48.58	41.36	33.37
Canned fish and seafood	6.01	3.30	4.68	5.83	5.68	8.01	8.58	8.27
Fresh fish and shellfish	20.50	15.98	16.48	19.71	23.86	30.71	18.84	17.36
Frozen fish and shellfish	9.26	5.64	7.80	8.38	11.34	9.85	13.93	7.74
Eggs	12.00	11.01	9.73	10.78	12.41	13.25	17.30	15.57
Dairy products	**115.57**	**90.18**	**93.22**	**112.62**	**120.79**	**123.83**	**143.02**	**165.36**
Fresh milk and cream	50.85	41.43	44.08	49.02	51.84	50.91	59.84	76.96
Fresh milk, all types	47.58	39.23	41.55	45.90	48.35	47.44	56.03	70.77
Cream	3.28	2.19	2.53	3.12	3.49	3.47	3.81	6.19
Other dairy products	64.72	48.76	49.14	63.61	68.95	72.93	83.17	88.40
Butter	4.66	3.40	3.93	4.27	6.22	4.94	5.08	4.43
Cheese	32.73	24.89	25.82	32.78	33.52	35.66	39.67	47.99
Ice cream and related products	19.06	13.11	13.50	18.27	20.05	23.73	27.21	26.07
Miscellaneous dairy products	8.26	7.37	5.90	8.29	9.16	8.60	11.21	9.91
Fruits and vegetables	**174.63**	**118.78**	**137.17**	**158.53**	**186.27**	**203.65**	**230.58**	**278.09**
Fresh fruits	53.21	33.17	40.63	46.83	58.47	60.86	74.20	90.64
Apples	10.15	6.20	8.77	10.32	11.03	11.34	11.31	11.69
Bananas	11.86	7.96	9.71	9.68	12.79	13.06	17.15	21.59
Oranges	6.54	5.67	5.77	5.31	7.95	7.42	8.16	7.67
Citrus fruits, excl. oranges	4.38	2.40	2.96	3.63	4.44	5.85	7.05	8.81
Other fresh fruits	20.27	10.96	13.42	17.88	22.26	23.20	30.54	40.87
Fresh vegetables	53.96	34.36	42.50	49.93	58.11	65.84	69.68	78.68
Potatoes	11.20	7.73	8.53	10.29	12.09	13.50	13.78	18.59
Lettuce	6.95	4.50	6.44	6.13	7.63	7.65	8.88	8.90
Tomatoes	8.40	5.63	7.15	7.98	8.76	9.92	10.19	11.40
Other fresh vegetables	27.40	16.52	20.38	25.53	29.63	34.77	36.84	39.79

	total consumer units	under 25	25 to 34	35 to 44	45 to 54	55 to 64	65 to 74	75+
Processed fruits	$37.23	$30.78	$29.78	$33.26	$38.83	$40.10	$48.42	$63.83
Frozen fruits and fruit juices	6.51	6.75	5.26	6.49	6.33	6.47	8.75	8.07
Frozen orange juice	3.80	4.46	3.07	3.46	3.74	3.56	5.37	5.54
Frozen fruits	0.64	0.21	0.51	0.49	0.51	1.34	1.18	0.63
Frozen fruit juices	2.08	2.08	1.68	2.53	2.09	1.57	2.21	1.91
Canned fruit	5.69	2.62	4.27	4.38	5.09	7.35	8.39	15.83
Dried fruit	2.36	0.96	1.23	1.75	2.87	2.80	4.56	5.47
Fresh fruit juices	7.16	5.11	6.05	6.19	9.00	7.76	8.17	9.59
Canned and bottled fruit juices	15.51	15.35	12.96	14.45	15.55	15.71	18.56	24.85
Processed vegetables	30.23	20.48	24.27	28.51	30.86	36.85	38.28	44.94
Frozen vegetables	9.93	6.81	7.77	10.58	9.72	12.61	11.80	11.03
Canned and dried vegetables and juices	20.30	13.67	16.50	17.93	21.13	24.25	26.48	33.92
Canned beans	4.18	4.07	3.14	3.70	4.19	4.79	5.43	7.41
Canned corn	2.72	2.53	2.46	2.58	2.82	2.55	2.37	5.13
Other canned and dried vegetables	10.82	5.99	8.76	9.56	11.38	13.55	14.49	17.59
Frozen vegetable juices	0.09	0.11	0.10	0.11	0.11	0.03	0.08	-
Fresh and canned vegetable juices	2.48	0.99	2.04	1.98	2.63	3.33	4.10	3.80
Other food at home	**330.17**	**259.54**	**275.24**	**316.92**	**361.48**	**375.38**	**384.62**	**400.19**
Sugar and other sweets	42.10	26.93	33.74	39.78	45.46	48.78	55.80	56.87
Candy and chewing gum	24.93	13.63	20.84	23.37	28.53	30.18	32.37	27.19
Sugar	7.32	6.41	6.31	7.27	7.85	6.89	9.02	8.56
Artificial sweeteners	1.36	0.52	0.59	1.07	1.40	1.23	2.76	4.64
Jams, preserves, other sweets	8.49	6.38	6.00	8.08	7.67	10.48	11.66	16.47
Fats and oils	31.70	25.07	23.91	29.86	32.49	34.50	41.94	53.70
Margarine	5.66	3.99	3.13	4.65	5.26	6.87	8.02	17.83
Fats and oils	9.24	7.38	8.06	8.38	9.81	9.43	11.99	13.17
Salad dressings	9.50	7.29	7.02	9.17	10.69	11.57	11.97	11.39
Nondairy cream and imitation milk	2.62	1.90	1.75	2.53	2.94	2.78	4.21	3.43
Peanut butter	4.68	4.52	3.95	5.14	3.78	3.85	5.75	7.89
Miscellaneous foods	144.65	124.07	130.90	144.44	151.63	149.20	156.34	164.50
Frozen prepared foods	26.46	17.56	21.98	24.09	30.99	29.61	28.64	40.59
Frozen meals	8.57	3.40	6.48	7.18	10.20	9.80	10.08	19.39
Other frozen prepared foods	17.88	14.17	15.51	16.92	20.79	19.81	18.57	21.20
Canned and packaged soups	11.82	9.74	9.53	10.98	11.46	14.05	15.36	18.27
Potato chips, nuts, and other snacks	29.63	20.19	23.85	32.51	33.96	30.17	33.38	25.81
Potato chips and other snacks	23.27	16.82	19.77	27.38	26.09	21.77	21.97	17.85
Nuts	6.36	3.37	4.08	5.13	7.88	8.40	11.41	7.95
Condiments and seasonings	31.90	28.58	25.37	32.50	34.46	34.80	36.83	35.11
Salt, spices and other seasonings	7.72	6.64	5.73	7.40	7.86	10.59	9.54	9.43
Olives, pickles, relishes	4.06	2.84	2.34	4.19	4.48	4.73	5.57	6.50
Sauces and gravies	14.57	13.48	13.04	15.43	16.11	14.20	14.36	12.57
Baking needs and misc. products	5.54	5.63	4.26	5.47	6.00	5.29	7.36	6.62
Other canned/packaged prepared foods	44.85	48.01	50.17	44.36	40.75	40.57	42.13	44.72
Prepared salads	4.39	1.92	2.69	4.38	4.93	5.71	7.37	4.89
Prepared desserts	3.20	1.84	2.25	2.86	3.20	3.45	5.12	6.52

	total consumer units	under 25	25 to 34	35 to 44	45 to 54	55 to 64	65 to 74	75+
Baby food	$11.24	$19.94	$22.29	$10.29	$6.19	$4.93	$2.78	$2.49
Miscellaneous prepared foods	26.02	24.31	22.95	26.83	26.43	26.47	26.88	30.81
Nonalcoholic beverages	93.16	74.11	73.77	87.43	105.95	117.64	105.12	109.57
Cola	35.78	32.51	29.66	35.34	41.94	43.27	37.42	27.42
Other carbonated drinks	15.56	15.36	13.51	14.71	16.05	19.81	16.42	16.45
Coffee	17.20	7.33	10.18	12.91	20.78	28.80	24.32	33.01
Roasted coffee	11.65	4.86	7.08	9.32	14.53	19.45	14.96	19.80
Instant and freeze-dried coffee	5.55	2.47	3.10	3.60	6.25	9.35	9.36	13.21
Noncarb. fruit flavored drinks incl. non-frozen lemonade	8.74	7.17	6.73	10.10	9.82	7.25	9.18	9.69
Tea	6.50	3.36	5.54	5.63	8.53	6.95	8.86	6.66
Nonalcoholic beer	0.26	-	0.22	0.20	0.09	0.55	0.66	0.52
Other nonalcoholic beverages	9.11	8.38	7.95	8.55	8.74	11.01	8.27	15.83
Food prepared by cu on out-of-town trips	18.56	9.36	12.93	15.41	25.95	25.26	25.42	15.55
FOOD AWAY FROM HOME	**679.38**	**588.41**	**609.17**	**634.58**	**819.67**	**825.46**	**664.56**	**506.09**
Meals at restaurants, carry-outs, other	**522.48**	**475.61**	**505.35**	**496.74**	**582.05**	**609.33**	**512.76**	**400.37**
Lunch	180.70	152.39	178.17	185.96	201.15	188.20	145.77	158.59
Dinner	260.72	240.09	247.25	233.21	291.64	328.20	289.82	188.78
Snacks and nonalcoholic beverages	40.69	55.12	44.79	42.48	43.84	35.99	28.52	13.45
Breakfast and brunch	40.38	28.02	35.14	35.10	45.41	56.94	48.64	39.55
Board (including at school)	**20.29**	**34.29**	**2.31**	**11.33**	**54.68**	**28.96**	**2.46**	**11.70**
Catered affairs	**22.44**	**5.23**	**14.96**	**11.96**	**49.66**	**37.65**	**14.49**	**9.35**
Food on out-of-town trips	**83.16**	**45.42**	**56.42**	**66.85**	**101.44**	**129.51**	**129.26**	**81.08**
School lunches	**21.50**	**1.38**	**16.63**	**41.78**	**24.61**	**5.54**	**2.87**	**1.97**
Meals as pay	**9.52**	**26.50**	**13.50**	**5.92**	**7.23**	**14.47**	**2.73**	**1.63**
ALCOHOLIC BEVERAGES	**111.21**	**123.31**	**123.91**	**92.50**	**104.17**	**153.43**	**128.23**	**51.56**
At home	**66.05**	**60.17**	**74.60**	**57.39**	**62.10**	**86.90**	**79.30**	**31.52**
Beer and ale	39.87	44.61	56.25	35.07	34.00	39.83	37.10	13.93
Whiskey	5.47	3.09	3.46	2.82	3.88	13.29	14.34	6.24
Wine	14.56	8.40	9.91	14.15	17.21	24.04	19.21	7.97
Other alcoholic beverages	6.14	4.07	4.97	5.34	7.01	9.75	8.64	3.37
Away from home	**45.16**	**63.14**	**49.32**	**35.11**	**42.06**	**66.53**	**48.94**	**20.04**
Beer and ale	15.42	30.28	19.59	11.45	12.92	20.90	12.19	4.05
Wine	6.32	7.34	6.56	5.11	6.10	10.57	6.54	2.37
Other alcoholic beverages	11.18	14.13	11.31	8.93	10.54	19.78	11.74	3.44
Alcoholic beverages purchased on trips	12.24	11.40	11.86	9.61	12.50	15.28	18.47	10.19

Note: Expenditures listed for items in a given category may not add to the total for that category because the listing is incomplete. (-) means insufficient data.

Age

indexed per capita spending

(indexed average annual per capita spending of consumer units on food and alcoholic beverages, by age of consumer unit reference person, 1994; index definition: an index of 100 is the per capita average for all consumer units; an index of 132 means that per capita spending by consumer units in the age group is 32 percent above the per capita average for all consumer units; an index of 68 indicates that per capita spending by the age group is 32 percent below the per capita average for all consumer units)

	total consumer units	under 25	25 to 34	35 to 44	45 to 54	55 to 64	65 to 74	75+
Per capita spending of cu, total	*$12,700.25*	*$9,208.87*	*$10,880.66*	*$11,746.15*	*$14,801.29*	*$15,319.17*	*$13,940.66*	*$12,870.41*
Per capita spending of cu, index	*100*	*73*	*86*	*92*	*117*	*121*	*110*	*101*
Food, per capita spending index	*100*	*79*	*84*	*95*	*114*	*117*	*112*	*108*
Alcoholic beverages, per capita spending index	*100*	*111*	*111*	*83*	*94*	*138*	*115*	*46*
FOOD AT HOME	**100**	**75**	**81**	**96**	**109**	**115**	**120**	**130**
Cereals and bakery products	**100**	**73**	**81**	**98**	**107**	**110**	**125**	**135**
Cereals and cereal products	100	88	87	102	104	97	109	129
Flour	100	98	105	83	100	87	123	149
Prepared flour mixes	100	87	77	97	98	106	128	164
Ready-to-eat and cooked cereals	100	88	85	104	101	95	115	130
Rice	100	89	97	103	111	95	82	101
Pasta, cornmeal, and other cereal products	100	86	87	100	116	100	91	120
Bakery products	100	64	77	95	108	118	134	138
Bread	100	67	79	89	107	120	138	150
White bread	100	77	85	96	99	114	130	131
Bread, other than white	100	58	73	83	115	127	145	167
Crackers and cookies	100	61	74	99	101	120	143	146
Cookies	100	59	76	99	101	117	140	146
Crackers	100	63	69	98	99	127	149	146
Frozen/refrigerated bakery products	100	70	86	92	117	105	125	117
Other bakery products	100	62	75	98	111	117	129	130
Biscuits and rolls	100	62	71	97	120	124	130	114
Cakes and cupcakes	100	71	79	103	106	129	121	92
Bread and cracker products	100	67	67	113	110	123	124	88
Sweetrolls, coffee cakes, doughnuts	100	45	74	88	118	91	154	193
Pies, tarts, turnovers	100	63	87	103	89	112	109	170
Meats, poultry, fish, and eggs	**100**	**73**	**79**	**98**	**114**	**120**	**113**	**114**
Beef	100	73	83	100	117	115	104	104
Ground beef	100	95	92	101	107	102	95	111
Roast	100	48	65	97	127	126	130	126
Chuck roast	100	62	72	91	97	147	130	171
Round roast	100	41	63	92	137	111	149	129
Other roast	100	44	60	109	144	121	106	78
Steak	100	67	83	96	127	129	96	81
Round steak	100	55	77	102	142	117	92	68
Sirloin steak	100	70	82	91	123	123	123	93
Other steak	100	69	85	97	125	136	82	80
Other beef	100	43	70	129	88	90	138	128
Pork	100	83	74	96	108	128	123	128
Bacon	100	84	72	86	102	122	127	205
Pork chops	100	84	87	100	114	121	89	95

	total consumer units	under 25	25 to 34	35 to 44	45 to 54	55 to 64	65 to 74	75+
Ham	100	70	57	96	102	137	159	151
Ham, not canned	100	68	57	95	107	139	160	139
Canned ham	100	95	58	113	40	107	151	303
Sausage	100	101	76	104	95	122	125	102
Other pork	100	84	76	90	118	133	118	106
Other meats	100	68	76	99	114	109	121	139
Frankfurters	100	94	79	101	101	112	102	153
Lunch meats (cold cuts)	100	67	75	98	116	110	123	134
Bologna, liverwurst, salami	100	85	78	98	108	106	122	135
Other lunchmeats	100	57	73	98	120	113	124	134
Lamb, organ meats and others	100	26	75	101	123	89	143	145
Lamb and organ meats	100	26	71	102	126	91	144	148
Mutton, goat and game	100	-	317	78	-	-	100	-
Poultry	100	64	81	100	120	118	103	108
Fresh and frozen chickens	100	70	84	101	119	116	94	102
Fresh and frozen whole chicken	100	52	77	101	117	131	101	123
Fresh and frozen chicken parts	100	77	87	101	120	110	91	94
Other poultry	100	41	69	97	121	124	138	128
Fish and seafood	100	70	81	95	114	136	116	93
Canned fish and seafood	100	55	78	97	95	133	143	138
Fresh fish and shellfish	100	78	80	96	116	150	92	85
Frozen fish and shellfish	100	61	84	91	122	106	150	84
Eggs	100	92	81	90	103	110	144	130
Dairy products	**100**	**78**	**81**	**97**	**105**	**107**	**124**	**143**
Fresh milk and cream	100	81	87	96	102	100	118	151
Fresh milk, all types	100	82	87	96	102	100	118	149
Cream	100	67	77	95	107	106	116	189
Other dairy products	100	75	76	98	107	113	129	137
Butter	100	73	84	92	134	106	109	95
Cheese	100	76	79	100	102	109	121	147
Ice cream and related products	100	69	71	96	105	125	143	137
Miscellaneous dairy products	100	89	71	100	111	104	136	120
Fruits and vegetables	**100**	**68**	**79**	**91**	**107**	**117**	**132**	**159**
Fresh fruits	100	62	76	88	110	114	139	170
Apples	100	61	86	102	109	112	111	115
Bananas	100	67	82	82	108	110	145	182
Oranges	100	87	88	81	121	113	125	117
Citrus fruits, excl. oranges	100	55	68	83	101	133	161	201
Other fresh fruits	100	54	66	88	110	114	151	202
Fresh vegetables	100	64	79	93	108	122	129	146
Potatoes	100	69	76	92	108	120	123	166
Lettuce	100	65	93	88	110	110	128	128
Tomatoes	100	67	85	95	104	118	121	136
Other fresh vegetables	100	60	74	93	108	127	134	145

	total consumer units	under 25	25 to 34	35 to 44	45 to 54	55 to 64	65 to 74	75+
Processed fruits	100	83	80	89	104	108	130	171
Frozen fruits and fruit juices	100	104	81	100	97	99	134	124
Frozen orange juice	100	117	81	91	99	94	141	146
Frozen fruits	100	32	80	77	79	209	184	98
Frozen fruit juices	100	100	81	122	100	76	106	92
Canned fruit	100	46	75	77	89	129	147	278
Dried fruit	100	41	52	74	122	119	193	232
Fresh fruit juices	100	71	85	86	126	108	114	134
Canned and bottled fruit juices	100	99	84	93	100	101	120	160
Processed vegetables	100	68	80	94	102	122	127	149
Frozen vegetables	100	69	78	107	98	127	119	111
Canned and dried vegetables and juices	100	67	81	88	104	119	130	167
Canned beans	100	97	75	89	100	115	130	178
Canned corn	100	93	90	95	103	94	87	188
Other canned and dried vegetables	100	55	81	88	105	125	134	163
Frozen vegetable juices	100	114	105	122	120	30	91	-
Fresh and canned vegetable juices	100	40	82	80	106	134	165	153
Other food at home	**100**	**79**	**83**	**96**	**109**	**114**	**116**	**121**
Sugar and other sweets	100	64	80	94	108	116	133	135
Candy and chewing gum	100	55	84	94	114	121	130	109
Sugar	100	87	86	99	107	94	123	117
Artificial sweeteners	100	38	43	79	103	91	204	342
Jams, preserves, other sweets	100	75	71	95	90	123	137	194
Fats and oils	100	79	75	94	102	109	132	169
Margarine	100	70	55	82	93	121	142	315
Fats and oils	100	80	87	91	106	102	130	143
Salad dressings	100	77	74	97	113	122	126	120
Nondairy cream and imitation milk	100	72	67	96	112	106	160	131
Peanut butter	100	97	84	110	81	82	123	169
Miscellaneous foods	100	86	90	100	105	103	108	114
Frozen prepared foods	100	66	83	91	117	112	108	153
Frozen meals	100	40	76	84	119	114	118	226
Other frozen prepared foods	100	79	87	95	116	111	104	119
Canned and packaged soups	100	82	81	93	97	119	130	155
Potato chips, nuts, and other snacks	100	68	80	110	115	102	113	87
Potato chips and other snacks	100	72	85	118	112	94	94	77
Nuts	100	53	64	81	124	132	179	125
Condiments and seasonings	100	90	80	102	108	109	115	110
Salt, spices and other seasonings	100	86	74	96	102	137	124	122
Olives, pickles, relishes	100	70	58	103	110	116	137	160
Sauces and gravies	100	93	89	106	111	97	99	86
Baking needs and misc. products	100	102	77	99	108	96	133	119
Other canned/packaged prepared foods	100	107	112	99	91	90	94	100
Prepared salads	100	44	61	100	112	130	168	112
Prepared desserts	100	58	70	89	100	108	160	204

	total consumer units	under 25	25 to 34	35 to 44	45 to 54	55 to 64	65 to 74	75+
Baby food	100	177	198	92	55	44	25	22
Miscellaneous prepared foods	100	93	88	103	102	102	103	118
Nonalcoholic beverages	100	80	79	94	114	126	113	118
Cola	100	91	83	99	117	121	105	77
Other carbonated drinks	100	99	87	95	103	127	106	106
Coffee	100	43	59	75	121	167	141	192
Roasted coffee	100	42	61	80	125	167	128	170
Instant and freeze-dried coffee	100	44	56	65	113	168	169	238
Noncarb. fruit flavored drinks								
incl. non-frozen lemonade	100	82	77	115	112	83	105	111
Tea	100	52	85	87	131	107	136	102
Nonalcoholic beer	100	-	83	75	35	208	248	197
Other nonalcoholic beverages	100	92	87	94	96	121	91	174
Food prepared by cu on out-of-town trips	100	50	70	83	140	136	137	84
FOOD AWAY FROM HOME	**100**	**87**	**90**	**93**	**121**	**122**	**98**	**74**
Meals at restaurants, carry-outs, other	**100**	**91**	**97**	**95**	**111**	**117**	**98**	**77**
Lunch	100	84	99	103	111	104	81	88
Dinner	100	92	95	89	112	126	111	72
Snacks and nonalcoholic beverages	100	135	110	104	108	88	70	33
Breakfast and brunch	100	69	87	87	112	141	120	98
Board (including at school)	**100**	**169**	**11**	**56**	**270**	**143**	**12**	**58**
Catered affairs	**100**	**23**	**67**	**53**	**221**	**168**	**65**	**42**
Food on out-of-town trips	**100**	**55**	**68**	**80**	**122**	**156**	**155**	**98**
School lunches	**100**	**6**	**77**	**194**	**114**	**26**	**13**	**9**
Meals as pay	**100**	**278**	**142**	**62**	**76**	**152**	**29**	**17**
ALCOHOLIC BEVERAGES	**100**	**111**	**111**	**83**	**94**	**138**	**115**	**46**
At home	**100**	**91**	**113**	**87**	**94**	**132**	**120**	**48**
Beer and ale	100	112	141	88	85	100	93	35
Whiskey	100	56	63	51	71	243	262	114
Wine	100	58	68	97	118	165	132	55
Other alcoholic beverages	100	66	81	87	114	159	141	55
Away from home	**100**	**140**	**109**	**78**	**93**	**147**	**108**	**44**
Beer and ale	100	196	127	74	84	136	79	26
Wine	100	116	104	81	97	167	104	37
Other alcoholic beverages	100	126	101	80	94	177	105	31
Alcoholic beverages purchased on trips	100	93	97	79	102	125	151	83

Note: (-) means insufficient data.

Age
total spending

(total annual spending on food and alcoholic beverages by consumer unit age groups, 1994; numbers in thousands)

	total consumer units	under 25	25 to 34	35 to 44	45 to 54	55 to 64	65 to 74	75+
Number of consumer units	102,210	7,453	20,606	22,825	17,812	12,015	12,038	9,463
Total spending of all cu's	$3,245,231,892	$137,267,342	$627,779,511	$857,939,024	$738,193,403	$404,931,693	$302,071,701	$182,688,987
Food, total spending	450,799,249	20,819,359	85,705,506	122,494,699	100,002,802	54,659,479	42,645,698	27,168,841
Alcoholic beverages, total spending	28,417,446	1,837,984	7,149,458	6,755,972	5,195,226	4,055,663	2,778,611	731,868
FOOD AT HOME	**$277,198,631**	**$12,048,520**	**$50,558,676**	**$76,145,341**	**$59,122,659**	**$32,839,999**	**$28,245,722**	**$19,985,004**
Cereals and bakery products	**43,815,383**	**1,865,337**	**7,982,764**	**12,226,440**	**9,114,044**	**4,975,171**	**4,637,640**	**3,277,889**
Cereals and cereal products	16,531,445	852,623	3,253,275	4,800,554	3,352,931	1,652,183	1,526,539	1,184,862
Flour	776,796	44,569	184,630	184,198	151,046	70,168	80,775	64,443
Prepared flour mixes	1,307,266	66,555	228,727	362,233	250,437	143,099	142,410	119,139
Ready-to-eat and cooked cereals	10,044,177	516,866	1,935,522	2,978,891	1,971,610	990,637	975,560	724,393
Rice	1,577,100	82,132	346,799	465,858	341,456	155,234	109,185	88,195
Pasta, cornmeal, other cereal products	2,826,107	142,501	557,392	809,603	638,560	293,046	218,610	188,692
Bakery products	27,282,915	1,012,788	4,729,489	7,425,886	5,760,935	3,323,109	3,111,101	2,092,932
Bread	7,790,446	305,573	1,383,487	1,987,373	1,631,579	970,812	909,110	647,269
White bread	3,848,207	172,611	737,283	1,051,548	744,720	454,287	425,423	280,862
Bread, other than white	3,942,240	132,962	646,410	935,597	886,859	516,525	483,687	366,407
Crackers and cookies	6,394,258	226,199	1,062,445	1,801,806	1,254,499	792,269	772,960	517,531
Cookies	4,391,964	152,339	750,264	1,240,082	869,047	529,501	520,042	355,052
Crackers	2,002,294	73,859	312,181	561,952	385,452	262,888	252,918	162,480
Frozen/refrigerated bakery products	2,203,648	89,511	426,956	582,494	505,326	238,978	233,778	143,364
Other bakery products	10,894,564	391,506	1,856,395	3,053,985	2,369,530	1,321,049	1,195,373	784,767
Biscuits and rolls	3,675,472	132,514	587,271	1,013,887	861,745	472,790	403,875	233,452
Cakes and cupcakes	3,187,930	132,440	565,635	935,825	659,756	425,091	327,193	163,521
Bread and cracker products	482,431	18,931	72,533	155,667	103,488	61,397	50,800	23,658
Sweetrolls, coffee cakes, doughnuts	2,240,443	59,102	374,617	561,723	517,082	210,383	292,523	240,739
Pies, tarts, turnovers	1,308,288	48,445	256,339	386,656	227,459	151,389	120,982	123,492
Meats, poultry, fish, and eggs	**74,863,715**	**3,199,796**	**13,402,555**	**20,966,360**	**16,666,332**	**9,285,913**	**7,178,621**	**4,732,068**
Beef	23,177,140	987,597	4,319,018	6,635,456	5,283,574	2,768,857	2,042,969	1,333,053
Ground beef	9,040,475	501,363	1,874,116	2,597,485	1,884,153	955,193	727,577	556,898
Roast	4,028,096	113,733	589,950	1,118,425	995,869	523,373	442,998	282,565
Chuck roast	1,253,095	45,240	203,175	327,082	236,365	190,318	138,317	119,139
Round roast	1,516,796	36,445	216,569	398,525	405,401	174,938	191,886	108,635
Other roast	1,258,205	32,048	170,412	393,047	354,103	158,117	112,916	54,791
Steak	8,662,298	336,205	1,624,577	2,387,267	2,155,608	1,155,242	703,621	390,443
Round steak	1,635,360	52,246	285,805	478,869	452,959	198,127	127,844	61,604
Sirloin steak	2,498,012	101,659	465,077	646,861	597,414	319,118	259,900	128,697
Other steak	4,528,925	182,300	873,694	1,261,766	1,105,235	637,997	315,877	200,048
Other beef	1,446,272	36,296	230,169	532,279	248,121	135,049	168,773	103,147
Pork	15,918,185	773,472	2,649,519	4,353,184	3,340,462	2,104,427	1,658,957	1,129,693
Bacon	2,328,344	114,478	376,472	575,418	464,003	292,685	250,872	264,585
Pork chops	4,018,897	196,983	786,531	1,151,293	897,903	503,909	302,876	212,728

	total consumer units	under 25	25 to 34	35 to 44	45 to 54	55 to 64	65 to 74	75+
Ham	$3,769,505	$154,575	$488,568	$1,034,201	$748,638	$533,947	$509,448	$316,064
Ham, not canned	3,491,494	139,148	452,302	944,270	726,551	503,308	473,936	269,222
Canned ham	278,011	15,428	36,267	89,931	21,909	30,638	35,512	46,842
Sausage	2,332,432	137,508	399,550	695,706	431,763	295,449	247,983	132,766
Other pork	3,467,985	169,928	598,398	896,338	798,156	478,557	347,898	203,549
Other meats	9,602,630	382,041	1,646,213	2,709,784	2,128,178	1,078,226	986,634	740,764
Frankfurters	1,917,460	104,789	341,854	551,680	377,971	221,677	166,124	162,669
Lunch meats (cold cuts)	6,711,109	262,569	1,138,688	1,875,302	1,515,801	767,038	702,297	499,457
Bologna, liverwurst, salami	2,425,443	120,366	428,399	678,816	512,807	266,252	250,511	181,500
Other lunchmeats	4,285,665	142,203	710,289	1,196,487	1,002,994	500,785	451,666	317,957
Lamb, organ meats and others	974,061	14,682	165,878	282,574	234,584	89,512	118,093	78,543
Lamb and organ meats	955,664	14,682	152,690	278,465	234,584	89,512	116,648	78,543
Mutton, goat and game	18,398	-	13,188	4,109	-	-	1,565	-
Poultry	13,959,842	521,337	2,555,762	4,002,364	3,256,212	1,700,243	1,219,088	833,880
Fresh and frozen chickens	11,027,437	450,459	2,099,339	3,187,511	2,565,819	1,325,255	875,765	625,883
Fresh and frozen whole chicken	3,021,328	91,970	525,659	869,176	688,434	410,913	257,613	206,956
Fresh and frozen chicken parts	8,006,109	358,489	1,573,886	2,318,335	1,877,385	914,342	618,151	418,927
Other poultry	2,932,405	70,878	456,217	814,853	690,393	374,988	343,324	207,997
Fish and seafood	9,140,640	371,234	1,670,528	2,478,110	2,039,118	1,284,163	896,109	473,718
Canned fish and seafood	1,536,216	49,115	269,733	426,143	283,389	211,824	185,987	117,341
Fresh fish and shellfish	5,239,285	238,198	950,555	1,439,801	1,190,020	811,854	408,329	246,417
Frozen fish and shellfish	2,366,162	83,995	450,241	612,167	565,709	260,485	301,913	109,865
Eggs	3,066,300	164,115	561,514	787,463	618,967	350,117	374,863	220,961
Dairy products	**29,530,513**	**1,344,223**	**5,378,372**	**8,225,674**	**6,024,197**	**3,273,246**	**3,098,942**	**2,347,203**
Fresh milk and cream	12,993,957	617,481	2,542,986	3,580,101	2,585,234	1,345,680	1,296,733	1,092,409
Fresh milk, all types	12,156,857	584,762	2,397,302	3,352,536	2,411,389	1,253,885	1,214,153	1,004,497
Cream	837,100	32,644	145,684	227,565	174,023	91,795	82,581	87,911
Other dairy products	16,536,556	726,742	2,835,180	4,645,801	3,438,963	1,927,687	1,802,209	1,254,794
Butter	1,190,747	50,680	226,460	311,790	310,285	130,483	110,027	62,834
Cheese	8,363,844	370,936	1,489,814	2,394,114	1,671,656	942,577	859,634	681,241
Ice cream and related products	4,869,284	195,343	778,701	1,334,578	1,000,144	627,303	589,621	370,098
Miscellaneous dairy products	2,111,659	109,783	340,205	605,319	456,700	227,324	242,927	140,715
Fruits and vegetables	**44,621,820**	**1,770,535**	**7,914,352**	**11,578,666**	**9,290,027**	**5,383,201**	**4,996,252**	**3,947,301**
Fresh fruits	13,595,974	494,432	2,344,345	3,420,098	2,916,181	1,608,809	1,607,795	1,286,589
Apples	2,593,068	92,343	505,877	753,682	550,213	299,654	244,973	165,981
Bananas	3,031,549	118,652	560,483	706,890	638,026	345,311	371,613	306,412
Oranges	1,672,156	84,442	332,993	388,025	396,317	196,085	176,718	108,919
Citrus fruits, excl. oranges	1,120,222	35,700	170,824	265,227	221,581	154,513	152,762	125,006
Other fresh fruits	5,178,981	163,295	774,167	1,306,275	1,110,044	613,246	661,729	580,177
Fresh vegetables	13,787,107	512,096	2,452,114	3,646,750	2,898,369	1,740,253	1,509,926	1,116,823
Potatoes	2,862,902	115,149	491,865	751,627	603,114	356,725	298,663	263,828
Lettuce	1,776,410	67,002	371,526	448,055	380,464	202,212	192,367	126,331
Tomatoes	2,147,432	83,846	412,738	582,494	436,928	262,287	220,777	161,817
Other fresh vegetables	7,001,385	246,173	1,175,984	1,864,574	1,477,862	919,027	798,240	564,846

	total consumer units	under 25	25 to 34	35 to 44	45 to 54	55 to 64	65 to 74	75+
Processed fruits	$9,513,707	$458,732	$1,717,922	$2,429,493	$1,936,699	$1,059,963	$1,049,112	$905,988
Frozen fruits and fruit juices	1,663,979	100,616	303,732	473,847	315,807	170,973	189,599	114,597
Frozen orange juice	969,973	66,481	177,006	252,673	186,492	94,077	116,287	78,638
Frozen fruits	163,536	3,056	29,467	36,064	25,293	35,324	25,521	8,895
Frozen fruit juices	530,470	31,004	97,054	185,111	104,022	41,572	47,791	27,064
Canned fruit	1,454,448	38,979	246,242	320,235	253,643	194,403	181,774	224,652
Dried fruit	602,017	14,235	70,679	127,592	143,030	74,133	98,712	77,691
Fresh fruit juices	1,829,559	76,095	349,272	452,163	448,684	205,216	177,079	136,173
Canned and bottled fruit juices	3,963,704	228,733	747,998	1,055,428	775,713	415,238	402,069	352,781
Processed vegetables	7,724,010	305,275	1,400,178	2,082,325	1,538,957	974,176	829,418	637,901
Frozen vegetables	2,537,874	101,510	448,387	773,083	484,843	333,296	255,687	156,518
Canned and dried vegetables and juices	5,186,135	203,765	951,791	1,309,470	1,053,936	640,880	573,731	481,477
Canned beans	1,067,072	60,593	181,333	270,476	209,113	126,518	117,732	105,229
Canned corn	696,050	37,712	141,975	188,078	140,537	67,524	51,282	72,770
Other canned and dried vegetables	2,764,781	89,212	505,465	697,989	567,668	358,047	314,071	249,634
Frozen vegetable juices	23,508	1,565	5,564	8,217	5,522	721	1,806	-
Fresh and canned vegetable juices	634,724	14,682	117,454	144,482	131,274	88,070	88,840	53,939
Other food at home	**84,367,200**	**3,868,629**	**15,880,632**	**23,147,974**	**18,028,060**	**9,922,468**	**8,334,148**	**5,680,544**
Sugar and other sweets	10,757,603	401,419	1,946,855	2,905,623	2,267,111	1,289,330	1,209,097	807,194
Candy and chewing gum	6,369,727	203,169	1,202,566	1,706,854	1,423,001	797,676	701,454	385,901
Sugar	1,871,465	95,473	364,314	530,910	391,686	182,147	195,377	121,505
Artificial sweeteners	346,492	7,677	34,000	78,062	69,823	32,441	59,829	65,862
Jams, preserves, other sweets	2,169,918	95,100	345,975	589,798	382,602	277,066	252,557	233,831
Fats and oils	8,100,143	373,693	1,379,366	2,181,157	1,620,180	911,939	908,869	762,245
Margarine	1,447,294	59,400	180,303	339,636	262,549	181,547	173,829	253,041
Fats and oils	2,360,029	110,006	464,871	611,938	489,474	249,191	259,900	186,894
Salad dressings	2,427,488	108,590	404,908	669,914	533,291	305,782	259,299	161,723
Nondairy cream and imitation milk	670,498	28,321	101,175	184,426	146,771	73,532	91,248	48,734
Peanut butter	1,195,857	67,375	228,108	375,471	188,273	101,767	124,593	111,947
Miscellaneous foods	36,961,180	1,849,313	7,552,305	10,549,943	7,562,263	3,943,804	3,387,614	2,334,995
Frozen prepared foods	6,760,169	261,749	1,268,299	1,759,808	1,545,547	782,657	620,679	576,202
Frozen meals	2,190,360	50,606	373,793	524,062	508,711	258,923	218,369	275,279
Other frozen prepared foods	4,569,809	211,143	894,713	1,235,746	1,036,658	523,614	402,430	300,923
Canned and packaged soups	3,020,306	145,184	549,562	802,071	571,765	371,504	332,730	259,286
Potato chips, nuts, and other snacks	7,570,695	300,878	1,375,863	2,374,713	1,693,921	797,436	723,243	366,313
Potato chips and other snacks	5,946,578	250,719	1,140,542	2,000,155	1,300,988	575,519	475,983	253,419
Nuts	1,624,117	50,159	235,527	374,787	392,933	221,917	247,140	112,894
Condiments and seasonings	8,150,225	426,013	1,463,644	2,373,800	1,718,858	919,868	797,999	498,416
Salt, spices and other seasonings	1,972,653	98,901	330,726	540,724	392,220	279,829	206,692	133,807
Olives, pickles, relishes	1,038,454	42,259	134,969	306,312	223,541	124,956	120,741	92,264
Sauces and gravies	3,723,510	200,933	752,119	1,127,327	803,677	375,228	311,062	178,378
Baking needs and misc. products	1,415,609	83,921	245,624	399,209	299,420	139,855	159,383	93,968
Other canned/packaged prepared foods	11,459,785	715,563	2,894,731	3,239,781	2,032,349	1,072,459	912,962	634,778
Prepared salads	1,121,244	28,545	155,163	319,550	245,806	151,029	159,744	69,458
Prepared desserts	816,658	27,427	129,612	208,621	159,774	91,194	110,870	92,548

	total consumer units	under 25	25 to 34	35 to 44	45 to 54	55 to 64	65 to 74	75+
Baby food	$2,873,123	$297,226	$1,286,020	$751,856	$308,504	$130,363	$60,190	$35,392
Miscellaneous prepared foods	6,648,761	362,290	1,324,142	1,959,755	1,318,266	699,754	582,398	437,285
Nonalcoholic beverages	23,803,687	1,104,684	4,256,375	6,385,979	5,284,286	3,109,482	2,277,710	1,555,339
Cola	9,142,685	484,594	1,711,122	2,581,051	2,091,841	1,143,828	810,880	389,213
Other carbonated drinks	3,974,947	228,956	779,319	1,074,145	800,471	523,614	355,723	233,452
Coffee	4,396,052	109,186	587,271	943,129	1,036,480	761,270	527,024	468,513
Roasted coffee	2,977,377	72,443	408,617	680,642	724,592	514,242	324,183	281,051
Instant and freeze-dried coffee	1,418,675	36,743	178,654	262,716	311,888	247,028	202,840	187,462
Noncarb. fruit flavored drinks								
incl. non-frozen lemonade	2,234,311	106,876	388,011	737,476	489,652	191,519	198,988	137,592
Tea	1,660,913	50,084	319,599	411,307	425,529	183,709	191,886	94,535
Nonalcoholic beer	67,459	-	12,570	14,380	4,631	14,538	14,205	7,381
Other nonalcoholic beverages	2,327,322	124,912	458,690	624,264	435,682	291,003	179,125	224,652
Food prepared by cu on out-of-town trips	4,743,566	139,520	745,731	1,125,273	1,294,220	667,794	550,739	220,677
FOOD AWAY FROM HOME	**173,599,597**	**8,770,839**	**35,147,036**	**46,349,358**	**40,879,965**	**21,819,360**	**14,399,976**	**7,183,742**
Meals at restaurants, carry-outs, other	**133,507,724**	**7,089,368**	**29,157,078**	**36,281,935**	**29,029,107**	**16,106,348**	**11,110,713**	**5,683,005**
Lunch	46,174,390	2,271,525	10,279,715	13,582,473	10,032,253	4,974,570	3,158,651	2,251,153
Dinner	66,619,456	3,578,707	14,265,534	17,033,385	14,545,279	8,675,311	6,279,984	2,679,638
Snacks and nonalcoholic beverages	10,396,801	821,544	2,583,992	3,102,602	2,186,423	951,228	618,031	190,869
Breakfast and brunch	10,318,100	417,592	2,027,630	2,563,704	2,264,974	1,505,119	1,054,047	561,345
Board (including at school)	**5,184,091**	**511,052**	**133,321**	**827,406**	**2,727,017**	**765,596**	**53,208**	**166,076**
Catered affairs	**5,732,959**	**77,884**	**863,391**	**873,513**	**2,476,937**	**995,082**	**313,951**	**132,671**
Food on out-of-town trips	**21,248,437**	**676,956**	**3,255,130**	**4,882,724**	**5,058,964**	**3,423,434**	**2,800,761**	**1,150,890**
School lunches	**5,494,810**	**20,570**	**959,415**	**3,051,246**	**1,227,247**	**146,463**	**62,116**	**28,010**
Meals as pay	**2,431,576**	**395,009**	**778,701**	**432,534**	**360,693**	**382,437**	**59,227**	**23,090**
ALCOHOLIC BEVERAGES	**28,417,446**	**1,837,984**	**7,149,458**	**6,755,972**	**5,195,226**	**4,055,663**	**2,778,611**	**731,868**
At home	**16,877,937**	**896,819**	**4,303,975**	**4,191,583**	**3,097,329**	**2,297,148**	**1,718,304**	**447,411**
Beer and ale	10,188,293	664,882	3,245,651	2,561,650	1,695,702	1,052,874	803,898	197,682
Whiskey	1,398,233	46,060	199,466	205,653	193,260	351,198	310,821	88,574
Wine	3,721,466	125,210	572,023	1,033,744	858,538	635,353	416,274	113,177
Other alcoholic beverages	1,568,924	60,667	286,836	390,308	349,828	257,722	187,311	47,883
Away from home	**11,540,531**	**941,165**	**2,845,689**	**2,564,389**	**2,097,897**	**1,758,515**	**1,060,427**	**284,458**
Beer and ale	3,941,218	451,279	1,130,239	836,536	644,260	552,450	264,234	57,440
Wine	1,613,896	109,410	378,326	373,417	304,407	279,349	141,687	33,594
Other alcoholic beverages	2,857,792	210,622	652,592	652,110	525,632	522,773	254,363	48,829
Alcoholic beverages purchased on trips	3,128,648	169,854	684,325	702,097	623,598	403,944	400,143	144,595

Note: Spending for items in a given category may not add to the total for that category because the listing is incomplete. Numbers may not add to total due to rounding. (-) means insufficient data.

Age
market shares

(percent of total annual spending on food accounted for by consumer unit age groups, 1994)

	total consumer units	under 25	25 to 34	35 to 44	45 to 54	55 to 64	65 to 74	75+
Share of total consumer units	100.0%	7.3%	20.2%	22.3%	17.4%	11.8%	11.8%	9.3%
Share of total spending	100.0	4.2	19.3	26.4	22.7	12.5	9.3	5.6
Share of food spending	100.0	4.6	19.0	27.2	22.2	12.1	9.5	6.0
Share of alcoholic beverages spending	100.0	6.5	25.2	23.8	18.3	14.3	9.8	2.6
FOOD AT HOME	100.0%	4.3%	18.2%	27.5%	21.3%	11.8%	10.2%	7.2%
Cereals and bakery products	100.0	4.3	18.2	27.9	20.8	11.4	10.6	7.5
Cereals and cereal products	100.0	5.2	19.7	29.0	20.3	10.0	9.2	7.2
Flour	100.0	5.7	23.8	23.7	19.4	9.0	10.4	8.3
Prepared flour mixes	100.0	5.1	17.5	27.7	19.2	10.9	10.9	9.1
Ready-to-eat and cooked cereals	100.0	5.1	19.3	29.7	19.6	9.9	9.7	7.2
Rice	100.0	5.2	22.0	29.5	21.7	9.8	6.9	5.6
Pasta, cornmeal, other cereal products	100.0	5.0	19.7	28.6	22.6	10.4	7.7	6.7
Bakery products	100.0	3.7	17.3	27.2	21.1	12.2	11.4	7.7
Bread	100.0	3.9	17.8	25.5	20.9	12.5	11.7	8.3
White bread	100.0	4.5	19.2	27.3	19.4	11.8	11.1	7.3
Bread, other than white	100.0	3.4	16.4	23.7	22.5	13.1	12.3	9.3
Crackers and cookies	100.0	3.5	16.6	28.2	19.6	12.4	12.1	8.1
Cookies	100.0	3.5	17.1	28.2	19.8	12.1	11.8	8.1
Crackers	100.0	3.7	15.6	28.1	19.3	13.1	12.6	8.1
Frozen/refrigerated bakery products	100.0	4.1	19.4	26.4	22.9	10.8	10.6	6.5
Other bakery products	100.0	3.6	17.0	28.0	21.7	12.1	11.0	7.2
Biscuits and rolls	100.0	3.6	16.0	27.6	23.4	12.9	11.0	6.4
Cakes and cupcakes	100.0	4.2	17.7	29.4	20.7	13.3	10.3	5.1
Bread and cracker products	100.0	3.9	15.0	32.3	21.5	12.7	10.5	4.9
Sweetrolls, coffee cakes, doughnuts	100.0	2.6	16.7	25.1	23.1	9.4	13.1	10.7
Pies, tarts, turnovers	100.0	3.7	19.6	29.6	17.4	11.6	9.2	9.4
Meats, poultry, fish, and eggs	100.0	4.3	17.9	28.0	22.3	12.4	9.6	6.3
Beef	100.0	4.3	18.6	28.6	22.8	11.9	8.8	5.8
Ground beef	100.0	5.5	20.7	28.7	20.8	10.6	8.0	6.2
Roast	100.0	2.8	14.6	27.8	24.7	13.0	11.0	7.0
Chuck roast	100.0	3.6	16.2	26.1	18.9	15.2	11.0	9.5
Round roast	100.0	2.4	14.3	26.3	26.7	11.5	12.7	7.2
Other roast	100.0	2.5	13.5	31.2	28.1	12.6	9.0	4.4
Steak	100.0	3.9	18.8	27.6	24.9	13.3	8.1	4.5
Round steak	100.0	3.2	17.5	29.3	27.7	12.1	7.8	3.8
Sirloin steak	100.0	4.1	18.6	25.9	23.9	12.8	10.4	5.2
Other steak	100.0	4.0	19.3	27.9	24.4	14.1	7.0	4.4
Other beef	100.0	2.5	15.9	36.8	17.2	9.3	11.7	7.1
Pork	100.0	4.9	16.6	27.3	21.0	13.2	10.4	7.1
Bacon	100.0	4.9	16.2	24.7	19.9	12.6	10.8	11.4
Pork chops	100.0	4.9	19.6	28.6	22.3	12.5	7.5	5.3

	total consumer units	under 25	25 to 34	35 to 44	45 to 54	55 to 64	65 to 74	75+
Ham	100.0%	4.1%	13.0%	27.4%	19.9%	14.2%	13.5%	8.4%
Ham, not canned	100.0	4.0	13.0	27.0	20.8	14.4	13.6	7.7
Canned ham	100.0	5.5	13.0	32.3	7.9	11.0	12.8	16.8
Sausage	100.0	5.9	17.1	29.8	18.5	12.7	10.6	5.7
Other pork	100.0	4.9	17.3	25.8	23.0	13.8	10.0	5.9
Other meats	100.0	4.0	17.1	28.2	22.2	11.2	10.3	7.7
Frankfurters	100.0	5.5	17.8	28.8	19.7	11.6	8.7	8.5
Lunch meats (cold cuts)	100.0	3.9	17.0	27.9	22.6	11.4	10.5	7.4
Bologna, liverwurst, salami	100.0	5.0	17.7	28.0	21.1	11.0	10.3	7.5
Other lunchmeats	100.0	3.3	16.6	27.9	23.4	11.7	10.5	7.4
Lamb, organ meats and others	100.0	1.5	17.0	29.0	24.1	9.2	12.1	8.1
Lamb and organ meats	100.0	1.5	16.0	29.1	24.5	9.4	12.2	8.2
Mutton, goat and game	100.0	-	71.7	22.3	-	-	8.5	-
Poultry	100.0	3.7	18.3	28.7	23.3	12.2	8.7	6.0
Fresh and frozen chickens	100.0	4.1	19.0	28.9	23.3	12.0	7.9	5.7
Fresh and frozen whole chicken	100.0	3.0	17.4	28.8	22.8	13.6	8.5	6.8
Fresh and frozen chicken parts	100.0	4.5	19.7	29.0	23.4	11.4	7.7	5.2
Other poultry	100.0	2.4	15.6	27.8	23.5	12.8	11.7	7.1
Fish and seafood	100.0	4.1	18.3	27.1	22.3	14.0	9.8	5.2
Canned fish and seafood	100.0	3.2	17.6	27.7	18.4	13.8	12.1	7.6
Fresh fish and shellfish	100.0	4.5	18.1	27.5	22.7	15.5	7.8	4.7
Frozen fish and shellfish	100.0	3.5	19.0	25.9	23.9	11.0	12.8	4.6
Eggs	100.0	5.4	18.3	25.7	20.2	11.4	12.2	7.2
Dairy products	**100.0**	**4.6**	**18.2**	**27.9**	**20.4**	**11.1**	**10.5**	**7.9**
Fresh milk and cream	100.0	4.8	19.6	27.6	19.9	10.4	10.0	8.4
Fresh milk, all types	100.0	4.8	19.7	27.6	19.8	10.3	10.0	8.3
Cream	100.0	3.9	17.4	27.2	20.8	11.0	9.9	10.5
Other dairy products	100.0	4.4	17.1	28.1	20.8	11.7	10.9	7.6
Butter	100.0	4.3	19.0	26.2	26.1	11.0	9.2	5.3
Cheese	100.0	4.4	17.8	28.6	20.0	11.3	10.3	8.1
Ice cream and related products	100.0	4.0	16.0	27.4	20.5	12.9	12.1	7.6
Miscellaneous dairy products	100.0	5.2	16.1	28.7	21.6	10.8	11.5	6.7
Fruits and vegetables	**100.0**	**4.0**	**17.7**	**25.9**	**20.8**	**12.1**	**11.2**	**8.8**
Fresh fruits	100.0	3.6	17.2	25.2	21.4	11.8	11.8	9.5
Apples	100.0	3.6	19.5	29.1	21.2	11.6	9.4	6.4
Bananas	100.0	3.9	18.5	23.3	21.0	11.4	12.3	10.1
Oranges	100.0	5.0	19.9	23.2	23.7	11.7	10.6	6.5
Citrus fruits, excl. oranges	100.0	3.2	15.2	23.7	19.8	13.8	13.6	11.2
Other fresh fruits	100.0	3.2	14.9	25.2	21.4	11.8	12.8	11.2
Fresh vegetables	100.0	3.7	17.8	26.5	21.0	12.6	11.0	8.1
Potatoes	100.0	4.0	17.2	26.3	21.1	12.5	10.4	9.2
Lettuce	100.0	3.8	20.9	25.2	21.4	11.4	10.8	7.1
Tomatoes	100.0	3.9	19.2	27.1	20.3	12.2	10.3	7.5
Other fresh vegetables	100.0	3.5	16.8	26.6	21.1	13.1	11.4	8.1

	total consumer units	under 25	25 to 34	35 to 44	45 to 54	55 to 64	65 to 74	75+
Processed fruits	100.0%	4.8%	18.1%	25.5%	20.4%	11.1%	11.0%	9.5%
Frozen fruits and fruit juices	100.0	6.0	18.3	28.5	19.0	10.3	11.4	6.9
Frozen orange juice	100.0	6.9	18.2	26.0	19.2	9.7	12.0	8.1
Frozen fruits	100.0	1.9	18.0	22.1	15.5	21.6	15.6	5.4
Frozen fruit juices	100.0	5.8	18.3	34.9	19.6	7.8	9.0	5.1
Canned fruit	100.0	2.7	16.9	22.0	17.4	13.4	12.5	15.4
Dried fruit	100.0	2.4	11.7	21.2	23.8	12.3	16.4	12.9
Fresh fruit juices	100.0	4.2	19.1	24.7	24.5	11.2	9.7	7.4
Canned and bottled fruit juices	100.0	5.8	18.9	26.6	19.6	10.5	10.1	8.9
Processed vegetables	100.0	4.0	18.1	27.0	19.9	12.6	10.7	8.3
Frozen vegetables	100.0	4.0	17.7	30.5	19.1	13.1	10.1	6.2
Canned and dried vegetables and juices	100.0	3.9	18.4	25.2	20.3	12.4	11.1	9.3
Canned beans	100.0	5.7	17.0	25.3	19.6	11.9	11.0	9.9
Canned corn	100.0	5.4	20.4	27.0	20.2	9.7	7.4	10.5
Other canned and dried vegetables	100.0	3.2	18.3	25.2	20.5	13.0	11.4	9.0
Frozen vegetable juices	100.0	6.7	23.7	35.0	23.5	3.1	7.7	-
Fresh and canned vegetable juices	100.0	2.3	18.5	22.8	20.7	13.9	14.0	8.5
Other food at home	**100.0**	**4.6**	**18.8**	**27.4**	**21.4**	**11.8**	**9.9**	**6.7**
Sugar and other sweets	100.0	3.7	18.1	27.0	21.1	12.0	11.2	7.5
Candy and chewing gum	100.0	3.2	18.9	26.8	22.3	12.5	11.0	6.1
Sugar	100.0	5.1	19.5	28.4	20.9	9.7	10.4	6.5
Artificial sweeteners	100.0	2.2	9.8	22.5	20.2	9.4	17.3	19.0
Jams, preserves, other sweets	100.0	4.4	15.9	27.2	17.6	12.8	11.6	10.8
Fats and oils	100.0	4.6	17.0	26.9	20.0	11.3	11.2	9.4
Margarine	100.0	4.1	12.5	23.5	18.1	12.5	12.0	17.5
Fats and oils	100.0	4.7	19.7	25.9	20.7	10.6	11.0	7.9
Salad dressings	100.0	4.5	16.7	27.6	22.0	12.6	10.7	6.7
Nondairy cream and imitation milk	100.0	4.2	15.1	27.5	21.9	11.0	13.6	7.3
Peanut butter	100.0	5.6	19.1	31.4	15.7	8.5	10.4	9.4
Miscellaneous foods	100.0	5.0	20.4	28.5	20.5	10.7	9.2	6.3
Frozen prepared foods	100.0	3.9	18.8	26.0	22.9	11.6	9.2	8.5
Frozen meals	100.0	2.3	17.1	23.9	23.2	11.8	10.0	12.6
Other frozen prepared foods	100.0	4.6	19.6	27.0	22.7	11.5	8.8	6.6
Canned and packaged soups	100.0	4.8	18.2	26.6	18.9	12.3	11.0	8.6
Potato chips, nuts, and other snacks	100.0	4.0	18.2	31.4	22.4	10.5	9.6	4.8
Potato chips and other snacks	100.0	4.2	19.2	33.6	21.9	9.7	8.0	4.3
Nuts	100.0	3.1	14.5	23.1	24.2	13.7	15.2	7.0
Condiments and seasonings	100.0	5.2	18.0	29.1	21.1	11.3	9.8	6.1
Salt, spices and other seasonings	100.0	5.0	16.8	27.4	19.9	14.2	10.5	6.8
Olives, pickles, relishes	100.0	4.1	13.0	29.5	21.5	12.0	11.6	8.9
Sauces and gravies	100.0	5.4	20.2	30.3	21.6	10.1	8.4	4.8
Baking needs and misc. products	100.0	5.9	17.4	28.2	21.2	9.9	11.3	6.6
Other canned/packaged prepared foods	100.0	6.2	25.3	28.3	17.7	9.4	8.0	5.5
Prepared salads	100.0	2.5	13.8	28.5	21.9	13.5	14.2	6.2
Prepared desserts	100.0	3.4	15.9	25.5	19.6	11.2	13.6	11.3

	total consumer units	under 25	25 to 34	35 to 44	45 to 54	55 to 64	65 to 74	75+
Baby food	100.0%	10.3%	44.8%	26.2%	10.7%	4.5%	2.1%	1.2%
Miscellaneous prepared foods	100.0	5.4	19.9	29.5	19.8	10.5	8.8	6.6
Nonalcoholic beverages	100.0	4.6	17.9	26.8	22.2	13.1	9.6	6.5
Cola	100.0	5.1	18.7	28.2	22.9	12.5	8.9	4.3
Other carbonated drinks	100.0	5.8	19.6	27.0	20.1	13.2	8.9	5.9
Coffee	100.0	2.5	13.4	21.5	23.6	17.3	12.0	10.7
Roasted coffee	100.0	2.4	13.7	22.9	24.3	17.3	10.9	9.4
Instant and freeze-dried coffee	100.0	2.6	12.6	18.5	22.0	17.4	14.3	13.2
Noncarb. fruit flavored drinks incl. non-frozen lemonade	100.0	4.8	17.4	33.0	21.9	8.6	8.9	6.2
Tea	100.0	3.0	19.2	24.8	25.6	11.1	11.6	5.7
Nonalcoholic beer	100.0	-	18.6	21.3	6.9	21.6	21.1	10.9
Other nonalcoholic beverages	100.0	5.4	19.7	26.8	18.7	12.5	7.7	9.7
Food prepared by cu on out-of-town trips	100.0	2.9	15.7	23.7	27.3	14.1	11.6	4.7
FOOD AWAY FROM HOME	**100.0**	**5.1**	**20.2**	**26.7**	**23.5**	**12.6**	**8.3**	**4.1**
Meals at restaurants, carry-outs, other	**100.0**	**5.3**	**21.8**	**27.2**	**21.7**	**12.1**	**8.3**	**4.3**
Lunch	100.0	4.9	22.3	29.4	21.7	10.8	6.8	4.9
Dinner	100.0	5.4	21.4	25.6	21.8	13.0	9.4	4.0
Snacks and nonalcoholic beverages	100.0	7.9	24.9	29.8	21.0	9.1	5.9	1.8
Breakfast and brunch	100.0	4.0	19.7	24.8	22.0	14.6	10.2	5.4
Board (including at school)	**100.0**	**9.9**	**2.6**	**16.0**	**52.6**	**14.8**	**1.0**	**3.2**
Catered affairs	**100.0**	**1.4**	**15.1**	**15.2**	**43.2**	**17.4**	**5.5**	**2.3**
Food on out-of-town trips	**100.0**	**3.2**	**15.3**	**23.0**	**23.8**	**16.1**	**13.2**	**5.4**
School lunches	**100.0**	**0.4**	**17.5**	**55.5**	**22.3**	**2.7**	**1.1**	**0.5**
Meals as pay	**100.0**	**16.2**	**32.0**	**17.8**	**14.8**	**15.7**	**2.4**	**0.9**
ALCOHOLIC BEVERAGES	**100.0**	**6.5**	**25.2**	**23.8**	**18.3**	**14.3**	**9.8**	**2.6**
At home	**100.0**	**5.3**	**25.5**	**24.8**	**18.4**	**13.6**	**10.2**	**2.7**
Beer and ale	100.0	6.5	31.9	25.1	16.6	10.3	7.9	1.9
Whiskey	100.0	3.3	14.3	14.7	13.8	25.1	22.2	6.3
Wine	100.0	3.4	15.4	27.8	23.1	17.1	11.2	3.0
Other alcoholic beverages	100.0	3.9	18.3	24.9	22.3	16.4	11.9	3.1
Away from home	**100.0**	**8.2**	**24.7**	**22.2**	**18.2**	**15.2**	**9.2**	**2.5**
Beer and ale	100.0	11.5	28.7	21.2	16.3	14.0	6.7	1.5
Wine	100.0	6.8	23.4	23.1	18.9	17.3	8.8	2.1
Other alcoholic beverages	100.0	7.4	22.8	22.8	18.4	18.3	8.9	1.7
Alcoholic beverages purchased on trips	100.0	5.4	21.9	22.4	19.9	12.9	12.8	4.6

Note: Numbers may not add to total due to rounding. (-) means insufficient data.

Age
projections of total spending to 2000

(total annual spending on food and alcoholic beverages by consumer unit age groups, 2000; numbers in thousands)

	total consumer units	under 25	25 to 34	35 to 44	45 to 54	55 to 64	65 to 74	75+
Number of consumer units	109,317	8,464	18,652	24,163	21,616	13,356	11,622	11,443
Total spending of all cu's	$3,470,883,620	$155,887,667	$568,249,221	$908,231,353	$895,844,858	$450,126,316	$291,632,938	$220,914,095
Food, total spending	482,144,815	23,643,507	77,578,331	129,675,330	121,359,790	60,760,050	41,171,981	32,853,540
Alcoholic beverages, total spending	30,393,406	2,087,307	6,471,498	7,152,006	6,304,739	4,508,318	2,682,590	885,002
FOOD AT HOME	**$296,473,170**	**$13,682,902**	**$45,764,361**	**$80,608,976**	**$71,749,124**	**$36,505,287**	**$27,269,628**	**$24,166,586**
Cereals and bakery products	**46,862,012**	**2,118,370**	**7,225,785**	**12,943,153**	**11,060,475**	**5,530,452**	**4,477,376**	**3,963,741**
Cereals and cereal products	17,680,932	968,282	2,944,778	5,081,962	4,068,996	1,836,584	1,473,786	1,432,778
Flour	830,809	50,615	167,122	194,995	183,304	77,999	77,984	77,927
Prepared flour mixes	1,398,164	75,584	207,037	383,467	303,921	159,070	137,488	144,067
Ready-to-eat and cooked cereals	10,742,582	586,978	1,751,982	3,153,513	2,392,675	1,101,202	941,847	875,962
Rice	1,686,761	93,273	313,913	493,167	414,379	172,560	105,412	106,649
Pasta, cornmeal, other cereal products	3,022,615	161,832	504,537	857,062	774,934	325,753	211,056	228,173
Bakery products	29,179,987	1,150,173	4,281,007	7,861,190	6,991,263	3,694,002	3,003,590	2,530,848
Bread	8,332,142	347,024	1,252,295	2,103,872	1,980,026	1,079,165	877,693	782,701
White bread	4,115,785	196,026	667,369	1,113,189	903,765	504,990	410,721	339,628
Bread, other than white	4,216,357	150,998	585,113	990,441	1,076,261	574,174	466,972	443,073
Crackers and cookies	6,838,872	256,882	961,697	1,907,427	1,522,415	880,695	746,249	625,818
Cookies	4,697,351	173,004	679,119	1,312,776	1,054,645	588,599	502,070	429,341
Crackers	2,141,520	83,878	282,578	594,893	467,770	292,229	244,178	196,476
Frozen/refrigerated bakery products	2,356,875	101,653	386,469	616,640	613,246	265,651	225,699	173,361
Other bakery products	11,652,099	444,614	1,680,359	3,233,009	2,875,576	1,468,492	1,154,065	948,968
Biscuits and rolls	3,931,039	150,490	531,582	1,073,320	1,045,782	525,559	389,918	282,299
Cakes and cupcakes	3,409,597	150,405	511,997	990,683	800,657	472,535	315,886	197,735
Bread and cracker products	515,976	21,499	65,655	164,792	125,589	68,249	49,045	28,608
Sweetrolls, coffee cakes, doughnuts	2,396,229	67,120	339,093	594,651	627,512	233,864	282,415	291,110
Pies, tarts, turnovers	1,399,258	55,016	232,031	409,321	276,036	168,286	116,801	149,331
Meats, poultry, fish, and eggs	**80,069,237**	**3,633,849**	**12,131,634**	**22,195,407**	**20,225,659**	**10,322,318**	**6,930,547**	**5,722,187**
Beef	24,788,723	1,121,565	3,909,459	7,024,426	6,411,954	3,077,890	1,972,370	1,611,975
Ground beef	9,669,089	569,373	1,696,399	2,749,749	2,286,540	1,061,802	702,434	673,421
Roast	4,308,183	129,161	534,007	1,183,987	1,208,551	581,787	427,690	341,688
Chuck roast	1,340,226	51,376	183,909	346,256	286,844	211,559	133,537	144,067
Round roast	1,622,264	41,389	196,033	421,886	491,980	194,463	185,255	131,366
Other roast	1,345,692	36,395	154,252	416,087	429,726	175,765	109,014	66,255
Steak	9,264,616	381,811	1,470,524	2,527,208	2,615,968	1,284,179	679,306	472,138
Round steak	1,749,072	59,333	258,703	506,940	549,695	220,240	123,426	74,494
Sirloin steak	2,671,707	115,449	420,976	684,779	725,001	354,735	250,919	155,625
Other steak	4,843,836	207,029	790,845	1,335,731	1,341,273	709,204	304,961	241,905
Other beef	1,546,836	41,220	208,343	563,481	301,111	150,121	162,940	124,729
Pork	17,025,030	878,394	2,398,274	4,608,367	4,053,865	2,339,303	1,601,628	1,366,065
Bacon	2,490,241	130,007	340,772	609,149	563,097	325,352	242,202	319,946
Pork chops	4,298,344	223,704	711,947	1,218,782	1,089,663	560,151	292,410	257,239

	total consumer units	under 25	25 to 34	35 to 44	45 to 54	55 to 64	65 to 74	75+
Ham	$4,031,611	$175,543	$442,239	$1,094,826	$908,520	$593,541	$491,843	$382,196
Ham, not canned	3,734,269	158,023	409,411	999,623	881,717	559,483	457,558	325,553
Canned ham	297,342	17,520	32,828	95,202	26,588	34,058	34,285	56,643
Sausage	2,494,614	156,161	361,662	736,488	523,972	328,424	239,413	160,545
Other pork	3,709,126	192,979	541,654	948,881	968,613	531,969	335,876	246,139
Other meats	10,270,332	433,865	1,490,108	2,868,631	2,582,680	1,198,567	952,539	895,758
Frankfurters	2,050,787	119,004	309,437	584,020	458,692	246,418	160,384	196,705
Lunch meats (cold cuts)	7,177,754	298,187	1,030,710	1,985,232	1,839,522	852,647	678,027	603,962
Bologna, liverwurst, salami	2,594,092	136,694	387,775	718,608	622,325	295,969	241,854	219,477
Other lunchmeats	4,583,662	161,493	642,934	1,266,624	1,217,197	556,678	436,057	384,485
Lamb, organ meats and others	1,041,791	16,674	150,149	299,138	284,683	99,502	114,012	94,977
Lamb and organ meats	1,022,114	16,674	138,211	294,789	284,683	99,502	112,617	94,977
Mutton, goat and game	19,677	-	11,937	4,349	-	-	1,511	-
Poultry	14,930,516	592,057	2,313,408	4,236,982	3,951,621	1,890,008	1,176,960	1,008,357
Fresh and frozen chickens	11,794,211	511,564	1,900,266	3,374,363	3,113,785	1,473,167	845,501	756,840
Fresh and frozen whole chicken	3,231,411	104,446	475,813	920,127	835,458	456,775	248,711	250,258
Fresh and frozen chicken parts	8,562,801	407,118	1,424,640	2,454,236	2,278,326	1,016,392	596,790	506,582
Other poultry	3,136,305	80,493	412,955	862,619	837,836	416,841	331,459	251,517
Fish and seafood	9,776,219	421,592	1,512,118	2,623,377	2,474,600	1,427,489	865,142	572,837
Canned fish and seafood	1,643,035	55,778	244,155	451,123	343,911	235,466	179,560	141,893
Fresh fish and shellfish	5,603,589	270,509	860,417	1,524,202	1,444,165	902,465	394,218	297,976
Frozen fish and shellfish	2,530,689	95,389	407,546	648,052	686,524	289,558	291,480	132,853
Eggs	3,279,510	186,377	508,267	833,624	751,156	389,194	361,909	267,194
Dairy products	**31,583,868**	**1,526,567**	**4,868,359**	**8,707,862**	**7,310,747**	**3,638,575**	**2,991,851**	**2,838,322**
Fresh milk and cream	13,897,470	701,242	2,301,843	3,789,967	3,137,346	1,495,872	1,251,922	1,320,980
Fresh milk, all types	13,002,164	664,085	2,169,974	3,549,061	2,926,374	1,393,832	1,172,195	1,214,674
Cream	895,306	37,072	131,870	240,905	211,188	102,040	79,727	106,305
Other dairy products	17,686,397	825,325	2,566,329	4,918,137	4,173,401	2,142,837	1,739,930	1,517,342
Butter	1,273,543	57,555	204,985	330,067	376,551	145,046	106,225	75,982
Cheese	8,945,410	421,253	1,348,540	2,534,457	2,028,662	1,047,778	829,927	823,782
Ice cream and related products	5,207,862	221,841	704,859	1,412,811	1,213,738	697,317	569,246	447,536
Miscellaneous dairy products	2,258,489	124,675	307,945	640,803	554,234	252,696	234,532	170,157
Fruits and vegetables	**47,724,523**	**2,010,708**	**7,163,860**	**12,257,407**	**11,274,041**	**5,984,022**	**4,823,595**	**4,773,219**
Fresh fruits	14,541,347	561,502	2,122,038	3,620,584	3,538,972	1,788,368	1,552,234	1,555,790
Apples	2,773,372	104,869	457,907	797,862	667,718	333,099	236,508	200,710
Bananas	3,242,342	134,747	507,334	748,328	774,285	383,851	358,771	370,524
Oranges	1,788,426	95,897	301,416	410,771	480,956	217,970	170,611	131,709
Citrus fruits, excl. oranges	1,198,114	40,543	154,625	280,774	268,903	171,758	147,483	151,162
Other fresh fruits	5,539,092	185,446	700,756	1,382,848	1,347,109	681,690	638,861	701,570
Fresh vegetables	14,745,770	581,561	2,219,588	3,860,523	3,517,356	1,934,483	1,457,747	1,350,503
Potatoes	3,061,969	130,769	445,223	795,688	731,918	396,540	288,342	319,031
Lettuce	1,899,929	76,091	336,296	474,320	461,718	224,781	185,720	152,764
Tomatoes	2,296,750	95,220	373,600	616,640	530,240	291,561	213,147	195,675
Other fresh vegetables	7,488,215	279,566	1,064,470	1,973,875	1,793,480	1,021,600	770,655	683,033

	total consumer units	under 25	25 to 34	35 to 44	45 to 54	55 to 64	65 to 74	75+
Processed fruits	$10,175,226	$520,959	$1,555,017	$2,571,910	$2,350,308	$1,178,266	$1,012,857	$1,095,553
Frozen fruits and fruit juices	1,779,681	114,264	274,930	501,624	383,252	190,056	183,047	138,575
Frozen orange juice	1,037,418	75,499	160,221	267,484	226,320	104,577	112,269	95,091
Frozen fruits	174,907	3,470	26,672	38,178	30,695	39,267	24,639	10,756
Frozen fruit juices	567,355	35,210	87,851	195,962	126,237	46,212	46,139	32,727
Canned fruit	1,555,581	44,267	222,891	339,007	307,812	216,100	175,492	271,657
Dried fruit	643,877	16,166	63,976	135,071	173,576	82,407	95,300	93,947
Fresh fruit juices	1,956,774	86,417	316,151	478,669	544,507	228,120	170,960	164,665
Canned and bottled fruit juices	4,239,313	259,760	677,068	1,117,297	941,377	461,583	388,175	426,595
Processed vegetables	8,261,086	346,685	1,267,403	2,204,390	1,867,622	1,082,904	800,756	771,373
Frozen vegetables	2,714,341	115,280	405,868	818,401	588,388	370,495	246,851	189,267
Canned and dried vegetables and juices	5,546,745	231,406	861,536	1,386,231	1,279,019	712,409	553,905	582,220
Canned beans	1,141,269	68,812	164,138	286,332	253,772	140,639	113,663	127,246
Canned corn	744,449	42,828	128,512	199,103	170,550	75,061	49,510	87,997
Other canned and dried vegetables	2,957,025	101,314	457,534	738,905	688,902	398,009	303,218	301,866
Frozen vegetable juices	25,143	1,777	5,036	8,699	6,701	801	1,743	-
Fresh and canned vegetable juices	678,859	16,674	106,316	152,952	159,310	97,899	85,770	65,225
Other food at home	**90,233,531**	**4,393,408**	**14,374,723**	**24,504,906**	**21,878,202**	**11,029,919**	**8,046,143**	**6,869,118**
Sugar and other sweets	11,505,614	455,871	1,762,241	3,075,950	2,751,284	1,433,232	1,167,314	976,088
Candy and chewing gum	6,812,635	230,729	1,088,531	1,806,909	1,726,902	886,705	677,214	466,646
Sugar	2,001,594	108,424	329,767	562,031	475,336	202,477	188,625	146,928
Artificial sweeteners	370,585	8,718	30,776	82,637	84,735	36,061	57,761	79,643
Jams, preserves, other sweets	2,320,800	108,001	313,167	624,372	464,312	307,989	243,830	282,757
Fats and oils	8,663,372	424,385	1,248,565	2,309,016	1,966,191	1,013,720	877,461	921,734
Margarine	1,547,929	67,458	163,205	359,545	318,620	201,809	167,822	305,986
Fats and oils	2,524,130	124,929	420,789	647,810	594,008	277,003	250,919	225,999
Salad dressings	2,596,279	123,320	366,512	709,184	647,183	339,910	250,338	195,561
Nondairy cream and imitation milk	717,120	32,163	91,581	195,237	178,116	81,739	88,095	58,931
Peanut butter	1,279,009	76,515	206,478	397,481	228,481	113,125	120,288	135,371
Miscellaneous foods	39,531,214	2,100,172	6,836,145	11,168,380	9,177,289	4,383,973	3,270,547	2,823,560
Frozen prepared foods	7,230,226	297,256	1,148,031	1,862,967	1,875,620	870,010	599,230	696,764
Frozen meals	2,342,663	57,471	338,347	554,782	617,353	287,822	210,823	332,877
Other frozen prepared foods	4,887,563	239,785	809,870	1,308,185	1,258,051	582,054	388,523	363,887
Canned and packaged soups	3,230,317	164,879	497,449	849,088	693,874	412,968	321,232	313,538
Potato chips, nuts, and other snacks	8,097,110	341,692	1,245,394	2,513,919	2,055,682	886,438	698,250	442,959
Potato chips and other snacks	6,360,063	284,729	1,032,388	2,117,404	1,578,833	639,752	459,534	306,444
Nuts	1,737,047	56,963	213,192	396,756	476,849	246,685	238,600	136,515
Condiments and seasonings	8,716,938	483,802	1,324,852	2,512,952	2,085,944	1,022,535	770,422	602,703
Salt, spices and other seasonings	2,109,818	112,317	299,365	572,421	475,984	311,061	199,550	161,804
Olives, pickles, relishes	1,110,661	47,991	122,171	324,267	271,281	138,902	116,569	111,569
Sauces and gravies	3,982,418	228,189	680,798	1,193,411	975,314	417,108	300,312	215,701
Baking needs and misc. products	1,514,040	95,305	222,332	422,611	363,365	155,464	153,875	113,629
Other canned/packaged prepared foods	12,256,622	812,629	2,620,233	3,429,696	2,466,386	1,192,157	881,412	767,596
Prepared salads	1,199,207	32,417	140,450	338,282	298,301	167,885	154,224	83,992
Prepared desserts	873,443	31,148	117,321	220,850	193,896	101,372	107,039	111,913

	total consumer units	under 25	25 to 34	35 to 44	45 to 54	55 to 64	65 to 74	75+
Baby food	$3,072,901	$337,544	$1,164,071	$795,929	$374,389	$144,913	$58,110	$42,797
Miscellaneous prepared foods	7,111,071	411,435	1,198,578	2,074,635	1,599,800	777,853	562,272	528,781
Nonalcoholic beverages	25,458,836	1,254,534	3,852,757	6,760,324	6,412,819	3,456,533	2,198,999	1,880,771
Cola	9,778,406	550,329	1,548,862	2,732,352	2,538,583	1,271,491	782,858	470,651
Other carbonated drinks	4,251,338	260,014	705,419	1,137,111	971,423	582,054	343,430	282,299
Coffee	4,701,724	123,998	531,582	998,415	1,257,835	846,236	508,811	566,543
Roasted coffee	3,184,404	82,270	369,869	720,541	879,339	571,637	312,980	339,857
Instant and freeze-dried coffee	1,517,320	41,728	161,713	278,116	378,496	274,599	195,831	226,686
Noncarb. fruit flavored drinks								
incl. non-frozen lemonade	2,389,670	121,374	351,217	780,707	594,224	212,895	192,112	166,381
Tea	1,776,401	56,878	289,293	435,417	516,406	204,213	185,255	114,316
Nonalcoholic beer	72,149	-	11,378	15,223	5,620	16,161	13,714	8,926
Other nonalcoholic beverages	2,489,148	141,857	415,194	660,858	528,727	323,482	172,935	271,657
Food prepared by cu on out-of-town trips	5,073,402	158,446	675,016	1,191,236	1,570,619	742,326	531,707	266,851
FOOD AWAY FROM HOME	**185,670,552**	**9,960,604**	**31,814,157**	**49,066,354**	**49,610,449**	**24,254,630**	**13,902,353**	**8,686,839**
Meals at restaurants, carry-outs, other	**142,790,959**	**8,051,041**	**26,392,207**	**38,408,780**	**35,228,676**	**17,903,985**	**10,726,757**	**6,872,094**
Lunch	49,385,048	2,579,658	9,304,923	14,378,676	12,174,780	5,529,785	3,049,497	2,722,175
Dinner	71,251,727	4,064,159	12,912,780	18,031,880	17,651,626	9,643,566	6,062,965	3,240,314
Snacks and nonalcoholic beverages	11,119,725	932,987	2,338,961	3,284,477	2,653,364	1,057,395	596,673	230,805
Breakfast and brunch	11,035,551	474,238	1,835,357	2,713,988	2,748,691	1,673,106	1,017,622	678,799
Board (including at school)	**5,544,558**	**580,376**	**120,678**	**875,909**	**3,309,410**	**851,044**	**51,369**	**200,825**
Catered affairs	**6,131,591**	**88,449**	**781,519**	**924,718**	**3,005,921**	**1,106,144**	**303,102**	**160,431**
Food on out-of-town trips	**22,725,911**	**768,785**	**2,946,456**	**5,168,949**	**6,139,376**	**3,805,525**	**2,703,975**	**1,391,698**
School lunches	**5,876,882**	**23,361**	**868,437**	**3,230,110**	**1,489,342**	**162,810**	**59,970**	**33,871**
Meals as pay	**2,600,651**	**448,592**	**704,859**	**457,889**	**437,724**	**425,121**	**57,180**	**27,921**
ALCOHOLIC BEVERAGES	**30,393,406**	**2,087,307**	**6,471,498**	**7,152,006**	**6,304,739**	**4,508,318**	**2,682,590**	**885,002**
At home	**18,051,516**	**1,018,473**	**3,895,843**	**4,437,293**	**3,758,806**	**2,553,534**	**1,658,924**	**541,025**
Beer and ale	10,896,719	755,073	2,937,877	2,711,813	2,057,843	1,170,386	776,117	239,044
Whiskey	1,495,457	52,308	180,551	217,709	234,534	390,396	300,080	107,106
Wine	3,980,232	142,195	517,780	1,094,342	1,041,891	706,265	401,889	136,858
Other alcoholic beverages	1,678,016	68,897	259,636	413,187	424,538	286,486	180,838	57,902
Away from home	**12,342,982**	**1,068,834**	**2,575,841**	**2,714,713**	**2,545,932**	**1,954,784**	**1,023,782**	**343,977**
Beer and ale	4,215,264	512,495	1,023,062	885,574	781,851	614,109	255,103	69,459
Wine	1,726,115	124,252	342,451	395,307	369,417	310,527	136,791	40,623
Other alcoholic beverages	3,056,503	239,193	590,709	690,337	637,888	581,120	245,573	59,046
Alcoholic beverages purchased on trips	3,346,193	192,895	619,433	743,254	756,776	449,029	386,315	174,849

Note: Spending for items in a given category may not add to the total for that category because the listing is incomplete. Numbers may not add to total due to rounding. (-) means insufficient data. Spending projections for 2000 account only for change in the age composition of consumer units and have not been adjusted for changes in price or spending patterns.
Source of consumer unit projections: TGE Demographics, Inc., Honeoye Falls, New York

Age
projections of market shares to 2000

(percent of total annual spending on food and alcoholic beverages accounted for by consumer unit age groups, 2000)

	total consumer units	under 25	25 to 34	35 to 44	45 to 54	55 to 64	65 to 74	75+
Share of total consumer units	100.0%	7.7%	17.1%	22.1%	19.8%	12.2%	10.6%	10.5%
Share of total spending	100.0	4.5	16.4	26.2	25.8	13.0	8.4	6.4
Share of food spending	100.0	4.9	16.1	26.9	25.2	12.6	8.5	6.8
Share of alcoholic beverages spending	100.0	6.9	21.3	23.5	20.7	14.8	8.8	2.9
FOOD AT HOME	100.0%	4.6%	15.4%	27.2%	24.2%	12.3%	9.2%	8.2%
Cereals and bakery products	100.0	4.5	15.4	27.6	23.6	11.8	9.6	8.5
Cereals and cereal products	100.0	5.5	16.7	28.7	23.0	10.4	8.3	8.1
Flour	100.0	6.1	20.1	23.5	22.1	9.4	9.4	9.4
Prepared flour mixes	100.0	5.4	14.8	27.4	21.7	11.4	9.8	10.3
Ready-to-eat and cooked cereals	100.0	5.5	16.3	29.4	22.3	10.3	8.8	8.2
Rice	100.0	5.5	18.6	29.2	24.6	10.2	6.2	6.3
Pasta, cornmeal, other cereal products	100.0	5.4	16.7	28.4	25.6	10.8	7.0	7.5
Bakery products	100.0	3.9	14.7	26.9	24.0	12.7	10.3	8.7
Bread	100.0	4.2	15.0	25.3	23.8	13.0	10.5	9.4
White bread	100.0	4.8	16.2	27.0	22.0	12.3	10.0	8.3
Bread, other than white	100.0	3.6	13.9	23.5	25.5	13.6	11.1	10.5
Crackers and cookies	100.0	3.8	14.1	27.9	22.3	12.9	10.9	9.2
Cookies	100.0	3.7	14.5	27.9	22.5	12.5	10.7	9.1
Crackers	100.0	3.9	13.2	27.8	21.8	13.6	11.4	9.2
Frozen/refrigerated bakery products	100.0	4.3	16.4	26.2	26.0	11.3	9.6	7.4
Other bakery products	100.0	3.8	14.4	27.7	24.7	12.6	9.9	8.1
Biscuits and rolls	100.0	3.8	13.5	27.3	26.6	13.4	9.9	7.2
Cakes and cupcakes	100.0	4.4	15.0	29.1	23.5	13.9	9.3	5.8
Bread and cracker products	100.0	4.2	12.7	31.9	24.3	13.2	9.5	5.5
Sweetrolls, coffee cakes, doughnuts	100.0	2.8	14.2	24.8	26.2	9.8	11.8	12.1
Pies, tarts, turnovers	100.0	3.9	16.6	29.3	19.7	12.0	8.3	10.7
Meats, poultry, fish, and eggs	100.0	4.5	15.2	27.7	25.3	12.9	8.7	7.1
Beef	100.0	4.5	15.8	28.3	25.9	12.4	8.0	6.5
Ground beef	100.0	5.9	17.5	28.4	23.6	11.0	7.3	7.0
Roast	100.0	3.0	12.4	27.5	28.1	13.5	9.9	7.9
Chuck roast	100.0	3.8	13.7	25.8	21.4	15.8	10.0	10.7
Round roast	100.0	2.6	12.1	26.0	30.3	12.0	11.4	8.1
Other roast	100.0	2.7	11.5	30.9	31.9	13.1	8.1	4.9
Steak	100.0	4.1	15.9	27.3	28.2	13.9	7.3	5.1
Round steak	100.0	3.4	14.8	29.0	31.4	12.6	7.1	4.3
Sirloin steak	100.0	4.3	15.8	25.6	27.1	13.3	9.4	5.8
Other steak	100.0	4.3	16.3	27.6	27.7	14.6	6.3	5.0
Other beef	100.0	2.7	13.5	36.4	19.5	9.7	10.5	8.1
Pork	100.0	5.2	14.1	27.1	23.8	13.7	9.4	8.0
Bacon	100.0	5.2	13.7	24.5	22.6	13.1	9.7	12.8
Pork chops	100.0	5.2	16.6	28.4	25.4	13.0	6.8	6.0

	total consumer units	under 25	25 to 34	35 to 44	45 to 54	55 to 64	65 to 74	75+
Ham	100.0%	4.4%	11.0%	27.2%	22.5%	14.7%	12.2%	9.5%
Ham, not canned	100.0	4.2	11.0	26.8	23.6	15.0	12.3	8.7
Canned ham	100.0	5.9	11.0	32.0	8.9	11.5	11.5	19.0
Sausage	100.0	6.3	14.5	29.5	21.0	13.2	9.6	6.4
Other pork	100.0	5.2	14.6	25.6	26.1	14.3	9.1	6.6
Other meats	100.0	4.2	14.5	27.9	25.1	11.7	9.3	8.7
Frankfurters	100.0	5.8	15.1	28.5	22.4	12.0	7.8	9.6
Lunch meats (cold cuts)	100.0	4.2	14.4	27.7	25.6	11.9	9.4	8.4
Bologna, liverwurst, salami	100.0	5.3	14.9	27.7	24.0	11.4	9.3	8.5
Other lunchmeats	100.0	3.5	14.0	27.6	26.6	12.1	9.5	8.4
Lamb, organ meats and others	100.0	1.6	14.4	28.7	27.3	9.6	10.9	9.1
Lamb and organ meats	100.0	1.6	13.5	28.8	27.9	9.7	11.0	9.3
Mutton, goat and game	100.0	-	60.7	22.1	-	-	7.7	-
Poultry	100.0	4.0	15.5	28.4	26.5	12.7	7.9	6.8
Fresh and frozen chickens	100.0	4.3	16.1	28.6	26.4	12.5	7.2	6.4
Fresh and frozen whole chicken	100.0	3.2	14.7	28.5	25.9	14.1	7.7	7.7
Fresh and frozen chicken parts	100.0	4.8	16.6	28.7	26.6	11.9	7.0	5.9
Other poultry	100.0	2.6	13.2	27.5	26.7	13.3	10.6	8.0
Fish and seafood	100.0	4.3	15.5	26.8	25.3	14.6	8.8	5.9
Canned fish and seafood	100.0	3.4	14.9	27.5	20.9	14.3	10.9	8.6
Fresh fish and shellfish	100.0	4.8	15.4	27.2	25.8	16.1	7.0	5.3
Frozen fish and shellfish	100.0	3.8	16.1	25.6	27.1	11.4	11.5	5.2
Eggs	100.0	5.7	15.5	25.4	22.9	11.9	11.0	8.1
Dairy products	**100.0**	**4.8**	**15.4**	**27.6**	**23.1**	**11.5**	**9.5**	**9.0**
Fresh milk and cream	100.0	5.0	16.6	27.3	22.6	10.8	9.0	9.5
Fresh milk, all types	100.0	5.1	16.7	27.3	22.5	10.7	9.0	9.3
Cream	100.0	4.1	14.7	26.9	23.6	11.4	8.9	11.9
Other dairy products	100.0	4.7	14.5	27.8	23.6	12.1	9.8	8.6
Butter	100.0	4.5	16.1	25.9	29.6	11.4	8.3	6.0
Cheese	100.0	4.7	15.1	28.3	22.7	11.7	9.3	9.2
Ice cream and related products	100.0	4.3	13.5	27.1	23.3	13.4	10.9	8.6
Miscellaneous dairy products	100.0	5.5	13.6	28.4	24.5	11.2	10.4	7.5
Fruits and vegetables	**100.0**	**4.2**	**15.0**	**25.7**	**23.6**	**12.5**	**10.1**	**10.0**
Fresh fruits	100.0	3.9	14.6	24.9	24.3	12.3	10.7	10.7
Apples	100.0	3.8	16.5	28.8	24.1	12.0	8.5	7.2
Bananas	100.0	4.2	15.6	23.1	23.9	11.8	11.1	11.4
Oranges	100.0	5.4	16.9	23.0	26.9	12.2	9.5	7.4
Citrus fruits, excl. oranges	100.0	3.4	12.9	23.4	22.4	14.3	12.3	12.6
Other fresh fruits	100.0	3.3	12.7	25.0	24.3	12.3	11.5	12.7
Fresh vegetables	100.0	3.9	15.1	26.2	23.9	13.1	9.9	9.2
Potatoes	100.0	4.3	14.5	26.0	23.9	13.0	9.4	10.4
Lettuce	100.0	4.0	17.7	25.0	24.3	11.8	9.8	8.0
Tomatoes	100.0	4.1	16.3	26.8	23.1	12.7	9.3	8.5
Other fresh vegetables	100.0	3.7	14.2	26.4	24.0	13.6	10.3	9.1

	total consumer units	under 25	25 to 34	35 to 44	45 to 54	55 to 64	65 to 74	75+
Processed fruits	100.0%	5.1%	15.3%	25.3%	23.1%	11.6%	10.0%	10.8%
Frozen fruits and fruit juices	100.0	6.4	15.4	28.2	21.5	10.7	10.3	7.8
Frozen orange juice	100.0	7.3	15.4	25.8	21.8	10.1	10.8	9.2
Frozen fruits	100.0	2.0	15.2	21.8	17.5	22.4	14.1	6.1
Frozen fruit juices	100.0	6.2	15.5	34.5	22.3	8.1	8.1	5.8
Canned fruit	100.0	2.8	14.3	21.8	19.8	13.9	11.3	17.5
Dried fruit	100.0	2.5	9.9	21.0	27.0	12.8	14.8	14.6
Fresh fruit juices	100.0	4.4	16.2	24.5	27.8	11.7	8.7	8.4
Canned and bottled fruit juices	100.0	6.1	16.0	26.4	22.2	10.9	9.2	10.1
Processed vegetables	100.0	4.2	15.3	26.7	22.6	13.1	9.7	9.3
Frozen vegetables	100.0	4.2	15.0	30.2	21.7	13.6	9.1	7.0
Canned and dried vegetables and juices	100.0	4.2	15.5	25.0	23.1	12.8	10.0	10.5
Canned beans	100.0	6.0	14.4	25.1	22.2	12.3	10.0	11.1
Canned corn	100.0	5.8	17.3	26.7	22.9	10.1	6.7	11.8
Other canned and dried vegetables	100.0	3.4	15.5	25.0	23.3	13.5	10.3	10.2
Frozen vegetable juices	100.0	7.1	20.0	34.6	26.7	3.2	6.9	-
Fresh and canned vegetable juices	100.0	2.5	15.7	22.5	23.5	14.4	12.6	9.6
Other food at home	**100.0**	**4.9**	**15.9**	**27.2**	**24.2**	**12.2**	**8.9**	**7.6**
Sugar and other sweets	100.0	4.0	15.3	26.7	23.9	12.5	10.1	8.5
Candy and chewing gum	100.0	3.4	16.0	26.5	25.3	13.0	9.9	6.8
Sugar	100.0	5.4	16.5	28.1	23.7	10.1	9.4	7.3
Artificial sweeteners	100.0	2.4	8.3	22.3	22.9	9.7	15.6	21.5
Jams, preserves, other sweets	100.0	4.7	13.5	26.9	20.0	13.3	10.5	12.2
Fats and oils	100.0	4.9	14.4	26.7	22.7	11.7	10.1	10.6
Margarine	100.0	4.4	10.5	23.2	20.6	13.0	10.8	19.8
Fats and oils	100.0	4.9	16.7	25.7	23.5	11.0	9.9	9.0
Salad dressings	100.0	4.7	14.1	27.3	24.9	13.1	9.6	7.5
Nondairy cream and imitation milk	100.0	4.5	12.8	27.2	24.8	11.4	12.3	8.2
Peanut butter	100.0	6.0	16.1	31.1	17.9	8.8	9.4	10.6
Miscellaneous foods	100.0	5.3	17.3	28.3	23.2	11.1	8.3	7.1
Frozen prepared foods	100.0	4.1	15.9	25.8	25.9	12.0	8.3	9.6
Frozen meals	100.0	2.5	14.4	23.7	26.4	12.3	9.0	14.2
Other frozen prepared foods	100.0	4.9	16.6	26.8	25.7	11.9	7.9	7.4
Canned and packaged soups	100.0	5.1	15.4	26.3	21.5	12.8	9.9	9.7
Potato chips, nuts, and other snacks	100.0	4.2	15.4	31.0	25.4	10.9	8.6	5.5
Potato chips and other snacks	100.0	4.5	16.2	33.3	24.8	10.1	7.2	4.8
Nuts	100.0	3.3	12.3	22.8	27.5	14.2	13.7	7.9
Condiments and seasonings	100.0	5.6	15.2	28.8	23.9	11.7	8.8	6.9
Salt, spices and other seasonings	100.0	5.3	14.2	27.1	22.6	14.7	9.5	7.7
Olives, pickles, relishes	100.0	4.3	11.0	29.2	24.4	12.5	10.5	10.0
Sauces and gravies	100.0	5.7	17.1	30.0	24.5	10.5	7.5	5.4
Baking needs and misc. products	100.0	6.3	14.7	27.9	24.0	10.3	10.2	7.5
Other canned/packaged prepared foods	100.0	6.6	21.4	28.0	20.1	9.7	7.2	6.3
Prepared salads	100.0	2.7	11.7	28.2	24.9	14.0	12.9	7.0
Prepared desserts	100.0	3.6	13.4	25.3	22.2	11.6	12.3	12.8

	total consumer units	under 25	25 to 34	35 to 44	45 to 54	55 to 64	65 to 74	75+
Baby food	100.0%	11.0%	37.9%	25.9%	12.2%	4.7%	1.9%	1.4%
Miscellaneous prepared foods	100.0	5.8	16.9	29.2	22.5	10.9	7.9	7.4
Nonalcoholic beverages	100.0	4.9	15.1	26.6	25.2	13.6	8.6	7.4
Cola	100.0	5.6	15.8	27.9	26.0	13.0	8.0	4.8
Other carbonated drinks	100.0	6.1	16.6	26.7	22.8	13.7	8.1	6.6
Coffee	100.0	2.6	11.3	21.2	26.8	18.0	10.8	12.0
Roasted coffee	100.0	2.6	11.6	22.6	27.6	18.0	9.8	10.7
Instant and freeze-dried coffee	100.0	2.8	10.7	18.3	24.9	18.1	12.9	14.9
Noncarb. fruit flavored drinks								
incl. non-frozen lemonade	100.0	5.1	14.7	32.7	24.9	8.9	8.0	7.0
Tea	100.0	3.2	16.3	24.5	29.1	11.5	10.4	6.4
Nonalcoholic beer	100.0	-	15.8	21.1	7.8	22.4	19.0	12.4
Other nonalcoholic beverages	100.0	5.7	16.7	26.5	21.2	13.0	6.9	10.9
Food prepared by cu on out-of-town trips	100.0	3.1	13.3	23.5	31.0	14.6	10.5	5.3
FOOD AWAY FROM HOME	**100.0**	**5.4**	**17.1**	**26.4**	**26.7**	**13.1**	**7.5**	**4.7**
Meals at restaurants, carry-outs, other	**100.0**	**5.6**	**18.5**	**26.9**	**24.7**	**12.5**	**7.5**	**4.8**
Lunch	100.0	5.2	18.8	29.1	24.7	11.2	6.2	5.5
Dinner	100.0	5.7	18.1	25.3	24.8	13.5	8.5	4.5
Snacks and nonalcoholic beverages	100.0	8.4	21.0	29.5	23.9	9.5	5.4	2.1
Breakfast and brunch	100.0	4.3	16.6	24.6	24.9	15.2	9.2	6.2
Board (including at school)	**100.0**	**10.5**	**2.2**	**15.8**	**59.7**	**15.3**	**0.9**	**3.6**
Catered affairs	**100.0**	**1.4**	**12.7**	**15.1**	**49.0**	**18.0**	**4.9**	**2.6**
Food on out-of-town trips	**100.0**	**3.4**	**13.0**	**22.7**	**27.0**	**16.7**	**11.9**	**6.1**
School lunches	**100.0**	**0.4**	**14.8**	**55.0**	**25.3**	**2.8**	**1.0**	**0.6**
Meals as pay	**100.0**	**17.2**	**27.1**	**17.6**	**16.8**	**16.3**	**2.2**	**1.1**
ALCOHOLIC BEVERAGES	**100.0**	**6.9**	**21.3**	**23.5**	**20.7**	**14.8**	**8.8**	**2.9**
At home	**100.0**	**5.6**	**21.6**	**24.6**	**20.8**	**14.1**	**9.2**	**3.0**
Beer and ale	100.0	6.9	27.0	24.9	18.9	10.7	7.1	2.2
Whiskey	100.0	3.5	12.1	14.6	15.7	26.1	20.1	7.2
Wine	100.0	3.6	13.0	27.5	26.2	17.7	10.1	3.4
Other alcoholic beverages	100.0	4.1	15.5	24.6	25.3	17.1	10.8	3.5
Away from home	**100.0**	**8.7**	**20.9**	**22.0**	**20.6**	**15.8**	**8.3**	**2.8**
Beer and ale	100.0	12.2	24.3	21.0	18.5	14.6	6.1	1.6
Wine	100.0	7.2	19.8	22.9	21.4	18.0	7.9	2.4
Other alcoholic beverages	100.0	7.8	19.3	22.6	20.9	19.0	8.0	1.9
Alcoholic beverages purchased on trips	100.0	5.8	18.5	22.2	22.6	13.4	11.5	5.2

Note: Numbers may not add to total due to rounding. (-) means insufficient data. Spending share projections for 2000 account only for change in the age composition of consumer units and have not been adjusted for changes in price or spending patterns.
Source of consumer unit projections: TGE Demographics, Inc., Honeoye Falls, New York

Spending by

Income

Not surprisingly, higher-income households spend more on food than those with lower incomes.

The average spending on food by households with annual incomes of $70,000 or more was nearly $8,000 in 1994, while households with annual incomes under $20,000 spent only about $2,900. As a share of income devoted to food, however, the lowest-income households spend much more than the wealthiest households.

On a per capita basis, households with incomes of $70,000 or more, which have an average of 3.1 people, spend $2,575 for each household member on food annually. Households with incomes under $20,000 have an average of 2.0 people in them and spend about $1,400 per capita annually on food.

What households buy varies greatly by income—although the highest-income households are also the biggest spenders in most categories. On a per capita basis, low-income households spend 16 percent more than average on white bread. They also spend more on a variety of pork products—23 percent more per capita on bacon and 17 percent more on pork chops. Less-expensive prepared meats—bologna, salami, and liverwurst—are also favored by lower-income households, whose per capita spending on these products is 13 percent above average. Low-income families spend 20 percent more than average on eggs, a less expensive source of protein than beef.

Other categories in which the poorest households spend more than those at the other end of the income scale include sugar; artificial sweeteners; margarine, fats, and oils; and instant coffee, when measured on a per capita basis. Households with incomes between $20,000 and $29,999 spend more per capita on flour; sausage and pork products excluding chops and canned ham; lamb and organ meats; bologna, salami, and liverwurst; cream; olives, pickles, and relishes. Middle-income households spend more per capita on a range of mid-priced meat products—households with incomes between $30,000 and $39,999 spend 33 percent more than average on round steak, 13 percent more on all ham, and almost two-and-a-half times more on canned ham. They also spend 28 percent more per capita on frozen fish and shellfish.

To get a sense of the differences that can inform shopping patterns by income, a good category on which to focus is roast beef and steak. Regardless of income, households spend about an average amount on the most popular type of beef—ground beef. But beyond hamburger, purchasing patterns are directly related to income. The wealthiest households spend 14 percent more per capita on roasts in general, but they spend 35 percent more on "other roasts," which include the more expensive tenderloins and standing rib cuts. On the other hand, households with incomes between $40,000 and $49,999 spend 31 percent more than average on moderately-priced round roast. Households with incomes ranging from $30,000 to $39,999 spend less than average on all roasts; they spend the most on less-expensive round steak.

High-income households spend more on all categories of food away from home. Their spending on alcoholic beverages, both at home and away from home, is also higher than expected in all categories except beer and ale consumed at home. In this category, households with incomes of $70,000 or more spend 13 percent less than average, while those with annual incomes between $20,000 and $29,999 spend 26 percent more than average.

Households with incomes below $20,000 account for about 38 percent of all households. They are the largest single market segment in the food industry, accounting for almost 24 percent of all household spending on food. But their dominance is limited to spending on food at home (28 percent), while households with the highest incomes account for the largest single share of spending on alcoholic beverages (21 percent) and food away from home (more than 26 percent).

Income
average spending

(average annual spending of consumer units on food and alcoholic beverages, by average before-tax income of consumer unit, 1994; complete income reporters only)

	total, complete income reporters	under $20,000	$20,000 to $29,999	$30,000 to $39,999	$40,000 to $49,999	$50,000 to $69,999	$70,000 or more
Number of consumer units							
(in thousands, add 000's)	85,994	32,208	13,975	10,922	8,280	10,510	10,099
Average number of persons per cu	2.5	2.0	2.5	2.8	2.9	3.1	3.1
Average before-tax income of cu	$36,838.00	$10,709.53	$24,721.00	$34,402.00	$44,388.00	$58,417.00	$110,955.00
Average spending of cu, total	32,762.99	16,999.29	27,041.91	32,474.52	40,299.65	48,177.01	69,506.28
Food, average spending	4,526.94	2,877.52	3,931.92	4,654.81	5,387.32	6,409.03	7,984.61
Alcoholic beverages, average spending	296.57	155.15	287.46	347.42	327.07	459.60	532.01
FOOD AT HOME	$2,764.21	$2,069.34	$2,597.85	$2,833.99	$3,175.54	$3,581.92	$4,022.95
Cereals and bakery products	439.36	324.83	396.10	437.08	524.69	577.64	662.60
Cereals and cereal products	166.94	128.21	150.43	165.52	202.11	207.94	245.76
Flour	7.93	7.34	9.42	6.83	10.55	6.21	8.44
Prepared flour mixes	13.20	12.31	11.66	10.92	15.88	15.73	15.46
Ready-to-eat and cooked cereals	102.02	75.37	89.29	96.03	128.24	133.10	158.92
Rice	15.47	12.01	16.19	17.44	15.39	17.75	21.51
Pasta, cornmeal, other cereal products	28.32	21.18	23.87	34.29	32.05	35.16	41.44
Bakery products	272.42	196.62	245.68	271.56	322.59	369.70	416.84
Bread	77.20	64.71	73.25	74.14	91.24	92.35	98.75
White bread	38.02	35.34	38.33	35.49	40.78	44.07	40.47
Bread, other than white	39.17	29.38	34.92	38.65	50.45	48.28	58.28
Crackers and cookies	64.36	45.56	53.88	64.93	71.76	88.61	109.52
Cookies	43.78	30.11	38.32	42.00	50.28	61.36	75.33
Crackers	20.58	15.45	15.57	22.93	21.48	27.25	34.19
Frozen/refrigerated bakery products	22.16	15.03	19.01	24.98	27.75	32.83	31.40
Other bakery products	108.70	71.32	99.53	107.51	131.84	155.91	177.17
Biscuits and rolls	37.26	21.63	30.11	34.96	43.57	59.49	72.93
Cakes and cupcakes	31.12	22.99	30.22	32.37	38.34	35.55	46.32
Bread and cracker products	4.68	2.38	4.55	5.20	5.37	8.28	7.74
Sweetrolls, coffee cakes, doughnuts	23.08	15.56	23.62	24.11	27.45	33.17	32.08
Pies, tarts, turnovers	12.55	8.76	11.04	10.87	17.12	19.42	18.10
Meats, poultry, fish, and eggs	728.89	588.78	721.58	768.02	789.87	863.60	968.79
Beef	226.73	178.31	217.25	240.05	269.39	281.06	291.53
Ground beef	89.79	72.37	93.81	95.31	98.99	109.63	106.97
Roast	37.79	30.48	34.24	36.55	44.98	46.08	53.34
Chuck roast	12.10	10.18	13.12	10.69	11.80	14.13	16.62
Round roast	14.18	10.61	11.39	15.58	21.50	18.65	17.42
Other roast	11.51	9.68	9.73	10.28	11.68	13.29	19.30
Steak	85.81	64.74	75.36	94.45	115.31	104.97	114.44
Round steak	16.44	12.06	17.33	24.53	21.20	15.74	17.20
Sirloin steak	24.09	19.66	18.36	20.12	30.12	30.52	38.62
Other steak	45.28	33.03	39.67	49.80	63.98	58.71	58.61
Other beef	13.34	10.71	13.84	13.74	10.11	20.38	16.78
Pork	154.66	137.62	167.03	164.10	150.04	165.40	177.46
Bacon	23.01	22.68	26.93	20.86	21.61	23.88	21.58
Pork chops	37.47	35.09	34.36	39.60	37.61	39.34	45.76

	total complete income reporters	less than $20,000	$20,000 to $29,999	$30,000 to $39,999	$40,000 to $49,999	$50,000 to $69,999	$70,000 or more
Ham	$36.74	$31.85	$36.04	$46.55	$36.16	$40.27	$40.25
Ham, not canned	33.91	29.07	35.10	39.10	34.48	37.52	38.36
Canned ham	2.84	2.77	0.94	7.45	1.69	2.74	1.89
Sausage	22.63	20.28	27.28	20.62	19.81	26.38	24.61
Other pork	34.80	27.72	42.43	36.47	34.85	35.53	45.26
Other meats	94.34	74.27	98.95	93.62	110.32	107.94	126.27
Frankfurters	19.13	15.43	21.39	16.72	25.99	24.50	19.40
Lunch meats (cold cuts)	65.67	49.88	65.74	68.48	75.01	77.77	93.34
Bologna, liverwurst, salami	23.25	20.95	26.37	24.46	21.56	21.99	27.48
Other lunchmeats	42.41	28.94	39.37	44.02	53.46	55.78	65.87
Lamb, organ meats and others	9.54	8.96	11.82	8.42	9.32	5.67	13.53
Lamb and organ meats	9.31	8.87	11.63	7.44	9.32	5.23	13.53
Mutton, goat and game	0.24	0.09	0.18	0.98	-	0.44	-
Poultry	135.32	106.92	125.36	138.20	151.33	169.07	192.49
Fresh and frozen chickens	107.49	85.90	96.57	113.39	115.83	135.20	152.67
Fresh and frozen whole chicken	29.05	23.91	31.75	30.77	30.96	34.21	33.59
Fresh and frozen chicken parts	78.44	61.98	64.82	82.62	84.87	100.99	119.07
Other poultry	27.83	21.02	28.79	24.81	35.50	33.87	39.82
Fish and seafood	87.13	62.18	82.28	100.88	77.96	107.27	149.29
Canned fish and seafood	15.60	10.62	15.24	15.54	17.15	19.63	27.09
Fresh fish and shellfish	48.29	33.65	45.45	52.06	43.26	60.40	88.89
Frozen fish and shellfish	23.23	17.92	21.59	33.28	17.55	27.24	33.32
Eggs	30.72	29.47	30.71	31.18	30.85	32.85	31.74
Dairy products	**297.87**	**229.14**	**274.61**	**300.11**	**330.56**	**390.39**	**433.09**
Fresh milk and cream	131.98	108.49	132.73	129.15	148.49	166.53	163.07
Fresh milk, all types	123.44	103.23	121.28	121.18	139.12	156.34	149.46
Cream	8.55	5.25	11.45	7.97	9.37	10.19	13.61
Other dairy products	165.88	120.65	141.88	170.96	182.07	223.86	270.02
Butter	11.78	7.82	12.74	13.46	14.07	12.99	18.58
Cheese	84.78	64.92	70.75	84.59	96.84	108.03	136.20
Ice cream and related products	48.15	32.02	42.08	54.88	50.92	70.77	76.90
Miscellaneous dairy products	21.17	15.89	16.31	18.03	20.24	32.07	38.35
Fruits and vegetables	**446.10**	**332.10**	**408.81**	**450.70**	**494.18**	**585.95**	**685.00**
Fresh fruits	135.12	101.73	122.95	130.75	141.83	174.27	221.59
Apples	25.34	16.41	21.12	31.34	25.41	36.17	43.34
Bananas	30.25	24.08	29.29	31.05	28.86	36.41	46.04
Oranges	16.05	13.71	15.56	15.38	17.32	18.62	21.24
Citrus fruits, excl. oranges	11.32	8.55	10.56	10.01	11.25	12.96	21.30
Other fresh fruits	52.17	38.98	46.41	42.97	59.00	70.11	89.67
Fresh vegetables	138.99	102.95	126.69	144.05	151.13	170.66	226.44
Potatoes	28.24	23.34	28.56	28.59	31.72	29.20	39.35
Lettuce	17.65	12.78	14.33	17.55	18.55	24.35	30.76
Tomatoes	21.59	16.03	21.67	22.99	21.17	29.55	30.65
Other fresh vegetables	71.52	50.79	62.14	74.92	79.69	87.56	125.68

	total complete income reporters	less than $20,000	$20,000 to $29,999	$30,000 to $39,999	$40,000 to $49,999	$50,000 to $69,999	$70,000 or more
Processed fruits	$95.31	$70.97	$83.47	$97.05	$108.66	$135.11	$138.02
Frozen fruits and fruit juices	16.38	11.73	14.89	17.13	20.49	23.06	22.60
Frozen orange juice	9.57	7.56	9.01	9.20	11.72	11.86	13.06
Frozen fruits	1.50	0.95	1.36	1.45	1.59	3.13	1.83
Frozen fruit juices	5.31	3.23	4.52	6.49	7.18	8.07	7.71
Canned fruit	14.88	11.27	12.49	14.39	15.82	19.74	24.58
Dried fruit	6.23	4.83	6.03	6.77	5.90	7.08	9.87
Fresh fruit juices	17.65	14.51	16.29	17.05	20.36	19.84	25.81
Canned and bottled fruit juices	40.18	28.62	33.77	41.70	46.10	65.40	55.16
Processed vegetables	76.68	56.45	75.70	78.85	92.55	105.90	98.95
Frozen vegetables	24.78	16.28	22.47	24.18	33.41	36.55	37.25
Canned and dried vegetables and juices	51.90	40.18	53.24	54.67	59.15	69.35	61.71
Canned beans	10.61	8.90	10.65	11.17	10.44	14.80	11.53
Canned corn	6.99	5.15	8.62	5.44	8.34	11.23	7.03
Other canned and dried vegetables	27.58	21.38	28.08	29.37	32.52	34.29	34.23
Frozen vegetable juices	0.23	0.17	0.13	0.16	0.33	0.47	0.28
Fresh and canned vegetable juices	6.49	4.58	5.75	8.52	7.52	8.57	8.64
Other food at home	**851.99**	**594.50**	**796.75**	**878.09**	**1,036.24**	**1,164.35**	**1,273.47**
Sugar and other sweets	110.67	83.12	101.67	118.26	124.91	156.70	147.85
Candy and chewing gum	66.52	43.38	58.02	74.64	80.08	106.99	93.79
Sugar	18.30	18.18	20.56	17.94	17.29	18.30	17.35
Artificial sweeteners	3.57	3.73	2.56	3.20	3.19	3.92	4.88
Jams, preserves, other sweets	22.28	17.83	20.53	22.48	24.35	27.50	31.83
Fats and oils	80.76	67.40	78.16	79.33	93.69	90.52	109.36
Margarine	14.68	14.52	14.03	13.69	14.45	14.52	18.09
Fats and oils	23.15	20.89	23.74	23.78	28.56	22.73	24.82
Salad dressings	24.33	16.95	24.42	23.44	27.50	31.56	39.37
Nondairy cream and imitation milk	6.71	5.44	6.40	5.99	6.48	8.67	10.15
Peanut butter	11.89	9.62	9.57	12.43	16.69	13.04	16.93
Miscellaneous foods	369.77	247.02	335.53	403.85	431.59	512.93	587.03
Frozen prepared foods	65.79	41.17	59.43	79.48	76.57	98.60	98.47
Frozen meals	20.54	14.88	21.51	26.69	24.03	22.52	25.75
Other frozen prepared foods	45.25	26.29	37.91	52.80	52.54	76.08	72.72
Canned and packaged soups	30.21	20.92	27.75	31.40	38.76	41.13	44.64
Potato chips, nuts, and other snacks	75.91	45.19	65.99	79.05	94.69	109.54	136.83
Potato chips and other snacks	59.81	35.28	51.85	61.42	73.79	92.34	104.88
Nuts	16.10	9.92	14.14	17.63	20.90	17.20	31.95
Condiments and seasonings	82.47	55.51	79.08	90.55	99.63	109.54	125.21
Salt, spices and other seasonings	19.68	14.15	18.18	27.28	24.17	22.83	24.99
Olives, pickles, relishes	10.76	7.22	13.11	10.81	13.94	12.38	14.69
Sauces and gravies	38.05	24.67	35.55	39.65	45.49	51.69	63.65
Baking needs and misc. products	13.98	9.48	12.24	12.82	16.03	22.64	21.87
Other canned/packaged prepared foods	115.39	84.23	103.28	123.37	121.94	154.12	181.87
Prepared salads	11.02	6.64	8.73	8.80	16.13	18.22	19.17
Prepared desserts	8.28	6.03	6.88	10.58	8.11	12.39	11.04

	total complete income reporters	less than $20,000	$20,000 to $29,999	$30,000 to $39,999	$40,000 to $49,999	$50,000 to $69,999	$70,000 or more
Baby food	$27.68	$20.30	$23.24	$33.45	$18.82	$43.40	$44.93
Miscellaneous prepared foods	68.41	51.25	64.43	70.55	78.88	80.12	106.73
Nonalcoholic beverages	241.81	176.93	242.70	236.58	300.37	322.53	328.03
Cola	93.27	67.45	99.17	96.13	109.44	138.65	107.55
Other carbonated drinks	40.20	29.29	39.93	38.06	50.87	54.39	55.49
Coffee	43.29	34.87	44.90	38.98	54.64	47.77	58.56
Roasted coffee	29.20	21.56	32.01	26.94	35.66	37.55	38.62
Instant and freeze-dried coffee	14.09	13.31	12.90	12.04	18.99	10.22	19.94
Noncarb. fruit flavored drinks incl. non-frozen lemonade	23.02	16.68	18.66	27.23	26.49	33.03	32.28
Tea	16.75	10.86	15.70	15.98	20.15	23.44	28.76
Nonalcoholic beer	0.76	0.54	0.71	0.20	1.55	0.81	1.41
Other nonalcoholic beverages	24.52	17.23	23.63	20.00	37.23	24.43	43.99
Food prepared by cu on out-of-town trips	48.98	20.02	38.70	40.07	85.68	81.66	101.19
FOOD AWAY FROM HOME	**1,762.72**	**808.17**	**1,334.07**	**1,820.82**	**2,211.78**	**2,827.12**	**3,961.66**
Meals at restaurants, carry-outs, other	**1,363.26**	**662.57**	**1,082.58**	**1,447.23**	**1,673.70**	**2,229.49**	**2,839.37**
Lunch	475.88	224.25	331.58	518.35	625.70	755.69	1,046.66
Dinner	668.88	326.23	570.46	695.66	749.58	1,115.84	1,395.44
Snacks and nonalcoholic beverages	110.46	52.36	93.58	123.49	141.16	184.17	211.46
Breakfast and brunch	108.05	59.74	86.96	109.72	157.25	173.79	185.80
Board (including at school)	**50.40**	**19.77**	**17.41**	**23.36**	**39.08**	**67.84**	**214.11**
Catered affairs	**55.38**	**7.36**	**19.41**	**53.06**	**111.38**	**90.40**	**178.50**
Food on out-of-town trips	**213.45**	**86.30**	**140.16**	**179.13**	**290.19**	**315.04**	**589.08**
School lunches	**54.93**	**14.48**	**40.08**	**86.57**	**79.17**	**106.22**	**97.04**
Meals as pay	**25.30**	**17.68**	**34.44**	**31.48**	**18.25**	**18.12**	**43.56**
ALCOHOLIC BEVERAGES	**296.57**	**155.15**	**287.46**	**347.42**	**327.07**	**459.60**	**532.01**
At home	**175.40**	**102.05**	**184.21**	**226.37**	**205.86**	**233.09**	**267.52**
Beer and ale	108.74	70.51	136.71	146.38	136.14	124.17	117.47
Whiskey	14.25	8.53	15.57	16.68	12.50	20.08	23.67
Wine	36.06	14.60	21.30	40.87	44.58	63.13	88.02
Other alcoholic beverages	**16.36**	**8.42**	**10.64**	**22.44**	**12.64**	**25.71**	**38.36**
Away from home	121.17	53.10	103.24	121.05	121.21	226.52	264.49
Beer and ale	42.50	21.28	38.66	54.46	39.97	79.89	70.35
Wine	16.74	6.55	14.05	15.55	14.41	36.42	37.93
Other alcoholic beverages	30.22	11.99	29.64	27.82	23.35	62.16	68.17
Alcoholic beverages purchased on trips	31.71	13.29	20.89	23.22	43.49	48.05	88.04

Note: Expenditures listed for items in a given category may not add to the total for that category because the listing is incomplete. (-) means insufficient data.

Income
indexed spending

(indexed average annual spending of consumer units on food and alcoholic beverages, by before-tax income of consumer unit, 1994; complete income reporters only; index definition: an index of 100 is the average for all consumer units; an index of 132 means that spending by consumer units in the income group is 32 percent above the average for all consumer units; an index of 68 indicates that spending by consumer units in the income group is 32 percent below the average for all consumer units)

	total, complete income reporters	under $20,000	$20,000 to $29,999	$30,000 to $39,999	$40,000 to $49,999	$50,000 to $69,999	$70,000 or more
Average spending of cu, total	*$32,762.99*	*$16,999.29*	*$27,041.91*	*$32,474.52*	*$40,299.65*	*$48,177.01*	*$69,506.28*
Average spending of cu, index	*100*	*52*	*83*	*99*	*123*	*147*	*212*
Food, spending index	*100*	*64*	*87*	*103*	*119*	*142*	*176*
Alcoholic beverages, spending index	*100*	*52*	*97*	*117*	*110*	*155*	*179*
FOOD AT HOME	**100**	**75**	**94**	**103**	**115**	**130**	**146**
Cereals and bakery products	**100**	**74**	**90**	**99**	**119**	**131**	**151**
Cereals and cereal products	100	77	90	99	121	125	147
Flour	100	93	119	86	133	78	106
Prepared flour mixes	100	93	88	83	120	119	117
Ready-to-eat and cooked cereals	100	74	88	94	126	130	156
Rice	100	78	105	113	99	115	139
Pasta, cornmeal, and other cereal products	100	75	84	121	113	124	146
Bakery products	100	72	90	100	118	136	153
Bread	100	84	95	96	118	120	128
White bread	100	93	101	93	107	116	106
Bread, other than white	100	75	89	99	129	123	149
Crackers and cookies	100	71	84	101	111	138	170
Cookies	100	69	88	96	115	140	172
Crackers	100	75	76	111	104	132	166
Frozen and refrigerated bakery products	100	68	86	113	125	148	142
Other bakery products	100	66	92	99	121	143	163
Biscuits and rolls	100	58	81	94	117	160	196
Cakes and cupcakes	100	74	97	104	123	114	149
Bread and cracker products	100	51	97	111	115	177	165
Sweetrolls, coffee cakes, doughnuts	100	67	102	104	119	144	139
Pies, tarts, turnovers	100	70	88	87	136	155	144
Meats, poultry, fish, and eggs	**100**	**81**	**99**	**105**	**108**	**118**	**133**
Beef	100	79	96	106	119	124	129
Ground beef	100	81	104	106	110	122	119
Roast	100	81	91	97	119	122	141
Chuck roast	100	84	108	88	98	117	137
Round roast	100	75	80	110	152	132	123
Other roast	100	84	85	89	101	115	168
Steak	100	75	88	110	134	122	133
Round steak	100	73	105	149	129	96	105
Sirloin steak	100	82	76	84	125	127	160
Other steak	100	73	88	110	141	130	129
Other beef	100	80	104	103	76	153	126
Pork	100	89	108	106	97	107	115
Bacon	100	99	117	91	94	104	94
Pork chops	100	94	92	106	100	105	122

	total complete income reporters	less than $20,000	$20,000 to $29,999	$30,000 to $39,999	$40,000 to $49,999	$50,000 to $69,999	$70,000 or more
Ham	100	87	98	127	98	110	110
Ham, not canned	100	86	104	115	102	111	113
Canned ham	100	98	33	262	60	96	67
Sausage	100	90	121	91	88	117	109
Other pork	100	80	122	105	100	102	130
Other meats	100	79	105	99	117	114	134
Frankfurters	100	81	112	87	136	128	101
Lunch meats (cold cuts)	100	76	100	104	114	118	142
Bologna, liverwurst, salami	100	90	113	105	93	95	118
Other lunchmeats	100	68	93	104	126	132	155
Lamb, organ meats and others	100	94	124	88	98	59	142
Lamb and organ meats	100	95	125	80	100	56	145
Mutton, goat and game	100	38	75	408	-	183	-
Poultry	100	79	93	102	112	125	142
Fresh and frozen chickens	100	80	90	105	108	126	142
Fresh and frozen whole chicken	100	82	109	106	107	118	116
Fresh and frozen chicken parts	100	79	83	105	108	129	152
Other poultry	100	76	103	89	128	122	143
Fish and seafood	100	71	94	116	89	123	171
Canned fish and seafood	100	68	98	100	110	126	174
Fresh fish and shellfish	100	70	94	108	90	125	184
Frozen fish and shellfish	100	77	93	143	76	117	143
Eggs	100	96	100	101	100	107	103
Dairy products	**100**	**77**	**92**	**101**	**111**	**131**	**145**
Fresh milk and cream	100	82	101	98	113	126	124
Fresh milk, all types	100	84	98	98	113	127	121
Cream	100	61	134	93	110	119	159
Other dairy products	100	73	86	103	110	135	163
Butter	100	66	108	114	119	110	158
Cheese	100	77	83	100	114	127	161
Ice cream and related products	100	67	87	114	106	147	160
Miscellaneous dairy products	100	75	77	85	96	151	181
Fruits and vegetables	**100**	**74**	**92**	**101**	**111**	**131**	**154**
Fresh fruits	100	75	91	97	105	129	164
Apples	100	65	83	124	100	143	171
Bananas	100	80	97	103	95	120	152
Oranges	100	85	97	96	108	116	132
Citrus fruits, excl. oranges	100	75	93	88	99	114	188
Other fresh fruits	100	75	89	82	113	134	172
Fresh vegetables	100	74	91	104	109	123	163
Potatoes	100	83	101	101	112	103	139
Lettuce	100	72	81	99	105	138	174
Tomatoes	100	74	100	106	98	137	142
Other fresh vegetables	100	71	87	105	111	122	176

	total complete income reporters	less than $20,000	$20,000 to $29,999	$30,000 to $39,999	$40,000 to $49,999	$50,000 to $69,999	$70,000 or more
Processed fruits	100	74	88	102	114	142	145
Frozen fruits and fruit juices	100	72	91	105	125	141	138
Frozen orange juice	100	79	94	96	122	124	136
Frozen fruits	100	64	91	97	106	209	122
Frozen fruit juices	100	61	85	122	135	152	145
Canned fruit	100	76	84	97	106	133	165
Dried fruit	100	77	97	109	95	114	158
Fresh fruit juices	100	82	92	97	115	112	146
Canned and bottled fruit juices	100	71	84	104	115	163	137
Processed vegetables	100	74	99	103	121	138	129
Frozen vegetables	100	66	91	98	135	147	150
Canned and dried vegetables and juices	100	77	103	105	114	134	119
Canned beans	100	84	100	105	98	139	109
Canned corn	100	74	123	78	119	161	101
Other canned and dried vegetables	100	78	102	106	118	124	124
Frozen vegetable juices	100	73	57	70	143	204	122
Fresh and canned vegetable juices	100	71	89	131	116	132	133
Other food at home	**100**	**70**	**94**	**103**	**122**	**137**	**149**
Sugar and other sweets	100	75	92	107	113	142	134
Candy and chewing gum	100	65	87	112	120	161	141
Sugar	100	99	112	98	94	100	95
Artificial sweeteners	100	105	72	90	89	110	137
Jams, preserves, other sweets	100	80	92	101	109	123	143
Fats and oils	100	83	97	98	116	112	135
Margarine	100	99	96	93	98	99	123
Fats and oils	100	90	103	103	123	98	107
Salad dressings	100	70	100	96	113	130	162
Nondairy cream and imitation milk	100	81	95	89	97	129	151
Peanut butter	100	81	80	105	140	110	142
Miscellaneous foods	100	67	91	109	117	139	159
Frozen prepared foods	100	63	90	121	116	150	150
Frozen meals	100	72	105	130	117	110	125
Other frozen prepared foods	100	58	84	117	116	168	161
Canned and packaged soups	100	69	92	104	128	136	148
Potato chips, nuts, and other snacks	100	60	87	104	125	144	180
Potato chips and other snacks	100	59	87	103	123	154	175
Nuts	100	62	88	110	130	107	198
Condiments and seasonings	100	67	96	110	121	133	152
Salt, spices and other seasonings	100	72	92	139	123	116	127
Olives, pickles, relishes	100	67	122	100	130	115	137
Sauces and gravies	100	65	93	104	120	136	167
Baking needs and misc. products	100	68	88	92	115	162	156
Other canned/packaged prepared foods	100	73	90	107	106	134	158
Prepared salads	100	60	79	80	146	165	174
Prepared desserts	100	73	83	128	98	150	133

	total complete income reporters	less than $20,000	$20,000 to $29,999	$30,000 to $39,999	$40,000 to $49,999	$50,000 to $69,999	$70,000 or more
Baby food	100	73	84	121	68	157	162
Miscellaneous prepared foods	100	75	94	103	115	117	156
Nonalcoholic beverages	100	73	100	98	124	133	136
Cola	100	72	106	103	117	149	115
Other carbonated drinks	100	73	99	95	127	135	138
Coffee	100	81	104	90	126	110	135
Roasted coffee	100	74	110	92	122	129	132
Instant and freeze-dried coffee	100	94	92	85	135	73	142
Noncarb. fruit flavored drinks incl. non-frozen lemonade	100	72	81	118	115	143	140
Tea	100	65	94	95	120	140	172
Nonalcoholic beer	100	71	93	26	204	107	186
Other nonalcoholic beverages	100	70	96	82	152	100	179
Food prepared by cu on out-of-town trips	100	41	79	82	175	167	207
FOOD AWAY FROM HOME	**100**	**46**	**76**	**103**	**125**	**160**	**225**
Meals at restaurants, carry-outs, other	**100**	**49**	**79**	**106**	**123**	**164**	**208**
Lunch	100	47	70	109	131	159	220
Dinner	100	49	85	104	112	167	209
Snacks and nonalcoholic beverages	100	47	85	112	128	167	191
Breakfast and brunch	100	55	80	102	146	161	172
Board (including at school)	**100**	**39**	**35**	**46**	**78**	**135**	**425**
Catered affairs	**100**	**13**	**35**	**96**	**201**	**163**	**322**
Food on out-of-town trips	**100**	**40**	**66**	**84**	**136**	**148**	**276**
School lunches	**100**	**26**	**73**	**158**	**144**	**193**	**177**
Meals as pay	**100**	**70**	**136**	**124**	**72**	**72**	**172**
ALCOHOLIC BEVERAGES	**100**	**52**	**97**	**117**	**110**	**155**	**179**
At home	**100**	**58**	**105**	**129**	**117**	**133**	**153**
Beer and ale	100	65	126	135	125	114	108
Whiskey	100	60	109	117	88	141	166
Wine	100	40	59	113	124	175	244
Other alcoholic beverages	100	51	65	137	77	157	234
Away from home	**100**	**44**	**85**	**100**	**100**	**187**	**218**
Beer and ale	100	50	91	128	94	188	166
Wine	100	39	84	93	86	218	227
Other alcoholic beverages	100	40	98	92	77	206	226
Alcoholic beverages purchased on trips	100	42	66	73	137	152	278

Note: (-) means insufficient data.

Income
average per capita spending

(average annual per capita spending of consumer units on food and alcoholic beverages, by before-tax income of consumer unit, 1994; complete income reporters only; per capita figures are calculated by dividing the average spending of consumer units by the average number of persons per consumer unit)

	total, complete income reporters	under $20,000	$20,000 to $29,999	$30,000 to $39,999	$40,000 to $49,999	$50,000 to $69,999	$70,000 or more
Average number of persons per cu	2.5	2.0	2.5	2.8	2.9	3.1	3.1
Per capita before-tax income of cu	$14,735.20	$5,354.77	$9,888.40	$12,286.43	$15,306.21	$18,844.19	$35,791.94
Per capita spending of cu, total	13,105.20	8,499.64	10,816.76	11,598.04	13,896.43	15,540.97	22,421.38
Food, per capita spending	1,810.78	1,438.76	1,572.77	1,662.43	1,857.70	2,067.43	2,575.68
Alcoholic beverages, per capita spending	118.63	77.57	114.98	124.08	112.78	148.26	171.62
FOOD AT HOME	**$1,105.68**	**$1,034.67**	**$1,039.14**	**$1,012.14**	**$1,095.01**	**$1,155.46**	**$1,297.73**
Cereals and bakery products	**175.74**	**162.42**	**158.44**	**156.10**	**180.93**	**186.34**	**213.74**
Cereals and cereal products	66.78	64.11	60.17	59.11	69.69	67.08	79.28
Flour	3.17	3.67	3.77	2.44	3.64	2.00	2.72
Prepared flour mixes	5.28	6.15	4.66	3.90	5.48	5.07	4.99
Ready-to-eat and cooked cereals	40.81	37.68	35.72	34.30	44.22	42.94	51.26
Rice	6.19	6.00	6.48	6.23	5.31	5.73	6.94
Pasta, cornmeal, and other cereal products	11.33	10.59	9.55	12.25	11.05	11.34	13.37
Bakery products	108.97	98.31	98.27	96.99	111.24	119.26	134.46
Bread	30.88	32.35	29.30	26.48	31.46	29.79	31.85
White bread	15.21	17.67	15.33	12.68	14.06	14.22	13.05
Bread, other than white	15.67	14.69	13.97	13.80	17.40	15.57	18.80
Crackers and cookies	25.74	22.78	21.55	23.19	24.74	28.58	35.33
Cookies	17.51	15.05	15.33	15.00	17.34	19.79	24.30
Crackers	8.23	7.72	6.23	8.19	7.41	8.79	11.03
Frozen and refrigerated bakery products	8.86	7.51	7.60	8.92	9.57	10.59	10.13
Other bakery products	43.48	35.66	39.81	38.40	45.46	50.29	57.15
Biscuits and rolls	14.90	10.82	12.04	12.49	15.02	19.19	23.53
Cakes and cupcakes	12.45	11.50	12.09	11.56	13.22	11.47	14.94
Bread and cracker products	1.87	1.19	1.82	1.86	1.85	2.67	2.50
Sweetrolls, coffee cakes, doughnuts	9.23	7.78	9.45	8.61	9.47	10.70	10.35
Pies, tarts, turnovers	5.02	4.38	4.42	3.88	5.90	6.26	5.84
Meats, poultry, fish, and eggs	**291.56**	**294.39**	**288.63**	**274.29**	**272.37**	**278.58**	**312.51**
Beef	90.69	89.16	86.90	85.73	92.89	90.66	94.04
Ground beef	35.92	36.19	37.52	34.04	34.13	35.36	34.51
Roast	15.12	15.24	13.70	13.05	15.51	14.86	17.21
Chuck roast	4.84	5.09	5.25	3.82	4.07	4.56	5.36
Round roast	5.67	5.31	4.56	5.56	7.41	6.02	5.62
Other roast	4.60	4.84	3.89	3.67	4.03	4.29	6.23
Steak	34.32	32.37	30.14	33.73	39.76	33.86	36.92
Round steak	6.58	6.03	6.93	8.76	7.31	5.08	5.55
Sirloin steak	9.64	9.83	7.34	7.19	10.39	9.85	12.46
Other steak	18.11	16.52	15.87	17.79	22.06	18.94	18.91
Other beef	5.34	5.36	5.54	4.91	3.49	6.57	5.41
Pork	61.86	68.81	66.81	58.61	51.74	53.35	57.25
Bacon	9.20	11.34	10.77	7.45	7.45	7.70	6.96
Pork chops	14.99	17.55	13.74	14.14	12.97	12.69	14.76

	total complete income reporters	less than $20,000	$20,000 to $29,999	$30,000 to $39,999	$40,000 to $49,999	$50,000 to $69,999	$70,000 or more
Ham	$14.70	$15.92	$14.42	$16.63	$12.47	$12.99	$12.98
Ham, not canned	13.56	14.53	14.04	13.96	11.89	12.10	12.37
Canned ham	1.14	1.39	0.38	2.66	0.58	0.88	0.61
Sausage	9.05	10.14	10.91	7.36	6.83	8.51	7.94
Other pork	13.92	13.86	16.97	13.03	12.02	11.46	14.60
Other meats	37.74	37.14	39.58	33.44	38.04	34.82	40.73
Frankfurters	7.65	7.72	8.56	5.97	8.96	7.90	6.26
Lunch meats (cold cuts)	26.27	24.94	26.30	24.46	25.87	25.09	30.11
Bologna, liverwurst, salami	9.30	10.47	10.55	8.74	7.43	7.09	8.86
Other lunchmeats	16.96	14.47	15.75	15.72	18.43	17.99	21.25
Lamb, organ meats and others	3.82	4.48	4.73	3.01	3.21	1.83	4.36
Lamb and organ meats	3.72	4.44	4.65	2.66	3.21	1.69	4.36
Mutton, goat and game	0.10	0.05	0.07	0.35	-	0.14	-
Poultry	54.13	53.46	50.14	49.36	52.18	54.54	62.09
Fresh and frozen chickens	43.00	42.95	38.63	40.50	39.94	43.61	49.25
Fresh and frozen whole chicken	11.62	11.95	12.70	10.99	10.68	11.04	10.84
Fresh and frozen chicken parts	31.38	30.99	25.93	29.51	29.27	32.58	38.41
Other poultry	11.13	10.51	11.52	8.86	12.24	10.93	12.85
Fish and seafood	34.85	31.09	32.91	36.03	26.88	34.60	48.16
Canned fish and seafood	6.24	5.31	6.10	5.55	5.91	6.33	8.74
Fresh fish and shellfish	19.32	16.83	18.18	18.59	14.92	19.48	28.67
Frozen fish and shellfish	9.29	8.96	8.64	11.89	6.05	8.79	10.75
Eggs	12.29	14.73	12.28	11.14	10.64	10.60	10.24
Dairy products	**119.15**	**114.57**	**109.84**	**107.18**	**113.99**	**125.93**	**139.71**
Fresh milk and cream	52.79	54.24	53.09	46.13	51.20	53.72	52.60
Fresh milk, all types	49.38	51.62	48.51	43.28	47.97	50.43	48.21
Cream	3.42	2.63	4.58	2.85	3.23	3.29	4.39
Other dairy products	66.35	60.32	56.75	61.06	62.78	72.21	87.10
Butter	4.71	3.91	5.10	4.81	4.85	4.19	5.99
Cheese	33.91	32.46	28.30	30.21	33.39	34.85	43.94
Ice cream and related products	19.26	16.01	16.83	19.60	17.56	22.83	24.81
Miscellaneous dairy products	8.47	7.95	6.52	6.44	6.98	10.35	12.37
Fruits and vegetables	**178.44**	**166.05**	**163.52**	**160.96**	**170.41**	**189.02**	**220.97**
Fresh fruits	54.05	50.86	49.18	46.70	48.91	56.22	71.48
Apples	10.14	8.20	8.45	11.19	8.76	11.67	13.98
Bananas	12.10	12.04	11.72	11.09	9.95	11.75	14.85
Oranges	6.42	6.86	6.22	5.49	5.97	6.01	6.85
Citrus fruits, excl. oranges	4.53	4.27	4.22	3.58	3.88	4.18	6.87
Other fresh fruits	20.87	19.49	18.56	15.35	20.34	22.62	28.93
Fresh vegetables	55.60	51.48	50.68	51.45	52.11	55.05	73.05
Potatoes	11.30	11.67	11.42	10.21	10.94	9.42	12.69
Lettuce	7.06	6.39	5.73	6.27	6.40	7.85	9.92
Tomatoes	8.64	8.01	8.67	8.21	7.30	9.53	9.89
Other fresh vegetables	28.61	25.40	24.86	26.76	27.48	28.25	40.54

	total complete income reporters	less than $20,000	$20,000 to $29,999	$30,000 to $39,999	$40,000 to $49,999	$50,000 to $69,999	$70,000 or more
Processed fruits	$38.12	$35.49	$33.39	$34.66	$37.47	$43.58	$44.52
Frozen fruits and fruit juices	6.55	5.87	5.96	6.12	7.07	7.44	7.29
Frozen orange juice	3.83	3.78	3.60	3.29	4.04	3.83	4.21
Frozen fruits	0.60	0.48	0.54	0.52	0.55	1.01	0.59
Frozen fruit juices	2.12	1.61	1.81	2.32	2.48	2.60	2.49
Canned fruit	5.95	5.64	5.00	5.14	5.46	6.37	7.93
Dried fruit	2.49	2.41	2.41	2.42	2.03	2.28	3.18
Fresh fruit juices	7.06	7.26	6.52	6.09	7.02	6.40	8.33
Canned and bottled fruit juices	16.07	14.31	13.51	14.89	15.90	21.10	17.79
Processed vegetables	30.67	28.23	30.28	28.16	31.91	34.16	31.92
Frozen vegetables	9.91	8.14	8.99	8.64	11.52	11.79	12.02
Canned and dried vegetables and juices	20.76	20.09	21.30	19.53	20.40	22.37	19.91
Canned beans	4.24	4.45	4.26	3.99	3.60	4.77	3.72
Canned corn	2.80	2.57	3.45	1.94	2.88	3.62	2.27
Other canned and dried vegetables	11.03	10.69	11.23	10.49	11.21	11.06	11.04
Frozen vegetable juices	0.09	0.08	0.05	0.06	0.11	0.15	0.09
Fresh and canned vegetable juices	2.60	2.29	2.30	3.04	2.59	2.76	2.79
Other food at home	**340.80**	**297.25**	**318.70**	**313.60**	**357.32**	**375.60**	**410.80**
Sugar and other sweets	44.27	41.56	40.67	42.24	43.07	50.55	47.69
Candy and chewing gum	26.61	21.69	23.21	26.66	27.61	34.51	30.25
Sugar	7.32	9.09	8.22	6.41	5.96	5.90	5.60
Artificial sweeteners	1.43	1.87	1.02	1.14	1.10	1.26	1.57
Jams, preserves, other sweets	8.91	8.92	8.21	8.03	8.40	8.87	10.27
Fats and oils	32.30	33.70	31.26	28.33	32.31	29.20	35.28
Margarine	5.87	7.26	5.61	4.89	4.98	4.68	5.84
Fats and oils	9.26	10.44	9.50	8.49	9.85	7.33	8.01
Salad dressings	9.73	8.47	9.77	8.37	9.48	10.18	12.70
Nondairy cream and imitation milk	2.68	2.72	2.56	2.14	2.23	2.80	3.27
Peanut butter	4.76	4.81	3.83	4.44	5.76	4.21	5.46
Miscellaneous foods	147.91	123.51	134.21	144.23	148.82	165.46	189.36
Frozen prepared foods	26.32	20.59	23.77	28.39	26.40	31.81	31.76
Frozen meals	8.22	7.44	8.60	9.53	8.29	7.26	8.31
Other frozen prepared foods	18.10	13.15	15.16	18.86	18.12	24.54	23.46
Canned and packaged soups	12.08	10.46	11.10	11.21	13.37	13.27	14.40
Potato chips, nuts, and other snacks	30.36	22.60	26.40	28.23	32.65	35.34	44.14
Potato chips and other snacks	23.92	17.64	20.74	21.94	25.44	29.79	33.83
Nuts	6.44	4.96	5.66	6.30	7.21	5.55	10.31
Condiments and seasonings	32.99	27.75	31.63	32.34	34.36	35.34	40.39
Salt, spices and other seasonings	7.87	7.07	7.27	9.74	8.33	7.36	8.06
Olives, pickles, relishes	4.30	3.61	5.24	3.86	4.81	3.99	4.74
Sauces and gravies	15.22	12.34	14.22	14.16	15.69	16.67	20.53
Baking needs and misc. products	5.59	4.74	4.90	4.58	5.53	7.30	7.05
Other canned/packaged prepared foods	46.16	42.11	41.31	44.06	42.05	49.72	58.67
Prepared salads	4.41	3.32	3.49	3.14	5.56	5.88	6.18
Prepared desserts	3.31	3.01	2.75	3.78	2.80	4.00	3.56

	total complete income reporters	less than $20,000	$20,000 to $29,999	$30,000 to $39,999	$40,000 to $49,999	$50,000 to $69,999	$70,000 or more
Baby food	$11.07	$10.15	$9.30	$11.95	$6.49	$14.00	$14.49
Miscellaneous prepared foods	27.36	25.63	25.77	25.20	27.20	25.85	34.43
Nonalcoholic beverages	96.72	88.47	97.08	84.49	103.58	104.04	105.82
Cola	37.31	33.73	39.67	34.33	37.74	44.73	34.69
Other carbonated drinks	16.08	14.65	15.97	13.59	17.54	17.55	17.90
Coffee	17.32	17.44	17.96	13.92	18.84	15.41	18.89
Roasted coffee	11.68	10.78	12.80	9.62	12.30	12.11	12.46
Instant and freeze-dried coffee	5.64	6.65	5.16	4.30	6.55	3.30	6.43
Noncarb. fruit flavored drinks incl. non-frozen lemonade	9.21	8.34	7.46	9.73	9.13	10.65	10.41
Tea	6.70	5.43	6.28	5.71	6.95	7.56	9.28
Nonalcoholic beer	0.30	0.27	0.28	0.07	0.53	0.26	0.45
Other nonalcoholic beverages	9.81	8.62	9.45	7.14	12.84	7.88	14.19
Food prepared by cu on out-of-town trips	19.59	10.01	15.48	14.31	29.54	26.34	32.64
FOOD AWAY FROM HOME	**705.09**	**404.09**	**533.63**	**650.29**	**762.68**	**911.97**	**1,277.95**
Meals at restaurants, carry-outs, other	**545.30**	**331.29**	**433.03**	**516.87**	**577.14**	**719.19**	**915.93**
Lunch	190.35	112.12	132.63	185.13	215.76	243.77	337.63
Dinner	267.55	163.11	228.18	248.45	258.48	359.95	450.14
Snacks and nonalcoholic beverages	44.18	26.18	37.43	44.10	48.68	59.41	68.21
Breakfast and brunch	43.22	29.87	34.78	39.19	54.22	56.06	59.94
Board (including at school)	**20.16**	**9.89**	**6.96**	**8.34**	**13.48**	**21.88**	**69.07**
Catered affairs	**22.15**	**3.68**	**7.76**	**18.95**	**38.41**	**29.16**	**57.58**
Food on out-of-town trips	**85.38**	**43.15**	**56.06**	**63.98**	**100.07**	**101.63**	**190.03**
School lunches	**21.97**	**7.24**	**16.03**	**30.92**	**27.30**	**34.26**	**31.30**
Meals as pay	**10.12**	**8.84**	**13.78**	**11.24**	**6.29**	**5.85**	**14.05**
ALCOHOLIC BEVERAGES	**118.63**	**77.57**	**114.98**	**124.08**	**112.78**	**148.26**	**171.62**
At home	**70.16**	**51.03**	**73.68**	**80.85**	**70.99**	**75.19**	**86.30**
Beer and ale	43.50	35.25	54.68	52.28	46.94	40.05	37.89
Whiskey	5.70	4.26	6.23	5.96	4.31	6.48	7.64
Wine	14.42	7.30	8.52	14.60	15.37	20.36	28.39
Other alcoholic beverages	6.54	4.21	4.26	8.01	4.36	8.29	12.37
Away from home	**48.47**	**26.55**	**41.30**	**43.23**	**41.80**	**73.07**	**85.32**
Beer and ale	17.00	10.64	15.46	19.45	13.78	25.77	22.69
Wine	6.70	3.27	5.62	5.55	4.97	11.75	12.24
Other alcoholic beverages	12.09	5.99	11.86	9.94	8.05	20.05	21.99
Alcoholic beverages purchased on trips	12.68	6.64	8.36	8.29	15.00	15.50	28.40

Note: Expenditures listed for items in a given category may not add to the total for that category because the listing is incomplete. (-) means insufficient data.

Income
indexed per capita spending

(indexed average annual per capita spending of consumer units on food and alcoholic beverages, by before-tax income of consumer unit, 1994; complete income reporters only; index definition: an index of 100 is the per capita average for all consumer units; an index of 132 means that per capita spending by consumer units in the income group is 32 percent above the per capita average for all consumer units; an index of 68 indicates that per capita spending by consumer units in the income group is 32 percent below the per capita average for all consumer units)

	total, complete income reporters	under $20,000	$20,000 to $29,999	$30,000 to $39,999	$40,000 to $49,999	$50,000 to $69,999	$70,000 or more
Per capita spending of cu, total	$13,105.20	$8,499.64	$10,816.76	$11,598.04	$13,896.43	$15,540.97	$22,421.38
Per capita spending of cu, index	100	65	83	88	106	119	171
Food, per capita spending index	100	79	87	92	103	114	142
Alcoholic beverages, per capita spending index	100	65	97	105	95	125	145
FOOD AT HOME	**100**	**94**	**94**	**92**	**99**	**105**	**117**
Cereals and bakery products	**100**	**92**	**90**	**89**	**103**	**106**	**122**
Cereals and cereal products	100	96	90	89	104	100	119
Flour	100	116	119	77	115	63	86
Prepared flour mixes	100	117	88	74	104	96	94
Ready-to-eat and cooked cereals	100	92	88	84	108	105	126
Rice	100	97	105	101	86	93	112
Pasta, cornmeal, and other cereal products	100	93	84	108	98	100	118
Bakery products	100	90	90	89	102	109	123
Bread	100	105	95	86	102	96	103
White bread	100	116	101	83	92	93	86
Bread, other than white	100	94	89	88	111	99	120
Crackers and cookies	100	88	84	90	96	111	137
Cookies	100	86	88	86	99	113	139
Crackers	100	94	76	99	90	107	134
Frozen and refrigerated bakery products	100	85	86	101	108	119	114
Other bakery products	100	82	92	88	105	116	131
Biscuits and rolls	100	73	81	84	101	129	158
Cakes and cupcakes	100	92	97	93	106	92	120
Bread and cracker products	100	63	97	99	99	143	133
Sweetrolls, coffee cakes, doughnuts	100	84	102	93	103	116	112
Pies, tarts, turnovers	100	87	88	77	118	125	116
Meats, poultry, fish, and eggs	**100**	**101**	**99**	**94**	**93**	**96**	**107**
Beef	100	98	96	95	102	100	104
Ground beef	100	101	104	95	95	98	96
Roast	100	101	91	86	103	98	114
Chuck roast	100	105	108	79	84	94	111
Round roast	100	94	80	98	131	106	99
Other roast	100	105	85	80	87	93	135
Steak	100	94	88	98	116	99	108
Round steak	100	92	105	133	111	77	84
Sirloin steak	100	102	76	75	108	102	129
Other steak	100	91	88	98	122	105	104
Other beef	100	100	104	92	65	123	101
Pork	100	111	108	95	84	86	93
Bacon	100	123	117	81	81	84	76
Pork chops	100	117	92	94	87	85	98

	total complete income reporters	less than $20,000	$20,000 to $29,999	$30,000 to $39,999	$40,000 to $49,999	$50,000 to $69,999	$70,000 or more
Ham	100	108	98	113	85	88	88
Ham, not canned	100	107	104	103	88	89	91
Canned ham	100	122	33	234	51	78	54
Sausage	100	112	121	81	75	94	88
Other pork	100	100	122	94	86	82	105
Other meats	100	98	105	89	101	92	108
Frankfurters	100	101	112	78	117	103	82
Lunch meats (cold cuts)	100	95	100	93	98	96	115
Bologna, liverwurst, salami	100	113	113	94	80	76	95
Other lunchmeats	100	85	93	93	109	106	125
Lamb, organ meats and others	100	117	124	79	84	48	114
Lamb and organ meats	100	119	125	71	86	45	117
Mutton, goat and game	100	47	75	365	-	148	-
Poultry	100	99	93	91	96	101	115
Fresh and frozen chickens	100	100	90	94	93	101	115
Fresh and frozen whole chicken	100	103	109	95	92	95	93
Fresh and frozen chicken parts	100	99	83	94	93	104	122
Other poultry	100	94	103	80	110	98	115
Fish and seafood	100	89	94	103	77	99	138
Canned fish and seafood	100	85	98	89	95	101	140
Fresh fish and shellfish	100	87	94	96	77	101	148
Frozen fish and shellfish	100	96	93	128	65	95	116
Eggs	100	120	100	91	87	86	83
Dairy products	**100**	**96**	**92**	**90**	**96**	**106**	**117**
Fresh milk and cream	100	103	101	87	97	102	100
Fresh milk, all types	100	105	98	88	97	102	98
Cream	100	77	134	83	94	96	128
Other dairy products	100	91	86	92	95	109	131
Butter	100	83	108	102	103	89	127
Cheese	100	96	83	89	98	103	130
Ice cream and related products	100	83	87	102	91	119	129
Miscellaneous dairy products	100	94	77	76	82	122	146
Fruits and vegetables	**100**	**93**	**92**	**90**	**95**	**106**	**124**
Fresh fruits	100	94	91	86	90	104	132
Apples	100	81	83	110	86	115	138
Bananas	100	100	97	92	82	97	123
Oranges	100	107	97	86	93	94	107
Citrus fruits, excl. oranges	100	94	93	79	86	92	152
Other fresh fruits	100	93	89	74	97	108	139
Fresh vegetables	100	93	91	93	94	99	131
Potatoes	100	103	101	90	97	83	112
Lettuce	100	91	81	89	91	111	141
Tomatoes	100	93	100	95	85	110	114
Other fresh vegetables	100	89	87	94	96	99	142

	total complete income reporters	less than $20,000	$20,000 to $29,999	$30,000 to $39,999	$40,000 to $49,999	$50,000 to $69,999	$70,000 or more
Processed fruits	100	93	88	91	98	114	117
Frozen fruits and fruit juices	100	90	91	93	108	114	111
Frozen orange juice	100	99	94	86	106	100	110
Frozen fruits	100	80	91	86	91	168	98
Frozen fruit juices	100	76	85	109	117	123	117
Canned fruit	100	95	84	86	92	107	133
Dried fruit	100	97	97	97	82	92	128
Fresh fruit juices	100	103	92	86	99	91	118
Canned and bottled fruit juices	100	89	84	93	99	131	111
Processed vegetables	100	92	99	92	104	111	104
Frozen vegetables	100	82	91	87	116	119	121
Canned and dried vegetables and juices	100	97	103	94	98	108	96
Canned beans	100	105	100	94	85	112	88
Canned corn	100	92	123	69	103	130	81
Other canned and dried vegetables	100	97	102	95	102	100	100
Frozen vegetable juices	100	91	57	62	124	165	98
Fresh and canned vegetable juices	100	88	89	117	100	106	107
Other food at home	**100**	**87**	**94**	**92**	**105**	**110**	**121**
Sugar and other sweets	100	94	92	95	97	114	108
Candy and chewing gum	100	82	87	100	104	130	114
Sugar	100	124	112	88	81	81	76
Artificial sweeteners	100	131	72	80	77	89	110
Jams, preserves, other sweets	100	100	92	90	94	100	115
Fats and oils	100	104	97	88	100	90	109
Margarine	100	124	96	83	85	80	99
Fats and oils	100	113	103	92	106	79	86
Salad dressings	100	87	100	86	97	105	130
Nondairy cream and imitation milk	100	101	95	80	83	104	122
Peanut butter	100	101	80	93	121	88	115
Miscellaneous foods	100	84	91	98	101	112	128
Frozen prepared foods	100	78	90	108	100	121	121
Frozen meals	100	91	105	116	101	88	101
Other frozen prepared foods	100	73	84	104	100	136	130
Canned and packaged soups	100	87	92	93	111	110	119
Potato chips, nuts, and other snacks	100	74	87	93	108	116	145
Potato chips and other snacks	100	74	87	92	106	125	141
Nuts	100	77	88	98	112	86	160
Condiments and seasonings	100	84	96	98	104	107	122
Salt, spices and other seasonings	100	90	92	124	106	94	102
Olives, pickles, relishes	100	84	122	90	112	93	110
Sauces and gravies	100	81	93	93	103	110	135
Baking needs and misc. products	100	85	88	82	99	131	126
Other canned/packaged prepared foods	100	91	90	95	91	108	127
Prepared salads	100	75	79	71	126	133	140
Prepared desserts	100	91	83	114	84	121	108

	total complete income reporters	less than $20,000	$20,000 to $29,999	$30,000 to $39,999	$40,000 to $49,999	$50,000 to $69,999	$70,000 or more
Baby food	100	92	84	108	59	126	131
Miscellaneous prepared foods	100	94	94	92	99	94	126
Nonalcoholic beverages	100	91	100	87	107	108	109
Cola	100	90	106	92	101	120	93
Other carbonated drinks	100	91	99	85	109	109	111
Coffee	100	101	104	80	109	89	109
Roasted coffee	100	92	110	82	105	104	107
Instant and freeze-dried coffee	100	118	92	76	116	58	114
Noncarb. fruit flavored drinks incl. non-frozen lemonade	100	91	81	106	99	116	113
Tea	100	81	94	85	104	113	138
Nonalcoholic beer	100	89	93	23	176	86	150
Other nonalcoholic beverages	100	88	96	73	131	80	145
Food prepared by cu on out-of-town trips	100	51	79	73	151	134	167
FOOD AWAY FROM HOME	**100**	**57**	**76**	**92**	**108**	**129**	**181**
Meals at restaurants, carry-outs, other	**100**	**61**	**79**	**95**	**106**	**132**	**168**
Lunch	100	59	70	97	113	128	177
Dinner	100	61	85	93	97	135	168
Snacks and nonalcoholic beverages	100	59	85	100	110	134	154
Breakfast and brunch	100	69	80	91	125	130	139
Board (including at school)	**100**	**49**	**35**	**41**	**67**	**109**	**343**
Catered affairs	**100**	**17**	**35**	**86**	**173**	**132**	**260**
Food on out-of-town trips	**100**	**51**	**66**	**75**	**117**	**119**	**223**
School lunches	**100**	**33**	**73**	**141**	**124**	**156**	**142**
Meals as pay	**100**	**87**	**136**	**111**	**62**	**58**	**139**
ALCOHOLIC BEVERAGES	**100**	**65**	**97**	**105**	**95**	**125**	**145**
At home	**100**	**73**	**105**	**115**	**101**	**107**	**123**
Beer and ale	100	81	126	120	108	92	87
Whiskey	100	75	109	105	76	114	134
Wine	100	51	59	101	107	141	197
Other alcoholic beverages	100	64	65	122	67	127	189
Away from home	**100**	**55**	**85**	**89**	**86**	**151**	**176**
Beer and ale	100	63	91	114	81	152	133
Wine	100	49	84	83	74	175	183
Other alcoholic beverages	100	50	98	82	67	166	182
Alcoholic beverages purchased on trips	100	52	66	65	118	122	224

Note: (-) means insufficient data.

(total annual spending on food and alcoholic beverages by before-tax income of consumer unit, 1994; complete income reporters only; numbers in thousands)

	total, complete income reporters	under $20,000	$20,000 to $29,999	$30,000 to $39,999	$40,000 to $49,999	$50,000 to $69,999	$70,000 or more
Number of consumer units	85,994	32,208	13,975	10,922	8,280	10,510	10,099
Total spending of all cu's	$2,817,420,562	$547,513,043	$377,910,692	$354,686,707	$333,681,102	$506,340,375	$701,943,922
Food, total spending	389,289,678	92,679,164	54,948,582	50,839,835	44,607,010	67,358,905	80,636,576
Alcoholic beverages, total spending	25,503,241	4,997,071	4,017,254	3,794,521	2,708,140	4,830,396	5,372,769
FOOD AT HOME	**$237,705,475**	**$66,649,303**	**$36,304,954**	**$30,952,839**	**$26,293,471**	**$37,645,979**	**$40,627,772**
Cereals and bakery products	**37,782,324**	**10,462,125**	**5,535,498**	**4,773,788**	**4,344,433**	**6,070,996**	**6,691,597**
Cereals and cereal products	14,355,838	4,129,388	2,102,259	1,807,809	1,673,471	2,185,449	2,481,930
Flour	681,932	236,407	131,645	74,597	87,354	65,267	85,236
Prepared flour mixes	1,135,121	396,480	162,949	119,268	131,486	165,322	156,131
Ready-to-eat and cooked cereals	8,773,108	2,427,517	1,247,828	1,048,840	1,061,827	1,398,881	1,604,933
Rice	1,330,327	386,818	226,255	190,480	127,429	186,553	217,229
Pasta, cornmeal, other cereal products	2,435,350	682,165	333,583	374,515	265,374	369,532	418,503
Bakery products	23,426,485	6,332,737	3,433,378	2,965,978	2,671,045	3,885,547	4,209,667
Bread	6,638,737	2,084,180	1,023,669	809,757	755,467	970,599	997,276
White bread	3,269,492	1,138,231	535,662	387,622	337,658	463,176	408,707
Bread, other than white	3,368,385	946,271	488,007	422,135	417,726	507,423	588,570
Crackers and cookies	5,534,574	1,467,396	752,973	709,165	594,173	931,291	1,106,042
Cookies	3,764,817	969,783	535,522	458,724	416,318	644,894	760,758
Crackers	1,769,757	497,614	217,591	250,441	177,854	286,398	345,285
Frozen and refrigerated bakery products	1,905,627	484,086	265,665	272,832	229,770	345,043	317,109
Other bakery products	9,347,548	2,297,075	1,390,932	1,174,224	1,091,635	1,638,614	1,789,240
Biscuits and rolls	3,204,136	696,659	420,787	381,833	360,760	625,240	736,520
Cakes and cupcakes	2,676,133	740,462	422,325	353,545	317,455	373,631	467,786
Bread and cracker products	402,452	76,655	63,586	56,794	44,464	87,023	78,166
Sweetrolls, coffee cakes, doughnuts	1,984,742	501,156	330,090	263,329	227,286	348,617	323,976
Pies, tarts, turnovers	1,079,225	282,142	154,284	118,722	141,754	204,104	182,792
Meats, poultry, fish, and eggs	**62,680,167**	**18,963,426**	**10,084,081**	**8,388,314**	**6,540,124**	**9,076,436**	**9,783,810**
Beef	19,497,420	5,743,008	3,036,069	2,621,826	2,230,549	2,953,941	2,944,161
Ground beef	7,721,401	2,330,893	1,310,995	1,040,976	819,637	1,152,211	1,080,290
Roast	3,249,713	981,700	478,504	399,199	372,434	484,301	538,681
Chuck roast	1,040,527	327,877	183,352	116,756	97,704	148,506	167,845
Round roast	1,219,395	341,727	159,175	170,165	178,020	196,012	175,925
Other roast	989,791	311,773	135,977	112,278	96,710	139,678	194,911
Steak	7,379,145	2,085,146	1,053,156	1,031,583	954,767	1,103,235	1,155,730
Round steak	1,413,741	388,428	242,187	267,917	175,536	165,427	173,703
Sirloin steak	2,071,595	633,209	256,581	219,751	249,394	320,765	390,023
Other steak	3,893,808	1,063,830	554,388	543,916	529,754	617,042	591,902
Other beef	1,147,160	344,948	193,414	150,068	83,711	214,194	169,461
Pork	13,299,832	4,432,465	2,334,244	1,792,300	1,242,331	1,738,354	1,792,169
Bacon	1,978,722	730,477	376,347	227,833	178,931	250,979	217,936
Pork chops	3,222,195	1,130,179	480,181	432,511	311,411	413,463	462,130

	total complete income reporters	less than $20,000	$20,000 to $29,999	$30,000 to $39,999	$40,000 to $49,999	$50,000 to $69,999	$70,000 or more
Ham	$3,159,420	$1,025,825	$503,659	$508,419	$299,405	$423,238	$406,485
Ham, not canned	2,916,057	936,287	490,523	427,050	285,494	394,335	387,398
Canned ham	244,223	89,216	13,137	81,369	13,993	28,797	19,087
Sausage	1,946,044	653,178	381,238	225,212	164,027	277,254	248,536
Other pork	2,992,591	892,806	592,959	398,325	288,558	373,420	457,081
Other meats	8,112,674	2,392,088	1,382,826	1,022,518	913,450	1,134,449	1,275,201
Frankfurters	1,645,065	496,969	298,925	182,616	215,197	257,495	195,921
Lunch meats (cold cuts)	5,647,226	1,606,535	918,717	747,939	621,083	817,363	942,641
Bologna, liverwurst, salami	1,999,361	674,758	368,521	267,152	178,517	231,115	277,521
Other lunchmeats	3,647,006	932,100	550,196	480,786	442,649	586,248	665,221
Lamb, organ meats and others	820,383	288,584	165,185	91,963	77,170	59,592	136,639
Lamb and organ meats	800,604	285,685	162,529	81,260	77,170	54,967	136,639
Mutton, goat and game	20,639	2,899	2,516	10,704	-	4,624	-
Poultry	11,636,708	3,443,679	1,751,906	1,509,420	1,253,012	1,776,926	1,943,957
Fresh and frozen chickens	9,243,495	2,766,667	1,349,566	1,238,446	959,072	1,420,952	1,541,814
Fresh and frozen whole chicken	2,498,126	770,093	443,706	336,070	256,349	359,547	339,225
Fresh and frozen chicken parts	6,745,369	1,996,252	905,860	902,376	702,724	1,061,405	1,202,488
Other poultry	2,393,213	677,012	402,340	270,975	293,940	355,974	402,142
Fish and seafood	7,492,657	2,002,693	1,149,863	1,101,811	645,509	1,127,408	1,507,680
Canned fish and seafood	1,341,506	342,049	212,979	169,728	142,002	206,311	273,582
Fresh fish and shellfish	4,152,650	1,083,799	635,164	568,599	358,193	634,804	897,700
Frozen fish and shellfish	1,997,641	577,167	301,720	363,484	145,314	286,292	336,499
Eggs	2,641,736	949,170	429,172	340,548	255,438	345,254	320,542
Dairy products	**25,615,033**	**7,380,141**	**3,837,675**	**3,277,801**	**2,737,037**	**4,102,999**	**4,373,776**
Fresh milk and cream	11,349,488	3,494,246	1,854,902	1,410,576	1,229,497	1,750,230	1,646,844
Fresh milk, all types	10,615,099	3,324,832	1,694,888	1,323,528	1,151,914	1,643,133	1,509,397
Cream	735,249	169,092	160,014	87,048	77,584	107,097	137,447
Other dairy products	14,264,685	3,885,895	1,982,773	1,867,225	1,507,540	2,352,769	2,726,932
Butter	1,013,009	251,867	178,042	147,010	116,500	136,525	187,639
Cheese	7,290,571	2,090,943	988,731	923,892	801,835	1,135,395	1,375,484
Ice cream and related products	4,140,611	1,031,300	588,068	599,399	421,618	743,793	776,613
Miscellaneous dairy products	1,820,493	511,785	227,932	196,924	167,587	337,056	387,297
Fruits and vegetables	**38,361,923**	**10,696,277**	**5,713,120**	**4,922,545**	**4,091,810**	**6,158,335**	**6,917,815**
Fresh fruits	11,619,509	3,276,520	1,718,226	1,428,052	1,174,352	1,831,578	2,237,837
Apples	2,179,088	528,533	295,152	342,295	210,395	380,147	437,691
Bananas	2,601,319	775,569	409,328	339,128	238,961	382,669	464,958
Oranges	1,380,204	441,572	217,451	167,980	143,410	195,696	214,503
Citrus fruits, excl. oranges	973,452	275,378	147,576	109,329	93,150	136,210	215,109
Other fresh fruits	4,486,307	1,255,468	648,580	469,318	488,520	736,856	905,577
Fresh vegetables	11,952,306	3,315,814	1,770,493	1,573,314	1,251,356	1,793,637	2,286,818
Potatoes	2,428,471	751,735	399,126	312,260	262,642	306,892	397,396
Lettuce	1,517,794	411,618	200,262	191,681	153,594	255,919	310,645
Tomatoes	1,856,610	516,294	302,838	251,097	175,288	310,571	309,534
Other fresh vegetables	6,150,291	1,635,844	868,407	818,276	659,833	920,256	1,269,242

	total complete income reporters	less than $20,000	$20,000 to $29,999	$30,000 to $39,999	$40,000 to $49,999	$50,000 to $69,999	$70,000 or more
Processed fruits	$8,196,088	$2,285,802	$1,166,493	$1,059,980	$899,705	$1,420,006	$1,393,864
Frozen fruits and fruit juices	1,408,582	377,800	208,088	187,094	169,657	242,361	228,237
Frozen orange juice	822,963	243,492	125,915	100,482	97,042	124,649	131,893
Frozen fruits	128,991	30,598	19,006	15,837	13,165	32,896	18,481
Frozen fruit juices	456,628	104,032	63,167	70,884	59,450	84,816	77,863
Canned fruit	1,279,591	362,984	174,548	157,168	130,990	207,467	248,233
Dried fruit	535,743	155,565	84,269	73,942	48,852	74,411	99,677
Fresh fruit juices	1,517,794	467,338	227,653	186,220	168,581	208,518	260,655
Canned and bottled fruit juices	3,455,239	921,793	471,936	455,447	381,708	687,354	557,061
Processed vegetables	6,594,020	1,818,142	1,057,908	861,200	766,314	1,113,009	999,296
Frozen vegetables	2,130,931	524,346	314,018	264,094	276,635	384,141	376,188
Canned and dried vegetables and juices	4,463,089	1,294,117	744,029	597,106	489,762	728,869	623,209
Canned beans	912,396	286,651	148,834	121,999	86,443	155,548	116,441
Canned corn	601,098	165,871	120,465	59,416	69,055	118,027	70,996
Other canned and dried vegetables	2,371,715	688,607	392,418	320,779	269,266	360,388	345,689
Frozen vegetable juices	19,779	5,475	1,817	1,748	2,732	4,940	2,828
Fresh and canned vegetable juices	558,101	147,513	80,356	93,055	62,266	90,071	87,255
Other food at home	**73,266,028**	**19,147,656**	**11,134,581**	**9,590,499**	**8,580,067**	**12,237,319**	**12,860,774**
Sugar and other sweets	9,516,956	2,677,129	1,420,838	1,291,636	1,034,255	1,646,917	1,493,137
Candy and chewing gum	5,720,321	1,397,183	810,830	815,218	663,062	1,124,465	947,185
Sugar	1,573,690	585,541	287,326	195,941	143,161	192,333	175,218
Artificial sweeteners	306,999	120,136	35,776	34,950	26,413	41,199	49,283
Jams, preserves, other sweets	1,915,946	574,269	286,907	245,527	201,618	289,025	321,451
Fats and oils	6,944,875	2,170,819	1,092,286	866,442	775,753	951,365	1,104,427
Margarine	1,262,392	467,660	196,069	149,522	119,646	152,605	182,691
Fats and oils	1,990,761	672,825	331,767	259,725	236,477	238,892	250,657
Salad dressings	2,092,234	545,926	341,270	256,012	227,700	331,696	397,598
Nondairy cream and imitation milk	577,020	175,212	89,440	65,423	53,654	91,122	102,505
Peanut butter	1,022,469	309,841	133,741	135,760	138,193	137,050	170,976
Miscellaneous foods	31,798,001	7,956,020	4,689,032	4,410,850	3,573,565	5,390,894	5,928,416
Frozen prepared foods	5,657,545	1,326,003	830,534	868,081	634,000	1,036,286	994,449
Frozen meals	1,766,317	479,255	300,602	291,508	198,968	236,685	260,049
Other frozen prepared foods	3,891,229	846,748	529,792	576,682	435,031	799,601	734,399
Canned and packaged soups	2,597,879	673,791	387,806	342,951	320,933	432,276	450,819
Potato chips, nuts, and other snacks	6,527,805	1,455,480	922,210	863,384	784,033	1,151,265	1,381,846
Potato chips and other snacks	5,143,301	1,136,298	724,604	670,829	610,981	970,493	1,059,183
Nuts	1,384,503	319,503	197,607	192,555	173,052	180,772	322,663
Condiments and seasonings	7,091,925	1,787,866	1,105,143	988,987	824,936	1,151,265	1,264,496
Salt, spices and other seasonings	1,692,362	455,743	254,066	297,952	200,128	239,943	252,374
Olives, pickles, relishes	925,295	232,542	183,212	118,067	115,423	130,114	148,354
Sauces and gravies	3,272,072	794,571	496,811	433,057	376,657	543,262	642,801
Baking needs and misc. products	1,202,196	305,332	171,054	140,020	132,728	237,946	220,865
Other canned/packaged prepared foods	9,922,848	2,712,880	1,443,338	1,347,447	1,009,663	1,619,801	1,836,705
Prepared salads	947,654	213,861	122,002	96,114	133,556	191,492	193,598
Prepared desserts	712,030	194,214	96,148	115,555	67,151	130,219	111,493

	total complete income reporters	less than $20,000	$20,000 to $29,999	$30,000 to $39,999	$40,000 to $49,999	$50,000 to $69,999	$70,000 or more
Baby food	$2,380,314	$653,822	$324,779	$365,341	$155,830	$456,134	$453,748
Miscellaneous prepared foods	5,882,850	1,650,660	900,409	770,547	653,126	842,061	1,077,866
Nonalcoholic beverages	20,794,209	5,698,561	3,391,733	2,583,927	2,487,064	3,389,790	3,312,775
Cola	8,020,660	2,172,430	1,385,901	1,049,932	906,163	1,457,212	1,086,147
Other carbonated drinks	3,456,959	943,372	558,022	415,691	421,204	571,639	560,394
Coffee	3,722,680	1,123,093	627,478	425,740	452,419	502,063	591,397
Roasted coffee	2,511,025	694,404	447,340	294,239	295,265	394,651	390,023
Instant and freeze-dried coffee	1,211,655	428,688	180,278	131,501	157,237	107,412	201,374
Noncarb. fruit flavored drinks incl. non-frozen lemonade	1,979,582	537,229	260,774	297,406	219,337	347,145	325,996
Tea	1,440,400	349,779	219,408	174,534	166,842	246,354	290,447
Nonalcoholic beer	65,355	17,392	9,922	2,184	12,834	8,513	14,240
Other nonalcoholic beverages	2,108,573	554,944	330,229	218,440	308,264	256,759	444,255
Food prepared by cu on out-of-town trips	4,211,986	644,804	540,833	437,645	709,430	858,247	1,021,918
FOOD AWAY FROM HOME	**151,583,344**	**26,029,539**	**18,643,628**	**19,886,996**	**18,313,538**	**29,713,031**	**40,008,804**
Meals at restaurants, carry-outs, other	**117,232,180**	**21,340,055**	**15,129,056**	**15,806,646**	**13,858,236**	**23,431,940**	**28,674,798**
Lunch	40,922,825	7,222,644	4,633,831	5,661,419	5,180,796	7,942,302	10,570,219
Dinner	57,519,667	10,507,216	7,972,179	7,597,999	6,206,522	11,727,478	14,092,549
Snacks and nonalcoholic beverages	9,498,897	1,686,411	1,307,781	1,348,758	1,168,805	1,935,627	2,135,535
Breakfast and brunch	9,291,652	1,924,106	1,215,266	1,198,362	1,302,030	1,826,533	1,876,394
Board (including at school)	**4,334,098**	**636,752**	**243,305**	**255,138**	**323,582**	**712,998**	**2,162,297**
Catered affairs	**4,762,348**	**237,051**	**271,255**	**579,521**	**922,226**	**950,104**	**1,802,672**
Food on out-of-town trips	**18,355,419**	**2,779,550**	**1,958,736**	**1,956,458**	**2,402,773**	**3,311,070**	**5,949,119**
School lunches	**4,723,650**	**466,372**	**560,118**	**945,518**	**655,528**	**1,116,372**	**980,007**
Meals as pay	**2,175,648**	**569,437**	**481,299**	**343,825**	**151,110**	**190,441**	**439,912**
ALCOHOLIC BEVERAGES	**25,503,241**	**4,997,071**	**4,017,254**	**3,794,521**	**2,708,140**	**4,830,396**	**5,372,769**
At home	**15,083,348**	**3,286,826**	**2,574,335**	**2,472,413**	**1,704,521**	**2,449,776**	**2,701,684**
Beer and ale	9,350,988	2,270,986	1,910,522	1,598,762	1,127,239	1,305,027	1,186,330
Whiskey	1,225,415	274,734	217,591	182,179	103,500	211,041	239,043
Wine	3,100,944	470,237	297,668	446,382	369,122	663,496	888,914
Other alcoholic beverages	1,406,862	271,191	148,694	245,090	104,659	270,212	387,398
Away from home	**10,419,893**	**1,710,245**	**1,442,779**	**1,322,108**	**1,003,619**	**2,380,725**	**2,671,085**
Beer and ale	3,654,745	685,386	540,274	594,812	330,952	839,644	710,465
Wine	1,439,540	210,962	196,349	169,837	119,315	382,774	383,055
Other alcoholic beverages	2,598,739	386,174	414,219	303,850	193,338	653,302	688,449
Alcoholic beverages purchased on trips	2,726,870	428,044	291,938	253,609	360,097	505,006	889,116

Note: Spending for items in a given category may not add to the total for that category because the listing is incomplete. Numbers may not add to total due to rounding. (-) means insufficient data.

Income

market shares

(percent of total annual spending on food accounted for by consumer unit before-tax income groups, 1994; complete income reporters only)

	total, complete income reporters	under $20,000	$20,000 to $29,999	$30,000 to $39,999	$40,000 to $49,999	$50,000 to $69,999	$70,000 or more
Share of total consumer units	*100.0%*	*37.5%*	*16.3%*	*12.7%*	*9.6%*	*12.2%*	*11.7%*
Share of total spending	*100.0*	*19.4*	*13.4*	*12.6*	*11.8*	*18.0*	*24.9*
Share of food spending	*100.0*	*23.8*	*14.1*	*13.1*	*11.5*	*17.3*	*20.7*
Share of alcoholic beverages spending	*100.0*	*19.6*	*15.8*	*14.9*	*10.6*	*18.9*	*21.1*
FOOD AT HOME	**100.0%**	**28.0%**	**15.3%**	**13.0%**	**11.1%**	**15.8%**	**17.1%**
Cereals and bakery products	**100.0**	**27.7**	**14.7**	**12.6**	**11.5**	**16.1**	**17.7**
Cereals and cereal products	100.0	28.8	14.6	12.6	11.7	15.2	17.3
Flour	100.0	34.7	19.3	10.9	12.8	9.6	12.5
Prepared flour mixes	100.0	34.9	14.4	10.5	11.6	14.6	13.8
Ready-to-eat and cooked cereals	100.0	27.7	14.2	12.0	12.1	15.9	18.3
Rice	100.0	29.1	17.0	14.3	9.6	14.0	16.3
Pasta, cornmeal, and other cereal products	100.0	28.0	13.7	15.4	10.9	15.2	17.2
Bakery products	100.0	27.0	14.7	12.7	11.4	16.6	18.0
Bread	100.0	31.4	15.4	12.2	11.4	14.6	15.0
White bread	100.0	34.8	16.4	11.9	10.3	14.2	12.5
Bread, other than white	100.0	28.1	14.5	12.5	12.4	15.1	17.5
Crackers and cookies	100.0	26.5	13.6	12.8	10.7	16.8	20.0
Cookies	100.0	25.8	14.2	12.2	11.1	17.1	20.2
Crackers	100.0	28.1	12.3	14.2	10.0	16.2	19.5
Frozen and refrigerated bakery products	100.0	25.4	13.9	14.3	12.1	18.1	16.6
Other bakery products	100.0	24.6	14.9	12.6	11.7	17.5	19.1
Biscuits and rolls	100.0	21.7	13.1	11.9	11.3	19.5	23.0
Cakes and cupcakes	100.0	27.7	15.8	13.2	11.9	14.0	17.5
Bread and cracker products	100.0	19.0	15.8	14.1	11.0	21.6	19.4
Sweetrolls, coffee cakes, doughnuts	100.0	25.3	16.6	13.3	11.5	17.6	16.3
Pies, tarts, turnovers	100.0	26.1	14.3	11.0	13.1	18.9	16.9
Meats, poultry, fish, and eggs	**100.0**	**30.3**	**16.1**	**13.4**	**10.4**	**14.5**	**15.6**
Beef	100.0	29.5	15.6	13.4	11.4	15.2	15.1
Ground beef	100.0	30.2	17.0	13.5	10.6	14.9	14.0
Roast	100.0	30.2	14.7	12.3	11.5	14.9	16.6
Chuck roast	100.0	31.5	17.6	11.2	9.4	14.3	16.1
Round roast	100.0	28.0	13.1	14.0	14.6	16.1	14.4
Other roast	100.0	31.5	13.7	11.3	9.8	14.1	19.7
Steak	100.0	28.3	14.3	14.0	12.9	15.0	15.7
Round steak	100.0	27.5	17.1	19.0	12.4	11.7	12.3
Sirloin steak	100.0	30.6	12.4	10.6	12.0	15.5	18.8
Other steak	100.0	27.3	14.2	14.0	13.6	15.8	15.2
Other beef	100.0	30.1	16.9	13.1	7.3	18.7	14.8
Pork	100.0	33.3	17.6	13.5	9.3	13.1	13.5
Bacon	100.0	36.9	19.0	11.5	9.0	12.7	11.0
Pork chops	100.0	35.1	14.9	13.4	9.7	12.8	14.3

	total complete income reporters	less than $20,000	$20,000 to $29,999	$30,000 to $39,999	$40,000 to $49,999	$50,000 to $69,999	$70,000 or more
Ham	100.0%	32.5%	15.9%	16.1%	9.5%	13.4%	12.9%
Ham, not canned	100.0	32.1	16.8	14.6	9.8	13.5	13.3
Canned ham	100.0	36.6	5.4	33.3	5.7	11.8	7.8
Sausage	100.0	33.6	19.6	11.6	8.4	14.2	12.8
Other pork	100.0	29.8	19.8	13.3	9.6	12.5	15.3
Other meats	100.0	29.5	17.0	12.6	11.3	14.0	15.7
Frankfurters	100.0	30.2	18.2	11.1	13.1	15.7	11.9
Lunch meats (cold cuts)	100.0	28.4	16.3	13.2	11.0	14.5	16.7
Bologna, liverwurst, salami	100.0	33.7	18.4	13.4	8.9	11.6	13.9
Other lunchmeats	100.0	25.6	15.1	13.2	12.1	16.1	18.2
Lamb, organ meats and others	100.0	35.2	20.1	11.2	9.4	7.3	16.7
Lamb and organ meats	100.0	35.7	20.3	10.1	9.6	6.9	17.1
Mutton, goat and game	100.0	14.2	12.2	51.9	-	22.4	-
Poultry	100.0	29.6	15.1	13.0	10.8	15.3	16.7
Fresh and frozen chickens	100.0	29.9	14.6	13.4	10.4	15.4	16.7
Fresh and frozen whole chicken	100.0	30.8	17.8	13.5	10.3	14.4	13.6
Fresh and frozen chicken parts	100.0	29.6	13.4	13.4	10.4	15.7	17.8
Other poultry	100.0	28.3	16.8	11.3	12.3	14.9	16.8
Fish and seafood	100.0	26.7	15.3	14.7	8.6	15.0	20.1
Canned fish and seafood	100.0	25.5	15.9	12.7	10.6	15.4	20.4
Fresh fish and shellfish	100.0	26.1	15.3	13.7	8.6	15.3	21.6
Frozen fish and shellfish	100.0	28.9	15.1	18.2	7.3	14.3	16.8
Eggs	100.0	35.9	16.2	12.9	9.7	13.1	12.1
Dairy products	**100.0**	**28.8**	**15.0**	**12.8**	**10.7**	**16.0**	**17.1**
Fresh milk and cream	100.0	30.8	16.3	12.4	10.8	15.4	14.5
Fresh milk, all types	100.0	31.3	16.0	12.5	10.9	15.5	14.2
Cream	100.0	23.0	21.8	11.8	10.6	14.6	18.7
Other dairy products	100.0	27.2	13.9	13.1	10.6	16.5	19.1
Butter	100.0	24.8	17.6	14.5	11.5	13.5	18.5
Cheese	100.0	28.7	13.6	12.7	11.0	15.6	18.9
Ice cream and related products	100.0	24.9	14.2	14.5	10.2	18.0	18.8
Miscellaneous dairy products	100.0	28.1	12.5	10.8	9.2	18.5	21.3
Fruits and vegetables	**100.0**	**27.9**	**14.9**	**12.8**	**10.7**	**16.1**	**18.0**
Fresh fruits	100.0	28.2	14.8	12.3	10.1	15.8	19.3
Apples	100.0	24.3	13.5	15.7	9.7	17.4	20.1
Bananas	100.0	29.8	15.7	13.0	9.2	14.7	17.9
Oranges	100.0	32.0	15.8	12.2	10.4	14.2	15.5
Citrus fruits, excl. oranges	100.0	28.3	15.2	11.2	9.6	14.0	22.1
Other fresh fruits	100.0	28.0	14.5	10.5	10.9	16.4	20.2
Fresh vegetables	100.0	27.7	14.8	13.2	10.5	15.0	19.1
Potatoes	100.0	31.0	16.4	12.9	10.8	12.6	16.4
Lettuce	100.0	27.1	13.2	12.6	10.1	16.9	20.5
Tomatoes	100.0	27.8	16.3	13.5	9.4	16.7	16.7
Other fresh vegetables	100.0	26.6	14.1	13.3	10.7	15.0	20.6

	total complete income reporters	less than $20,000	$20,000 to $29,999	$30,000 to $39,999	$40,000 to $49,999	$50,000 to $69,999	$70,000 or more
Processed fruits	100.0%	27.9%	14.2%	12.9%	11.0%	17.3%	17.0%
Frozen fruits and fruit juices	100.0	26.8	14.8	13.3	12.0	17.2	16.2
Frozen orange juice	100.0	29.6	15.3	12.2	11.8	15.1	16.0
Frozen fruits	100.0	23.8	14.7	12.3	10.2	25.5	14.3
Frozen fruit juices	100.0	22.8	13.8	15.5	13.0	18.6	17.1
Canned fruit	100.0	28.4	13.6	12.3	10.2	16.2	19.4
Dried fruit	100.0	29.0	15.7	13.8	9.1	13.9	18.6
Fresh fruit juices	100.0	30.8	15.0	12.3	11.1	13.7	17.2
Canned and bottled fruit juices	100.0	26.7	13.7	13.2	11.0	19.9	16.1
Processed vegetables	100.0	27.6	16.0	13.1	11.6	16.9	15.2
Frozen vegetables	100.0	24.6	14.7	12.4	13.0	18.0	17.7
Canned and dried vegetables and juices	100.0	29.0	16.7	13.4	11.0	16.3	14.0
Canned beans	100.0	31.4	16.3	13.4	9.5	17.0	12.8
Canned corn	100.0	27.6	20.0	9.9	11.5	19.6	11.8
Other canned and dried vegetables	100.0	29.0	16.5	13.5	11.4	15.2	14.6
Frozen vegetable juices	100.0	27.2	9.2	8.8	13.8	25.0	14.3
Fresh and canned vegetable juices	100.0	26.4	14.4	16.7	11.2	16.1	15.6
Other food at home	**100.0**	**26.1**	**15.2**	**13.1**	**11.7**	**16.7**	**17.6**
Sugar and other sweets	100.0	28.1	14.9	13.6	10.9	17.3	15.7
Candy and chewing gum	100.0	24.4	14.2	14.3	11.6	19.7	16.6
Sugar	100.0	37.2	18.3	12.5	9.1	12.2	11.1
Artificial sweeteners	100.0	39.2	11.7	11.4	8.6	13.4	16.1
Jams, preserves, other sweets	100.0	30.0	15.0	12.8	10.5	15.1	16.8
Fats and oils	100.0	31.3	15.7	12.5	11.2	13.7	15.9
Margarine	100.0	37.0	15.5	11.8	9.5	12.1	14.5
Fats and oils	100.0	33.8	16.7	13.0	11.9	12.0	12.6
Salad dressings	100.0	26.1	16.3	12.2	10.9	15.9	19.0
Nondairy cream and imitation milk	100.0	30.4	15.5	11.3	9.3	15.8	17.8
Peanut butter	100.0	30.3	13.1	13.3	13.5	13.4	16.7
Miscellaneous foods	100.0	25.0	14.7	13.9	11.2	17.0	18.6
Frozen prepared foods	100.0	23.4	14.7	15.3	11.2	18.3	17.6
Frozen meals	100.0	27.1	17.0	16.5	11.3	13.4	14.7
Other frozen prepared foods	100.0	21.8	13.6	14.8	11.2	20.5	18.9
Canned and packaged soups	100.0	25.9	14.9	13.2	12.4	16.6	17.4
Potato chips, nuts, and other snacks	100.0	22.3	14.1	13.2	12.0	17.6	21.2
Potato chips and other snacks	100.0	22.1	14.1	13.0	11.9	18.9	20.6
Nuts	100.0	23.1	14.3	13.9	12.5	13.1	23.3
Condiments and seasonings	100.0	25.2	15.6	13.9	11.6	16.2	17.8
Salt, spices and other seasonings	100.0	26.9	15.0	17.6	11.8	14.2	14.9
Olives, pickles, relishes	100.0	25.1	19.8	12.8	12.5	14.1	16.0
Sauces and gravies	100.0	24.3	15.2	13.2	11.5	16.6	19.6
Baking needs and misc. products	100.0	25.4	14.2	11.6	11.0	19.8	18.4
Other canned/packaged prepared foods	100.0	27.3	14.5	13.6	10.2	16.3	18.5
Prepared salads	100.0	22.6	12.9	10.1	14.1	20.2	20.4
Prepared desserts	100.0	27.3	13.5	16.2	9.4	18.3	15.7

	total complete income reporters	less than $20,000	$20,000 to $29,999	$30,000 to $39,999	$40,000 to $49,999	$50,000 to $69,999	$70,000 or more
Baby food	100.0%	27.5%	13.6%	15.3%	6.5%	19.2%	19.1%
Miscellaneous prepared foods	100.0	28.1	15.3	13.1	11.1	14.3	18.3
Nonalcoholic beverages	100.0	27.4	16.3	12.4	12.0	16.3	15.9
Cola	100.0	27.1	17.3	13.1	11.3	18.2	13.5
Other carbonated drinks	100.0	27.3	16.1	12.0	12.2	16.5	16.2
Coffee	100.0	30.2	16.9	11.4	12.2	13.5	15.9
Roasted coffee	100.0	27.7	17.8	11.7	11.8	15.7	15.5
Instant and freeze-dried coffee	100.0	35.4	14.9	10.9	13.0	8.9	16.6
Noncarb. fruit flavored drinks incl. non-frozen lemonade	100.0	27.1	13.2	15.0	11.1	17.5	16.5
Tea	100.0	24.3	15.2	12.1	11.6	17.1	20.2
Nonalcoholic beer	100.0	26.6	15.2	3.3	19.6	13.0	21.8
Other nonalcoholic beverages	100.0	26.3	15.7	10.4	14.6	12.2	21.1
Food prepared by cu on out-of-town trips	100.0	15.3	12.8	10.4	16.8	20.4	24.3
FOOD AWAY FROM HOME	**100.0**	**17.2**	**12.3**	**13.1**	**12.1**	**19.6**	**26.4**
Meals at restaurants, carry-outs, other	**100.0**	**18.2**	**12.9**	**13.5**	**11.8**	**20.0**	**24.5**
Lunch	100.0	17.6	11.3	13.8	12.7	19.4	25.8
Dinner	100.0	18.3	13.9	13.2	10.8	20.4	24.5
Snacks and nonalcoholic beverages	100.0	17.8	13.8	14.2	12.3	20.4	22.5
Breakfast and brunch	100.0	20.7	13.1	12.9	14.0	19.7	20.2
Board (including at school)	**100.0**	**14.7**	**5.6**	**5.9**	**7.5**	**16.5**	**49.9**
Catered affairs	**100.0**	**5.0**	**5.7**	**12.2**	**19.4**	**20.0**	**37.9**
Food on out-of-town trips	**100.0**	**15.1**	**10.7**	**10.7**	**13.1**	**18.0**	**32.4**
School lunches	**100.0**	**9.9**	**11.9**	**20.0**	**13.9**	**23.6**	**20.7**
Meals as pay	**100.0**	**26.2**	**22.1**	**15.8**	**6.9**	**8.8**	**20.2**
ALCOHOLIC BEVERAGES	**100.0**	**19.6**	**15.8**	**14.9**	**10.6**	**18.9**	**21.1**
At home	**100.0**	**21.8**	**17.1**	**16.4**	**11.3**	**16.2**	**17.9**
Beer and ale	100.0	24.3	20.4	17.1	12.1	14.0	12.7
Whiskey	100.0	22.4	17.8	14.9	8.4	17.2	19.5
Wine	100.0	15.2	9.6	14.4	11.9	21.4	28.7
Other alcoholic beverages	100.0	19.3	10.6	17.4	7.4	19.2	27.5
Away from home	**100.0**	**16.4**	**13.8**	**12.7**	**9.6**	**22.8**	**25.6**
Beer and ale	100.0	18.8	14.8	16.3	9.1	23.0	19.4
Wine	100.0	14.6	13.6	11.8	8.3	26.6	26.6
Other alcoholic beverages	100.0	14.9	15.9	11.7	7.4	25.1	26.5
Alcoholic beverages purchased on trips	100.0	15.7	10.7	9.3	13.2	18.5	32.6

Note: Numbers may not add to total due to rounding. (-) means insufficient data.

Spending by
Consumer Unit Type

Food spending is directly related to household size—the more people in the household, the more food the household buys. Consequently, married couples with children spend the most on food because they have the largest households. But after adjusting for household size, spending on food shows some surprising patterns.

Single-person households spend the most, per capita, on food overall—40 percent more than average. On a per capita basis, married couples without children at home rank second, spending 32 percent more than average. On food at home, people who live alone spend 28 percent more than average, while couples without children spend 24 percent above average. On food away from home, singles spend 59 percent above average, while married couples with no children spend 44 percent more. Single-person households spend 129 percent more than average on alcohol, while married couples without children spend 54 percent above average in this category.

On a per capita basis, food spending by families with children falls below average because families benefit from economies of scale. Married couples whose oldest child is under age 6 spend 14 percent less than average on food at home per capita, while those whose oldest child is aged 6 to 17 spend 12 percent less than average. Married couples with children aged 18 or older at home spend 2 percent more than average on food per capita.

Although the largest households spend less on food per capita than smaller households, they control the largest share of spending on most categories of food. Married couples with children account for at least 40 percent of household spending on cereals and cereal products; cookies; pies, tarts, and turnovers; sirloin steak; frankfurters; poultry; milk; apples; frozen fruit juices; peanut butter; potato chips and other snacks; prepared desserts; baby food; cola; lunch away from home; and snacks and non-alcoholic beverages consumed away from home.

Married couples without children at home control the largest share of the market for frozen fruits; artificial sweeteners; nonalcoholic beer; catered affairs; food on out-of-town trips; whiskey consumed at home; and wine and other alcoholic beverages consumed away from home, including on trips.

Chapter 4

Single-person households control the largest share of spending in only one food category: beer and ale consumed away from home.

Not surprisingly, considering their low incomes, single-parent households spend much less than average on food. On a per capita basis, they spend 17 percent less on food at home, half as much on food away from home, and 72 percent less on alcoholic beverages. The only categories in which single parents spend significantly more than average are "other" roasts and beef; pork chops; lamb and organ meats; frozen vegetable juices; baby food; and school lunches. Single parents control just 6 percent of household spending on food.

Consumer Unit Type
average spending

(average annual spending of consumer units on food and alcoholic beverages, by type of consumer unit, 1994)

	total married couples	married couples, no children	married couples with children total	oldest child under 6	oldest child 6 to 17	oldest child 18 or older	single parent at least one child < 18	single person
Number of consumer units								
(in thousands, add 000's)	53,578	22,017	27,572	5,529	14,965	7,079	7,065	29,097
Average number of persons per cu	3.2	2.0	4.0	3.5	4.2	3.8	2.9	1.0
Average before-tax income of cu	$48,919.00	$45,100.00	$52,005.00	$45,202.00	$51,947.00	$58,006.00	$19,069.00	$21,347.00
Average spending of cu, total	40,730.97	36,198.09	44,087.86	38,559.51	44,145.34	48,489.12	21,671.03	19,345.48
Food, average spending	5,614.31	4,649.93	6,276.43	4,879.51	6,557.92	6,921.14	3,598.78	2,464.41
Alcoholic beverages, average spending	306.67	342.56	288.36	267.30	263.64	353.70	89.11	255.20
FOOD AT HOME	**$3,432.32**	**$2,689.19**	**$3,894.71**	**$3,282.50**	**$4,014.53**	**$4,205.29**	**$2,625.90**	**$1,385.55**
Cereals and bakery products	**550.14**	**422.15**	**636.28**	**533.77**	**665.08**	**671.92**	**408.62**	**219.59**
Cereals and cereal products	204.77	145.44	243.45	219.21	255.65	241.69	179.83	77.38
Flour	9.53	6.84	10.76	13.52	8.52	12.54	6.87	3.15
Prepared flour mixes	16.32	12.59	19.12	16.84	19.83	19.80	16.06	6.61
Ready-to-eat and cooked cereals	125.68	90.71	150.61	126.53	164.11	146.30	105.84	47.05
Rice	18.89	11.17	22.20	21.79	23.27	20.54	19.65	7.24
Pasta, cornmeal, other cereal products	34.34	24.14	40.75	40.53	39.92	42.52	31.41	13.34
Bakery products	345.38	276.71	392.84	314.56	409.42	430.23	228.80	142.21
Bread	94.53	81.69	102.55	82.49	103.25	118.83	66.14	42.27
White bread	45.88	34.79	52.62	43.17	53.39	59.48	42.14	19.79
Bread, other than white	48.65	46.90	49.93	39.32	49.86	59.35	24.00	22.47
Crackers and cookies	82.71	66.89	94.51	77.09	97.66	103.84	54.47	32.43
Cookies	57.17	44.09	66.69	54.82	67.30	75.96	37.93	21.06
Crackers	25.54	22.80	27.82	22.28	30.36	27.89	16.54	11.37
Frozen and refrigerated bakery products	28.23	22.26	32.57	28.42	35.39	30.92	21.23	11.07
Other bakery products	139.91	105.87	163.20	126.56	173.12	176.64	86.96	56.44
Biscuits and rolls	48.59	38.49	57.09	42.90	59.55	64.88	28.23	17.54
Cakes and cupcakes	40.82	30.82	45.38	32.67	48.65	50.37	29.05	16.31
Bread and cracker products	6.22	4.59	7.50	7.14	6.92	8.92	3.75	2.00
Sweetrolls, coffee cakes, doughnuts	27.78	21.44	31.72	21.04	35.83	33.37	16.57	12.31
Pies, tarts, turnovers	16.50	10.53	21.51	22.81	22.17	19.11	9.35	8.28
Meats, poultry, fish, and eggs	**908.64**	**700.02**	**1,026.03**	**807.98**	**1,071.72**	**1,131.18**	**802.47**	**348.36**
Beef	284.18	213.97	320.60	255.11	332.40	355.79	267.16	98.51
Ground beef	110.30	75.91	129.92	113.60	142.33	120.84	111.88	39.31
Roast	50.62	37.85	55.77	39.89	53.06	74.82	45.67	14.84
Chuck roast	15.52	12.56	16.01	10.33	17.39	18.39	10.50	5.24
Round roast	19.62	13.78	21.87	18.41	19.12	30.10	16.84	5.86
Other roast	15.48	11.51	17.89	11.14	16.55	26.33	18.33	3.74
Steak	105.77	88.95	114.89	90.69	114.58	136.71	91.33	37.68
Round steak	20.10	14.70	22.53	14.79	23.54	27.41	19.68	4.54
Sirloin steak	32.88	26.97	36.94	29.84	36.04	44.87	18.59	11.18
Other steak	52.80	47.28	55.42	46.06	54.99	64.43	53.06	21.96
Other beef	17.49	11.26	20.01	10.93	22.43	23.42	18.28	6.68
Pork	187.63	159.35	201.91	156.67	218.57	210.17	184.83	74.43
Bacon	26.21	24.81	26.12	23.81	26.01	28.36	25.08	14.29
Pork chops	46.90	36.35	53.38	45.71	56.82	53.64	57.05	17.66

	total married couples	married couples, no children	married couples with children				single parent at least one child < 18	single person
			total	oldest child under 6	oldest child 6 to 17	oldest child 18 or older		
Ham	$47.37	$44.03	$48.02	$30.93	$55.12	$49.61	$39.52	$15.30
Ham, not canned	44.90	42.48	44.90	30.04	51.85	44.81	38.15	14.44
Canned ham	2.48	1.55	3.12	0.89	3.27	4.80	1.37	0.87
Sausage	26.62	20.47	30.86	21.77	33.10	34.61	21.28	12.22
Other pork	40.53	33.69	43.53	34.45	47.53	43.95	41.90	14.95
Other meats	120.44	93.03	139.47	100.54	151.24	151.42	91.45	42.47
Frankfurters	22.97	15.07	28.58	26.64	29.92	27.75	22.11	8.19
Lunch meats (cold cuts)	85.43	69.63	96.51	65.72	102.60	112.04	55.33	30.94
Bologna, liverwurst, salami	28.92	22.05	32.70	25.29	34.51	35.78	23.04	12.08
Other lunchmeats	56.51	47.58	63.81	40.43	68.08	76.26	32.28	18.86
Lamb, organ meats and others	12.03	8.33	14.38	8.17	18.72	11.63	14.01	3.33
Lamb and organ meats	11.70	8.33	13.97	8.17	17.90	11.63	14.01	3.33
Mutton, goat and game	0.32	-	0.41	-	0.82	-	-	-
Poultry	168.78	116.64	202.63	168.13	199.35	239.08	145.14	71.92
Fresh and frozen chickens	133.39	88.89	163.62	142.47	160.60	187.85	115.15	54.09
Fresh and frozen whole chicken	38.30	25.47	46.36	39.50	45.19	54.57	30.59	13.16
Fresh and frozen chicken parts	95.09	63.42	117.26	102.97	115.42	133.28	84.56	40.92
Other poultry	35.39	27.75	39.01	25.66	38.75	51.23	29.99	17.83
Fish and seafood	111.56	88.27	122.70	95.12	130.70	131.80	82.96	44.41
Canned fish and seafood	18.24	15.28	20.00	15.77	19.34	24.96	13.92	9.55
Fresh fish and shellfish	66.05	49.19	72.44	57.13	80.57	70.53	41.75	24.00
Frozen fish and shellfish	27.27	23.79	30.25	22.22	30.78	36.31	27.29	10.86
Eggs	36.05	28.76	38.73	32.40	39.46	42.91	30.92	16.62
Dairy products	**367.07**	**280.02**	**423.15**	**346.27**	**445.67**	**448.12**	**268.17**	**150.96**
Fresh milk and cream	159.77	109.94	189.69	162.41	198.58	196.87	123.24	65.57
Fresh milk, all types	149.36	101.12	178.62	155.31	186.17	184.81	116.41	62.25
Cream	10.40	8.82	11.08	7.10	12.40	12.06	6.83	3.32
Other dairy products	207.30	170.08	233.46	183.86	247.09	251.25	144.93	85.40
Butter	14.45	11.57	15.26	14.32	14.37	17.77	11.23	5.52
Cheese	104.42	82.30	121.51	93.24	130.58	129.22	73.48	44.78
Ice cream and related products	62.79	53.80	68.54	53.44	71.22	76.75	38.49	22.33
Miscellaneous dairy products	25.65	22.40	28.14	22.86	30.92	27.51	21.73	12.77
Fruits and vegetables	**548.32**	**457.76**	**603.48**	**510.57**	**615.94**	**661.52**	**374.16**	**251.75**
Fresh fruits	170.20	143.05	187.63	151.56	192.99	209.14	113.97	77.66
Apples	33.39	24.63	38.76	31.99	41.58	39.40	26.20	13.01
Bananas	37.20	33.93	38.33	34.51	38.37	41.62	24.20	18.61
Oranges	20.58	16.93	22.78	16.33	27.12	20.24	17.39	8.63
Citrus fruits, excl. oranges	13.30	11.69	14.06	12.15	13.23	17.29	8.08	7.03
Other fresh fruits	65.73	55.87	73.70	56.58	72.70	90.60	38.10	30.37
Fresh vegetables	167.75	136.64	186.36	146.48	186.46	221.16	111.45	76.36
Potatoes	34.12	27.96	37.31	31.88	36.34	43.89	26.64	14.33
Lettuce	21.71	16.80	25.19	17.82	25.92	30.27	15.99	10.61
Tomatoes	26.15	19.22	29.54	24.21	29.63	34.06	19.20	11.53
Other fresh vegetables	85.77	72.67	94.32	72.58	94.57	112.93	49.60	39.88

	total married couples	married couples, no children	married couples with children			single parent at least one child < 18	single person
			total	oldest child under 6	oldest child 6 to 17	oldest child 18 or older		
Processed fruits	$115.55	$94.14	$128.93	$122.97	$129.69	$132.74	$80.24	$56.83
Frozen fruits and fruit juices	20.87	17.47	23.12	20.76	23.52	24.43	14.47	9.01
Frozen orange juice	11.83	10.70	12.64	10.82	13.27	13.03	9.11	6.45
Frozen fruits	1.99	2.53	1.72	1.52	1.71	1.93	0.77	0.74
Frozen fruit juices	7.04	4.25	8.76	8.42	8.54	9.47	4.60	1.82
Canned fruit	17.92	19.40	17.16	14.23	16.81	20.37	9.56	9.16
Dried fruit	7.25	6.99	7.11	5.08	6.65	9.74	5.19	3.86
Fresh fruit juices	20.69	14.86	23.86	21.11	23.21	27.50	17.68	13.25
Canned and bottled fruit juices	48.82	35.42	57.69	61.80	59.48	50.70	33.34	21.55
Processed vegetables	94.82	83.94	100.56	89.55	106.79	98.48	68.49	40.91
Frozen vegetables	32.47	26.00	36.49	29.86	41.36	33.12	22.03	11.92
Canned and dried vegetables and juices	62.36	57.94	64.07	59.69	65.43	65.36	46.47	28.99
Canned beans	12.46	10.83	13.52	12.97	13.34	14.33	10.03	6.77
Canned corn	7.76	4.96	9.38	8.34	10.33	8.48	8.93	4.33
Other canned and dried vegetables	33.87	33.46	33.64	30.65	33.85	35.88	23.63	14.05
Frozen vegetable juices	0.27	0.23	0.30	0.32	0.28	0.33	0.44	0.09
Fresh and canned vegetable juices	8.00	8.45	7.23	7.42	7.63	6.33	3.44	3.75
Other food at home	**1,058.14**	**829.23**	**1,205.77**	**1,083.92**	**1,216.13**	**1,292.55**	**772.49**	**414.88**
Sugar and other sweets	134.40	107.15	149.56	130.49	163.07	140.81	97.72	51.84
Candy and chewing gum	81.98	64.87	91.49	85.02	101.57	78.16	47.51	31.69
Sugar	21.97	15.75	25.34	19.04	27.51	26.78	22.99	7.79
Artificial sweeteners	4.10	5.08	3.35	0.82	3.97	4.42	4.57	1.94
Jams, preserves, other sweets	26.35	21.44	29.37	25.61	30.02	31.45	22.65	10.43
Fats and oils	99.01	80.07	109.37	82.88	111.11	129.35	71.12	41.09
Margarine	16.45	14.50	17.67	13.91	17.84	20.65	11.25	10.17
Fats and oils	28.80	20.74	32.50	24.21	31.33	41.97	21.42	10.08
Salad dressings	31.21	26.12	33.86	23.40	34.39	42.04	23.47	10.76
Nondairy cream and imitation milk	8.11	8.58	7.90	7.42	8.03	8.07	5.45	3.90
Peanut butter	14.44	10.13	17.44	13.94	19.52	16.61	9.52	6.19
Miscellaneous foods	468.15	345.37	551.00	558.90	552.31	541.59	371.66	171.46
Frozen prepared foods	81.39	66.00	93.39	69.34	94.46	112.49	66.07	37.64
Frozen meals	22.09	20.89	23.56	16.65	19.82	36.68	24.35	18.11
Other frozen prepared foods	59.30	45.10	69.83	52.68	74.64	75.81	41.73	19.53
Canned and packaged soups	37.23	33.69	39.31	36.73	41.38	37.67	29.51	16.03
Potato chips, nuts, and other snacks	99.94	76.67	119.06	88.24	134.77	116.50	62.79	33.33
Potato chips and other snacks	78.52	53.90	98.10	69.12	113.82	93.90	53.97	25.14
Nuts	21.42	22.77	20.96	19.12	20.95	22.60	8.82	8.19
Condiments and seasonings	102.15	80.98	114.78	92.38	121.56	121.63	78.05	37.91
Salt, spices and other seasonings	24.32	21.04	25.53	20.95	24.73	31.06	17.16	9.04
Olives, pickles, relishes	13.23	12.40	13.49	9.87	14.91	13.98	11.38	4.55
Sauces and gravies	46.36	32.46	55.57	46.67	59.84	55.34	39.14	16.96
Baking needs and misc. products	18.24	15.08	20.19	14.89	22.08	21.25	10.37	7.37
Other canned/packaged prepared foods	147.44	88.03	184.46	272.22	160.15	153.30	135.24	46.53
Prepared salads	13.91	14.87	13.26	9.69	14.53	14.03	8.87	6.85
Prepared desserts	10.67	8.73	12.24	8.95	12.38	14.86	7.20	4.00

	total married couples	married couples, no children	married couples with children				single parent at least one child < 18	single person
			total	oldest child under 6	oldest child 6 to 17	oldest child 18 or older		
Baby food	$40.25	$8.17	$59.16	$165.22	$31.22	$18.80	$52.58	$4.38
Miscellaneous prepared foods	82.61	56.26	99.79	88.36	102.02	105.62	66.59	31.31
Nonalcoholic beverages	292.05	227.34	334.21	265.14	331.82	399.30	209.14	124.78
Cola	114.79	87.00	134.38	95.98	135.75	165.47	82.14	41.08
Other carbonated drinks	49.51	36.51	57.93	46.97	59.74	64.12	40.47	17.75
Coffee	51.10	53.36	48.43	41.37	46.36	58.54	27.47	29.93
Roasted coffee	34.88	36.13	34.44	31.72	31.08	43.17	19.15	19.10
Instant and freeze-dried coffee	16.23	17.23	13.99	9.64	15.28	15.37	8.31	10.83
Noncarb. fruit flavored drinks incl. non-frozen lemonade	27.06	13.47	35.51	22.65	41.90	34.76	28.54	10.39
Tea	21.66	18.08	23.44	20.58	21.77	29.11	13.33	8.62
Nonalcoholic beer	0.91	1.44	0.39	0.36	0.51	0.20	-	0.61
Other nonalcoholic beverages	27.01	17.49	34.12	37.23	25.80	47.10	17.18	16.40
Food prepared by cu on out-of-town trips	64.53	69.30	61.63	46.51	57.83	81.49	22.85	25.71
FOOD AWAY FROM HOME	**2,182.00**	**1,960.74**	**2,381.72**	**1,597.01**	**2,543.39**	**2,715.85**	**972.88**	**1,078.86**
Meals at restaurants, carry-outs, other	**1,630.77**	**1,435.57**	**1,811.05**	**1,370.83**	**1,901.57**	**2,026.59**	**767.51**	**867.57**
Lunch	559.76	432.75	670.82	463.93	748.60	705.65	324.82	294.36
Dinner	816.84	780.66	862.56	671.38	859.17	1,036.67	324.96	439.43
Snacks and nonalcoholic beverages	126.93	87.98	155.70	139.79	165.26	151.64	72.58	63.40
Breakfast and brunch	127.24	134.18	121.98	95.73	128.54	132.63	45.16	70.38
Board (including at school)	**72.65**	**52.23**	**87.99**	**6.72**	**61.41**	**207.65**	**26.99**	**31.46**
Catered affairs	**86.22**	**106.63**	**58.64**	**8.49**	**66.57**	**81.05**	**4.44**	**28.00**
Food on out-of-town trips	**287.14**	**344.12**	**253.98**	**169.50**	**264.77**	**297.15**	**68.12**	**127.53**
School lunches	**85.20**	**0.23**	**151.20**	**6.07**	**235.51**	**86.33**	**84.05**	**0.10**
Meals as pay	**20.01**	**21.97**	**18.85**	**35.40**	**13.57**	**17.08**	**21.76**	**24.20**
ALCOHOLIC BEVERAGES	**306.67**	**342.56**	**288.36**	**267.30**	**263.64**	**353.70**	**89.11**	**255.20**
At home	**183.24**	**185.84**	**185.72**	**173.64**	**174.29**	**217.86**	**62.94**	**144.31**
Beer and ale	104.74	97.97	109.74	127.00	106.08	101.50	39.09	97.75
Whiskey	15.73	20.22	13.81	4.44	10.47	28.33	2.45	9.29
Wine	44.56	49.97	42.08	31.64	43.92	47.77	16.54	26.83
Other alcoholic beverages	18.21	17.69	20.09	10.56	13.82	40.27	4.86	10.45
Away from home	**123.43**	**156.72**	**102.65**	**93.67**	**89.35**	**135.84**	**26.17**	**110.88**
Beer and ale	39.22	46.97	35.02	29.64	31.23	46.86	7.76	41.81
Wine	17.66	22.82	14.37	13.46	12.17	19.32	4.05	13.62
Other alcoholic beverages	31.07	40.58	24.97	24.69	19.73	35.09	7.52	25.48
Alcoholic beverages purchased on trips	35.48	46.34	28.29	25.88	26.22	34.57	6.85	29.97

Note: Average spending figures for total consumer units can be found in other average spending tables. Expenditures listed for items in a given category may not add to the total for that category because the listing is incomplete. (-) means insufficient data.

Consumer Unit Type
indexed spending

(indexed average annual spending of consumer units on food and alcoholic beverages, by type of consumer unit, 1994; index definition: an index of 100 is the average for all consumer units; an index of 132 means that spending by consumer unit type is 32 percent above the average for all consumer units; an index of 68 indicates that spending by the consumer unit type is 32 percent below the average for all consumer units)

	total married couples	married couples, no children	married couples with children			single parent at least one child < 18	single person
			total	oldest child under 6	oldest child 6 to 17	oldest child 18 or older	
Average spending of cu, total	$40,730.97	$36,198.09	$44,087.86	$38,559.51	$44,145.34	$48,489.12	$21,671.03	$19,345.48
Average spending of cu, index	128	114	139	121	139	153	68	61
Food, spending index	127	105	142	111	149	157	82	56
Alcoholic beverages, spending index	110	123	104	96	95	127	32	92
FOOD AT HOME	**127**	**99**	**144**	**121**	**148**	**155**	**97**	**51**
Cereals and bakery products	**128**	**98**	**148**	**125**	**155**	**157**	**95**	**51**
Cereals and cereal products	127	90	151	136	158	149	111	48
Flour	125	90	142	178	112	165	90	41
Prepared flour mixes	128	98	149	132	155	155	126	52
Ready-to-eat and cooked cereals	128	92	153	129	167	149	108	48
Rice	122	72	144	141	151	133	127	47
Pasta, cornmeal, and other cereal products	124	87	147	147	144	154	114	48
Bakery products	129	104	147	118	153	161	86	53
Bread	124	107	135	108	135	156	87	55
White bread	122	92	140	115	142	158	112	53
Bread, other than white	126	122	129	102	129	154	62	58
Crackers and cookies	132	107	151	123	156	166	87	52
Cookies	133	103	155	128	157	177	88	49
Crackers	130	116	142	114	155	142	84	58
Frozen and refrigerated bakery products	131	103	151	132	164	143	98	51
Other bakery products	131	99	153	119	162	166	82	53
Biscuits and rolls	135	107	159	119	166	180	79	49
Cakes and cupcakes	131	99	145	105	156	161	93	52
Bread and cracker products	132	97	159	151	147	189	79	42
Sweetrolls, coffee cakes, doughnuts	127	98	145	96	163	152	76	56
Pies, tarts, turnovers	129	82	168	178	173	149	73	65
Meats, poultry, fish, and eggs	**124**	**96**	**140**	**110**	**146**	**154**	**110**	**48**
Beef	125	94	141	113	147	157	118	43
Ground beef	125	86	147	128	161	137	126	44
Roast	128	96	142	101	135	190	116	38
Chuck roast	127	102	131	84	142	150	86	43
Round roast	132	93	147	124	129	203	113	39
Other roast	126	94	145	90	134	214	149	30
Steak	125	105	136	107	135	161	108	44
Round steak	126	92	141	92	147	171	123	28
Sirloin steak	135	110	151	122	147	184	76	46
Other steak	119	107	125	104	124	145	120	50
Other beef	124	80	141	77	159	166	129	47
Pork	120	102	130	101	140	135	119	48
Bacon	115	109	115	105	114	124	110	63
Pork chops	119	92	136	116	145	136	145	45

	total married couples	married couples, no children	married couples with children				single parent at least one child < 18	single person
			total	oldest child under 6	oldest child 6 to 17	oldest child 18 or older		
Ham	128	119	130	84	149	135	107	41
Ham, not canned	131	124	131	88	152	131	112	42
Canned ham	91	57	115	33	120	176	50	32
Sausage	117	90	135	95	145	152	93	54
Other pork	119	99	128	102	140	130	123	44
Other meats	128	99	148	107	161	161	97	45
Frankfurters	122	80	152	142	159	148	118	44
Lunch meats (cold cuts)	130	106	147	100	156	171	84	47
Bologna, liverwurst, salami	122	93	138	107	145	151	97	51
Other lunchmeats	135	113	152	96	162	182	77	45
Lamb, organ meats and others	126	87	151	86	196	122	147	35
Lamb and organ meats	125	89	149	87	191	124	150	36
Mutton, goat and game	178	-	228	-	456	-	-	-
Poultry	124	85	148	123	146	175	106	53
Fresh and frozen chickens	124	82	152	132	149	174	107	50
Fresh and frozen whole chicken	130	86	157	134	153	185	103	45
Fresh and frozen chicken parts	121	81	150	131	147	170	108	52
Other poultry	123	97	136	89	135	179	105	62
Fish and seafood	125	99	137	106	146	147	93	50
Canned fish and seafood	121	102	133	105	129	166	93	64
Fresh fish and shellfish	129	96	141	111	157	138	81	47
Frozen fish and shellfish	118	103	131	96	133	157	118	47
Eggs	120	96	129	108	132	143	103	55
Dairy products	**127**	**97**	**146**	**120**	**154**	**155**	**93**	**52**
Fresh milk and cream	126	86	149	128	156	155	97	52
Fresh milk, all types	126	85	150	131	157	155	98	52
Cream	127	108	135	87	151	147	83	41
Other dairy products	128	105	144	114	153	155	90	53
Butter	124	99	131	123	123	153	96	47
Cheese	128	101	148	114	160	158	90	55
Ice cream and related products	132	113	144	112	149	161	81	47
Miscellaneous dairy products	124	108	136	111	150	133	105	62
Fruits and vegetables	**126**	**105**	**138**	**117**	**141**	**152**	**86**	**58**
Fresh fruits	128	108	141	114	145	157	86	58
Apples	132	97	153	126	164	155	103	51
Bananas	125	114	129	116	129	140	82	63
Oranges	126	103	139	100	166	124	106	53
Citrus fruits, excl. oranges	121	107	128	111	121	158	74	64
Other fresh fruits	130	110	145	112	143	179	75	60
Fresh vegetables	124	101	138	109	138	164	83	57
Potatoes	122	100	133	114	130	157	95	51
Lettuce	125	97	145	106	149	174	92	61
Tomatoes	124	91	141	115	141	162	91	55
Other fresh vegetables	125	106	138	104	138	165	72	58

	total married couples	married couples, no children	married couples with children				single parent at least one child < 18	single person
			total	oldest child under 6	oldest child 6 to 17	oldest child 18 or older		
Processed fruits	124	101	139	132	139	143	86	61
Frozen fruits and fruit juices	128	107	142	128	144	150	89	55
Frozen orange juice	125	113	133	114	140	137	96	68
Frozen fruits	124	158	108	95	107	121	48	46
Frozen fruit juices	136	82	169	162	165	182	89	35
Canned fruit	126	136	121	100	118	143	67	64
Dried fruit	123	119	121	86	113	165	88	66
Fresh fruit juices	116	83	133	118	130	154	99	74
Canned and bottled fruit juices	126	91	149	159	153	131	86	56
Processed vegetables	125	111	133	118	141	130	91	54
Frozen vegetables	131	105	147	120	167	133	89	48
Canned and dried vegetables and juices	123	114	126	118	129		92	57
Canned beans	119	104	130	124	128	137	96	65
Canned corn	114	73	138	122	152	125	131	64
Other canned and dried vegetables	125	124	124	113	125	133	87	52
Frozen vegetable juices	117	100	130	139	122	143	191	39
Fresh and canned vegetable juices	129	136	116	119	123	102	55	60
Other food at home	**128**	**100**	**146**	**131**	**147**	**157**	**94**	**50**
Sugar and other sweets	128	102	142	124	155	134	93	49
Candy and chewing gum	132	104	147	136	163	125	76	51
Sugar	120	86	138	104	150	146	126	43
Artificial sweeteners	121	150	99	24	117	130	135	57
Jams, preserves, other sweets	124	101	138	121	141	148	107	49
Fats and oils	125	101	138	105	140	163	90	52
Margarine	116	102	125	98	126	146	79	72
Fats and oils	125	90	141	105	136	182	93	44
Salad dressings	131	110	143	99	145	177	99	45
Nondairy cream and imitation milk	124	131	120	113	122	123	83	59
Peanut butter	123	87	149	119	167	142	81	53
Miscellaneous foods	129	96	152	155	153	150	103	47
Frozen prepared foods	123	100	141	105	143	170	100	57
Frozen meals	103	97	110	78	92	171	114	85
Other frozen prepared foods	133	101	156	118	167	170	93	44
Canned and packaged soups	126	114	133	124	140	127	100	54
Potato chips, nuts, and other snacks	135	104	161	119	182	157	85	45
Potato chips and other snacks	135	93	169	119	196	161	93	43
Nuts	135	143	132	120	132	142	56	52
Condiments and seasonings	128	102	144	116	152	153	98	48
Salt, spices and other seasonings	126	109	132	109	128	161	89	47
Olives, pickles, relishes	130	122	133	97	147	138	112	45
Sauces and gravies	127	89	153	128	164	152	107	47
Baking needs and misc. products	132	109	146	108	159	153	75	53
Other canned/packaged prepared foods	132	79	165	243	143	137	121	42
Prepared salads	127	136	121	88	132	128	81	62
Prepared desserts	134	109	153	112	155	186	90	50

	total married couples	married couples, no children	married couples with children				single parent at least one child < 18	single person
			total	oldest child under 6	oldest child 6 to 17	oldest child 18 or older		
Baby food	143	29	210	588	111	67	187	16
Miscellaneous prepared foods	127	86	153	136	157	162	102	48
Nonalcoholic beverages	125	98	144	114	142	171	90	54
Cola	128	97	150	107	152	185	92	46
Other carbonated drinks	127	94	149	121	154	165	104	46
Coffee	119	124	113	96	108	136	64	70
Roasted coffee	120	124	118	109	107	148	66	66
Instant and freeze-dried coffee	117	124	101	69	110	111	60	78
Noncarb. fruit flavored drinks incl. non-frozen lemonade	124	62	162	104	192	159	131	48
Tea	133	111	144	127	134	179	82	53
Nonalcoholic beer	138	218	59	55	77	30	-	92
Other nonalcoholic beverages	119	77	150	164	113	207	75	72
Food prepared by cu on out-of-town trips	139	149	133	100	125	176	49	55
FOOD AWAY FROM HOME	**128**	**115**	**140**	**94**	**150**	**160**	**57**	**64**
Meals at restaurants, carry-outs, other	**125**	**110**	**139**	**105**	**146**	**155**	**59**	**66**
Lunch	124	96	148	103	166	156	72	65
Dinner	125	120	132	103	132	159	50	67
Snacks and nonalcoholic beverages	125	86	153	137	162	149	71	62
Breakfast and brunch	126	133	121	95	127	131	45	70
Board (including at school)	**143**	**103**	**173**	**13**	**121**	**409**	**53**	**62**
Catered affairs	**154**	**190**	**105**	**15**	**119**	**144**	**8**	**50**
Food on out-of-town trips	**138**	**166**	**122**	**82**	**127**	**143**	**33**	**61**
School lunches	**158**	**0**	**281**	**11**	**438**	**161**	**156**	**0**
Meals as pay	**84**	**92**	**79**	**149**	**57**	**72**	**91**	**102**
ALCOHOLIC BEVERAGES	**110**	**123**	**104**	**96**	**95**	**127**	**32**	**92**
At home	**111**	**113**	**112**	**105**	**106**	**132**	**38**	**87**
Beer and ale	105	98	110	127	106	102	39	98
Whiskey	115	148	101	32	77	207	18	68
Wine	122	137	116	87	121	131	45	74
Other alcoholic beverages	119	115	131	69	90	262	32	68
Away from home	**109**	**139**	**91**	**83**	**79**	**120**	**23**	**98**
Beer and ale	102	122	91	77	81	122	20	108
Wine	112	145	91	85	77	122	26	86
Other alcoholic beverages	111	145	89	88	71	126	27	91
Alcoholic beverages purchased on trips	116	151	92	85	86	113	22	98

Note: Spending index for total consumer units is 100. (-) means insufficient data.

Consumer Unit Type
average per capita spending

(average annual per capita spending of consumer units on food and alcoholic beverages, by type of consumer unit, 1994; per capita figures are calculated by dividing the average spending of consumer units by the average number of persons per consumer unit)

	total married couples	married couples, no children	married couples with children				single parent at least one child < 18	single person
			total	oldest child under 6	oldest child 6 to 17	oldest child 18 or older		
Average number of persons per cu	3.2	2.0	4.0	3.5	4.2	3.8	2.9	1.0
Per capita before-tax income of cu	$15,287.19	$22,550.00	$13,001.25	$12,914.86	$12,368.33	$15,264.74	$6,575.52	$21,347.00
Per capita spending of cu, total	12,728.43	18,099.05	11,021.97	11,017.00	10,510.80	12,760.29	7,472.77	19,345.48
Food, per capita spending	1,754.47	2,324.97	1,569.11	1,394.15	1,561.41	1,821.35	1,240.96	2,464.41
Alcoholic beverages, per capita spending	95.83	171.28	72.09	76.37	62.77	93.08	30.73	255.20
FOOD AT HOME	**$1,072.60**	**$1,344.60**	**$973.68**	**$937.86**	**$955.84**	**$1,106.66**	**$905.48**	**$1,385.55**
Cereals and bakery products	**171.92**	**211.08**	**159.07**	**152.51**	**158.35**	**176.82**	**140.90**	**219.59**
Cereals and cereal products	63.99	72.72	60.86	62.63	60.87	63.60	62.01	77.38
Flour	2.98	3.42	2.69	3.86	2.03	3.30	2.37	3.15
Prepared flour mixes	5.10	6.30	4.78	4.81	4.72	5.21	5.54	6.61
Ready-to-eat and cooked cereals	39.28	45.36	37.65	36.15	39.07	38.50	36.50	47.05
Rice	5.90	5.59	5.55	6.23	5.54	5.41	6.78	7.24
Pasta, cornmeal, and other cereal products	10.73	12.07	10.19	11.58	9.50	11.19	10.83	13.34
Bakery products	107.93	138.36	98.21	89.87	97.48	113.22	78.90	142.21
Bread	29.54	40.85	25.64	23.57	24.58	31.27	22.81	42.27
White bread	14.34	17.40	13.16	12.33	12.71	15.65	14.53	19.79
Bread, other than white	15.20	23.45	12.48	11.23	11.87	15.62	8.28	22.47
Crackers and cookies	25.85	33.45	23.63	22.03	23.25	27.33	18.78	32.43
Cookies	17.87	22.05	16.67	15.66	16.02	19.99	13.08	21.06
Crackers	7.98	11.40	6.96	6.37	7.23	7.34	5.70	11.37
Frozen and refrigerated bakery products	8.82	11.13	8.14	8.12	8.43	8.14	7.32	11.07
Other bakery products	43.72	52.94	40.80	36.16	41.22	46.48	29.99	56.44
Biscuits and rolls	15.18	19.25	14.27	12.26	14.18	17.07	9.73	17.54
Cakes and cupcakes	12.76	15.41	11.35	9.33	11.58	13.26	10.02	16.31
Bread and cracker products	1.94	2.30	1.88	2.04	1.65	2.35	1.29	2.00
Sweetrolls, coffee cakes, doughnuts	8.68	10.72	7.93	6.01	8.53	8.78	5.71	12.31
Pies, tarts, turnovers	5.16	5.27	5.38	6.52	5.28	5.03	3.22	8.28
Meats, poultry, fish, and eggs	**283.95**	**350.01**	**256.51**	**230.85**	**255.17**	**297.68**	**276.71**	**348.36**
Beef	88.81	106.99	80.15	72.89	79.14	93.63	92.12	98.51
Ground beef	34.47	37.96	32.48	32.46	33.89	31.80	38.58	39.31
Roast	15.82	18.93	13.94	11.40	12.63	19.69	15.75	14.84
Chuck roast	4.85	6.28	4.00	2.95	4.14	4.84	3.62	5.24
Round roast	6.13	6.89	5.47	5.26	4.55	7.92	5.81	5.86
Other roast	4.84	5.76	4.47	3.18	3.94	6.93	6.32	3.74
Steak	33.05	44.48	28.72	25.91	27.28	35.98	31.49	37.68
Round steak	6.28	7.35	5.63	4.23	5.60	7.21	6.79	4.54
Sirloin steak	10.28	13.49	9.24	8.53	8.58	11.81	6.41	11.18
Other steak	16.50	23.64	13.86	13.16	13.09	16.96	18.30	21.96
Other beef	5.47	5.63	5.00	3.12	5.34	6.16	6.30	6.68
Pork	58.63	79.68	50.48	44.76	52.04	55.31	63.73	74.43
Bacon	8.19	12.41	6.53	6.80	6.19	7.46	8.65	14.29
Pork chops	14.66	18.18	13.35	13.06	13.53	14.12	19.67	17.66

	total married couples	married couples, no children	married couples with children				single parent at least one child < 18	single person
			total	oldest child under 6	oldest child 6 to 17	oldest child 18 or older		
Ham	$14.80	$22.02	$12.01	$8.84	$13.12	$13.06	$13.63	$15.30
Ham, not canned	14.03	21.24	11.23	8.58	12.35	11.79	13.16	14.44
Canned ham	0.78	0.78	0.78	0.25	0.78	1.26	0.47	0.87
Sausage	8.32	10.24	7.72	6.22	7.88	9.11	7.34	12.22
Other pork	12.67	16.85	10.88	9.84	11.32	11.57	14.45	14.95
Other meats	37.64	46.52	34.87	28.73	36.01	39.85	31.53	42.47
Frankfurters	7.18	7.54	7.15	7.61	7.12	7.30	7.62	8.19
Lunch meats (cold cuts)	26.70	34.82	24.13	18.78	24.43	29.48	19.08	30.94
Bologna, liverwurst, salami	9.04	11.03	8.18	7.23	8.22	9.42	7.94	12.08
Other lunchmeats	17.66	23.79	15.95	11.55	16.21	20.07	11.13	18.86
Lamb, organ meats and others	3.76	4.17	3.60	2.33	4.46	3.06	4.83	3.33
Lamb and organ meats	3.66	4.17	3.49	2.33	4.26	3.06	4.83	3.33
Mutton, goat and game	0.10	-	0.10	-	0.20	-	-	-
Poultry	52.74	58.32	50.66	48.04	47.46	62.92	50.05	71.92
Fresh and frozen chickens	41.68	44.45	40.91	40.71	38.24	49.43	39.71	54.09
Fresh and frozen whole chicken	11.97	12.74	11.59	11.29	10.76	14.36	10.55	13.16
Fresh and frozen chicken parts	29.72	31.71	29.32	29.42	27.48	35.07	29.16	40.92
Other poultry	11.06	13.88	9.75	7.33	9.23	13.48	10.34	17.83
Fish and seafood	34.86	44.14	30.68	27.18	31.12	34.68	28.61	44.41
Canned fish and seafood	5.70	7.64	5.00	4.51	4.60	6.57	4.80	9.55
Fresh fish and shellfish	20.64	24.60	18.11	16.32	19.18	18.56	14.40	24.00
Frozen fish and shellfish	8.52	11.90	7.56	6.35	7.33	9.56	9.41	10.86
Eggs	11.27	14.38	9.68	9.26	9.40	11.29	10.66	16.62
Dairy products	**114.71**	**140.01**	**105.79**	**98.93**	**106.11**	**117.93**	**92.47**	**150.96**
Fresh milk and cream	49.93	54.97	47.42	46.40	47.28	51.81	42.50	65.57
Fresh milk, all types	46.68	50.56	44.66	44.37	44.33	48.63	40.14	62.25
Cream	3.25	4.41	2.77	2.03	2.95	3.17	2.36	3.32
Other dairy products	64.78	85.04	58.37	52.53	58.83	66.12	49.98	85.40
Butter	4.52	5.79	3.82	4.09	3.42	4.68	3.87	5.52
Cheese	32.63	41.15	30.38	26.64	31.09	34.01	25.34	44.78
Ice cream and related products	19.62	26.90	17.14	15.27	16.96	20.20	13.27	22.33
Miscellaneous dairy products	8.02	11.20	7.04	6.53	7.36	7.24	7.49	12.77
Fruits and vegetables	**171.35**	**228.88**	**150.87**	**145.88**	**146.65**	**174.08**	**129.02**	**251.75**
Fresh fruits	53.19	71.53	46.91	43.30	45.95	55.04	39.30	77.66
Apples	10.43	12.32	9.69	9.14	9.90	10.37	9.03	13.01
Bananas	11.63	16.97	9.58	9.86	9.14	10.95	8.34	18.61
Oranges	6.43	8.47	5.70	4.67	6.46	5.33	6.00	8.63
Citrus fruits, excl. oranges	4.16	5.85	3.52	3.47	3.15	4.55	2.79	7.03
Other fresh fruits	20.54	27.94	18.43	16.17	17.31	23.84	13.14	30.37
Fresh vegetables	52.42	68.32	46.59	41.85	44.40	58.20	38.43	76.36
Potatoes	10.66	13.98	9.33	9.11	8.65	11.55	9.19	14.33
Lettuce	6.78	8.40	6.30	5.09	6.17	7.97	5.51	10.61
Tomatoes	8.17	9.61	7.39	6.92	7.05	8.96	6.62	11.53
Other fresh vegetables	26.80	36.34	23.58	20.74	22.52	29.72	17.10	39.88

	total married couples	married couples, no children	married couples with children				single parent at least one child < 18	single person
			total	oldest child under 6	oldest child 6 to 17	oldest child 18 or older		
Processed fruits	$36.11	$47.07	$32.23	$35.13	$30.88	$34.93	$27.67	$56.83
Frozen fruits and fruit juices	6.52	8.74	5.78	5.93	5.60	6.43	4.99	9.01
Frozen orange juice	3.70	5.35	3.16	3.09	3.16	3.43	3.14	6.45
Frozen fruits	0.62	1.27	0.43	0.43	0.41	0.51	0.27	0.74
Frozen fruit juices	2.20	2.13	2.19	2.41	2.03	2.49	1.59	1.82
Canned fruit	5.60	9.70	4.29	4.07	4.00	5.36	3.30	9.16
Dried fruit	2.27	3.50	1.78	1.45	1.58	2.56	1.79	3.86
Fresh fruit juices	6.47	7.43	5.97	6.03	5.53	7.24	6.10	13.25
Canned and bottled fruit juices	15.26	17.71	14.42	17.66	14.16	13.34	11.50	21.55
Processed vegetables	29.63	41.97	25.14	25.59	25.43	25.92	23.62	40.91
Frozen vegetables	10.15	13.00	9.12	8.53	9.85	8.72	7.60	11.92
Canned and dried vegetables and juices	19.49	28.97	16.02	17.05	15.58	17.20	16.02	28.99
Canned beans	3.89	5.42	3.38	3.71	3.18	3.77	3.46	6.77
Canned corn	2.43	2.48	2.35	2.38	2.46	2.23	3.08	4.33
Other canned and dried vegetables	10.58	16.73	8.41	8.76	8.06	9.44	8.15	14.05
Frozen vegetable juices	0.08	0.12	0.08	0.09	0.07	0.09	0.15	0.09
Fresh and canned vegetable juices	2.50	4.23	1.81	2.12	1.82	1.67	1.19	3.75
Other food at home	**330.67**	**414.62**	**301.44**	**309.69**	**289.55**	**340.14**	**266.38**	**414.88**
Sugar and other sweets	42.00	53.58	37.39	37.28	38.83	37.06	33.70	51.84
Candy and chewing gum	25.62	32.44	22.87	24.29	24.18	20.57	16.38	31.69
Sugar	6.87	7.88	6.34	5.44	6.55	7.05	7.93	7.79
Artificial sweeteners	1.28	2.54	0.84	0.23	0.95	1.16	1.58	1.94
Jams, preserves, other sweets	8.23	10.72	7.34	7.32	7.15	8.28	7.81	10.43
Fats and oils	30.94	40.04	27.34	23.68	26.45	34.04	24.52	41.09
Margarine	5.14	7.25	4.42	3.97	4.25	5.43	3.88	10.17
Fats and oils	9.00	10.37	8.13	6.92	7.46	11.04	7.39	10.08
Salad dressings	9.75	13.06	8.47	6.69	8.19	11.06	8.09	10.76
Nondairy cream and imitation milk	2.53	4.29	1.98	2.12	1.91	2.12	1.88	3.90
Peanut butter	4.51	5.07	4.36	3.98	4.65	4.37	3.28	6.19
Miscellaneous foods	146.30	172.69	137.75	159.69	131.50	142.52	128.16	171.46
Frozen prepared foods	25.43	33.00	23.35	19.81	22.49	29.60	22.78	37.64
Frozen meals	6.90	10.45	5.89	4.76	4.72	9.65	8.40	18.11
Other frozen prepared foods	18.53	22.55	17.46	15.05	17.77	19.95	14.39	19.53
Canned and packaged soups	11.63	16.85	9.83	10.49	9.85	9.91	10.18	16.03
Potato chips, nuts, and other snacks	31.23	38.34	29.77	25.21	32.09	30.66	21.65	33.33
Potato chips and other snacks	24.54	26.95	24.53	19.75	27.10	24.71	18.61	25.14
Nuts	6.69	11.39	5.24	5.46	4.99	5.95	3.04	8.19
Condiments and seasonings	31.92	40.49	28.70	26.39	28.94	32.01	26.91	37.91
Salt, spices and other seasonings	7.60	10.52	6.38	5.99	5.89	8.17	5.92	9.04
Olives, pickles, relishes	4.13	6.20	3.37	2.82	3.55	3.68	3.92	4.55
Sauces and gravies	14.49	16.23	13.89	13.33	14.25	14.56	13.50	16.96
Baking needs and misc. products	5.70	7.54	5.05	4.25	5.26	5.59	3.58	7.37
Other canned/packaged prepared foods	46.08	44.02	46.12	77.78	38.13	40.34	46.63	46.53
Prepared salads	4.35	7.44	3.32	2.77	3.46	3.69	3.06	6.85
Prepared desserts	3.33	4.37	3.06	2.56	2.95	3.91	2.48	4.00

	total married couples	married couples, no children	married couples with children				single parent at least one child < 18	single person
			total	oldest child under 6	oldest child 6 to 17	oldest child 18 or older		
Baby food	$12.58	$4.09	$14.79	$47.21	$7.43	$4.95	$18.13	$4.38
Miscellaneous prepared foods	25.82	28.13	24.95	25.25	24.29	27.79	22.96	31.31
Nonalcoholic beverages	91.27	113.67	83.55	75.75	79.00	105.08	72.12	124.78
Cola	35.87	43.50	33.60	27.42	32.32	43.54	28.32	41.08
Other carbonated drinks	15.47	18.26	14.48	13.42	14.22	16.87	13.96	17.75
Coffee	15.97	26.68	12.11	11.82	11.04	15.41	9.47	29.93
Roasted coffee	10.90	18.07	8.61	9.06	7.40	11.36	6.60	19.10
Instant and freeze-dried coffee	5.07	8.62	3.50	2.75	3.64	4.04	2.87	10.83
Noncarb. fruit flavored drinks incl. non-frozen lemonade	8.46	6.74	8.88	6.47	9.98	9.15	9.84	10.39
Tea	6.77	9.04	5.86	5.88	5.18	7.66	4.60	8.62
Nonalcoholic beer	0.28	0.72	0.10	0.10	0.12	0.05	-	0.61
Other nonalcoholic beverages	8.44	8.75	8.53	10.64	6.14	12.39	5.92	16.40
Food prepared by cu on out-of-town trips	20.17	34.65	15.41	13.29	13.77	21.44	7.88	25.71
FOOD AWAY FROM HOME	**681.88**	**980.37**	**595.43**	**456.29**	**605.57**	**714.70**	**335.48**	**1,078.86**
Meals at restaurants, carry-outs, other	**509.62**	**717.79**	**452.76**	**391.67**	**452.75**	**533.31**	**264.66**	**867.57**
Lunch	174.93	216.38	167.71	132.55	178.24	185.70	112.01	294.36
Dinner	255.26	390.33	215.64	191.82	204.56	272.81	112.06	439.43
Snacks and nonalcoholic beverages	39.67	43.99	38.93	39.94	39.35	39.91	25.03	63.40
Breakfast and brunch	39.76	67.09	30.50	27.35	30.60	34.90	15.57	70.38
Board (including at school)	**22.70**	**26.12**	**22.00**	**1.92**	**14.62**	**54.64**	**9.31**	**31.46**
Catered affairs	**26.94**	**53.32**	**14.66**	**2.43**	**15.85**	**21.33**	**1.53**	**28.00**
Food on out-of-town trips	**89.73**	**172.06**	**63.50**	**48.43**	**63.04**	**78.20**	**23.49**	**127.53**
School lunches	**26.63**	**0.12**	**37.80**	**1.73**	**56.07**	**22.72**	**28.98**	**0.10**
Meals as pay	**6.25**	**10.99**	**4.71**	**10.11**	**3.23**	**4.49**	**7.50**	**24.20**
ALCOHOLIC BEVERAGES	**95.83**	**171.28**	**72.09**	**76.37**	**62.77**	**93.08**	**30.73**	**255.20**
At home	**57.26**	**92.92**	**46.43**	**49.61**	**41.50**	**57.33**	**21.70**	**144.31**
Beer and ale	32.73	48.99	27.44	36.29	25.26	26.71	13.48	97.75
Whiskey	4.92	10.11	3.45	1.27	2.49	7.46	0.84	9.29
Wine	13.93	24.99	10.52	9.04	10.46	12.57	5.70	26.83
Other alcoholic beverages	5.69	8.85	5.02	3.02	3.29	10.60	1.68	10.45
Away from home	**38.57**	**78.36**	**25.66**	**26.76**	**21.27**	**35.75**	**9.02**	**110.88**
Beer and ale	12.26	23.49	8.76	8.47	7.44	12.33	2.68	41.81
Wine	5.52	11.41	3.59	3.85	2.90	5.08	1.40	13.62
Other alcoholic beverages	9.71	20.29	6.24	7.05	4.70	9.23	2.59	25.48
Alcoholic beverages purchased on trips	11.09	23.17	7.07	7.39	6.24	9.10	2.36	29.97

Note: Average spending figures for total consumer units can be found on other average spending tables. Expenditures listed for items in a given category may not add to the total for that category because the listing is incomplete. (-) means insufficient data.

Consumer Unit Type
indexed per capita spending

(indexed average annual per capita spending of consumer units on food and alcoholic beverages, by type of consumer unit, 1994; index definition: an index of 100 is the per capita average for all consumer units; an index of 132 means that per capita spending by the consumer unit type is 32 percent above the per capita average for all consumer units; an index of 68 indicates that per capita spending by the consumer unit type is 32 percent below the per capita average for all consumer units)

	total married couples	married couples, no children	married couples with children				single parent at least one child < 18	single person
			total	oldest child under 6	oldest child 6 to 17	oldest child 18 or older		
Per capita spending of cu, total	$15,287.19	$22,550.00	$13,001.25	$12,914.86	$12,368.33	$15,264.74	$6,575.52	$21,347.00
Per capita spending of cu, index	100	143	87	87	83	100	59	152
Food, per capita spending index	99	132	89	79	89	103	70	140
Alcoholic beverages, per capita spending index	86	154	65	69	56	84	28	229
FOOD AT HOME	**99**	**124**	**90**	**86**	**88**	**102**	**83**	**128**
Cereals and bakery products	**100**	**123**	**93**	**89**	**92**	**103**	**82**	**128**
Cereals and cereal products	99	112	94	97	94	98	96	120
Flour	98	113	88	127	67	109	78	104
Prepared flour mixes	100	123	93	94	92	102	108	129
Ready-to-eat and cooked cereals	100	115	96	92	99	98	93	120
Rice	96	90	90	101	90	88	110	117
Pasta, cornmeal, and other cereal products	97	109	92	105	86	101	98	121
Bakery products	101	130	92	84	91	106	74	133
Bread	97	134	84	77	81	103	75	139
White bread	95	116	87	82	84	104	96	131
Bread, other than white	99	152	81	73	77	101	54	146
Crackers and cookies	103	134	94	88	93	109	75	130
Cookies	104	128	97	91	93	116	76	123
Crackers	102	145	89	81	92	94	73	145
Frozen and refrigerated bakery products	102	129	94	94	98	94	85	128
Other bakery products	103	124	96	85	97	109	70	132
Biscuits and rolls	106	134	99	85	99	119	68	122
Cakes and cupcakes	102	124	91	75	93	106	80	131
Bread and cracker products	103	122	99	108	87	124	68	106
Sweetrolls, coffee cakes, doughnuts	99	122	90	69	97	100	65	140
Pies, tarts, turnovers	101	103	105	127	103	98	63	162
Meats, poultry, fish, and eggs	**97**	**119**	**88**	**79**	**87**	**102**	**94**	**119**
Beef	98	118	88	80	87	103	102	109
Ground beef	97	107	92	92	96	90	109	111
Roast	100	120	88	72	80	125	100	94
Chuck roast	99	128	82	60	84	99	74	107
Round roast	103	116	92	89	77	133	98	99
Other roast	98	117	91	65	80	141	128	76
Steak	98	131	85	76	80	106	93	111
Round steak	98	115	88	66	88	113	106	71
Sirloin steak	105	138	94	87	88	121	66	114
Other steak	93	133	78	74	74	96	103	124
Other beef	97	99	88	55	94	109	111	118
Pork	94	128	81	72	84	89	102	119
Bacon	90	136	72	75	68	82	95	157
Pork chops	93	116	85	83	86	90	125	112

	total married couples	married couples, no children	married couples with children			single parent at least one child < 18	single person
			total	oldest child under 6	oldest child 6 to 17	oldest child 18 or older		
Ham	100	149	81	60	89	88	92	104
Ham, not canned	103	155	82	63	90	86	96	106
Canned ham	71	71	72	23	72	116	43	80
Sausage	91	112	85	68	86	100	80	134
Other pork	93	124	80	73	83	85	106	110
Other meats	100	124	93	76	96	106	84	113
Frankfurters	96	100	95	101	95	97	102	109
Lunch meats (cold cuts)	102	133	92	71	93	112	73	118
Bologna, liverwurst, salami	95	116	86	76	87	99	84	127
Other lunchmeats	105	142	95	69	97	120	66	112
Lamb, organ meats and others	99	109	94	61	117	80	127	87
Lamb and organ meats	98	111	93	62	114	82	129	89
Mutton, goat and game	139	-	142	-	271	-	-	-
Poultry	97	107	93	88	87	115	92	132
Fresh and frozen chickens	97	103	95	94	89	115	92	125
Fresh and frozen whole chicken	101	108	98	95	91	121	89	111
Fresh and frozen chicken parts	95	101	94	94	88	112	93	131
Other poultry	96	121	85	64	80	117	90	155
Fish and seafood	97	123	86	76	87	97	80	124
Canned fish and seafood	95	127	83	75	77	109	80	159
Fresh fish and shellfish	101	120	88	80	94	91	70	117
Frozen fish and shellfish	92	128	82	69	79	103	102	117
Eggs	94	120	81	77	78	94	89	139
Dairy products	**99**	**121**	**92**	**86**	**92**	**102**	**80**	**131**
Fresh milk and cream	98	108	93	91	93	102	84	129
Fresh milk, all types	98	106	94	93	93	102	84	131
Cream	99	135	85	62	90	97	72	101
Other dairy products	100	131	90	81	91	102	77	132
Butter	97	124	82	88	73	100	83	118
Cheese	100	126	93	81	95	104	77	137
Ice cream and related products	103	141	90	80	89	106	70	117
Miscellaneous dairy products	97	136	85	79	89	88	91	155
Fruits and vegetables	**98**	**131**	**86**	**84**	**84**	**100**	**74**	**144**
Fresh fruits	100	134	88	81	86	103	74	146
Apples	103	121	95	90	98	102	89	128
Bananas	98	143	81	83	77	92	70	157
Oranges	98	129	87	71	99	81	92	132
Citrus fruits, excl. oranges	95	133	80	79	72	104	64	160
Other fresh fruits	101	138	91	80	85	118	65	150
Fresh vegetables	97	127	86	78	82	108	71	142
Potatoes	95	125	83	81	77	103	82	128
Lettuce	98	121	91	73	89	115	79	153
Tomatoes	97	114	88	82	84	107	79	137
Other fresh vegetables	98	133	86	76	82	108	62	146

	total married couples	married couples, no children	married couples with children			single parent at least one child < 18	single person
			total	oldest child under 6	oldest child 6 to 17	oldest child 18 or older		
Processed fruits	97	126	87	94	83	94	74	153
Frozen fruits and fruit juices	100	134	89	91	86	99	77	138
Frozen orange juice	97	141	83	81	83	90	83	170
Frozen fruits	97	198	67	68	64	79	41	116
Frozen fruit juices	106	102	105	116	98	120	76	88
Canned fruit	98	170	75	71	70	94	58	161
Dried fruit	96	148	75	62	67	109	76	164
Fresh fruit juices	90	104	83	84	77	101	85	185
Canned and bottled fruit juices	98	114	93	114	91	86	74	139
Processed vegetables	98	139	83	85	84	86	78	135
Frozen vegetables	102	131	92	86	99	88	76	120
Canned and dried vegetables and juices	96	143	79	84	77	85	79	143
Canned beans	93	130	81	89	76	90	83	162
Canned corn	89	91	86	87	90	82	113	159
Other canned and dried vegetables	98	155	78	81	74	87	75	130
Frozen vegetable juices	92	125	82	99	72	94	165	98
Fresh and canned vegetable juices	101	170	73	85	73	67	48	151
Other food at home	**100**	**126**	**91**	**94**	**88**	**103**	**81**	**126**
Sugar and other sweets	100	127	89	89	92	88	80	123
Candy and chewing gum	103	130	92	97	97	83	66	127
Sugar	94	108	86	74	89	96	108	106
Artificial sweeteners	94	187	62	17	70	86	116	143
Jams, preserves, other sweets	97	126	86	86	84	97	92	123
Fats and oils	98	126	86	75	83	107	77	130
Margarine	91	128	78	70	75	96	68	180
Fats and oils	97	112	88	75	81	120	80	109
Salad dressings	103	137	89	70	86	116	85	113
Nondairy cream and imitation milk	97	163	75	81	73	81	72	149
Peanut butter	96	108	93	85	99	93	70	132
Miscellaneous foods	101	119	95	110	91	99	89	119
Frozen prepared foods	96	125	88	75	85	112	86	142
Frozen meals	81	122	69	55	55	113	98	211
Other frozen prepared foods	104	126	98	84	99	112	80	109
Canned and packaged soups	98	143	83	89	83	84	86	136
Potato chips, nuts, and other snacks	105	129	100	85	108	103	73	112
Potato chips and other snacks	105	116	105	85	116	106	80	108
Nuts	105	179	82	86	78	94	48	129
Condiments and seasonings	100	127	90	83	91	100	84	119
Salt, spices and other seasonings	98	136	83	78	76	106	77	117
Olives, pickles, relishes	102	153	83	69	87	91	97	112
Sauces and gravies	99	111	95	92	98	100	93	116
Baking needs and misc. products	103	136	91	77	95	101	65	133
Other canned/packaged prepared foods	103	98	103	173	85	90	104	104
Prepared salads	99	169	76	63	79	84	70	156
Prepared desserts	104	137	96	80	92	122	78	125

	total married couples	married couples, no children	married couples with children			single parent at least one child < 18	single person
			total	oldest child under 6	oldest child 6 to 17	oldest child 18 or older	
Baby food	112	36	132	420	66	44	161	39
Miscellaneous prepared foods	99	108	96	97	93	107	88	120
Nonalcoholic beverages	98	122	90	81	85	113	77	134
Cola	100	122	94	77	90	122	79	115
Other carbonated drinks	99	117	93	86	91	108	90	114
Coffee	93	155	70	69	64	90	55	174
Roasted coffee	94	155	74	78	64	97	57	164
Instant and freeze-dried coffee	91	155	63	50	66	73	52	195
Noncarb. fruit flavored drinks incl. non-frozen lemonade	97	77	102	74	114	105	113	119
Tea	104	139	90	90	80	118	71	133
Nonalcoholic beer	108	273	37	39	46	20	-	231
Other nonalcoholic beverages	93	96	94	117	67	136	65	180
Food prepared by cu on out-of-town trips	109	187	83	72	74	116	42	138
FOOD AWAY FROM HOME	**100**	**144**	**88**	**67**	**89**	**105**	**49**	**159**
Meals at restaurants, carry-outs, other	**98**	**137**	**87**	**75**	**87**	**102**	**51**	**166**
Lunch	97	120	93	73	99	103	62	163
Dinner	98	150	83	74	78	105	43	169
Snacks and nonalcoholic beverages	97	108	96	98	97	98	62	156
Breakfast and brunch	98	166	76	68	76	86	39	174
Board (including at school)	**112**	**129**	**108**	**9**	**72**	**269**	**46**	**155**
Catered affairs	**120**	**238**	**65**	**11**	**71**	**95**	**7**	**125**
Food on out-of-town trips	**108**	**207**	**76**	**58**	**76**	**94**	**28**	**153**
School lunches	**124**	**1**	**176**	**8**	**261**	**106**	**135**	**0**
Meals as pay	**66**	**115**	**50**	**106**	**34**	**47**	**79**	**254**
ALCOHOLIC BEVERAGES	**86**	**154**	**65**	**69**	**56**	**84**	**28**	**229**
At home	**87**	**141**	**70**	**75**	**63**	**87**	**33**	**218**
Beer and ale	82	123	69	91	63	67	34	245
Whiskey	90	185	63	23	46	136	15	170
Wine	96	172	72	62	72	86	39	184
Other alcoholic beverages	93	144	82	49	54	173	27	170
Away from home	**85**	**174**	**57**	**59**	**47**	**79**	**20**	**246**
Beer and ale	79	152	57	55	48	80	17	271
Wine	87	181	57	61	46	80	22	216
Other alcoholic beverages	87	181	56	63	42	83	23	228
Alcoholic beverages purchased on trips	91	189	58	60	51	74	19	245

Note: Spending index for total consumer units is 100. (-) means insufficient data.

Consumer Unit Type
total spending

(total annual spending on food and alcoholic beverages by consumer unit types, 1994; numbers in thousands)

	total married couples	married couples, no children	married couples with children total	oldest child under 6	oldest child 6 to 17	oldest child 18 or older	single parent at least one child < 18	single person
Number of consumer units	53,578	22,017	27,572	5,529	14,965	7,079	7,065	29,097
Total spending of all cu's	$2,182,283,911	$796,973,348	$1,215,590,476	$213,195,531	$660,635,013	$343,254,480	$153,105,827	$562,895,432
Food, total spending	300,803,501	102,377,509	173,053,728	26,978,811	98,139,273	48,994,750	25,425,381	71,706,938
Alcoholic beverages, total spending	16,430,765	7,542,144	7,950,662	1,477,902	3,945,373	2,503,842	629,562	7,425,554
FOOD AT HOME	$183,896,841	$59,207,896	$107,384,944	$18,148,943	$60,077,441	$29,769,248	$18,551,984	$40,315,348
Cereals and bakery products	29,475,401	9,294,477	17,543,512	2,951,214	9,952,922	4,756,522	2,886,900	6,389,410
Cereals and cereal products	10,971,167	3,202,152	6,712,403	1,212,012	3,825,802	1,710,924	1,270,499	2,251,526
Flour	510,598	150,596	296,675	74,752	127,502	88,771	48,537	91,656
Prepared flour mixes	874,393	277,194	527,177	93,108	296,756	140,164	113,464	192,331
Ready-to-eat and cooked cereals	6,733,683	1,997,162	4,152,619	699,584	2,455,906	1,035,658	747,760	1,369,014
Rice	1,012,088	245,92?	612,098	120,477	348,236	145,403	138,827	210,662
Pasta, cornmeal, other cereal products	1,839,869	531,490	1,123,559	224,090	597,403	300,999	221,912	388,154
Bakery products	18,504,770	6,092,324	10,831,384	1,739,202	6,126,970	3,045,598	1,616,472	4,137,884
Bread	5,064,728	1,798,569	2,827,509	456,087	1,545,136	841,198	467,279	1,229,930
White bread	2,458,159	765,971	1,450,839	238,687	798,981	421,059	297,719	575,830
Bread, other than white	2,606,570	1,032,597	1,376,670	217,400	746,155	420,139	169,560	653,810
Crackers and cookies	4,431,436	1,472,717	2,605,830	426,231	1,461,482	735,083	384,831	943,616
Cookies	3,063,054	970,730	1,838,777	303,100	1,007,145	537,721	267,975	612,783
Crackers	1,368,382	501,988	767,053	123,186	454,337	197,433	116,855	330,833
Frozen/refrigerated bakery products	1,512,507	490,098	898,020	157,134	529,611	218,883	149,990	322,104
Other bakery products	7,496,098	2,330,940	4,499,750	699,750	2,590,741	1,250,435	614,372	1,642,235
Biscuits and rolls	2,603,355	847,434	1,574,085	237,194	891,166	459,286	199,445	510,361
Cakes and cupcakes	2,187,054	678,564	1,251,217	180,632	728,047	356,569	205,238	474,572
Bread and cracker products	333,255	101,058	206,790	39,477	103,558	63,145	26,494	58,194
Sweetrolls, coffee cakes, doughnuts	1,488,397	472,044	874,584	116,330	536,196	236,226	117,067	358,184
Pies, tarts, turnovers	884,037	231,839	593,074	126,116	331,774	135,280	66,058	240,923
Meats, poultry, fish, and eggs	48,683,114	15,412,340	28,289,699	4,467,321	16,038,290	8,007,623	5,669,451	10,136,231
Beef	15,225,796	4,710,977	8,839,583	1,410,503	4,974,366	2,518,637	1,887,485	2,866,345
Ground beef	5,909,653	1,671,310	3,582,154	628,094	2,129,968	855,426	790,432	1,143,803
Roast	2,712,118	833,343	1,537,690	220,552	794,043	529,651	322,659	431,799
Chuck roast	831,531	276,534	441,428	57,115	260,241	130,183	74,183	152,468
Round roast	1,051,200	303,394	603,000	101,789	286,131	213,078	118,975	170,508
Other roast	829,387	253,416	493,263	61,593	247,671	186,390	129,501	108,823
Steak	5,666,945	1,958,412	3,167,747	501,425	1,714,690	967,770	645,246	1,096,375
Round steak	1,076,918	323,650	621,197	81,774	352,276	194,035	139,039	132,100
Sirloin steak	1,761,645	593,798	1,018,510	164,985	539,339	317,635	131,338	325,304
Other steak	2,828,918	1,040,964	1,528,040	254,666	822,925	456,100	374,869	638,970
Other beef	937,079	247,911	551,716	60,432	335,665	165,790	129,148	194,368
Pork	10,052,840	3,508,409	5,567,063	866,228	3,270,900	1,487,793	1,305,824	2,165,690
Bacon	1,404,279	546,242	720,181	131,645	389,240	200,760	177,190	415,796
Pork chops	2,512,808	800,318	1,471,793	252,731	850,311	379,718	403,058	513,853

	total married couples	married couples, no children	married couples with children				single parent at least one child < 18	single person
			total	oldest child under 6	oldest child 6 to 17	oldest child 18 or older		
Ham	$2,537,990	$969,409	$1,324,007	$171,012	$824,871	$351,189	$279,209	$445,184
Ham, not canned	2,405,652	935,282	1,237,983	166,091	775,935	317,210	269,530	420,161
Canned ham	132,873	34,126	86,025	4,921	48,936	33,979	9,679	25,314
Sausage	1,426,246	450,688	850,872	120,366	495,342	245,004	150,343	355,565
Other pork	2,171,516	741,753	1,200,209	190,474	711,286	311,122	296,024	435,000
Other meats	6,452,934	2,048,242	3,845,467	555,886	2,263,307	1,071,902	646,094	1,235,750
Frankfurters	1,230,687	331,796	788,008	147,293	447,753	196,442	156,207	238,304
Lunch meats (cold cuts)	4,577,169	1,533,044	2,660,974	363,366	1,535,409	793,131	390,906	900,261
Bologna, liverwurst, salami	1,549,476	485,475	901,604	139,828	516,442	253,287	162,778	351,492
Other lunchmeats	3,027,693	1,047,569	1,759,369	223,537	1,018,817	539,845	228,058	548,769
Lamb, organ meats and others	644,543	183,402	396,485	45,172	280,145	82,329	98,981	96,893
Lamb and organ meats	626,863	183,402	385,181	45,172	267,874	82,329	98,981	96,893
Mutton, goat and game	17,145	#VALUE!	11,305	-	12,271	-	-	-
Poultry	9,042,895	2,568,063	5,586,914	929,591	2,983,273	1,692,447	1,025,414	2,092,656
Fresh and frozen chickens	7,146,769	1,957,091	4,511,331	787,717	2,403,379	1,329,790	813,535	1,573,857
Fresh and frozen whole chicken	2,052,037	560,773	1,278,238	218,396	676,268	386,301	216,118	382,917
Fresh and frozen chicken parts	5,094,732	1,396,318	3,233,093	569,321	1,727,260	943,489	597,416	1,190,649
Other poultry	1,896,125	610,972	1,075,584	141,874	579,894	362,657	211,879	518,800
Fish and seafood	5,977,162	1,943,441	3,383,084	525,918	1,955,926	933,012	586,112	1,292,198
Canned fish and seafood	977,263	336,420	551,440	87,192	289,423	176,692	98,345	277,876
Fresh fish and shellfish	3,538,827	1,083,016	1,997,316	315,872	1,205,730	499,282	294,964	698,328
Frozen fish and shellfish	1,461,072	523,784	834,053	122,854	460,623	257,038	192,804	315,993
Eggs	1,931,487	633,209	1,067,864	179,140	590,519	303,760	218,450	483,592
Dairy products	**19,666,876**	**6,165,200**	**11,667,092**	**1,914,527**	**6,669,452**	**3,172,241**	**1,894,621**	**4,392,483**
Fresh milk and cream	8,560,157	2,420,549	5,230,133	897,965	2,971,750	1,393,643	870,691	1,907,890
Fresh milk, all types	8,002,410	2,226,359	4,924,911	858,709	2,786,034	1,308,270	822,437	1,811,288
Cream	557,211	194,190	305,498	39,256	185,566	85,373	48,254	96,602
Other dairy products	11,106,719	3,744,651	6,436,959	1,016,562	3,697,702	1,778,599	1,023,930	2,484,884
Butter	774,202	254,737	420,749	79,175	215,047	125,794	79,340	160,615
Cheese	5,594,615	1,811,999	3,350,274	515,524	1,954,130	914,748	519,136	1,302,964
Ice cream and related products	3,364,163	1,184,515	1,889,785	295,470	1,065,807	543,313	271,932	649,736
Miscellaneous dairy products	1,374,276	493,181	775,876	126,393	462,718	194,743	153,522	371,569
Fruits and vegetables	**29,377,889**	**10,078,502**	**16,639,151**	**2,822,942**	**9,217,542**	**4,682,900**	**2,643,440**	**7,325,170**
Fresh fruits	9,118,976	3,149,532	5,173,334	837,975	2,888,095	1,480,502	805,198	2,259,673
Apples	1,788,969	542,279	1,068,691	176,873	622,245	278,913	185,103	378,552
Bananas	1,993,102	747,037	1,056,835	190,806	574,207	294,628	170,973	541,495
Oranges	1,102,635	372,748	628,090	90,289	405,851	143,279	122,860	251,107
Citrus fruits, excl. oranges	712,587	257,379	387,662	67,177	197,987	122,396	57,085	204,552
Other fresh fruits	3,521,682	1,230,090	2,032,056	312,831	1,087,956	641,357	269,177	883,676
Fresh vegetables	8,987,710	3,008,403	5,138,318	809,888	2,790,374	1,565,592	787,394	2,221,847
Potatoes	1,828,081	615,595	1,028,711	176,265	543,828	310,697	188,212	416,960
Lettuce	1,163,178	369,886	694,539	98,527	387,893	214,281	112,969	308,719
Tomatoes	1,401,065	423,167	814,477	133,857	443,413	241,111	135,648	335,488
Other fresh vegetables	4,595,385	1,599,975	2,600,591	401,295	1,415,240	799,431	350,424	1,160,388

	total married couples	married couples, no children	married couples with children				single parent at least one child < 18	single person
			total	oldest child under 6	oldest child 6 to 17	oldest child 18 or older		
Processed fruits	$6,190,938	$2,072,680	$3,554,858	$679,901	$1,940,811	$939,666	$566,896	$1,653,583
Frozen fruits and fruit juices	1,118,173	384,637	637,465	114,782	351,977	172,940	102,231	262,164
Frozen orange juice	633,828	235,582	348,510	59,824	198,586	92,239	64,362	187,676
Frozen fruits	106,620	55,703	47,424	8,404	25,590	13,662	5,440	21,532
Frozen fruit juices	377,189	93,572	241,531	46,554	127,801	67,038	32,499	52,957
Canned fruit	960,118	427,130	473,136	78,678	251,562	144,199	67,541	266,529
Dried fruit	388,441	153,899	196,037	28,087	99,517	68,949	36,667	112,314
Fresh fruit juices	1,108,529	327,173	657,868	116,717	347,338	194,673	124,909	385,535
Canned and bottled fruit juices	2,615,678	779,842	1,590,629	341,692	890,118	358,905	235,547	627,040
Processed vegetables	5,080,266	1,848,107	2,772,640	495,122	1,598,112	697,140	483,882	1,190,358
Frozen vegetables	1,739,678	572,442	1,006,102	165,096	618,952	234,456	155,642	346,836
Canned and dried vegetables and juices	3,341,124	1,275,665	1,766,538	330,026	979,160	462,683	328,311	843,522
Canned beans	667,582	238,444	372,773	71,711	199,633	101,442	70,862	196,987
Canned corn	415,765	109,204	258,625	46,112	154,588	60,030	63,090	125,990
Other canned and dried vegetables	1,814,687	736,689	927,522	169,464	506,565	253,995	166,946	408,813
Frozen vegetable juices	14,466	5,064	8,272	1,769	4,190	2,336	3,109	2,619
Fresh and canned vegetable juices	428,624	186,044	199,346	41,025	114,183	44,810	24,304	109,114
Other food at home	**56,693,025**	**18,257,157**	**33,245,490**	**5,992,994**	**18,199,385**	**9,149,961**	**5,457,642**	**12,071,763**
Sugar and other sweets	7,200,883	2,359,122	4,123,668	721,479	2,440,343	996,794	690,392	1,508,388
Candy and chewing gum	4,392,324	1,428,243	2,522,562	470,076	1,519,995	553,295	335,658	922,084
Sugar	1,177,109	346,768	698,674	105,272	411,687	189,576	162,424	226,666
Artificial sweeteners	219,670	111,846	92,366	4,534	59,411	31,289	32,287	56,448
Jams, preserves, other sweets	1,411,780	472,044	809,790	141,598	449,249	222,635	160,022	303,482
Fats and oils	5,304,758	1,762,901	3,015,550	458,244	1,662,761	915,669	502,463	1,195,596
Margarine	881,358	319,247	487,197	76,908	266,976	146,181	79,481	295,916
Fats and oils	1,543,046	456,633	896,090	133,857	468,853	297,106	151,332	293,298
Salad dressings	1,672,169	575,084	933,588	129,379	514,646	297,601	165,816	313,084
Nondairy cream and imitation milk	434,518	188,906	217,819	41,025	120,169	57,128	38,504	113,478
Peanut butter	773,666	223,032	480,856	77,074	292,117	117,582	67,259	180,110
Miscellaneous foods	25,082,541	7,604,011	15,192,172	3,090,158	8,265,319	3,833,916	2,625,778	4,988,972
Frozen prepared foods	4,360,713	1,453,122	2,574,949	383,381	1,413,594	796,317	466,785	1,095,211
Frozen meals	1,183,538	459,935	649,596	92,058	296,606	259,658	172,033	526,947
Other frozen prepared foods	3,177,175	992,967	1,925,353	291,268	1,116,988	536,659	294,822	568,264
Canned and packaged soups	1,994,709	741,753	1,083,855	203,080	619,252	266,666	208,488	466,425
Potato chips, nuts, and other snacks	5,354,585	1,688,043	3,282,722	487,879	2,016,833	824,704	443,611	969,803
Potato chips and other snacks	4,206,945	1,186,716	2,704,813	382,164	1,703,316	664,718	381,298	731,499
Nuts	1,147,641	501,327	577,909	105,714	313,517	159,985	62,313	238,304
Condiments and seasonings	5,472,993	1,782,937	3,164,714	510,769	1,819,145	861,019	551,423	1,103,067
Salt, spices and other seasonings	1,303,017	463,238	703,913	115,833	370,084	219,874	121,235	263,037
Olives, pickles, relishes	708,837	273,011	371,946	54,571	223,128	98,964	80,400	132,391
Sauces and gravies	2,483,876	714,672	1,532,176	258,038	895,506	391,752	276,524	493,485
Baking needs and misc. products	977,263	332,016	556,679	82,327	330,427	150,429	73,264	214,445
Other canned/packaged prepared foods	7,899,540	1,938,157	5,085,931	1,505,104	2,396,645	1,085,211	955,471	1,353,883
Prepared salads	745,270	327,393	365,605	53,576	217,441	99,318	62,667	199,314
Prepared desserts	571,677	192,208	337,481	49,485	185,267	105,194	50,868	116,388

	total married couples	married couples, no children	married couples with children				single parent at least one child < 18	single person
			total	oldest child under 6	oldest child 6 to 17	oldest child 18 or older		
Baby food	$2,156,515	$179,879	$1,631,160	$913,501	$467,207	$133,085	$371,478	$127,445
Miscellaneous prepared foods	4,426,079	1,238,676	2,751,410	488,542	1,526,729	747,684	470,458	911,027
Nonalcoholic beverages	15,647,455	5,005,345	9,214,838	1,465,959	4,965,686	2,826,645	1,477,574	3,630,724
Cola	6,150,219	1,915,479	3,705,125	530,673	2,031,499	1,171,362	580,319	1,195,305
Other carbonated drinks	2,652,647	803,841	1,597,246	259,697	894,009	453,905	285,921	516,472
Coffee	2,737,836	1,174,827	1,335,312	228,735	693,777	414,405	194,076	870,873
Roasted coffee	1,868,801	795,474	949,580	175,380	465,112	305,600	135,295	555,753
Instant and freeze-dried coffee	869,571	379,353	385,732	53,300	228,665	108,804	58,710	315,121
Noncarb. fruit flavored drinks incl. non-frozen lemonade	1,449,821	296,569	979,082	125,232	627,034	246,066	201,635	302,318
Tea	1,160,499	398,067	646,288	113,787	325,788	206,070	94,176	250,816
Nonalcoholic beer	48,756	31,704	10,753	1,990	7,632	1,416	-	17,749
Other nonalcoholic beverages	1,447,142	385,077	940,757	205,845	386,097	333,421	121,377	477,191
Food prepared by cu on out-of-town trips	3,457,388	1,525,778	1,699,262	257,154	865,426	576,868	161,435	748,084
FOOD AWAY FROM HOME	**116,907,196**	**43,169,613**	**65,668,784**	**8,829,868**	**38,061,831**	**19,225,502**	**6,873,397**	**31,391,589**
Meals at restaurants, carry-outs, other	**87,373,395**	**31,606,945**	**49,934,271**	**7,579,319**	**28,456,995**	**14,346,231**	**5,422,458**	**25,243,684**
Lunch	29,990,821	9,527,857	18,495,849	2,565,069	11,202,799	4,995,296	2,294,853	8,564,993
Dinner	43,764,654	17,187,791	23,782,504	3,712,060	12,857,479	7,338,587	2,295,842	12,786,095
Snacks and nonalcoholic beverages	6,800,656	1,937,056	4,292,960	772,899	2,473,116	1,073,460	512,778	1,844,750
Breakfast and brunch	6,817,265	2,954,241	3,363,233	529,291	1,923,601	938,888	319,055	2,047,847
Board (including at school)	**3,892,442**	**1,149,948**	**2,426,060**	**37,155**	**919,001**	**1,469,954**	**190,684**	**915,392**
Catered affairs	**4,619,495**	**2,347,673**	**1,616,822**	**46,941**	**996,220**	**573,753**	**31,369**	**814,716**
Food on out-of-town trips	**15,384,387**	**7,576,490**	**7,002,737**	**937,166**	**3,962,283**	**2,103,525**	**481,268**	**3,710,740**
School lunches	**4,564,846**	**5,064**	**4,168,886**	**33,561**	**3,524,407**	**611,130**	**593,813**	**2,910**
Meals as pay	**1,072,096**	**483,713**	**519,732**	**195,727**	**203,075**	**120,909**	**153,734**	**704,147**
ALCOHOLIC BEVERAGES	**16,430,765**	**7,542,144**	**7,950,662**	**1,477,902**	**3,945,373**	**2,503,842**	**629,562**	**7,425,554**
At home	**9,817,633**	**4,091,639**	**5,120,672**	**960,056**	**2,608,250**	**1,542,231**	**444,671**	**4,198,988**
Beer and ale	5,611,760	2,157,005	3,025,751	702,183	1,587,487	718,519	276,171	2,844,232
Whiskey	842,782	445,184	380,769	24,549	156,684	200,548	17,309	270,311
Wine	2,387,436	1,100,189	1,160,230	174,938	657,263	338,164	116,855	780,673
Other alcoholic beverages	975,655	389,481	553,921	58,386	206,816	285,071	34,336	304,064
Away from home	**6,613,133**	**3,450,504**	**2,830,266**	**517,901**	**1,337,123**	**961,611**	**184,891**	**3,226,275**
Beer and ale	2,101,329	1,034,138	965,571	163,880	467,357	331,722	54,824	1,216,546
Wine	946,187	502,428	396,210	74,420	182,124	136,766	28,613	396,301
Other alcoholic beverages	1,664,668	893,450	688,473	136,511	295,259	248,402	53,129	741,392
Alcoholic beverages purchased on trips	1,900,947	1,020,268	780,012	143,091	392,382	244,721	48,395	872,037

Note: Total spending figures for total consumer units can be found on other total spending tables. Spending for items in a given category may not add to the total for that category because the listing is incomplete. Numbers will not add to total because not all household types are shown. (-) means insufficient data

market shares

(percent of total annual spending on food accounted for by types of consumer units, 1994)

	total married couples	married couples, no children	married couples with children			single parent at least one child < 18	single person
			total	oldest child under 6	oldest child 6 to 17	oldest child 18 or older		
Share of total consumer units	52.4%	21.5%	27.0%	5.4%	14.6%	6.9%	6.9%	28.5%
Share of total spending	67.2	24.6	37.5	6.6	20.4	10.6	4.7	17.3
Share of food spending	66.7	22.7	38.4	6.0	21.8	10.9	5.6	15.9
Share of alcoholic beverages spending	57.8	26.5	28.0	5.2	13.9	8.8	2.2	26.1
FOOD AT HOME	**66.3%**	**21.4%**	**38.7%**	**6.5%**	**21.7%**	**10.7%**	**6.7%**	**14.5%**
Cereals and bakery products	**67.3**	**21.2**	**40.0**	**6.7**	**22.7**	**10.9**	**6.6**	**14.6**
Cereals and cereal products	66.4	19.4	40.6	7.3	23.1	10.3	7.7	13.6
Flour	65.7	19.4	38.2	9.6	16.4	11.4	6.2	11.8
Prepared flour mixes	66.9	21.2	40.3	7.1	22.7	10.7	8.7	14.7
Ready-to-eat and cooked cereals	67.0	19.9	41.3	7.0	24.5	10.3	7.4	13.6
Rice	64.2	15.6	38.8	7.6	22.1	9.2	8.8	13.4
Pasta, cornmeal, and other cereal products	65.1	18.8	39.8	7.9	21.1	10.7	7.9	13.7
Bakery products	67.8	22.3	39.7	6.4	22.5	11.2	5.9	15.2
Bread	65.0	23.1	36.3	5.9	19.8	10.8	6.0	15.8
White bread	63.9	19.9	37.7	6.2	20.8	10.9	7.7	15.0
Bread, other than white	66.1	26.2	34.9	5.5	18.9	10.7	4.3	16.6
Crackers and cookies	69.3	23.0	40.8	6.7	22.9	11.5	6.0	14.8
Cookies	69.7	22.1	41.9	6.9	22.9	12.2	6.1	14.0
Crackers	68.3	25.1	38.3	6.2	22.7	9.9	5.8	16.5
Frozen and refrigerated bakery products	68.6	22.2	40.8	7.1	24.0	9.9	6.8	14.6
Other bakery products	68.8	21.4	41.3	6.4	23.8	11.5	5.6	15.1
Biscuits and rolls	70.8	23.1	42.8	6.5	24.2	12.5	5.4	13.9
Cakes and cupcakes	68.6	21.3	39.2	5.7	22.8	11.2	6.4	14.9
Bread and cracker products	69.1	20.9	42.9	8.2	21.5	13.1	5.5	12.1
Sweetrolls, coffee cakes, doughnuts	66.4	21.1	39.0	5.2	23.9	10.5	5.2	16.0
Pies, tarts, turnovers	67.6	17.7	45.3	9.6	25.4	10.3	5.0	18.4
Meats, poultry, fish, and eggs	**65.0**	**20.6**	**37.8**	**6.0**	**21.4**	**10.7**	**7.6**	**13.5**
Beef	65.7	20.3	38.1	6.1	21.5	10.9	8.1	12.4
Ground beef	65.4	18.5	39.6	6.9	23.6	9.5	8.7	12.7
Roast	67.3	20.7	38.2	5.5	19.7	13.1	8.0	10.7
Chuck roast	66.4	22.1	35.2	4.6	20.8	10.4	5.9	12.2
Round roast	69.3	20.0	39.8	6.7	18.9	14.0	7.8	11.2
Other roast	65.9	20.1	39.2	4.9	19.7	14.8	10.3	8.6
Steak	65.4	22.6	36.6	5.8	19.8	11.2	7.4	12.7
Round steak	65.9	19.8	38.0	5.0	21.5	11.9	8.5	8.1
Sirloin steak	70.5	23.8	40.8	6.6	21.6	12.7	5.3	13.0
Other steak	62.5	23.0	33.7	5.6	18.2	10.1	8.3	14.1
Other beef	64.8	17.1	38.1	4.2	23.2	11.5	8.9	13.4
Pork	63.2	22.0	35.0	5.4	20.5	9.3	8.2	13.6
Bacon	60.3	23.5	30.9	5.7	16.7	8.6	7.6	17.9
Pork chops	62.5	19.9	36.6	6.3	21.2	9.4	10.0	12.8

	total married couples	married couples, no children	married couples with children				single parent at least one child < 18	single person
			total	oldest child under 6	oldest child 6 to 17	oldest child 18 or older		
Ham	67.3%	25.7%	35.1%	4.5%	21.9%	9.3%	7.4%	11.8%
Ham, not canned	68.9	26.8	35.5	4.8	22.2	9.1	7.7	12.0
Canned ham	47.8	12.3	30.9	1.8	17.6	12.2	3.5	9.1
Sausage	61.1	19.3	36.5	5.2	21.2	10.5	6.4	15.2
Other pork	62.6	21.4	34.6	5.5	20.5	9.0	8.5	12.5
Other meats	67.2	21.3	40.0	5.8	23.6	11.2	6.7	12.9
Frankfurters	64.2	17.3	41.1	7.7	23.4	10.2	8.1	12.4
Lunch meats (cold cuts)	68.2	22.8	39.7	5.4	22.9	11.8	5.8	13.4
Bologna, liverwurst, salami	63.9	20.0	37.2	5.8	21.3	10.4	6.7	14.5
Other lunchmeats	70.6	24.4	41.1	5.2	23.8	12.6	5.3	12.8
Lamb, organ meats and others	66.2	18.8	40.7	4.6	28.8	8.5	10.2	9.9
Lamb and organ meats	65.6	19.2	40.3	4.7	28.0	8.6	10.4	10.1
Mutton, goat and game	93.2	-	61.4	0.0	66.7	0.0	0.0	0.0
Poultry	64.8	18.4	40.0	6.7	21.4	12.1	7.3	15.0
Fresh and frozen chickens	64.8	17.7	40.9	7.1	21.8	12.1	7.4	14.3
Fresh and frozen whole chicken	67.9	18.6	42.3	7.2	22.4	12.8	7.2	12.7
Fresh and frozen chicken parts	63.6	17.4	40.4	7.1	21.6	11.8	7.5	14.9
Other poultry	64.7	20.8	36.7	4.8	19.8	12.4	7.2	17.7
Fish and seafood	65.4	21.3	37.0	5.8	21.4	10.2	6.4	14.1
Canned fish and seafood	63.6	21.9	35.9	5.7	18.8	11.5	6.4	18.1
Fresh fish and shellfish	67.5	20.7	38.1	6.0	23.0	9.5	5.6	13.3
Frozen fish and shellfish	61.7	22.1	35.2	5.2	19.5	10.9	8.1	13.4
Eggs	63.0	20.7	34.8	5.8	19.3	9.9	7.1	15.8
Dairy products	**66.6**	**20.9**	**39.5**	**6.5**	**22.6**	**10.7**	**6.4**	**14.9**
Fresh milk and cream	65.9	18.6	40.3	6.9	22.9	10.7	6.7	14.7
Fresh milk, all types	65.8	18.3	40.5	7.1	22.9	10.8	6.8	14.9
Cream	66.6	23.2	36.5	4.7	22.2	10.2	5.8	11.5
Other dairy products	67.2	22.6	38.9	6.1	22.4	10.8	6.2	15.0
Butter	65.0	21.4	35.3	6.6	18.1	10.6	6.7	13.5
Cheese	66.9	21.7	40.1	6.2	23.4	10.9	6.2	15.6
Ice cream and related products	69.1	24.3	38.8	6.1	21.9	11.2	5.6	13.3
Miscellaneous dairy products	65.1	23.4	36.7	6.0	21.9	9.2	7.3	17.6
Fruits and vegetables	**65.8**	**22.6**	**37.3**	**6.3**	**20.7**	**10.5**	**5.9**	**16.4**
Fresh fruits	67.1	23.2	38.1	6.2	21.2	10.9	5.9	16.6
Apples	69.0	20.9	41.2	6.8	24.0	10.8	7.1	14.6
Bananas	65.7	24.6	34.9	6.3	18.9	9.7	5.6	17.9
Oranges	65.9	22.3	37.6	5.4	24.3	8.6	7.3	15.0
Citrus fruits, excl. oranges	63.6	23.0	34.6	6.0	17.7	10.9	5.1	18.3
Other fresh fruits	68.0	23.8	39.2	6.0	21.0	12.4	5.2	17.1
Fresh vegetables	65.2	21.8	37.3	5.9	20.2	11.4	5.7	16.1
Potatoes	63.9	21.5	35.9	6.2	19.0	10.9	6.6	14.6
Lettuce	65.5	20.8	39.1	5.5	21.8	12.1	6.4	17.4
Tomatoes	65.2	19.7	37.9	6.2	20.6	11.2	6.3	15.6
Other fresh vegetables	65.6	22.9	37.1	5.7	20.2	11.4	5.0	16.6

	total married couples	married couples, no children	married couples with children				single parent at least one child < 18	single person
			total	oldest child under 6	oldest child 6 to 17	oldest child 18 or older		
Processed fruits	65.1%	21.8%	37.4%	7.1%	20.4%	9.9%	6.0%	17.4%
Frozen fruits and fruit juices	67.2	23.1	38.3	6.9	21.2	10.4	6.1	15.8
Frozen orange juice	65.3	24.3	35.9	6.2	20.5	9.5	6.6	19.3
Frozen fruits	65.2	34.1	29.0	5.1	15.6	8.4	3.3	13.2
Frozen fruit juices	71.1	17.6	45.5	8.8	24.1	12.6	6.1	10.0
Canned fruit	66.0	29.4	32.5	5.4	17.3	9.9	4.6	18.3
Dried fruit	64.5	25.6	32.6	4.7	16.5	11.5	6.1	18.7
Fresh fruit juices	60.6	17.9	36.0	6.4	19.0	10.6	6.8	21.1
Canned and bottled fruit juices	66.0	19.7	40.1	8.6	22.5	9.1	5.9	15.8
Processed vegetables	65.8	23.9	35.9	6.4	20.7	9.0	6.3	15.4
Frozen vegetables	68.5	22.6	39.6	6.5	24.4	9.2	6.1	13.7
Canned and dried vegetables and juices	64.4	24.6	34.1	6.4	18.9	8.9	6.3	16.3
Canned beans	62.6	22.3	34.9	6.7	18.7	9.5	6.6	18.5
Canned corn	59.7	15.7	37.2	6.6	22.2	8.6	9.1	18.1
Other canned and dried vegetables	65.6	26.6	33.5	6.1	18.3	9.2	6.0	14.8
Frozen vegetable juices	61.5	21.5	35.2	7.5	17.8	9.9	13.2	11.1
Fresh and canned vegetable juices	67.5	29.3	31.4	6.5	18.0	7.1	3.8	17.2
Other food at home	**67.2**	**21.6**	**39.4**	**7.1**	**21.6**	**10.8**	**6.5**	**14.3**
Sugar and other sweets	66.9	21.9	38.3	6.7	22.7	9.3	6.4	14.0
Candy and chewing gum	69.0	22.4	39.6	7.4	23.9	8.7	5.3	14.5
Sugar	62.9	18.5	37.3	5.6	22.0	10.1	8.7	12.1
Artificial sweeteners	63.4	32.3	26.7	1.3	17.1	9.0	9.3	16.3
Jams, preserves, other sweets	65.1	21.8	37.3	6.5	20.7	10.3	7.4	14.0
Fats and oils	65.5	21.8	37.2	5.7	20.5	11.3	6.2	14.8
Margarine	60.9	22.1	33.7	5.3	18.4	10.1	5.5	20.4
Fats and oils	65.4	19.3	38.0	5.7	19.9	12.6	6.4	12.4
Salad dressings	68.9	23.7	38.5	5.3	21.2	12.3	6.8	12.9
Nondairy cream and imitation milk	64.8	28.2	32.5	6.1	17.9	8.5	5.7	16.9
Peanut butter	64.7	18.7	40.2	6.4	24.4	9.8	5.6	15.1
Miscellaneous foods	67.9	20.6	41.1	8.4	22.4	10.4	7.1	13.5
Frozen prepared foods	64.5	21.5	38.1	5.7	20.9	11.8	6.9	16.2
Frozen meals	54.0	21.0	29.7	4.2	13.5	11.9	7.9	24.1
Other frozen prepared foods	69.5	21.7	42.1	6.4	24.4	11.7	6.5	12.4
Canned and packaged soups	66.0	24.6	35.9	6.7	20.5	8.8	6.9	15.4
Potato chips, nuts, and other snacks	70.7	22.3	43.4	6.4	26.6	10.9	5.9	12.8
Potato chips and other snacks	70.7	20.0	45.5	6.4	28.6	11.2	6.4	12.3
Nuts	70.7	30.9	35.6	6.5	19.3	9.9	3.8	14.7
Condiments and seasonings	67.2	21.9	38.8	6.3	22.3	10.6	6.8	13.5
Salt, spices and other seasonings	66.1	23.5	35.7	5.9	18.8	11.1	6.1	13.3
Olives, pickles, relishes	68.3	26.3	35.8	5.3	21.5	9.5	7.7	12.7
Sauces and gravies	66.7	19.2	41.1	6.9	24.1	10.5	7.4	13.3
Baking needs and misc. products	69.0	23.5	39.3	5.8	23.3	10.6	5.2	15.1
Other canned/packaged prepared foods	68.9	16.9	44.4	13.1	20.9	9.5	8.3	11.8
Prepared salads	66.5	29.2	32.6	4.8	19.4	8.9	5.6	17.8
Prepared desserts	70.0	23.5	41.3	6.1	22.7	12.9	6.2	14.3

	total married couples	married couples, no children	married couples with children				single parent at least one child < 18	single person
			total	oldest child under 6	oldest child 6 to 17	oldest child 18 or older		
Baby food	75.1%	6.3%	56.8%	31.8%	16.3%	4.6%	12.9%	4.4%
Miscellaneous prepared foods	66.6	18.6	41.4	7.3	23.0	11.2	7.1	13.7
Nonalcoholic beverages	65.7	21.0	38.7	6.2	20.9	11.9	6.2	15.3
Cola	67.3	21.0	40.5	5.8	22.2	12.8	6.3	13.1
Other carbonated drinks	66.7	20.2	40.2	6.5	22.5	11.4	7.2	13.0
Coffee	62.3	26.7	30.4	5.2	15.8	9.4	4.4	19.8
Roasted coffee	62.8	26.7	31.9	5.9	15.6	10.3	4.5	18.7
Instant and freeze-dried coffee	61.3	26.7	27.2	3.8	16.1	7.7	4.1	22.2
Noncarb. fruit flavored drinks incl. non-frozen lemonade	64.9	13.3	43.8	5.6	28.1	11.0	9.0	13.5
Tea	69.9	24.0	38.9	6.9	19.6	12.4	5.7	15.1
Nonalcoholic beer	72.3	47.0	15.9	3.0	11.3	2.1	0.0	26.3
Other nonalcoholic beverages	62.2	16.5	40.4	8.8	16.6	14.3	5.2	20.5
Food prepared by cu on out-of-town trips	72.9	32.2	35.8	5.4	18.2	12.2	3.4	15.8
FOOD AWAY FROM HOME	**67.3**	**24.9**	**37.8**	**5.1**	**21.9**	**11.1**	**4.0**	**18.1**
Meals at restaurants, carry-outs, other	**65.4**	**23.7**	**37.4**	**5.7**	**21.3**	**10.7**	**4.1**	**18.9**
Lunch	65.0	20.6	40.1	5.6	24.3	10.8	5.0	18.5
Dinner	65.7	25.8	35.7	5.6	19.3	11.0	3.4	19.2
Snacks and nonalcoholic beverages	65.4	18.6	41.3	7.4	23.8	10.3	4.9	17.7
Breakfast and brunch	66.1	28.6	32.6	5.1	18.6	9.1	3.1	19.8
Board (including at school)	**75.1**	**22.2**	**46.8**	**0.7**	**17.7**	**28.4**	**3.7**	**17.7**
Catered affairs	**80.6**	**41.0**	**28.2**	**0.8**	**17.4**	**10.0**	**0.5**	**14.2**
Food on out-of-town trips	**72.4**	**35.7**	**33.0**	**4.4**	**18.6**	**9.9**	**2.3**	**17.5**
School lunches	**83.1**	**0.1**	**75.9**	**0.6**	**64.1**	**11.1**	**10.8**	**0.1**
Meals as pay	**44.1**	**19.9**	**21.4**	**8.0**	**8.4**	**5.0**	**6.3**	**29.0**
ALCOHOLIC BEVERAGES	**57.8**	**26.5**	**28.0**	**5.2**	**13.9**	**8.8**	**2.2**	**26.1**
At home	**58.2**	**24.2**	**30.3**	**5.7**	**15.5**	**9.1**	**2.6**	**24.9**
Beer and ale	55.1	21.2	29.7	6.9	15.6	7.1	2.7	27.9
Whiskey	60.3	31.8	27.2	1.8	11.2	14.3	1.2	19.3
Wine	64.2	29.6	31.2	4.7	17.7	9.1	3.1	21.0
Other alcoholic beverages	62.2	24.8	35.3	3.7	13.2	18.2	2.2	19.4
Away from home	**57.3**	**29.9**	**24.5**	**4.5**	**11.6**	**8.3**	**1.6**	**28.0**
Beer and ale	53.3	26.2	24.5	4.2	11.9	8.4	1.4	30.9
Wine	58.6	31.1	24.5	4.6	11.3	8.5	1.8	24.6
Other alcoholic beverages	58.3	31.3	24.1	4.8	10.3	8.7	1.9	25.9
Alcoholic beverages purchased on trips	60.8	32.6	24.9	4.6	12.5	7.8	1.5	27.9

Note: Market share for total consumer units is 100.0%. Numbers will not add to total because not all household types are shown; (-) means insufficient data.

Chapter 5

Spending by
Region

Households in the West spend 5 percent more on food overall than do those in other regions of the country. Northeasterners spend 7 percent more. Households in the South spend 4 percent less than average on food, while those in the Midwest spend 5 percent less.

Some spending patterns reflect regional food traditions, while others are driven by the ethnic and racial composition of regions. Southerners, for example, spend more than average on chuck roast and pork, both popular barbecue meats. The heavily Hispanic South sees greater than average expenditures on canned beans and corn, as well as fats and oils—important elements of the Hispanic diet. Spending on rice is 39 percent greater than average in the West, which has large Hispanic and Asian populations. A few spending patterns are attributable to regional characteristics. It is not surprising, for example, that in the land-locked Midwest, households spend 38 percent less than average on fresh fish and shellfish.

When examining spending by region, the cost of transporting fresh food must be considered. Northeasterners, for example, spend 31 percent more on oranges than average, while Southerners spend 21 percent less. In this case, more spending may not indicate greater consumption, but merely the higher price paid for the product. The same is probably true for fresh fruit juices. Spending in the Northeast is 50 percent higher than average, while in the West, where much of the juice fruit is produced, it is 16 percent lower.

Considering that the most recent wave of coffee culture began in Seattle, it is not surprising that households in the West spend the most on coffee—30 percent more than average on all coffee, and 33 percent more on roasted coffee. Spending on alcoholic beverages at home is highest in the Northeast; Southerners spend the most for beer and ale, while Westerners spend 40 percent more than average on wine at home. Away-from-home alcoholic beverage spending is highest in the West, which also has the greatest household spending on food away from home and on alcohol purchased while on trips. But Midwesterners spend the most on beer and ale away from home— 15 percent more than average.

Region

average spending

(average annual spending of consumer units on food and alcoholic beverages, by region in which consumer unit lives, 1994)

	total consumer units	Northeast	Midwest	South	West
Number of consumer units (in thousands, add 000's)	102,210	20,473	25,983	34,374	21,380
Average number of persons per cu	2.5	2.5	2.5	2.5	2.7
Average before-tax income of cu	$36,838.00	$39,464.00	$33,628.00	$34,002.00	$42,219.00
Average spending of cu, total	31,750.63	32,565.23	30,335.31	30,086.12	35,367.64
Food, average spending	4,410.52	4,706.02	4,200.68	4,251.14	4,638.92
Alcoholic beverages, average spending	278.03	313.15	246.45	261.83	308.83
FOOD AT HOME	**$2,712.05**	**$2,934.47**	**$2,536.85**	**$2,618.34**	**$2,862.40**
Cereals and bakery products	**428.68**	**481.07**	**412.01**	**402.12**	**441.34**
Cereals and cereal products	161.74	170.76	154.56	152.25	177.15
Flour	7.60	5.23	6.51	7.60	11.23
Prepared flour mixes	12.79	11.36	13.64	12.76	13.19
Ready-to-eat and cooked cereals	98.27	101.73	100.64	93.49	99.77
Rice	15.43	18.70	9.20	14.47	21.41
Pasta, cornmeal, and other cereal products	27.65	33.74	24.58	23.93	31.54
Bakery products	266.93	310.31	257.45	249.86	264.20
Bread	76.22	89.48	76.79	69.08	74.25
White bread	37.65	41.97	38.45	37.96	32.00
Bread, other than white	38.57	47.51	38.34	31.12	42.25
Crackers and cookies	62.56	68.42	58.93	63.08	60.47
Cookies	42.97	48.04	39.58	44.12	40.34
Crackers	19.59	20.37	19.35	18.96	20.13
Frozen and refrigerated bakery products	21.56	21.55	20.84	23.59	19.19
Other bakery products	106.59	130.86	100.89	94.12	110.28
Biscuits and rolls	35.96	48.70	31.96	30.90	36.70
Cakes and cupcakes	31.19	37.12	27.85	30.95	29.94
Bread and cracker products	4.72	6.37	4.71	3.75	4.74
Sweetrolls, coffee cakes, doughnuts	21.92	25.65	23.75	17.55	23.15
Pies, tarts, turnovers	12.80	13.03	12.61	10.97	15.76
Meats, poultry, fish, and eggs	**732.45**	**840.14**	**646.59**	**749.69**	**705.41**
Beef	226.76	238.32	203.84	240.02	222.11
Ground beef	88.45	84.52	87.42	94.02	84.50
Roast	39.41	42.63	33.86	39.55	42.84
Chuck roast	12.26	10.05	10.77	14.49	12.60
Round roast	14.84	20.78	11.56	12.09	17.53
Other roast	12.31	11.80	11.53	12.97	12.70
Steak	84.75	94.86	71.19	91.12	81.24
Round steak	16.00	15.72	14.33	16.69	17.22
Sirloin steak	24.44	32.56	19.61	25.48	20.79
Other steak	44.31	46.58	37.24	48.95	43.23
Other beef	14.15	16.31	11.38	15.33	13.53
Pork	155.74	161.16	146.41	169.69	139.35
Bacon	22.78	16.51	20.09	29.69	20.98
Pork chops	39.32	43.08	39.78	43.06	29.11

	total consumer units	Northeast	Midwest	South	West
Ham	$36.88	$44.22	$31.95	$38.08	$33.87
Ham, not canned	34.16	41.15	31.15	36.07	28.00
Canned ham	2.72	3.07	0.79	2.01	5.88
Sausage	22.82	24.63	21.27	26.60	16.88
Other pork	33.93	32.72	33.33	32.26	38.52
Other meats	93.95	111.09	95.44	86.83	87.08
Frankfurters	18.76	20.50	17.91	18.60	18.35
Lunch meats (cold cuts)	65.66	78.23	69.58	60.11	57.70
Bologna, liverwurst, salami	23.73	28.58	23.59	20.77	23.98
Other lunchmeats	41.93	49.65	45.99	39.33	33.72
Lamb, organ meats and others	9.53	12.36	7.94	8.13	11.02
Lamb and organ meats	9.35	12.36	7.48	8.08	10.78
Mutton, goat and game	0.18	-	0.46	0.05	0.25
Poultry	136.58	177.63	114.12	135.69	125.80
Fresh and frozen chickens	107.89	145.08	87.85	105.07	101.02
Fresh and frozen whole chicken	29.56	39.89	24.57	28.05	28.13
Fresh and frozen chicken parts	78.33	105.19	63.28	77.02	72.89
Other poultry	28.69	32.55	26.27	30.62	24.78
Fish and seafood	89.43	122.53	62.13	86.48	95.54
Canned fish and seafood	15.03	18.51	12.23	14.70	15.60
Fresh fish and shellfish	51.26	74.65	31.76	52.13	51.04
Frozen fish and shellfish	23.15	29.37	18.13	19.65	28.91
Eggs	30.00	29.42	24.65	30.97	35.53
Dairy products	**288.92**	**319.12**	**268.66**	**271.32**	**312.93**
Fresh milk and cream	127.13	132.36	121.51	122.41	136.58
Fresh milk, all types	118.94	122.63	114.58	115.80	125.80
Cream	8.19	9.74	6.93	6.61	10.78
Other dairy products	161.79	186.76	147.15	148.91	176.34
Butter	11.65	18.04	10.02	9.14	11.53
Cheese	81.83	96.31	72.13	77.21	87.18
Ice cream and related products	47.64	49.31	44.36	44.29	55.44
Miscellaneous dairy products	20.66	23.10	20.65	18.27	22.19
Fruits and vegetables	**436.57**	**509.17**	**400.65**	**404.06**	**462.83**
Fresh fruits	133.02	157.58	120.20	117.62	149.83
Apples	25.37	28.06	23.85	23.16	28.18
Bananas	29.66	32.19	26.84	26.87	35.17
Oranges	16.36	21.49	15.70	12.96	17.70
Citrus fruits, excl. oranges	10.96	13.22	9.69	8.92	13.65
Other fresh fruits	50.67	62.62	44.12	45.71	55.14
Fresh vegetables	134.89	168.27	113.07	123.93	147.03
Potatoes	28.01	31.70	25.22	29.83	24.91
Lettuce	17.38	23.29	14.87	14.92	18.69
Tomatoes	21.01	27.02	14.98	19.94	24.30
Other fresh vegetables	68.50	86.26	58.00	59.23	79.13

	total consumer units	Northeast	Midwest	South	West
Processed fruits	$93.08	$106.55	$95.25	$82.46	$94.61
Frozen fruits and fruit juices	16.28	12.50	19.55	13.55	20.36
Frozen orange juice	9.49	7.09	11.42	8.60	10.89
Frozen fruits	1.60	0.99	1.90	1.70	1.65
Frozen fruit juices	5.19	4.42	6.23	3.25	7.82
Canned fruit	14.23	13.76	16.94	12.07	14.88
Dried fruit	5.89	5.42	6.75	4.99	6.78
Fresh fruit juices	17.90	26.77	15.36	16.32	14.98
Canned and bottled fruit juices	38.78	48.10	36.66	35.53	37.61
Processed vegetables	75.57	76.78	72.14	80.05	71.37
Frozen vegetables	24.83	29.95	23.26	24.34	22.60
Canned and dried vegetables and juices	50.74	46.83	48.87	55.71	48.77
Canned beans	10.44	9.76	10.09	12.73	7.84
Canned corn	6.81	6.19	6.99	7.73	5.69
Other canned and dried vegetables	27.05	23.75	24.79	29.88	28.41
Frozen vegetable juices	0.23	0.21	0.28	0.16	0.30
Fresh and canned vegetable juices	6.21	6.92	6.72	5.21	6.53
Other food at home	**825.43**	**784.97**	**808.94**	**791.16**	**939.89**
Sugar and other sweets	105.25	103.00	105.22	101.14	114.10
Candy and chewing gum	62.32	61.23	68.69	53.33	70.11
Sugar	18.31	17.66	15.02	21.36	18.01
Artificial sweeteners	3.39	3.36	1.95	4.98	2.63
Jams, preserves, other sweets	21.23	20.75	19.55	21.47	23.36
Fats and oils	79.25	81.94	67.03	83.01	85.50
Margarine	14.16	14.59	11.90	15.96	13.59
Fats and oils	23.09	25.51	15.65	26.03	25.06
Salad dressings	23.75	23.55	21.99	22.85	27.53
Nondairy cream and imitation milk	6.56	7.22	5.64	6.26	7.54
Peanut butter	11.70	11.07	11.86	11.90	11.78
Miscellaneous foods	361.62	332.56	357.42	343.85	423.51
Frozen prepared foods	66.14	55.57	71.78	62.82	74.83
Frozen meals	21.43	15.91	22.42	20.06	27.77
Other frozen prepared foods	44.71	39.66	49.36	42.76	47.05
Canned and packaged soups	29.55	28.99	27.60	28.97	33.39
Potato chips, nuts, and other snacks	74.07	70.84	73.53	72.46	80.44
Potato chips and other snacks	58.18	54.16	58.71	57.98	61.72
Nuts	15.89	16.68	14.82	14.48	18.71
Condiments and seasonings	79.74	71.40	80.21	74.67	95.42
Salt, spices and other seasonings	19.30	16.42	17.56	20.24	22.71
Olives, pickles, relishes	10.16	7.51	11.73	7.58	14.99
Sauces and gravies	36.43	34.44	37.23	34.20	40.97
Baking needs and misc. products	13.85	13.04	13.68	12.66	16.76
Other canned/packaged prepared foods	112.12	105.74	104.30	104.93	139.44
Prepared salads	10.97	12.64	11.67	8.94	11.79
Prepared desserts	7.99	7.88	8.80	7.28	8.24

	total consumer units	Northeast	Midwest	South	West
Baby food	$28.11	$32.19	$26.17	$25.65	$30.51
Miscellaneous prepared foods	65.05	53.03	57.66	63.05	88.89
Nonalcoholic beverages	232.89	222.64	233.62	227.08	251.29
Cola	89.45	73.14	100.45	91.64	88.26
Other carbonated drinks	38.89	35.90	43.44	37.33	38.74
Coffee	43.01	44.88	38.97	36.88	56.04
Roasted coffee	29.13	31.39	26.73	23.69	38.65
Instant and freeze-dried coffee	13.88	13.49	12.24	13.18	17.40
Noncarb. fruit flavored drinks incl. non-frozen lemonade	21.86	21.73	21.87	19.98	24.99
Tea	16.25	24.28	12.26	14.60	16.02
Nonalcoholic beer	0.66	1.48	0.76	0.29	0.36
Other nonalcoholic beverages	22.77	21.22	15.88	26.36	26.87
Food prepared by cu on out-of-town trips	46.41	44.83	45.65	36.08	65.47
FOOD AWAY FROM HOME	**1,698.46**	**1,771.55**	**1,663.83**	**1,632.79**	**1,776.52**
Meals at restaurants, carry-outs, other	**1,306.21**	**1,273.27**	**1,271.56**	**1,314.96**	**1,366.17**
Lunch	451.76	449.38	434.70	474.04	438.87
Dinner	651.79	629.06	639.32	644.65	700.45
Snacks and nonalcoholic beverages	101.72	108.61	100.17	92.73	111.47
Breakfast and brunch	100.95	86.22	97.36	103.53	115.38
Board (including at school)	**50.72**	**60.77**	**70.75**	**40.66**	**32.91**
Catered affairs	**56.09**	**136.28**	**49.43**	**21.12**	**43.66**
Food on out-of-town trips	**207.89**	**227.36**	**188.89**	**182.51**	**253.13**
School lunches	**53.76**	**47.66**	**59.97**	**58.71**	**44.10**
Meals as pay	**23.79**	**26.22**	**23.23**	**14.84**	**36.56**
ALCOHOLIC BEVERAGES	**278.03**	**313.15**	**246.45**	**261.83**	**308.83**
At home	**165.13**	**187.19**	**132.00**	**168.13**	**179.39**
Beer and ale	99.68	99.84	88.30	107.99	100.00
Whiskey	13.68	16.56	5.00	17.82	14.82
Wine	36.41	49.86	21.26	30.74	51.07
Other alcoholic beverages	15.35	20.92	17.45	11.58	13.50
Away from home	**112.91**	**125.96**	**114.45**	**93.70**	**129.44**
Beer and ale	38.56	40.10	44.24	31.31	41.84
Wine	15.79	17.92	14.64	13.96	18.08
Other alcoholic beverages	27.96	32.68	26.23	24.55	31.02
Alcoholic beverages purchased on trips	30.61	35.27	29.34	23.88	38.50

Note: Expenditures listed for items in a given category may not add to the total for that category because the listing is incomplete. (-) means insufficient data.

Region

indexed spending

(indexed average annual spending of consumer units on food and alcoholic beverages, by region in which consumer unit lives, 1994; index definition: an index of 100 is the average for all consumer units; an index of 132 means that spending by consumer units in the region is 32 percent above the average for all consumer units; an index of 68 indicates that spending by consumer units in the region is 32 percent below the average for all consumer units)

	total consumer units	Northeast	Midwest	South	West
Average spending of cu, total	*$31,751.63*	*$32,565.23*	*$30,335.31*	*$30,086.12*	*$35,368.64*
Average spending of cu, index	*100*	*103*	*96*	*95*	*111*
Food, spending index	*100*	*107*	*95*	*96*	*105*
Alcoholic beverages, spending index	*100*	*113*	*89*	*94*	*111*
FOOD AT HOME	**100**	**108**	**94**	**97**	**106**
Cereals and bakery products	**100**	**112**	**96**	**94**	**103**
Cereals and cereal products	100	106	96	94	110
Flour	100	69	86	100	148
Prepared flour mixes	100	89	107	100	103
Ready-to-eat and cooked cereals	100	104	102	95	102
Rice	100	121	60	94	139
Pasta, cornmeal, and other cereal products	100	122	89	87	114
Bakery products	100	116	96	94	99
Bread	100	117	101	91	97
White bread	100	111	102	101	85
Bread, other than white	100	123	99	81	110
Crackers and cookies	100	109	94	101	97
Cookies	100	112	92	103	94
Crackers	100	104	99	97	103
Frozen and refrigerated bakery products	100	100	97	109	89
Other bakery products	100	123	95	88	103
Biscuits and rolls	100	135	89	86	102
Cakes and cupcakes	100	119	89	99	96
Bread and cracker products	100	135	100	79	100
Sweetrolls, coffee cakes, doughnuts	100	117	108	80	106
Pies, tarts, turnovers	100	102	99	86	123
Meats, poultry, fish, and eggs	**100**	**115**	**88**	**102**	**96**
Beef	100	105	90	106	98
Ground beef	100	96	99	106	96
Roast	100	108	86	100	109
Chuck roast	100	82	88	118	103
Round roast	100	140	78	81	118
Other roast	100	96	94	105	103
Steak	100	112	84	108	96
Round steak	100	98	90	104	108
Sirloin steak	100	133	80	104	85
Other steak	100	105	84	110	98
Other beef	100	115	80	108	96
Pork	100	103	94	109	89
Bacon	100	72	88	130	92
Pork chops	100	110	101	110	74

	total consumer units	Northeast	Midwest	South	West
Ham	100	120	87	103	92
Ham, not canned	100	120	91	106	82
Canned ham	100	113	29	74	216
Sausage	100	108	93	117	74
Other pork	100	96	98	95	114
Other meats	100	118	102	92	93
Frankfurters	100	109	95	99	98
Lunch meats (cold cuts)	100	119	106	92	88
Bologna, liverwurst, salami	100	120	99	88	101
Other lunchmeats	100	118	110	94	80
Lamb, organ meats and others	100	130	83	85	116
Lamb and organ meats	100	132	80	86	115
Mutton, goat and game	100	-	256	28	139
Poultry	100	130	84	99	92
Fresh and frozen chickens	100	134	81	97	94
Fresh and frozen whole chicken	100	135	83	95	95
Fresh and frozen chicken parts	100	134	81	98	93
Other poultry	100	113	92	107	86
Fish and seafood	100	137	69	97	107
Canned fish and seafood	100	123	81	98	104
Fresh fish and shellfish	100	146	62	102	100
Frozen fish and shellfish	100	127	78	85	125
Eggs	100	98	82	103	118
Dairy products	**100**	**110**	**93**	**94**	**108**
Fresh milk and cream	100	104	96	96	107
Fresh milk, all types	100	103	96	97	106
Cream	100	119	85	81	132
Other dairy products	100	115	91	92	109
Butter	100	155	86	78	99
Cheese	100	118	88	94	107
Ice cream and related products	100	104	93	93	116
Miscellaneous dairy products	100	112	100	88	107
Fruits and vegetables	**100**	**117**	**92**	**93**	**106**
Fresh fruits	100	118	90	88	113
Apples	100	111	94	91	111
Bananas	100	109	90	91	119
Oranges	100	131	96	79	108
Citrus fruits, excl. oranges	100	121	88	81	125
Other fresh fruits	100	124	87	90	109
Fresh vegetables	100	125	84	92	109
Potatoes	100	113	90	106	89
Lettuce	100	134	86	86	108
Tomatoes	100	129	71	95	116
Other fresh vegetables	100	126	85	86	116

	total consumer units	Northeast	Midwest	South	West
Processed fruits	100	114	102	89	102
Frozen fruits and fruit juices	100	77	120	83	125
Frozen orange juice	100	75	120	91	115
Frozen fruits	100	62	119	106	103
Frozen fruit juices	100	85	120	63	151
Canned fruit	100	97	119	85	105
Dried fruit	100	92	115	85	115
Fresh fruit juices	100	150	86	91	84
Canned and bottled fruit juices	100	124	95	92	97
Processed vegetables	100	102	95	106	94
Frozen vegetables	100	121	94	98	91
Canned and dried vegetables and juices	100	92	96	110	96
Canned beans	100	93	97	122	75
Canned corn	100	91	103	114	84
Other canned and dried vegetables	100	88	92	110	105
Frozen vegetable juices	100	91	122	70	130
Fresh and canned vegetable juices	100	111	108	84	105
Other food at home	**100**	**95**	**98**	**96**	**114**
Sugar and other sweets	100	98	100	96	108
Candy and chewing gum	100	98	110	86	113
Sugar	100	96	82	117	98
Artificial sweeteners	100	99	58	147	78
Jams, preserves, other sweets	100	98	92	101	110
Fats and oils	100	103	85	105	108
Margarine	100	103	84	113	96
Fats and oils	100	110	68	113	109
Salad dressings	100	99	93	96	116
Nondairy cream and imitation milk	100	110	86	95	115
Peanut butter	100	95	101	102	101
Miscellaneous foods	100	92	99	95	117
Frozen prepared foods	100	84	109	95	113
Frozen meals	100	74	105	94	130
Other frozen prepared foods	100	89	110	96	105
Canned and packaged soups	100	98	93	98	113
Potato chips, nuts, and other snacks	100	96	99	98	109
Potato chips and other snacks	100	93	101	100	106
Nuts	100	105	93	91	118
Condiments and seasonings	100	90	101	94	120
Salt, spices and other seasonings	100	85	91	105	118
Olives, pickles, relishes	100	74	115	75	148
Sauces and gravies	100	95	102	94	112
Baking needs and misc. products	100	94	99	91	121
Other canned/packaged prepared foods	100	94	93	94	124
Prepared salads	100	115	106	81	107
Prepared desserts	100	99	110	91	103

	total consumer units	Northeast	Midwest	South	West
Baby food	100	115	93	91	109
Miscellaneous prepared foods	100	82	89	97	137
Nonalcoholic beverages	100	96	100	98	108
Cola	100	82	112	102	99
Other carbonated drinks	100	92	112	96	100
Coffee	100	104	91	86	130
Roasted coffee	100	108	92	81	133
Instant and freeze-dried coffee	100	97	88	95	125
Noncarb. fruit flavored drinks incl. non-frozen lemonade	100	99	100	91	114
Tea	100	149	75	90	99
Nonalcoholic beer	100	224	115	44	55
Other nonalcoholic beverages	100	93	70	116	118
Food prepared by cu on out-of-town trips	100	97	98	78	141
FOOD AWAY FROM HOME	**100**	**104**	**98**	**96**	**105**
Meals at restaurants, carry-outs, other	**100**	**97**	**97**	**101**	**105**
Lunch	100	99	96	105	97
Dinner	100	97	98	99	107
Snacks and nonalcoholic beverages	100	107	98	91	110
Breakfast and brunch	100	85	96	103	114
Board (including at school)	**100**	**120**	**139**	**80**	**65**
Catered affairs	**100**	**243**	**88**	**38**	**78**
Food on out-of-town trips	**100**	**109**	**91**	**88**	**122**
School lunches	**100**	**89**	**112**	**109**	**82**
Meals as pay	**100**	**110**	**98**	**62**	**154**
ALCOHOLIC BEVERAGES	**100**	**113**	**89**	**94**	**111**
At home	**100**	**113**	**80**	**102**	**109**
Beer and ale	100	100	89	108	100
Whiskey	100	121	37	130	108
Wine	100	137	58	84	140
Other alcoholic beverages	100	136	114	75	88
Away from home	**100**	**112**	**101**	**83**	**115**
Beer and ale	100	104	115	81	109
Wine	100	113	93	88	115
Other alcoholic beverages	100	117	94	88	111
Alcoholic beverages purchased on trips	100	115	96	78	126

Note: (-) means insufficient data.

Region

average per capita spending

(average annual per capita spending of consumer units on food and alcoholic beverages, by region in which consumer unit lives, 1994; per capita figures are calculated by dividing the average spending of consumer units by the average number of persons per consumer unit)

	total consumer units	Northeast	Midwest	South	West
Average number of persons per cu	*2.5*	*2.5*	*2.5*	*2.5*	*2.7*
Per capita before-tax income of cu	*$14,735.20*	*$15,785.60*	*$13,451.20*	*$13,600.80*	*$15,636.67*
Per capita spending of cu, total	*12,700.25*	*13,026.09*	*12,134.12*	*12,034.45*	*13,099.13*
Food, per capita spending	*1,764.21*	*1,882.41*	*1,680.27*	*1,700.46*	*1,718.12*
Alcoholic beverages, per capita spending	*111.21*	*125.26*	*98.58*	*104.73*	*114.38*
FOOD AT HOME	**$1,084.82**	**$1,173.79**	**$1,014.74**	**$1,047.34**	**$1,060.15**
Cereals and bakery products	**171.47**	**192.43**	**164.80**	**160.85**	**163.46**
Cereals and cereal products	64.70	68.30	61.82	60.90	65.61
Flour	3.04	2.09	2.60	3.04	4.16
Prepared flour mixes	5.12	4.54	5.46	5.10	4.89
Ready-to-eat and cooked cereals	39.31	40.69	40.26	37.40	36.95
Rice	6.17	7.48	3.68	5.79	7.93
Pasta, cornmeal, and other cereal products	11.06	13.50	9.83	9.57	11.68
Bakery products	106.77	124.12	102.98	99.94	97.85
Bread	30.49	35.79	30.72	27.63	27.50
White bread	15.06	16.79	15.38	15.18	11.85
Bread, other than white	15.43	19.00	15.34	12.45	15.65
Crackers and cookies	25.02	27.37	23.57	25.23	22.40
Cookies	17.19	19.22	15.83	17.65	14.94
Crackers	7.84	8.15	7.74	7.58	7.46
Frozen and refrigerated bakery products	8.62	8.62	8.34	9.44	7.11
Other bakery products	42.64	52.34	40.36	37.65	40.84
Biscuits and rolls	14.38	19.48	12.78	12.36	13.59
Cakes and cupcakes	12.48	14.85	11.14	12.38	11.09
Bread and cracker products	1.89	2.55	1.88	1.50	1.76
Sweetrolls, coffee cakes, doughnuts	8.77	10.26	9.50	7.02	8.57
Pies, tarts, turnovers	5.12	5.21	5.04	4.39	5.84
Meats, poultry, fish, and eggs	**292.98**	**336.06**	**258.64**	**299.88**	**261.26**
Beef	90.70	95.33	81.54	96.01	82.26
Ground beef	35.38	33.81	34.97	37.61	31.30
Roast	15.76	17.05	13.54	15.82	15.87
Chuck roast	4.90	4.02	4.31	5.80	4.67
Round roast	5.94	8.31	4.62	4.84	6.49
Other roast	4.92	4.72	4.61	5.19	4.70
Steak	33.90	37.94	28.48	36.45	30.09
Round steak	6.40	6.29	5.73	6.68	6.38
Sirloin steak	9.78	13.02	7.84	10.19	7.70
Other steak	17.72	18.63	14.90	19.58	16.01
Other beef	5.66	6.52	4.55	6.13	5.01
Pork	62.30	64.46	58.56	67.88	51.61
Bacon	9.11	6.60	8.04	11.88	7.77
Pork chops	15.73	17.23	15.91	17.22	10.78

	total consumer units	Northeast	Midwest	South	West
Ham	$14.75	$17.69	$12.78	$15.23	$12.54
Ham, not canned	13.66	16.46	12.46	14.43	10.37
Canned ham	1.09	1.23	0.32	0.80	2.18
Sausage	9.13	9.85	8.51	10.64	6.25
Other pork	13.57	13.09	13.33	12.90	14.27
Other meats	37.58	44.44	38.18	34.73	32.25
Frankfurters	7.50	8.20	7.16	7.44	6.80
Lunch meats (cold cuts)	26.26	31.29	27.83	24.04	21.37
Bologna, liverwurst, salami	9.49	11.43	9.44	8.31	8.88
Other lunchmeats	16.77	19.86	18.40	15.73	12.49
Lamb, organ meats and others	3.81	4.94	3.18	3.25	4.08
Lamb and organ meats	3.74	4.94	2.99	3.23	3.99
Mutton, goat and game	0.07	-	0.18	0.02	0.09
Poultry	54.63	71.05	45.65	54.28	46.59
Fresh and frozen chickens	43.16	58.03	35.14	42.03	37.41
Fresh and frozen whole chicken	11.82	15.96	9.83	11.22	10.42
Fresh and frozen chicken parts	31.33	42.08	25.31	30.81	27.00
Other poultry	11.48	13.02	10.51	12.25	9.18
Fish and seafood	35.77	49.01	24.85	34.59	35.39
Canned fish and seafood	6.01	7.40	4.89	5.88	5.78
Fresh fish and shellfish	20.50	29.86	12.70	20.85	18.90
Frozen fish and shellfish	9.26	11.75	7.25	7.86	10.71
Eggs	12.00	11.77	9.86	12.39	13.16
Dairy products	**115.57**	**127.65**	**107.46**	**108.53**	**115.90**
Fresh milk and cream	50.85	52.94	48.60	48.96	50.59
Fresh milk, all types	47.58	49.05	45.83	46.32	46.59
Cream	3.28	3.90	2.77	2.64	3.99
Other dairy products	64.72	74.70	58.86	59.56	65.31
Butter	4.66	7.22	4.01	3.66	4.27
Cheese	32.73	38.52	28.85	30.88	32.29
Ice cream and related products	19.06	19.72	17.74	17.72	20.53
Miscellaneous dairy products	8.26	9.24	8.26	7.31	8.22
Fruits and vegetables	**174.63**	**203.67**	**160.26**	**161.62**	**171.42**
Fresh fruits	53.21	63.03	48.08	47.05	55.49
Apples	10.15	11.22	9.54	9.26	10.44
Bananas	11.86	12.88	10.74	10.75	13.03
Oranges	6.54	8.60	6.28	5.18	6.56
Citrus fruits, excl. oranges	4.38	5.29	3.88	3.57	5.06
Other fresh fruits	20.27	25.05	17.65	18.28	20.42
Fresh vegetables	53.96	67.31	45.23	49.57	54.46
Potatoes	11.20	12.68	10.09	11.93	9.23
Lettuce	6.95	9.32	5.95	5.97	6.92
Tomatoes	8.40	10.81	5.99	7.98	9.00
Other fresh vegetables	27.40	34.50	23.20	23.69	29.31

	total consumer units	Northeast	Midwest	South	West
Processed fruits	$37.23	$42.62	$38.10	$32.98	$35.04
Frozen fruits and fruit juices	6.51	5.00	7.82	5.42	7.54
Frozen orange juice	3.80	2.84	4.57	3.44	4.03
Frozen fruits	0.64	0.40	0.76	0.68	0.61
Frozen fruit juices	2.08	1.77	2.49	1.30	2.90
Canned fruit	5.69	5.50	6.78	4.83	5.51
Dried fruit	2.36	2.17	2.70	2.00	2.51
Fresh fruit juices	7.16	10.71	6.14	6.53	5.55
Canned and bottled fruit juices	15.51	19.24	14.66	14.21	13.93
Processed vegetables	30.23	30.71	28.86	32.02	26.43
Frozen vegetables	9.93	11.98	9.30	9.74	8.37
Canned and dried vegetables and juices	20.30	18.73	19.55	22.28	18.06
Canned beans	4.18	3.90	4.04	5.09	2.90
Canned corn	2.72	2.48	2.80	3.09	2.11
Other canned and dried vegetables	10.82	9.50	9.92	11.95	10.52
Frozen vegetable juices	0.09	0.08	0.11	0.06	0.11
Fresh and canned vegetable juices	2.48	2.77	2.69	2.08	2.42
Other food at home	**330.17**	**313.99**	**323.58**	**316.46**	**348.11**
Sugar and other sweets	42.10	41.20	42.09	40.46	42.26
Candy and chewing gum	24.93	24.49	27.48	21.33	25.97
Sugar	7.32	7.06	6.01	8.54	6.67
Artificial sweeteners	1.36	1.34	0.78	1.99	0.97
Jams, preserves, other sweets	8.49	8.30	7.82	8.59	8.65
Fats and oils	31.70	32.78	26.81	33.20	31.67
Margarine	5.66	5.84	4.76	6.38	5.03
Fats and oils	9.24	10.20	6.26	10.41	9.28
Salad dressings	9.50	9.42	8.80	9.14	10.20
Nondairy cream and imitation milk	2.62	2.89	2.26	2.50	2.79
Peanut butter	4.68	4.43	4.74	4.76	4.36
Miscellaneous foods	144.65	133.02	142.97	137.54	156.86
Frozen prepared foods	26.46	22.23	28.71	25.13	27.71
Frozen meals	8.57	6.36	8.97	8.02	10.29
Other frozen prepared foods	17.88	15.86	19.74	17.10	17.43
Canned and packaged soups	11.82	11.60	11.04	11.59	12.37
Potato chips, nuts, and other snacks	29.63	28.34	29.41	28.98	29.79
Potato chips and other snacks	23.27	21.66	23.48	23.19	22.86
Nuts	6.36	6.67	5.93	5.79	6.93
Condiments and seasonings	31.90	28.56	32.08	29.87	35.34
Salt, spices and other seasonings	7.72	6.57	7.02	8.10	8.41
Olives, pickles, relishes	4.06	3.00	4.69	3.03	5.55
Sauces and gravies	14.57	13.78	14.89	13.68	15.17
Baking needs and misc. products	5.54	5.22	5.47	5.06	6.21
Other canned/packaged prepared foods	44.85	42.30	41.72	41.97	51.64
Prepared salads	4.39	5.06	4.67	3.58	4.37
Prepared desserts	3.20	3.15	3.52	2.91	3.05

	total consumer units	Northeast	Midwest	South	West
Baby food	$11.24	$12.88	$10.47	$10.26	$11.30
Miscellaneous prepared foods	26.02	21.21	23.06	25.22	32.92
Nonalcoholic beverages	93.16	89.06	93.45	90.83	93.07
Cola	35.78	29.26	40.18	36.66	32.69
Other carbonated drinks	15.56	14.36	17.38	14.93	14.35
Coffee	17.20	17.95	15.59	14.75	20.76
Roasted coffee	11.65	12.56	10.69	9.48	14.31
Instant and freeze-dried coffee	5.55	5.40	4.90	5.27	6.44
Noncarb. fruit flavored drinks incl. non-frozen lemonade	8.74	8.69	8.75	7.99	9.26
Tea	6.50	9.71	4.90	5.84	5.93
Nonalcoholic beer	0.26	0.59	0.30	0.12	0.13
Other nonalcoholic beverages	9.11	8.49	6.35	10.54	9.95
Food prepared by cu on out-of-town trips	18.56	17.93	18.26	14.43	24.25
FOOD AWAY FROM HOME	**679.38**	**708.62**	**665.53**	**653.12**	**657.97**
Meals at restaurants, carry-outs, other	**522.48**	**509.31**	**508.62**	**525.98**	**505.99**
Lunch	180.70	179.75	173.88	189.62	162.54
Dinner	260.72	251.62	255.73	257.86	259.43
Snacks and nonalcoholic beverages	40.69	43.44	40.07	37.09	41.29
Breakfast and brunch	40.38	34.49	38.94	41.41	42.73
Board (including at school)	**20.29**	**24.31**	**28.30**	**16.26**	**12.19**
Catered affairs	**22.44**	**54.51**	**19.77**	**8.45**	**16.17**
Food on out-of-town trips	**83.16**	**90.94**	**75.56**	**73.00**	**93.75**
School lunches	**21.50**	**19.06**	**23.99**	**23.48**	**16.33**
Meals as pay	**9.52**	**10.49**	**9.29**	**5.94**	**13.54**
ALCOHOLIC BEVERAGES	**111.21**	**125.26**	**98.58**	**104.73**	**114.38**
At home	**66.05**	**74.88**	**52.80**	**67.25**	**66.44**
Beer and ale	39.87	39.94	35.32	43.20	37.04
Whiskey	5.47	6.62	2.00	7.13	5.49
Wine	14.56	19.94	8.50	12.30	18.91
Other alcoholic beverages	6.14	8.37	6.98	4.63	5.00
Away from home	**45.16**	**50.38**	**45.78**	**37.48**	**47.94**
Beer and ale	15.42	16.04	17.70	12.52	15.50
Wine	6.32	7.17	5.86	5.58	6.70
Other alcoholic beverages	11.18	13.07	10.49	9.82	11.49
Alcoholic beverages purchased on trips	12.24	14.11	11.74	9.55	14.26

Note: Expenditures listed for items in a given category may not add to the total for that category because the listing is incomplete. (-) means insufficient data.

Region

indexed per capita spending

(indexed average annual per capita spending of consumer units on food and alcoholic beverages, by region in which consumer unit lives, 1994; index definition: an index of 100 is the per capita average for all consumer units; an index of 132 means that per capita spending by consumer units in the region is 32 percent above the per capita average for all consumer units; an index of 68 indicates that per capita spending by consumer units in the region is 32 percent below the per capita average for all consumer units)

	total consumer units	Northeast	Midwest	South	West
Per capita spending of cu, total	*$12,700.25*	*$13,026.09*	*$12,134.12*	*$12,034.45*	*$13,099.13*
Per capita spending of cu, index	*100*	*103*	*96*	*95*	*103*
Food, per capita spending	*100*	*107*	*95*	*96*	*97*
Alcoholic beverages, per capita spending	*100*	*113*	*89*	*94*	*103*
FOOD AT HOME	**100**	**108**	**94**	**97**	**98**
Cereals and bakery products	**100**	**112**	**96**	**94**	**95**
Cereals and cereal products	100	106	96	94	101
Flour	100	69	86	100	137
Prepared flour mixes	100	89	107	100	95
Ready-to-eat and cooked cereals	100	104	102	95	94
Rice	100	121	60	94	128
Pasta, cornmeal, and other cereal products	100	122	89	87	106
Bakery products	100	116	96	94	92
Bread	100	117	101	91	90
White bread	100	111	102	101	79
Bread, other than white	100	123	99	81	101
Crackers and cookies	100	109	94	101	89
Cookies	100	112	92	103	87
Crackers	100	104	99	97	95
Frozen and refrigerated bakery products	100	100	97	109	82
Other bakery products	100	123	95	88	96
Biscuits and rolls	100	135	89	86	94
Cakes and cupcakes	100	119	89	99	89
Bread and cracker products	100	135	100	79	93
Sweetrolls, coffee cakes, doughnuts	100	117	108	80	98
Pies, tarts, turnovers	100	102	99	86	114
Meats, poultry, fish, and eggs	**100**	**115**	**88**	**102**	**89**
Beef	100	105	90	106	91
Ground beef	100	96	99	106	88
Roast	100	108	86	100	101
Chuck roast	100	82	88	118	95
Round roast	100	140	78	81	109
Other roast	100	96	94	105	96
Steak	100	112	84	108	89
Round steak	100	98	90	104	100
Sirloin steak	100	133	80	104	79
Other steak	100	105	84	110	90
Other beef	100	115	80	108	89
Pork	100	103	94	109	83
Bacon	100	72	88	130	85
Pork chops	100	110	101	110	69

	total consumer units	Northeast	Midwest	South	West
Ham	100	120	87	103	85
Ham, not canned	100	120	91	106	76
Canned ham	100	113	29	74	200
Sausage	100	108	93	117	68
Other pork	100	96	98	95	105
Other meats	100	118	102	92	86
Frankfurters	100	109	95	99	91
Lunch meats (cold cuts)	100	119	106	92	81
Bologna, liverwurst, salami	100	120	99	88	94
Other lunchmeats	100	118	110	94	74
Lamb, organ meats and others	100	130	83	85	107
Lamb and organ meats	100	132	80	86	107
Mutton, goat and game	100	-	256	28	129
Poultry	100	130	84	99	85
Fresh and frozen chickens	100	134	81	97	87
Fresh and frozen whole chicken	100	135	83	95	88
Fresh and frozen chicken parts	100	134	81	98	86
Other poultry	100	113	92	107	80
Fish and seafood	100	137	69	97	99
Canned fish and seafood	100	123	81	98	96
Fresh fish and shellfish	100	146	62	102	92
Frozen fish and shellfish	100	127	78	85	116
Eggs	100	98	82	103	110
Dairy products	**100**	**110**	**93**	**94**	**100**
Fresh milk and cream	100	104	96	96	99
Fresh milk, all types	100	103	96	97	98
Cream	100	119	85	81	122
Other dairy products	100	115	91	92	101
Butter	100	155	86	78	92
Cheese	100	118	88	94	99
Ice cream and related products	100	104	93	93	108
Miscellaneous dairy products	100	112	100	88	99
Fruits and vegetables	**100**	**117**	**92**	**93**	**98**
Fresh fruits	100	118	90	88	104
Apples	100	111	94	91	103
Bananas	100	109	90	91	110
Oranges	100	131	96	79	100
Citrus fruits, excl. oranges	100	121	88	81	115
Other fresh fruits	100	124	87	90	101
Fresh vegetables	100	125	84	92	101
Potatoes	100	113	90	106	82
Lettuce	100	134	86	86	100
Tomatoes	100	129	71	95	107
Other fresh vegetables	100	126	85	86	107

	total consumer units	Northeast	Midwest	South	West
Processed fruits	100	114	102	89	94
Frozen fruits and fruit juices	100	77	120	83	116
Frozen orange juice	100	75	120	91	106
Frozen fruits	100	62	119	106	95
Frozen fruit juices	100	85	120	63	140
Canned fruit	100	97	119	85	97
Dried fruit	100	92	115	85	107
Fresh fruit juices	100	150	86	91	77
Canned and bottled fruit juices	100	124	95	92	90
Processed vegetables	100	102	95	106	87
Frozen vegetables	100	121	94	98	84
Canned and dried vegetables and juices	100	92	96	110	89
Canned beans	100	93	97	122	70
Canned corn	100	91	103	114	77
Other canned and dried vegetables	100	88	92	110	97
Frozen vegetable juices	100	91	122	70	121
Fresh and canned vegetable juices	100	111	108	84	97
Other food at home	**100**	**95**	**98**	**96**	**105**
Sugar and other sweets	100	98	100	96	100
Candy and chewing gum	100	98	110	86	104
Sugar	100	96	82	117	91
Artificial sweeteners	100	99	58	147	72
Jams, preserves, other sweets	100	98	92	101	102
Fats and oils	100	103	85	105	100
Margarine	100	103	84	113	89
Fats and oils	100	110	68	113	100
Salad dressings	100	99	93	96	107
Nondairy cream and imitation milk	100	110	86	95	106
Peanut butter	100	95	101	102	93
Miscellaneous foods	100	92	99	95	108
Frozen prepared foods	100	84	109	95	105
Frozen meals	100	74	105	94	120
Other frozen prepared foods	100	89	110	96	97
Canned and packaged soups	100	98	93	98	105
Potato chips, nuts, and other snacks	100	96	99	98	101
Potato chips and other snacks	100	93	101	100	98
Nuts	100	105	93	91	109
Condiments and seasonings	100	90	101	94	111
Salt, spices and other seasonings	100	85	91	105	109
Olives, pickles, relishes	100	74	115	75	137
Sauces and gravies	100	95	102	94	104
Baking needs and misc. products	100	94	99	91	112
Other canned/packaged prepared foods	100	94	93	94	115
Prepared salads	100	115	106	81	100
Prepared desserts	100	99	110	91	95

	total consumer units	Northeast	Midwest	South	West
Baby food	100	115	93	91	100
Miscellaneous prepared foods	100	82	89	97	127
Nonalcoholic beverages	100	96	100	98	100
Cola	100	82	112	102	91
Other carbonated drinks	100	92	112	96	92
Coffee	100	104	91	86	121
Roasted coffee	100	108	92	81	123
Instant and freeze-dried coffee	100	97	88	95	116
Noncarb. fruit flavored drinks incl.					
non-frozen lemonade	100	99	100	91	106
Tea	100	149	75	90	91
Nonalcoholic beer	100	224	115	44	51
Other nonalcoholic beverages	100	93	70	116	109
Food prepared by cu on out-of-town trips	100	97	98	78	131
FOOD AWAY FROM HOME	**100**	**104**	**98**	**96**	**97**
Meals at restaurants, carry-outs, other	**100**	**97**	**97**	**101**	**97**
Lunch	100	99	96	105	90
Dinner	100	97	98	99	100
Snacks and nonalcoholic beverages	100	107	98	91	101
Breakfast and brunch	100	85	96	103	106
Board (including at school)	**100**	**120**	**139**	**80**	**60**
Catered affairs	**100**	**243**	**88**	**38**	**72**
Food on out-of-town trips	**100**	**109**	**91**	**88**	**113**
School lunches	**100**	**89**	**112**	**109**	**76**
Meals as pay	**100**	**110**	**98**	**62**	**142**
ALCOHOLIC BEVERAGES	**100**	**113**	**89**	**94**	**103**
At home	**100**	**113**	**80**	**102**	**101**
Beer and ale	100	100	89	108	93
Whiskey	100	121	37	130	100
Wine	100	137	58	84	130
Other alcoholic beverages	100	136	114	75	81
Away from home	**100**	**112**	**101**	**83**	**106**
Beer and ale	100	104	115	81	100
Wine	100	113	93	88	106
Other alcoholic beverages	100	117	94	88	103
Alcoholic beverages purchased on trips	100	115	96	78	116

Note: (-) means insufficient data.

Region
total spending

(total annual spending on food and alcoholic beverages by consumer units in region, 1994; numbers in thousands)

	total consumer units	Northeast	Midwest	South	West
Number of consumer units	102,210	20,473	25,983	34,374	21,380
Total spending of all cu's	$3,245,231,892	$666,707,954	$788,202,360	$1,034,180,289	$756,160,143
Food, total spending	450,799,249	96,346,347	109,146,268	146,128,686	99,180,110
Alcoholic beverages, total spending	28,417,446	6,411,120	6,403,510	9,000,144	6,602,785
FOOD AT HOME	**$277,198,631**	**$60,077,404**	**$65,914,974**	**$90,002,819**	**$61,198,112**
Cereals and bakery products	**43,815,383**	**9,848,946**	**10,705,256**	**13,822,473**	**9,435,849**
Cereals and cereal products	16,531,445	3,495,969	4,015,932	5,233,442	3,787,467
Flour	776,796	107,074	169,149	261,242	240,097
Prepared flour mixes	1,307,266	232,573	354,408	438,612	282,002
Ready-to-eat and cooked cereals	10,044,177	2,082,718	2,614,929	3,213,625	2,133,083
Rice	1,577,100	382,845	239,044	497,392	457,746
Pasta, cornmeal, and other cereal products	2,826,107	690,759	638,662	822,570	674,325
Bakery products	27,282,915	6,352,977	6,689,323	8,588,688	5,648,596
Bread	7,790,446	1,831,924	1,995,235	2,374,556	1,587,465
White bread	3,848,207	859,252	999,046	1,304,837	684,160
Bread, other than white	3,942,240	972,672	996,188	1,069,719	903,305
Crackers and cookies	6,394,258	1,400,763	1,531,178	2,168,312	1,292,849
Cookies	4,391,964	983,523	1,028,407	1,516,581	862,469
Crackers	2,002,294	417,035	502,771	651,731	430,379
Frozen and refrigerated bakery products	2,203,648	441,193	541,486	810,883	410,282
Other bakery products	10,894,564	2,679,097	2,621,425	3,235,281	2,357,786
Biscuits and rolls	3,675,472	997,035	830,417	1,062,157	784,646
Cakes and cupcakes	3,187,930	759,958	723,627	1,063,875	640,117
Bread and cracker products	482,431	130,413	122,380	128,903	101,341
Sweetrolls, coffee cakes, doughnuts	2,240,443	525,132	617,096	603,264	494,947
Pies, tarts, turnovers	1,308,288	266,763	327,646	377,083	336,949
Meats, poultry, fish, and eggs	**74,863,715**	**17,200,186**	**16,800,348**	**25,769,844**	**15,081,666**
Beef	23,177,140	4,879,125	5,296,375	8,250,447	4,748,712
Ground beef	9,040,475	1,730,378	2,271,434	3,231,843	1,806,610
Roast	4,028,096	872,764	879,784	1,359,492	915,919
Chuck roast	1,253,095	205,754	279,837	498,079	269,388
Round roast	1,516,796	425,429	300,363	415,582	374,791
Other roast	1,258,205	241,581	299,584	445,831	271,526
Steak	8,662,298	1,942,069	1,849,730	3,132,159	1,736,911
Round steak	1,635,360	321,836	372,336	573,702	368,164
Sirloin steak	2,498,012	666,601	509,527	875,850	444,490
Other steak	4,528,925	953,632	967,607	1,682,607	924,257
Other beef	1,446,272	333,915	295,687	526,953	289,271
Pork	15,918,185	3,299,429	3,804,171	5,832,924	2,979,303
Bacon	2,328,344	338,009	521,998	1,020,564	448,552
Pork chops	4,018,897	881,977	1,033,604	1,480,144	622,372

	total consumer units	Northeast	Midwest	South	West
Ham	$3,769,505	$905,316	$830,157	$1,308,962	$724,141
Ham, not canned	3,491,494	842,464	809,370	1,239,870	598,640
Canned ham	278,011	62,852	20,527	69,092	125,714
Sausage	2,332,432	504,250	552,658	914,348	360,894
Other pork	3,467,985	669,877	866,013	1,108,905	823,558
Other meats	9,602,630	2,274,346	2,479,818	2,984,694	1,861,770
Frankfurters	1,917,460	419,697	465,356	639,356	392,323
Lunch meats (cold cuts)	6,711,109	1,601,603	1,807,897	2,066,221	1,233,626
Bologna, liverwurst, salami	2,425,443	585,118	612,939	713,948	512,692
Other lunchmeats	4,285,665	1,016,484	1,194,958	1,351,929	720,934
Lamb, organ meats and others	974,061	253,046	206,305	279,461	235,608
Lamb and organ meats	955,664	253,046	194,353	277,742	230,476
Mutton, goat and game	18,398	-	11,952	1,719	5,345
Poultry	13,959,842	3,636,619	2,965,180	4,664,208	2,689,604
Fresh and frozen chickens	11,027,437	2,970,223	2,282,607	3,611,676	2,159,808
Fresh and frozen whole chicken	3,021,328	816,668	638,402	964,191	601,419
Fresh and frozen chicken parts	8,006,109	2,153,555	1,644,204	2,647,485	1,558,388
Other poultry	2,932,405	666,396	682,573	1,052,532	529,796
Fish and seafood	9,140,640	2,508,557	1,614,324	2,972,664	2,042,645
Canned fish and seafood	1,536,216	378,955	317,772	505,298	333,528
Fresh fish and shellfish	5,239,285	1,528,309	825,220	1,791,917	1,091,235
Frozen fish and shellfish	2,366,162	601,292	471,072	675,449	618,096
Eggs	3,066,300	602,316	640,481	1,064,563	759,631
Dairy products	**29,530,513**	**6,533,344**	**6,980,593**	**9,326,354**	**6,690,443**
Fresh milk and cream	12,993,957	2,709,806	3,157,194	4,207,721	2,920,080
Fresh milk, all types	12,156,857	2,510,604	2,977,132	3,980,509	2,689,604
Cream	837,100	199,407	180,062	227,212	230,476
Other dairy products	16,536,556	3,823,537	3,823,398	5,118,632	3,770,149
Butter	1,190,747	369,333	260,350	314,178	246,511
Cheese	8,363,844	1,971,755	1,874,154	2,654,017	1,863,908
Ice cream and related products	4,869,284	1,009,524	1,152,606	1,522,424	1,185,307
Miscellaneous dairy products	2,111,659	472,926	536,549	628,013	474,422
Fruits and vegetables	**44,621,820**	**10,424,237**	**10,410,089**	**13,889,158**	**9,895,305**
Fresh fruits	13,595,974	3,226,135	3,123,157	4,043,070	3,203,365
Apples	2,593,068	574,472	619,695	796,102	602,488
Bananas	3,031,549	659,026	697,384	923,629	751,935
Oranges	1,672,156	439,965	407,933	445,487	378,426
Citrus fruits, excl. oranges	1,120,222	270,653	251,775	306,616	291,837
Other fresh fruits	5,178,981	1,282,019	1,146,370	1,571,236	1,178,893
Fresh vegetables	13,787,107	3,444,992	2,937,898	4,259,970	3,143,501
Potatoes	2,862,902	648,994	655,291	1,025,376	532,576
Lettuce	1,776,410	476,816	386,367	512,860	399,592
Tomatoes	2,147,432	553,180	389,225	685,418	519,534
Other fresh vegetables	7,001,385	1,766,001	1,507,014	2,035,972	1,691,799

	total consumer units	Northeast	Midwest	South	West
Processed fruits	$9,513,707	$2,181,398	$2,474,881	$2,834,480	$2,022,762
Frozen fruits and fruit juices	1,663,979	255,913	507,968	465,768	435,297
Frozen orange juice	969,973	145,154	296,726	295,616	232,828
Frozen fruits	163,536	20,268	49,368	58,436	35,277
Frozen fruit juices	530,470	90,491	161,874	111,716	167,192
Canned fruit	1,454,448	281,708	440,152	414,894	318,134
Dried fruit	602,017	110,964	175,385	171,526	144,956
Fresh fruit juices	1,829,559	548,062	399,099	560,984	320,272
Canned and bottled fruit juices	3,963,704	984,751	952,537	1,221,308	804,102
Processed vegetables	7,724,010	1,571,917	1,874,414	2,751,639	1,525,891
Frozen vegetables	2,537,874	613,166	604,365	836,663	483,188
Canned and dried vegetables and juices	5,186,135	958,751	1,269,789	1,914,976	1,042,703
Canned beans	1,067,072	199,816	262,168	437,581	167,619
Canned corn	696,050	126,728	181,621	265,711	121,652
Other canned and dried vegetables	2,764,781	486,234	644,119	1,027,095	607,406
Frozen vegetable juices	23,508	4,299	7,275	5,500	6,414
Fresh and canned vegetable juices	634,724	141,673	174,606	179,089	139,611
Other food at home	**84,367,200**	**16,070,691**	**21,018,688**	**27,195,334**	**20,094,848**
Sugar and other sweets	10,757,603	2,108,719	2,733,931	3,476,586	2,439,458
Candy and chewing gum	6,369,727	1,253,562	1,784,772	1,833,165	1,498,952
Sugar	1,871,465	361,553	390,265	734,229	385,054
Artificial sweeteners	346,492	68,789	50,667	171,183	56,229
Jams, preserves, other sweets	2,169,918	424,815	507,968	738,010	499,437
Fats and oils	8,100,143	1,677,558	1,741,640	2,853,386	1,827,990
Margarine	1,447,294	298,701	309,198	548,609	290,554
Fats and oils	2,360,029	522,266	406,634	894,755	535,783
Salad dressings	2,427,488	482,139	571,366	785,446	588,591
Nondairy cream and imitation milk	670,498	147,815	146,544	215,181	161,205
Peanut butter	1,195,857	226,636	308,158	409,051	251,856
Miscellaneous foods	36,961,180	6,808,501	9,286,844	11,819,500	9,054,644
Frozen prepared foods	6,760,169	1,137,685	1,865,060	2,159,375	1,599,865
Frozen meals	2,190,360	325,725	582,539	689,542	593,723
Other frozen prepared foods	4,569,809	811,959	1,282,521	1,469,832	1,005,929
Canned and packaged soups	3,020,306	593,512	717,131	995,815	713,878
Potato chips, nuts, and other snacks	7,570,695	1,450,307	1,910,530	2,490,740	1,719,807
Potato chips and other snacks	5,946,578	1,108,818	1,525,462	1,993,005	1,319,574
Nuts	1,624,117	341,490	385,068	497,736	400,020
Condiments and seasonings	8,150,225	1,461,772	2,084,096	2,566,707	2,040,080
Salt, spices and other seasonings	1,972,653	336,167	456,261	695,730	485,540
Olives, pickles, relishes	1,038,454	153,752	304,781	260,555	320,486
Sauces and gravies	3,723,510	705,090	967,347	1,175,591	875,939
Baking needs and misc. products	1,415,609	266,968	355,447	435,175	358,329
Other canned/packaged prepared foods	11,459,785	2,164,815	2,710,027	3,606,864	2,981,227
Prepared salads	1,121,244	258,779	303,222	307,304	252,070
Prepared desserts	816,658	161,327	228,650	250,243	176,171

	total consumer units	Northeast	Midwest	South	West
Baby food	$2,873,123	$659,026	$679,975	$881,693	$652,304
Miscellaneous prepared foods	6,648,761	1,085,683	1,498,180	2,167,281	1,900,468
Nonalcoholic beverages	23,803,687	4,558,109	6,070,148	7,805,648	5,372,580
Cola	9,142,685	1,497,395	2,609,992	3,150,033	1,886,999
Other carbonated drinks	3,974,947	734,981	1,128,702	1,283,181	828,261
Coffee	4,396,052	918,828	1,012,558	1,267,713	1,198,135
Roasted coffee	2,977,377	642,647	694,526	814,320	826,337
Instant and freeze-dried coffee	1,418,675	276,181	318,032	453,049	372,012
Noncarb. fruit flavored drinks incl.					
non-frozen lemonade	2,234,311	444,878	568,248	686,793	534,286
Tea	1,660,913	497,084	318,552	501,860	342,508
Nonalcoholic beer	67,459	30,300	19,747	9,968	7,697
Other nonalcoholic beverages	2,327,322	434,437	412,610	906,099	574,481
Food prepared by cu on out-of-town trips	4,743,566	917,805	1,186,124	1,240,214	1,399,749
FOOD AWAY FROM HOME	**173,599,597**	**36,268,943**	**43,231,295**	**56,125,523**	**37,981,998**
Meals at restaurants, carry-outs, other	**133,507,724**	**26,067,657**	**33,038,943**	**45,200,435**	**29,208,715**
Lunch	46,174,390	9,200,157	11,294,810	16,294,651	9,383,041
Dinner	66,619,456	12,878,745	16,611,452	22,159,199	14,975,621
Snacks and nonalcoholic beverages	10,396,801	2,223,573	2,602,717	3,187,501	2,383,229
Breakfast and brunch	10,318,100	1,765,182	2,529,705	3,558,740	2,466,824
Board (including at school)	**5,184,091**	**1,244,144**	**1,838,297**	**1,397,647**	**703,616**
Catered affairs	**5,732,959**	**2,790,060**	**1,284,340**	**725,979**	**933,451**
Food on out-of-town trips	**21,248,437**	**4,654,741**	**4,907,929**	**6,273,599**	**5,411,919**
School lunches	**5,494,810**	**975,743**	**1,558,201**	**2,018,098**	**942,858**
Meals as pay	**2,431,576**	**536,802**	**603,585**	**510,110**	**781,653**
ALCOHOLIC BEVERAGES	**28,417,446**	**6,411,120**	**6,403,510**	**9,000,144**	**6,602,785**
At home	**16,877,937**	**3,832,341**	**3,429,756**	**5,779,301**	**3,835,358**
Beer and ale	10,188,293	2,044,024	2,294,299	3,712,048	2,138,000
Whiskey	1,398,233	339,033	129,915	612,545	316,852
Wine	3,721,466	1,020,784	552,399	1,056,657	1,091,877
Other alcoholic beverages	1,568,924	428,295	453,403	398,051	288,630
Away from home	**11,540,531**	**2,578,779**	**2,973,754**	**3,220,844**	**2,767,427**
Beer and ale	3,941,218	820,967	1,149,488	1,076,250	894,539
Wine	1,613,896	366,876	380,391	479,861	386,550
Other alcoholic beverages	2,857,792	669,058	681,534	843,882	663,208
Alcoholic beverages purchased on trips	3,128,648	722,083	762,341	820,851	823,130

Note: Spending for items in a given category may not add to the total for that category because the listing is incomplete. Numbers may not add to total due to rounding. (-) means insufficient data.

Region

market shares

(percent of total annual spending on food accounted for by consumer units in region, 1994)

	total consumer units	Northeast	Midwest	South	West
Share of total consumer units	100.0%	20.0%	25.4%	33.6%	20.9%
Share of total spending	100.0	20.5	24.3	31.9	23.3
Share of food spending	100.0	21.4	24.2	32.4	22.0
Share of alcoholic beverages spending	100.0	22.6	22.5	31.7	23.2
FOOD AT HOME	**100.0%**	**21.7%**	**23.8%**	**32.5%**	**22.1%**
Cereals and bakery products	**100.0**	**22.5**	**24.4**	**31.5**	**21.5**
Cereals and cereal products	100.0	21.1	24.3	31.7	22.9
Flour	100.0	13.8	21.8	33.6	30.9
Prepared flour mixes	100.0	17.8	27.1	33.6	21.6
Ready-to-eat and cooked cereals	100.0	20.7	26.0	32.0	21.2
Rice	100.0	24.3	15.2	31.5	29.0
Pasta, cornmeal, and other cereal products	100.0	24.4	22.6	29.1	23.9
Bakery products	100.0	23.3	24.5	31.5	20.7
Bread	100.0	23.5	25.6	30.5	20.4
White bread	100.0	22.3	26.0	33.9	17.8
Bread, other than white	100.0	24.7	25.3	27.1	22.9
Crackers and cookies	100.0	21.9	23.9	33.9	20.2
Cookies	100.0	22.4	23.4	34.5	19.6
Crackers	100.0	20.8	25.1	32.5	21.5
Frozen and refrigerated bakery products	100.0	20.0	24.6	36.8	18.6
Other bakery products	100.0	24.6	24.1	29.7	21.6
Biscuits and rolls	100.0	27.1	22.6	28.9	21.3
Cakes and cupcakes	100.0	23.8	22.7	33.4	20.1
Bread and cracker products	100.0	27.0	25.4	26.7	21.0
Sweetrolls, coffee cakes, doughnuts	100.0	23.4	27.5	26.9	22.1
Pies, tarts, turnovers	100.0	20.4	25.0	28.8	25.8
Meats, poultry, fish, and eggs	**100.0**	**23.0**	**22.4**	**34.4**	**20.1**
Beef	100.0	21.1	22.9	35.6	20.5
Ground beef	100.0	19.1	25.1	35.7	20.0
Roast	100.0	21.7	21.8	33.8	22.7
Chuck roast	100.0	16.4	22.3	39.7	21.5
Round roast	100.0	28.0	19.8	27.4	24.7
Other roast	100.0	19.2	23.8	35.4	21.6
Steak	100.0	22.4	21.4	36.2	20.1
Round steak	100.0	19.7	22.8	35.1	22.5
Sirloin steak	100.0	26.7	20.4	35.1	17.8
Other steak	100.0	21.1	21.4	37.2	20.4
Other beef	100.0	23.1	20.4	36.4	20.0
Pork	100.0	20.7	23.9	36.6	18.7
Bacon	100.0	14.5	22.4	43.8	19.3
Pork chops	100.0	21.9	25.7	36.8	15.5

	total consumer units	Northeast	Midwest	South	West
Ham	100.0%	24.0%	22.0%	34.7%	19.2%
Ham, not canned	100.0	24.1	23.2	35.5	17.1
Canned ham	100.0	22.6	7.4	24.9	45.2
Sausage	100.0	21.6	23.7	39.2	15.5
Other pork	100.0	19.3	25.0	32.0	23.7
Other meats	100.0	23.7	25.8	31.1	19.4
Frankfurters	100.0	21.9	24.3	33.3	20.5
Lunch meats (cold cuts)	100.0	23.9	26.9	30.8	18.4
Bologna, liverwurst, salami	100.0	24.1	25.3	29.4	21.1
Other lunchmeats	100.0	23.7	27.9	31.5	16.8
Lamb, organ meats and others	100.0	26.0	21.2	28.7	24.2
Lamb and organ meats	100.0	26.5	20.3	29.1	24.1
Mutton, goat and game	100.0	-	65.0	9.3	29.1
Poultry	100.0	26.1	21.2	33.4	19.3
Fresh and frozen chickens	100.0	26.9	20.7	32.8	19.6
Fresh and frozen whole chicken	100.0	27.0	21.1	31.9	19.9
Fresh and frozen chicken parts	100.0	26.9	20.5	33.1	19.5
Other poultry	100.0	22.7	23.3	35.9	18.1
Fish and seafood	100.0	27.4	17.7	32.5	22.3
Canned fish and seafood	100.0	24.7	20.7	32.9	21.7
Fresh fish and shellfish	100.0	29.2	15.8	34.2	20.8
Frozen fish and shellfish	100.0	25.4	19.9	28.5	26.1
Eggs	100.0	19.6	20.9	34.7	24.8
Dairy products	**100.0**	**22.1**	**23.6**	**31.6**	**22.7**
Fresh milk and cream	100.0	20.9	24.3	32.4	22.5
Fresh milk, all types	100.0	20.7	24.5	32.7	22.1
Cream	100.0	23.8	21.5	27.1	27.5
Other dairy products	100.0	23.1	23.1	31.0	22.8
Butter	100.0	31.0	21.9	26.4	20.7
Cheese	100.0	23.6	22.4	31.7	22.3
Ice cream and related products	100.0	20.7	23.7	31.3	24.3
Miscellaneous dairy products	100.0	22.4	25.4	29.7	22.5
Fruits and vegetables	**100.0**	**23.4**	**23.3**	**31.1**	**22.2**
Fresh fruits	100.0	23.7	23.0	29.7	23.6
Apples	100.0	22.2	23.9	30.7	23.2
Bananas	100.0	21.7	23.0	30.5	24.8
Oranges	100.0	26.3	24.4	26.6	22.6
Citrus fruits, excl. oranges	100.0	24.2	22.5	27.4	26.1
Other fresh fruits	100.0	24.8	22.1	30.3	22.8
Fresh vegetables	100.0	25.0	21.3	30.9	22.8
Potatoes	100.0	22.7	22.9	35.8	18.6
Lettuce	100.0	26.8	21.7	28.9	22.5
Tomatoes	100.0	25.8	18.1	31.9	24.2
Other fresh vegetables	100.0	25.2	21.5	29.1	24.2

	total consumer units	Northeast	Midwest	South	West
Processed fruits	100.0%	22.9%	26.0%	29.8%	21.3%
Frozen fruits and fruit juices	100.0	15.4	30.5	28.0	26.2
Frozen orange juice	100.0	15.0	30.6	30.5	24.0
Frozen fruits	100.0	12.4	30.2	35.7	21.6
Frozen fruit juices	100.0	17.1	30.5	21.1	31.5
Canned fruit	100.0	19.4	30.3	28.5	21.9
Dried fruit	100.0	18.4	29.1	28.5	24.1
Fresh fruit juices	100.0	30.0	21.8	30.7	17.5
Canned and bottled fruit juices	100.0	24.8	24.0	30.8	20.3
Processed vegetables	100.0	20.4	24.3	35.6	19.8
Frozen vegetables	100.0	24.2	23.8	33.0	19.0
Canned and dried vegetables and juices	100.0	18.5	24.5	36.9	20.1
Canned beans	100.0	18.7	24.6	41.0	15.7
Canned corn	100.0	18.2	26.1	38.2	17.5
Other canned and dried vegetables	100.0	17.6	23.3	37.1	22.0
Frozen vegetable juices	100.0	18.3	30.9	23.4	27.3
Fresh and canned vegetable juices	100.0	22.3	27.5	28.2	22.0
Other food at home	**100.0**	**19.0**	**24.9**	**32.2**	**23.8**
Sugar and other sweets	100.0	19.6	25.4	32.3	22.7
Candy and chewing gum	100.0	19.7	28.0	28.8	23.5
Sugar	100.0	19.3	20.9	39.2	20.6
Artificial sweeteners	100.0	19.9	14.6	49.4	16.2
Jams, preserves, other sweets	100.0	19.6	23.4	34.0	23.0
Fats and oils	100.0	20.7	21.5	35.2	22.6
Margarine	100.0	20.6	21.4	37.9	20.1
Fats and oils	100.0	22.1	17.2	37.9	22.7
Salad dressings	100.0	19.9	23.5	32.4	24.2
Nondairy cream and imitation milk	100.0	22.0	21.9	32.1	24.0
Peanut butter	100.0	19.0	25.8	34.2	21.1
Miscellaneous foods	100.0	18.4	25.1	32.0	24.5
Frozen prepared foods	100.0	16.8	27.6	31.9	23.7
Frozen meals	100.0	14.9	26.6	31.5	27.1
Other frozen prepared foods	100.0	17.8	28.1	32.2	22.0
Canned and packaged soups	100.0	19.7	23.7	33.0	23.6
Potato chips, nuts, and other snacks	100.0	19.2	25.2	32.9	22.7
Potato chips and other snacks	100.0	18.6	25.7	33.5	22.2
Nuts	100.0	21.0	23.7	30.6	24.6
Condiments and seasonings	100.0	17.9	25.6	31.5	25.0
Salt, spices and other seasonings	100.0	17.0	23.1	35.3	24.6
Olives, pickles, relishes	100.0	14.8	29.3	25.1	30.9
Sauces and gravies	100.0	18.9	26.0	31.6	23.5
Baking needs and misc. products	100.0	18.9	25.1	30.7	25.3
Other canned/packaged prepared foods	100.0	18.9	23.6	31.5	26.0
Prepared salads	100.0	23.1	27.0	27.4	22.5
Prepared desserts	100.0	19.8	28.0	30.6	21.6

	total consumer units	Northeast	Midwest	South	West
Baby food	100.0%	22.9%	23.7%	30.7%	22.7%
Miscellaneous prepared foods	100.0	16.3	22.5	32.6	28.6
Nonalcoholic beverages	100.0	19.1	25.5	32.8	22.6
Cola	100.0	16.4	28.5	34.5	20.6
Other carbonated drinks	100.0	18.5	28.4	32.3	20.8
Coffee	100.0	20.9	23.0	28.8	27.3
Roasted coffee	100.0	21.6	23.3	27.4	27.8
Instant and freeze-dried coffee	100.0	19.5	22.4	31.9	26.2
Noncarb. fruit flavored drinks incl.					
non-frozen lemonade	100.0	19.9	25.4	30.7	23.9
Tea	100.0	29.9	19.2	30.2	20.6
Nonalcoholic beer	100.0	44.9	29.3	14.8	11.4
Other nonalcoholic beverages	100.0	18.7	17.7	38.9	24.7
Food prepared by cu on out-of-town trips	100.0	19.3	25.0	26.1	29.5
FOOD AWAY FROM HOME	**100.0**	**20.9**	**24.9**	**32.3**	**21.9**
Meals at restaurants, carry-outs, other	**100.0**	**19.5**	**24.7**	**33.9**	**21.9**
Lunch	100.0	19.9	24.5	35.3	20.3
Dinner	100.0	19.3	24.9	33.3	22.5
Snacks and nonalcoholic beverages	100.0	21.4	25.0	30.7	22.9
Breakfast and brunch	100.0	17.1	24.5	34.5	23.9
Board (including at school)	**100.0**	**24.0**	**35.5**	**27.0**	**13.6**
Catered affairs	**100.0**	**48.7**	**22.4**	**12.7**	**16.3**
Food on out-of-town trips	**100.0**	**21.9**	**23.1**	**29.5**	**25.5**
School lunches	**100.0**	**17.8**	**28.4**	**36.7**	**17.2**
Meals as pay	**100.0**	**22.1**	**24.8**	**21.0**	**32.1**
ALCOHOLIC BEVERAGES	**100.0**	**22.6**	**22.5**	**31.7**	**23.2**
At home	**100.0**	**22.7**	**20.3**	**34.2**	**22.7**
Beer and ale	100.0	20.1	22.5	36.4	21.0
Whiskey	100.0	24.2	9.3	43.8	22.7
Wine	100.0	27.4	14.8	28.4	29.3
Other alcoholic beverages	100.0	27.3	28.9	25.4	18.4
Away from home	**100.0**	**22.3**	**25.8**	**27.9**	**24.0**
Beer and ale	100.0	20.8	29.2	27.3	22.7
Wine	100.0	22.7	23.6	29.7	24.0
Other alcoholic beverages	100.0	23.4	23.8	29.5	23.2
Alcoholic beverages purchased on trips	100.0	23.1	24.4	26.2	26.3

Note: Numbers may not add to total due to rounding. (-) means insufficient data.

Chapter 6

Spending by
Race & Hispanic Origin

White households spend more on food than black households, but Hispanic households spend more on food than those headed by non-Hispanics. Behind these spending patterns are the greater incomes of whites relative to blacks and the larger household size of Hispanics relative to non-Hispanics.

White and "other" households (including Asians and Native Americans) spend 3 percent more than average on food, while black households spend 23 percent less. Hispanic households spend 2 percent more than average on food, while non-Hispanic households spend an average amount.

After adjusting for household size, however, the spending patterns change. On a per capita basis, Hispanic households spend 25 percent less than average on food, while non-Hispanics continue to spend an average amount. Black households spend 31 percent less than average on food, after adjusting for household size, while white households spend 3 percent more. Whites spend more than average on many foods, including every category of food away from home. But blacks and Hispanics outspend whites in a number of food-at-home categories. Blacks spend more per capita than whites on some meats—they spend 24 percent more on pork in general, 36 percent more on bacon and pork chops, and 48 percent more on sausage. They also spend 34 percent more on whole chickens, both fresh and frozen, and 26 percent more on fresh fish and shellfish. Spending on beef among blacks is higher than average for roasts, but lower than average for steak. Blacks spend significantly less than average on dairy products. Their genetic predisposition to lactose intolerance may account for the 33 to 51 percent below-average spending in dairy categories.

Hispanic spending patterns reveal ethnic food traditions. Hispanics spend more per capita than any other group on flour and rice. They also spend more on beef, particularly steak. Spending on lamb and organ meats is 68 percent higher per capita among Hispanics, whose cuisines include many dishes making use of these less-common cuts. Per capita egg consumption among Hispanics is 57 percent higher than average as well. Other foods on which Hispanic spending is considerably above average include tropical fruits such as bananas, oranges and other citrus fruits. Fresh vegetable spending is slightly higher than average, but per capita spending on tomatoes, the backbone of many Hispanic recipes, is 48 percent higher than average. Not surprisingly, given the ingredients commonly used in many Hispanic cuisines, per capita fat and oil spending is 76 percent higher than average. And given the comparatively high birth rate among Hispanics, it is also not surprising that their spending on baby food is 43 percent higher than average.

Race & Hispanic Origin

average spending

(average annual spending of consumer units on food and alcoholic beverages, by race and Hispanic origin of consumer unit reference person, 1994)

	total consumer units	race white and other	race black	Hispanic origin non-Hispanic	Hispanic origin Hispanic
Number of consumer units (in thousands, add 000's)	102,210	90,740	11,470	94,479	7,730
Average number of persons per cu	2.5	2.5	2.8	2.5	3.4
Average before-tax income of cu	$36,838.00	$38,212.00	$25,250.00	$37,708.00	$26,821.00
Average spending of cu, total	31,750.63	32,934.93	22,418.27	32,185.56	26,437.49
Food, average spending	4,410.52	4,541.71	3,389.94	4,403.81	4,495.88
Alcoholic beverages, average spending	278.03	294.58	149.49	283.49	210.75
FOOD AT HOME	**$2,712.05**	**$2,753.59**	**$2,390.00**	**$2,662.67**	**$3,322.31**
Cereals and bakery products	**428.68**	**439.76**	**342.97**	**424.51**	**480.09**
Cereals and cereal products	161.74	162.63	154.93	156.35	228.38
Flour	7.60	7.04	11.94	6.57	20.39
Prepared flour mixes	12.79	12.67	13.75	12.66	14.39
Ready-to-eat and cooked cereals	98.27	99.65	87.62	96.74	117.22
Rice	15.43	14.99	18.79	13.57	38.36
Pasta, cornmeal, and other cereal products	27.65	28.28	22.83	26.81	38.02
Bakery products	266.93	277.13	188.04	268.16	251.71
Bread	76.22	77.65	65.12	75.12	89.85
White bread	37.65	37.52	38.66	36.98	45.95
Bread, other than white	38.57	40.13	26.46	38.14	43.90
Crackers and cookies	62.56	64.82	45.01	63.18	54.79
Cookies	42.97	44.21	33.33	43.02	42.37
Crackers	19.59	20.61	11.68	20.17	12.42
Frozen and refrigerated bakery products	21.56	22.43	14.84	22.09	15.02
Other bakery products	106.59	112.22	63.07	107.77	92.06
Biscuits and rolls	35.96	38.08	19.53	36.72	26.50
Cakes and cupcakes	31.19	32.40	21.85	31.18	31.35
Bread and cracker products	4.72	5.08	1.97	4.91	2.41
Sweetrolls, coffee cakes, doughnuts	21.92	23.09	12.88	21.88	22.44
Pies, tarts, turnovers	12.80	13.57	6.85	13.08	9.37
Meats, poultry, fish, and eggs	**732.45**	**716.27**	**857.65**	**708.53**	**1,027.96**
Beef	226.76	223.69	250.47	215.63	364.23
Ground beef	88.45	87.77	93.70	84.85	132.97
Roast	39.41	38.40	47.20	38.30	53.06
Chuck roast	12.26	11.91	14.96	12.00	15.46
Round roast	14.84	14.88	14.52	14.17	23.07
Other roast	12.31	11.61	17.72	12.13	14.53
Steak	84.75	83.99	90.61	79.57	148.70
Round steak	16.00	15.82	17.43	13.88	42.22
Sirloin steak	24.44	24.72	22.28	22.93	43.00
Other steak	44.31	43.45	50.90	42.75	63.47
Other beef	14.15	13.53	18.97	12.91	29.51
Pork	155.74	147.93	216.10	152.19	199.58
Bacon	22.78	21.23	34.78	22.56	25.55
Pork chops	39.32	36.64	60.08	38.16	53.70

	total consumer units	race		Hispanic origin	
		white and other	black	non-Hispanic	Hispanic
Ham	$36.88	$37.39	$32.97	$36.40	$42.86
Ham, not canned	34.16	34.47	31.77	33.76	39.10
Canned ham	2.72	2.92	1.20	2.64	3.76
Sausage	22.82	20.88	37.86	22.72	24.06
Other pork	33.93	31.79	50.42	32.35	53.40
Other meats	93.95	94.72	87.95	92.32	114.07
Frankfurters	18.76	18.65	19.58	18.30	24.42
Lunch meats (cold cuts)	65.66	66.90	56.04	65.48	67.88
Bologna, liverwurst, salami	23.73	23.65	24.29	22.95	33.36
Other lunchmeats	41.93	43.25	31.75	42.53	34.52
Lamb, organ meats and others	9.53	9.17	12.34	8.54	21.77
Lamb and organ meats	9.35	8.98	12.20	8.39	21.25
Mutton, goat and game	0.18	0.19	0.14	0.16	0.53
Poultry	136.58	133.09	163.58	133.04	180.34
Fresh and frozen chickens	107.89	103.88	138.97	103.48	162.48
Fresh and frozen whole chicken	29.56	27.63	44.47	27.77	51.70
Fresh and frozen chicken parts	78.33	76.24	94.51	75.71	110.78
Other poultry	28.69	29.22	24.61	29.56	17.86
Fish and seafood	89.43	87.38	105.26	88.10	105.88
Canned fish and seafood	15.03	15.41	12.03	14.91	16.51
Fresh fish and shellfish	51.26	48.55	72.15	49.51	72.83
Frozen fish and shellfish	23.15	23.41	21.08	23.68	16.54
Eggs	30.00	29.45	34.27	27.26	63.86
Dairy products	**288.92**	**301.36**	**192.67**	**284.72**	**340.78**
Fresh milk and cream	127.13	131.44	93.82	122.64	182.70
Fresh milk, all types	118.94	122.84	88.79	114.42	174.78
Cream	8.19	8.60	5.03	8.21	7.92
Other dairy products	161.79	169.92	98.85	162.09	158.08
Butter	11.65	11.84	10.20	11.39	14.84
Cheese	81.83	86.64	44.65	81.53	85.59
Ice cream and related products	47.64	49.66	31.98	48.36	38.71
Miscellaneous dairy products	20.66	21.78	12.03	20.80	18.94
Fruits and vegetables	**436.57**	**445.18**	**369.99**	**425.93**	**568.05**
Fresh fruits	133.02	137.51	98.31	128.90	183.96
Apples	25.37	26.14	19.39	24.93	30.74
Bananas	29.66	30.47	23.37	28.13	48.63
Oranges	16.36	16.36	16.33	15.74	23.98
Citrus fruits, excl. oranges	10.96	11.43	7.37	10.44	17.48
Other fresh fruits	50.67	53.10	31.85	49.66	63.13
Fresh vegetables	134.89	138.40	107.75	130.42	190.19
Potatoes	28.01	28.07	27.51	27.56	33.54
Lettuce	17.38	18.21	10.90	16.84	23.96
Tomatoes	21.01	21.73	15.47	19.29	42.30
Other fresh vegetables	68.50	70.39	53.87	66.72	90.40

	total consumer units	race		Hispanic origin	
		white and other	black	non-Hispanic	Hispanic
Processed fruits	$93.08	$93.44	$90.33	$91.62	$111.13
Frozen fruits and fruit juices	16.28	16.71	12.94	16.18	17.51
Frozen orange juice	9.49	9.73	7.61	9.42	10.43
Frozen fruits	1.60	1.60	1.57	1.62	1.33
Frozen fruit juices	5.19	5.38	3.77	5.15	5.75
Canned fruit	14.23	15.00	8.33	14.49	11.06
Dried fruit	5.89	6.03	4.81	5.95	5.15
Fresh fruit juices	17.90	17.28	22.64	17.40	23.99
Canned and bottled fruit juices	38.78	38.41	41.61	37.59	53.42
Processed vegetables	75.57	75.83	73.59	74.99	82.76
Frozen vegetables	24.83	25.23	21.78	25.39	17.99
Canned and dried vegetables and juices	50.74	50.60	51.81	49.61	64.78
Canned beans	10.44	10.28	11.67	10.32	12.00
Canned corn	6.81	6.58	8.58	6.72	7.88
Other canned and dried vegetables	27.05	27.24	25.57	26.15	38.13
Frozen vegetable juices	0.23	0.20	0.45	0.24	0.10
Fresh and canned vegetable juices	6.21	6.30	5.54	6.17	6.66
Other food at home	**825.43**	**851.02**	**626.73**	**818.97**	**905.43**
Sugar and other sweets	105.25	107.56	87.41	104.36	116.24
Candy and chewing gum	62.32	65.25	39.66	62.66	58.05
Sugar	18.31	17.17	27.08	17.32	30.47
Artificial sweeteners	3.39	3.46	2.90	3.30	4.50
Jams, preserves, other sweets	21.23	21.68	17.77	21.07	23.21
Fats and oils	79.25	80.38	70.56	76.99	107.17
Margarine	14.16	14.61	10.68	14.41	11.02
Fats and oils	23.09	22.37	28.67	20.47	55.39
Salad dressings	23.75	24.56	17.48	23.63	25.26
Nondairy cream and imitation milk	6.56	6.89	4.06	6.71	4.71
Peanut butter	11.70	11.96	9.65	11.77	10.80
Miscellaneous foods	361.62	373.66	268.49	359.36	389.48
Frozen prepared foods	66.14	69.90	37.10	68.24	40.21
Frozen meals	21.43	22.75	11.25	22.27	11.10
Other frozen prepared foods	44.71	47.15	25.84	45.97	29.12
Canned and packaged soups	29.55	30.72	20.48	29.70	27.68
Potato chips, nuts, and other snacks	74.07	78.19	42.16	75.42	57.30
Potato chips and other snacks	58.18	61.31	33.95	59.35	43.68
Nuts	15.89	16.88	8.20	16.07	13.62
Condiments and seasonings	79.74	81.35	67.28	79.89	77.99
Salt, spices and other seasonings	19.30	18.50	25.53	18.88	24.50
Olives, pickles, relishes	10.16	10.69	6.07	10.48	6.32
Sauces and gravies	36.43	37.54	27.83	36.43	36.40
Baking needs and misc. products	13.85	14.62	7.86	14.10	10.77
Other canned/packaged prepared foods	112.12	113.50	101.47	106.12	186.29
Prepared salads	10.97	11.50	6.94	11.45	5.12
Prepared desserts	7.99	8.54	3.76	8.03	7.49

	total consumer units	race		Hispanic origin	
		white and other	black	non-Hispanic	Hispanic
Baby food	$28.11	$26.30	$42.10	$25.97	$54.59
Miscellaneous prepared foods	65.05	67.17	48.67	60.67	119.10
Nonalcoholic beverages	232.89	238.89	186.51	230.13	266.99
Cola	89.45	92.11	68.89	88.50	101.19
Other carbonated drinks	38.89	39.85	31.48	38.66	41.75
Coffee	43.01	45.59	23.07	42.89	44.48
Roasted coffee	29.13	30.95	15.06	29.41	25.66
Instant and freeze-dried coffee	13.88	14.64	8.01	13.48	18.83
Noncarb. fruit flavored drinks incl. non-frozen lemonade	21.86	21.03	28.26	20.72	35.82
Tea	16.25	16.73	12.48	16.39	14.53
Nonalcoholic beer	0.66	0.68	0.54	0.72	-
Other nonalcoholic beverages	22.77	22.90	21.79	22.25	29.21
Food prepared by cu on out-of-town trips	46.41	50.54	13.76	48.12	25.55
FOOD AWAY FROM HOME	**1,698.46**	**1,788.12**	**999.94**	**1,741.15**	**1,173.57**
Meals at restaurants, carry-outs, other	**1,306.21**	**1,367.26**	**834.03**	**1,330.98**	**1,000.31**
Lunch	451.76	468.36	323.33	457.22	384.34
Dinner	651.79	685.34	392.27	667.25	460.72
Snacks and nonalcoholic beverages	101.72	107.58	56.36	104.15	71.71
Breakfast and brunch	100.95	105.98	62.07	102.36	83.53
Board (including at school)	**50.72**	**54.56**	**20.28**	**54.11**	**9.17**
Catered affairs	**56.09**	**60.71**	**19.60**	**59.60**	**13.25**
Food on out-of-town trips	**207.89**	**226.69**	**59.19**	**218.14**	**82.65**
School lunches	**53.76**	**54.74**	**45.98**	**54.18**	**48.64**
Meals as pay	**23.79**	**24.16**	**20.86**	**24.14**	**19.55**
ALCOHOLIC BEVERAGES	**278.03**	**294.58**	**149.49**	**283.49**	**210.75**
At home	**165.13**	**170.81**	**121.15**	**166.32**	**150.36**
Beer and ale	99.68	102.75	75.98	97.67	124.58
Whiskey	13.68	14.16	9.99	14.34	4.51
Wine	36.41	38.82	17.74	38.09	15.65
Other alcoholic beverages	15.35	15.08	17.43	16.14	5.63
Away from home	**112.91**	**123.77**	**28.34**	**117.17**	**60.39**
Beer and ale	38.56	42.52	7.88	40.03	20.28
Wine	15.79	17.20	4.90	16.10	11.97
Other alcoholic beverages	27.96	30.44	8.78	28.97	15.40
Alcoholic beverages purchased on trips	30.61	33.62	6.78	32.07	12.74

Note: Expenditures listed for items in a given category may not add to the total for that category because the listing is incomplete. Persons of other race include Asians, Native Americans, and Hispanics who did not identify themselves as either white or black. Hispanics may be of any race. (-) means insufficient data.

Race & Hispanic Origin
indexed spending

(indexed average annual spending of consumer units on food and alcoholic beverages, by race and Hispanic origin of consumer unit reference person, 1994; index definition: an index of 100 is the average for all consumer units; an index of 132 means that spending by consumer units in the racial/ethnic group is 32 percent above the average for all consumer units; an index of 68 indicates that spending by consumer units in the racial/ethnic group is 32 percent below the average for all consumer units)

	total consumer units	race white and other	race black	Hispanic origin non-Hispanic	Hispanic origin Hispanic
Average spending of cu, total	*$31,750.63*	*$32,934.93*	*$22,418.27*	*$32,185.56*	*$26,437.49*
Average spending of cu, index	*100*	*104*	*71*	*101*	*83*
Food, spending index	*100*	*103*	*77*	*100*	*102*
Alcoholic beverages, spending index	*100*	*106*	*54*	*102*	*76*
FOOD AT HOME	**100**	**102**	**88**	**98**	**123**
Cereals and bakery products	**100**	**103**	**80**	**99**	**112**
Cereals and cereal products	100	101	96	97	141
Flour	100	93	157	86	268
Prepared flour mixes	100	99	108	99	113
Ready-to-eat and cooked cereals	100	101	89	98	119
Rice	100	97	122	88	249
Pasta, cornmeal, and other cereal products	100	102	83	97	138
Bakery products	100	104	70	100	94
Bread	100	102	85	99	118
White bread	100	100	103	98	122
Bread, other than white	100	104	69	99	114
Crackers and cookies	100	104	72	101	88
Cookies	100	103	78	100	99
Crackers	100	105	60	103	63
Frozen and refrigerated bakery products	100	104	69	102	70
Other bakery products	100	105	59	101	86
Biscuits and rolls	100	106	54	102	74
Cakes and cupcakes	100	104	70	100	101
Bread and cracker products	100	108	42	104	51
Sweetrolls, coffee cakes, doughnuts	100	105	59	100	102
Pies, tarts, turnovers	100	106	54	102	73
Meats, poultry, fish, and eggs	**100**	**98**	**117**	**97**	**140**
Beef	100	99	110	95	161
Ground beef	100	99	106	96	150
Roast	100	97	120	97	135
Chuck roast	100	97	122	98	126
Round roast	100	100	98	95	155
Other roast	100	94	144	99	118
Steak	100	99	107	94	175
Round steak	100	99	109	87	264
Sirloin steak	100	101	91	94	176
Other steak	100	98	115	96	143
Other beef	100	96	134	91	209
Pork	100	95	139	98	128
Bacon	100	93	153	99	112
Pork chops	100	93	153	97	137

	total consumer units	race		Hispanic origin	
		white and other	black	non-Hispanic	Hispanic
Ham	100	101	89	99	116
Ham, not canned	100	101	93	99	114
Canned ham	100	107	44	97	138
Sausage	100	91	166	100	105
Other pork	100	94	149	95	157
Other meats	100	101	94	98	121
Frankfurters	100	99	104	98	130
Lunch meats (cold cuts)	100	102	85	100	103
Bologna, liverwurst, salami	100	100	102	97	141
Other lunchmeats	100	103	76	101	82
Lamb, organ meats and others	100	96	129	90	228
Lamb and organ meats	100	96	130	90	227
Mutton, goat and game	100	106	78	89	294
Poultry	100	97	120	97	132
Fresh and frozen chickens	100	96	129	96	151
Fresh and frozen whole chicken	100	93	150	94	175
Fresh and frozen chicken parts	100	97	121	97	141
Other poultry	100	102	86	103	62
Fish and seafood	100	98	118	99	118
Canned fish and seafood	100	103	80	99	110
Fresh fish and shellfish	100	95	141	97	142
Frozen fish and shellfish	100	101	91	102	71
Eggs	100	98	114	91	213
Dairy products	**100**	**104**	**67**	**99**	**118**
Fresh milk and cream	100	103	74	96	144
Fresh milk, all types	100	103	75	96	147
Cream	100	105	61	100	97
Other dairy products	100	105	61	100	98
Butter	100	102	88	98	127
Cheese	100	106	55	100	105
Ice cream and related products	100	104	67	102	81
Miscellaneous dairy products	100	105	58	101	92
Fruits and vegetables	**100**	**102**	**85**	**98**	**130**
Fresh fruits	100	103	74	97	138
Apples	100	103	76	98	121
Bananas	100	103	79	95	164
Oranges	100	100	100	96	147
Citrus fruits, excl. oranges	100	104	67	95	159
Other fresh fruits	100	105	63	98	125
Fresh vegetables	100	103	80	97	141
Potatoes	100	100	98	98	120
Lettuce	100	105	63	97	138
Tomatoes	100	103	74	92	201
Other fresh vegetables	100	103	79	97	132

	total consumer units	race		Hispanic origin	
		white and other	black	non-Hispanic	Hispanic
Processed fruits	100	100	97	98	119
Frozen fruits and fruit juices	100	103	79	99	108
Frozen orange juice	100	103	80	99	110
Frozen fruits	100	100	98	101	83
Frozen fruit juices	100	104	73	99	111
Canned fruit	100	105	59	102	78
Dried fruit	100	102	82	101	87
Fresh fruit juices	100	97	126	97	134
Canned and bottled fruit juices	100	99	107	97	138
Processed vegetables	100	100	97	99	110
Frozen vegetables	100	102	88	102	72
Canned and dried vegetables and juices	100	100	102	98	128
Canned beans	100	98	112	99	115
Canned corn	100	97	126	99	116
Other canned and dried vegetables	100	101	95	97	141
Frozen vegetable juices	100	87	196	104	43
Fresh and canned vegetable juices	100	101	89	99	107
Other food at home	**100**	**103**	**76**	**99**	**110**
Sugar and other sweets	100	102	83	99	110
Candy and chewing gum	100	105	64	101	93
Sugar	100	94	148	95	166
Artificial sweeteners	100	102	86	97	133
Jams, preserves, other sweets	100	102	84	99	109
Fats and oils	100	101	89	97	135
Margarine	100	103	75	102	78
Fats and oils	100	97	124	89	240
Salad dressings	100	103	74	99	106
Nondairy cream and imitation milk	100	105	62	102	72
Peanut butter	100	102	82	101	92
Miscellaneous foods	100	103	74	99	108
Frozen prepared foods	100	106	56	103	61
Frozen meals	100	106	52	104	52
Other frozen prepared foods	100	105	58	103	65
Canned and packaged soups	100	104	69	101	94
Potato chips, nuts, and other snacks	100	106	57	102	77
Potato chips and other snacks	100	105	58	102	75
Nuts	100	106	52	101	86
Condiments and seasonings	100	102	84	100	98
Salt, spices and other seasonings	100	96	132	98	127
Olives, pickles, relishes	100	105	60	103	62
Sauces and gravies	100	103	76	100	100
Baking needs and misc. products	100	106	57	102	78
Other canned/packaged prepared foods	100	101	91	95	166
Prepared salads	100	105	63	104	47
Prepared desserts	100	107	47	101	94

	total consumer units	race		Hispanic origin	
		white and other	black	non-Hispanic	Hispanic
Baby food	100	94	150	92	194
Miscellaneous prepared foods	100	103	75	93	183
Nonalcoholic beverages	100	103	80	99	115
Cola	100	103	77	99	113
Other carbonated drinks	100	102	81	99	107
Coffee	100	106	54	100	103
Roasted coffee	100	106	52	101	88
Instant and freeze-dried coffee	100	105	58	97	136
Noncarb. fruit flavored drinks incl. non-frozen lemonade	100	96	129	95	164
Tea	100	103	77	101	89
Nonalcoholic beer	100	103	82	109	-
Other nonalcoholic beverages	100	101	96	98	128
Food prepared by cu on out-of-town trips	100	109	30	104	55
FOOD AWAY FROM HOME	**100**	**105**	**59**	**103**	**69**
Meals at restaurants, carry-outs, other	**100**	**105**	**64**	**102**	**77**
Lunch	100	104	72	101	85
Dinner	100	105	60	102	71
Snacks and nonalcoholic beverages	100	106	55	102	70
Breakfast and brunch	100	105	61	101	83
Board (including at school)	**100**	**108**	**40**	**107**	**18**
Catered affairs	**100**	**108**	**35**	**106**	**24**
Food on out-of-town trips	**100**	**109**	**28**	**105**	**40**
School lunches	**100**	**102**	**86**	**101**	**90**
Meals as pay	**100**	**102**	**88**	**101**	**82**
ALCOHOLIC BEVERAGES	**100**	**106**	**54**	**102**	**76**
At home	**100**	**103**	**73**	**101**	**91**
Beer and ale	100	103	76	98	125
Whiskey	100	104	73	105	33
Wine	100	107	49	105	43
Other alcoholic beverages	100	98	114	105	37
Away from home	**100**	**110**	**25**	**104**	**53**
Beer and ale	100	110	20	104	53
Wine	100	109	31	102	76
Other alcoholic beverages	100	109	31	104	55
Alcoholic beverages purchased on trips	100	110	22	105	42

Note: Persons of other race include Asians, Native Americans, and Hispanics who did not identify themselves as either white or black. Hispanics may be of any race. (-) means insufficient data.

Race & Hispanic Origin

average per capita spending

(average annual per capita spending of consumer units on food and alcoholic beverages, by race and Hispanic origin of consumer unit reference person, 1994; per capita figures are calculated by dividing the average spending consumer units by the average number of persons per consumer unit)

	total consumer units	race		Hispanic origin	
		white and other	black	non-Hispanic	Hispanic
Average number of persons per cu	2.5	2.5	2.8	2.5	3.4
Per capita before-tax income of cu	$14,735.20	$15,284.80	$9,017.86	$15,083.20	$7,888.53
Per capita spending of cu, total	12,700.25	13,173.97	8,006.53	12,874.22	7,775.73
Food, per capita spending	1,764.21	1,816.68	1,210.69	1,761.52	1,322.32
Alcoholic beverages, per capita spending	111.21	117.83	53.39	113.40	61.99
FOOD AT HOME	**$1,084.82**	**$1,101.44**	**$853.57**	**$1,065.07**	**$977.15**
Cereals and bakery products	**171.47**	**175.90**	**122.49**	**169.80**	**141.20**
Cereals and cereal products	64.70	65.05	55.33	62.54	67.17
Flour	3.04	2.82	4.26	2.63	6.00
Prepared flour mixes	5.12	5.07	4.91	5.06	4.23
Ready-to-eat and cooked cereals	39.31	39.86	31.29	38.70	34.48
Rice	6.17	6.00	6.71	5.43	11.28
Pasta, cornmeal, and other cereal products	11.06	11.31	8.15	10.72	11.18
Bakery products	106.77	110.85	67.16	107.26	74.03
Bread	30.49	31.06	23.26	30.05	26.43
White bread	15.06	15.01	13.81	14.79	13.51
Bread, other than white	15.43	16.05	9.45	15.26	12.91
Crackers and cookies	25.02	25.93	16.08	25.27	16.11
Cookies	17.19	17.68	11.90	17.21	12.46
Crackers	7.84	8.24	4.17	8.07	3.65
Frozen and refrigerated bakery products	8.62	8.97	5.30	8.84	4.42
Other bakery products	42.64	44.89	22.53	43.11	27.08
Biscuits and rolls	14.38	15.23	6.98	14.69	7.79
Cakes and cupcakes	12.48	12.96	7.80	12.47	9.22
Bread and cracker products	1.89	2.03	0.70	1.96	0.71
Sweetrolls, coffee cakes, doughnuts	8.77	9.24	4.60	8.75	6.60
Pies, tarts, turnovers	5.12	5.43	2.45	5.23	2.76
Meats, poultry, fish, and eggs	**292.98**	**286.51**	**306.30**	**283.41**	**302.34**
Beef	90.70	89.48	89.45	86.25	107.13
Ground beef	35.38	35.11	33.46	33.94	39.11
Roast	15.76	15.36	16.86	15.32	15.61
Chuck roast	4.90	4.76	5.34	4.80	4.55
Round roast	5.94	5.95	5.19	5.67	6.79
Other roast	4.92	4.64	6.33	4.85	4.27
Steak	33.90	33.60	32.36	31.83	43.74
Round steak	6.40	6.33	6.23	5.55	12.42
Sirloin steak	9.78	9.89	7.96	9.17	12.65
Other steak	17.72	17.38	18.18	17.10	18.67
Other beef	5.66	5.41	6.78	5.16	8.68
Pork	62.30	59.17	77.18	60.88	58.70
Bacon	9.11	8.49	12.42	9.02	7.51
Pork chops	15.73	14.66	21.46	15.26	15.79

	total consumer units	race		Hispanic origin	
		white and other	black	non-Hispanic	Hispanic
Ham	$14.75	$14.96	$11.78	$14.56	$12.61
Ham, not canned	13.66	13.79	11.35	13.50	11.50
Canned ham	1.09	1.17	0.43	1.06	1.11
Sausage	9.13	8.35	13.52	9.09	7.08
Other pork	13.57	12.72	18.01	12.94	15.71
Other meats	37.58	37.89	31.41	36.93	33.55
Frankfurters	7.50	7.46	6.99	7.32	7.18
Lunch meats (cold cuts)	26.26	26.76	20.01	26.19	19.96
Bologna, liverwurst, salami	9.49	9.46	8.68	9.18	9.81
Other lunchmeats	16.77	17.30	11.34	17.01	10.15
Lamb, organ meats and others	3.81	3.67	4.41	3.42	6.40
Lamb and organ meats	3.74	3.59	4.36	3.36	6.25
Mutton, goat and game	0.07	0.08	0.05	0.06	0.16
Poultry	54.63	53.24	58.42	53.22	53.04
Fresh and frozen chickens	43.16	41.55	49.63	41.39	47.79
Fresh and frozen whole chicken	11.82	11.05	15.88	11.11	15.21
Fresh and frozen chicken parts	31.33	30.50	33.75	30.28	32.58
Other poultry	11.48	11.69	8.79	11.82	5.25
Fish and seafood	35.77	34.95	37.59	35.24	31.14
Canned fish and seafood	6.01	6.16	4.30	5.96	4.86
Fresh fish and shellfish	20.50	19.42	25.77	19.80	21.42
Frozen fish and shellfish	9.26	9.36	7.53	9.47	4.86
Eggs	12.00	11.78	12.24	10.90	18.78
Dairy products	**115.57**	**120.54**	**68.81**	**113.89**	**100.23**
Fresh milk and cream	50.85	52.58	33.51	49.06	53.74
Fresh milk, all types	47.58	49.14	31.71	45.77	51.41
Cream	3.28	3.44	1.80	3.28	2.33
Other dairy products	64.72	67.97	35.30	64.84	46.49
Butter	4.66	4.74	3.64	4.56	4.36
Cheese	32.73	34.66	15.95	32.61	25.17
Ice cream and related products	19.06	19.86	11.42	19.34	11.39
Miscellaneous dairy products	8.26	8.71	4.30	8.32	5.57
Fruits and vegetables	**174.63**	**178.07**	**132.14**	**170.37**	**167.07**
Fresh fruits	53.21	55.00	35.11	51.56	54.11
Apples	10.15	10.46	6.93	9.97	9.04
Bananas	11.86	12.19	8.35	11.25	14.30
Oranges	6.54	6.54	5.83	6.30	7.05
Citrus fruits, excl. oranges	4.38	4.57	2.63	4.18	5.14
Other fresh fruits	20.27	21.24	11.38	19.86	18.57
Fresh vegetables	53.96	55.36	38.48	52.17	55.94
Potatoes	11.20	11.23	9.83	11.02	9.86
Lettuce	6.95	7.28	3.89	6.74	7.05
Tomatoes	8.40	8.69	5.53	7.72	12.44
Other fresh vegetables	27.40	28.16	19.24	26.69	26.59

	total	race		Hispanic origin	
	consumer units	white and other	black	non-Hispanic	Hispanic
Processed fruits	$37.23	$37.38	$32.26	$36.65	$32.69
Frozen fruits and fruit juices	6.51	6.68	4.62	6.47	5.15
Frozen orange juice	3.80	3.89	2.72	3.77	3.07
Frozen fruits	0.64	0.64	0.56	0.65	0.39
Frozen fruit juices	2.08	2.15	1.35	2.06	1.69
Canned fruit	5.69	6.00	2.98	5.80	3.25
Dried fruit	2.36	2.41	1.72	2.38	1.51
Fresh fruit juices	7.16	6.91	8.09	6.96	7.06
Canned and bottled fruit juices	15.51	15.36	14.86	15.04	15.71
Processed vegetables	30.23	30.33	26.28	30.00	24.34
Frozen vegetables	9.93	10.09	7.78	10.16	5.29
Canned and dried vegetables and juices	20.30	20.24	18.50	19.84	19.05
Canned beans	4.18	4.11	4.17	4.13	3.53
Canned corn	2.72	2.63	3.06	2.69	2.32
Other canned and dried vegetables	10.82	10.90	9.13	10.46	11.21
Frozen vegetable juices	0.09	0.08	0.16	0.10	0.03
Fresh and canned vegetable juices	2.48	2.52	1.98	2.47	1.96
Other food at home	**330.17**	**340.41**	**223.83**	**327.59**	**266.30**
Sugar and other sweets	42.10	43.02	31.22	41.74	34.19
Candy and chewing gum	24.93	26.10	14.16	25.06	17.07
Sugar	7.32	6.87	9.67	6.93	8.96
Artificial sweeteners	1.36	1.38	1.04	1.32	1.32
Jams, preserves, other sweets	8.49	8.67	6.35	8.43	6.83
Fats and oils	31.70	32.15	25.20	30.80	31.52
Margarine	5.66	5.84	3.81	5.76	3.24
Fats and oils	9.24	8.95	10.24	8.19	16.29
Salad dressings	9.50	9.82	6.24	9.45	7.43
Nondairy cream and imitation milk	2.62	2.76	1.45	2.68	1.39
Peanut butter	4.68	4.78	3.45	4.71	3.18
Miscellaneous foods	144.65	149.46	95.89	143.74	114.55
Frozen prepared foods	26.46	27.96	13.25	27.30	11.83
Frozen meals	8.57	9.10	4.02	8.91	3.26
Other frozen prepared foods	17.88	18.86	9.23	18.39	8.56
Canned and packaged soups	11.82	12.29	7.31	11.88	8.14
Potato chips, nuts, and other snacks	29.63	31.28	15.06	30.17	16.85
Potato chips and other snacks	23.27	24.52	12.13	23.74	12.85
Nuts	6.36	6.75	2.93	6.43	4.01
Condiments and seasonings	31.90	32.54	24.03	31.96	22.94
Salt, spices and other seasonings	7.72	7.40	9.12	7.55	7.21
Olives, pickles, relishes	4.06	4.28	2.17	4.19	1.86
Sauces and gravies	14.57	15.02	9.94	14.57	10.71
Baking needs and misc. products	5.54	5.85	2.81	5.64	3.17
Other canned/packaged prepared foods	44.85	45.40	36.24	42.45	54.79
Prepared salads	4.39	4.60	2.48	4.58	1.51
Prepared desserts	3.20	3.42	1.34	3.21	2.20

	total consumer units	race		Hispanic origin	
		white and other	*black*	*non-Hispanic*	*Hispanic*
Baby food	$11.24	$10.52	$15.04	$10.39	$16.06
Miscellaneous prepared foods	26.02	26.87	17.38	24.27	35.03
Nonalcoholic beverages	93.16	95.56	66.61	92.05	78.53
Cola	35.78	36.84	24.60	35.40	29.76
Other carbonated drinks	15.56	15.94	11.24	15.46	12.28
Coffee	17.20	18.24	8.24	17.16	13.08
Roasted coffee	11.65	12.38	5.38	11.76	7.55
Instant and freeze-dried coffee	5.55	5.86	2.86	5.39	5.54
Noncarb. fruit flavored drinks incl.					
non-frozen lemonade	8.74	8.41	10.09	8.29	10.54
Tea	6.50	6.69	4.46	6.56	4.27
Nonalcoholic beer	0.26	0.27	0.19	0.29	-
Other nonalcoholic beverages	9.11	9.16	7.78	8.90	8.59
Food prepared by cu on out-of-town trips	18.56	20.22	4.91	19.25	7.51
FOOD AWAY FROM HOME	**679.38**	**715.25**	**357.12**	**696.46**	**345.17**
Meals at restaurants, carry-outs, other	**522.48**	**546.90**	**297.87**	**532.39**	**294.21**
Lunch	180.70	187.34	115.48	182.89	113.04
Dinner	260.72	274.14	140.10	266.90	135.51
Snacks and nonalcoholic beverages	40.69	43.03	20.13	41.66	21.09
Breakfast and brunch	40.38	42.39	22.17	40.94	24.57
Board (including at school)	**20.29**	**21.82**	**7.24**	**21.64**	**2.70**
Catered affairs	**22.44**	**24.28**	**7.00**	**23.84**	**3.90**
Food on out-of-town trips	**83.16**	**90.68**	**21.14**	**87.26**	**24.31**
School lunches	**21.50**	**21.90**	**16.42**	**21.67**	**14.31**
Meals as pay	**9.52**	**9.66**	**7.45**	**9.66**	**5.75**
ALCOHOLIC BEVERAGES	**111.21**	**117.83**	**53.39**	**113.40**	**61.99**
At home	**66.05**	**68.32**	**43.27**	**66.53**	**44.22**
Beer and ale	39.87	41.10	27.14	39.07	36.64
Whiskey	5.47	5.66	3.57	5.74	1.33
Wine	14.56	15.53	6.34	15.24	4.60
Other alcoholic beverages	6.14	6.03	6.23	6.46	1.66
Away from home	**45.16**	**49.51**	**10.12**	**46.87**	**17.76**
Beer and ale	15.42	17.01	2.81	16.01	5.96
Wine	6.32	6.88	1.75	6.44	3.52
Other alcoholic beverages	11.18	12.18	3.14	11.59	4.53
Alcoholic beverages purchased on trips	12.24	13.45	2.42	12.83	3.75

Note: Expenditures listed for items in a given category may not add to the total for that category because the listing is incomplete. Persons of other race include Asians, Native Americans, and Hispanics who did not identify themselves as either white or black. Hispanics may be of any race. (-) means insufficient data.

Race & Hispanic Origin
indexed per capita spending

(indexed average annual per capita spending of consumer units on food and alcoholic beverages, by race and Hispanic origin of consumer unit reference person, 1994; index definition: an index of 100 is the per capita average for all consumer units; an index of 132 means that per capita spending by consumer units in the racial/ethnic group is 32 percent above the per capita average for all consumer units; an index of 68 indicates that per capita spending by consumer units in the racial/ethnic group is 32 percent below the per capita average for all consumer units

	total consumer units	race white and other	race black	Hispanic origin non-Hispanic	Hispanic origin Hispanic
Per capita spending of cu, total	$12,700.25	$13,173.97	$8,006.53	$12,874.22	$7,775.73
Per capita spending of cu, index	100	104	63	101	61
Food, per capita spending index	100	103	69	100	75
Alcoholic beverages, per capita spending index	100	106	48	102	56
FOOD AT HOME	100	102	79	98	90
Cereals and bakery products	100	103	71	99	82
Cereals and cereal products	100	101	86	97	104
Flour	100	93	140	86	197
Prepared flour mixes	100	99	96	99	83
Ready-to-eat and cooked cereals	100	101	80	98	88
Rice	100	97	109	88	183
Pasta, cornmeal, and other cereal products	100	102	74	97	101
Bakery products	100	104	63	100	69
Bread	100	102	76	99	87
White bread	100	100	92	98	90
Bread, other than white	100	104	61	99	84
Crackers and cookies	100	104	64	101	64
Cookies	100	103	69	100	73
Crackers	100	105	53	103	47
Frozen and refrigerated bakery products	100	104	61	102	51
Other bakery products	100	105	53	101	64
Biscuits and rolls	100	106	48	102	54
Cakes and cupcakes	100	104	63	100	74
Bread and cracker products	100	108	37	104	38
Sweetrolls, coffee cakes, doughnuts	100	105	52	100	75
Pies, tarts, turnovers	100	106	48	102	54
Meats, poultry, fish, and eggs	100	98	105	97	103
Beef	100	99	99	95	118
Ground beef	100	99	95	96	111
Roast	100	97	107	97	99
Chuck roast	100	97	109	98	93
Round roast	100	100	87	95	114
Other roast	100	94	129	99	87
Steak	100	99	95	94	129
Round steak	100	99	97	87	194
Sirloin steak	100	101	81	94	129
Other steak	100	98	103	96	105
Other beef	100	96	120	91	153
Pork	100	95	124	98	94
Bacon	100	93	136	99	82
Pork chops	100	93	136	97	100

	total consumer units	race		Hispanic origin	
		white and other	black	non-Hispanic	Hispanic
Ham	100	101	80	99	85
Ham, not canned	100	101	83	99	84
Canned ham	100	107	39	97	102
Sausage	100	91	148	100	78
Other pork	100	94	133	95	116
Other meats	100	101	84	98	89
Frankfurters	100	99	93	98	96
Lunch meats (cold cuts)	100	102	76	100	76
Bologna, liverwurst, salami	100	100	91	97	103
Other lunchmeats	100	103	68	101	61
Lamb, organ meats and others	100	96	116	90	168
Lamb and organ meats	100	96	117	90	167
Mutton, goat and game	100	106	69	89	217
Poultry	100	97	107	97	97
Fresh and frozen chickens	100	96	115	96	111
Fresh and frozen whole chicken	100	93	134	94	129
Fresh and frozen chicken parts	100	97	108	97	104
Other poultry	100	102	77	103	46
Fish and seafood	100	98	105	99	87
Canned fish and seafood	100	103	71	99	81
Fresh fish and shellfish	100	95	126	97	104
Frozen fish and shellfish	100	101	81	102	53
Eggs	100	98	102	91	157
Dairy products	**100**	**104**	**60**	**99**	**87**
Fresh milk and cream	100	103	66	96	106
Fresh milk, all types	100	103	67	96	108
Cream	100	105	55	100	71
Other dairy products	100	105	55	100	72
Butter	100	102	78	98	94
Cheese	100	106	49	100	77
Ice cream and related products	100	104	60	102	60
Miscellaneous dairy products	100	105	52	101	67
Fruits and vegetables	**100**	**102**	**76**	**98**	**96**
Fresh fruits	100	103	66	97	102
Apples	100	103	68	98	89
Bananas	100	103	70	95	121
Oranges	100	100	89	96	108
Citrus fruits, excl. oranges	100	104	60	95	117
Other fresh fruits	100	105	56	98	92
Fresh vegetables	100	103	71	97	104
Potatoes	100	100	88	98	88
Lettuce	100	105	56	97	101
Tomatoes	100	103	66	92	148
Other fresh vegetables	100	103	70	97	97

	total consumer units	race		Hispanic origin	
		white and other	black	non-Hispanic	Hispanic
Processed fruits	100	100	87	98	88
Frozen fruits and fruit juices	100	103	71	99	79
Frozen orange juice	100	103	72	99	81
Frozen fruits	100	100	88	101	61
Frozen fruit juices	100	104	65	99	81
Canned fruit	100	105	52	102	57
Dried fruit	100	102	73	101	64
Fresh fruit juices	100	97	113	97	99
Canned and bottled fruit juices	100	99	96	97	101
Processed vegetables	100	100	87	99	81
Frozen vegetables	100	102	78	102	53
Canned and dried vegetables and juices	100	100	91	98	94
Canned beans	100	98	100	99	85
Canned corn	100	97	112	99	85
Other canned and dried vegetables	100	101	84	97	104
Frozen vegetable juices	100	87	175	104	32
Fresh and canned vegetable juices	100	101	80	99	79
Other food at home	**100**	**103**	**68**	**99**	**81**
Sugar and other sweets	100	102	74	99	81
Candy and chewing gum	100	105	57	101	68
Sugar	100	94	132	95	122
Artificial sweeteners	100	102	76	97	98
Jams, preserves, other sweets	100	102	75	99	80
Fats and oils	100	101	79	97	99
Margarine	100	103	67	102	57
Fats and oils	100	97	111	89	176
Salad dressings	100	103	66	99	78
Nondairy cream and imitation milk	100	105	55	102	53
Peanut butter	100	102	74	101	68
Miscellaneous foods	100	103	66	99	79
Frozen prepared foods	100	106	50	103	45
Frozen meals	100	106	47	104	38
Other frozen prepared foods	100	105	52	103	48
Canned and packaged soups	100	104	62	101	69
Potato chips, nuts, and other snacks	100	106	51	102	57
Potato chips and other snacks	100	105	52	102	55
Nuts	100	106	46	101	63
Condiments and seasonings	100	102	75	100	72
Salt, spices and other seasonings	100	96	118	98	93
Olives, pickles, relishes	100	105	53	103	46
Sauces and gravies	100	103	68	100	73
Baking needs and misc. products	100	106	51	102	57
Other canned/packaged prepared foods	100	101	81	95	122
Prepared salads	100	105	56	104	34
Prepared desserts	100	107	42	101	69

	total consumer units	race		Hispanic origin	
		white and other	black	non-Hispanic	Hispanic
Baby food	100	94	134	92	143
Miscellaneous prepared foods	100	103	67	93	135
Nonalcoholic beverages	100	103	72	99	84
Cola	100	103	69	99	83
Other carbonated drinks	100	102	72	99	79
Coffee	100	106	48	100	76
Roasted coffee	100	106	46	101	65
Instant and freeze-dried coffee	100	105	52	97	100
Noncarb. fruit flavored drinks incl. non-frozen lemonade	100	96	115	95	120
Tea	100	103	69	101	66
Nonalcoholic beer	100	103	73	109	-
Other nonalcoholic beverages	100	101	85	98	94
Food prepared by cu on out-of-town trips	100	109	26	104	40
FOOD AWAY FROM HOME	**100**	**105**	**53**	**103**	**51**
Meals at restaurants, carry-outs, other	**100**	**105**	**57**	**102**	**56**
Lunch	100	104	64	101	63
Dinner	100	105	54	102	52
Snacks and nonalcoholic beverages	100	106	49	102	52
Breakfast and brunch	100	105	55	101	61
Board (including at school)	**100**	**108**	**36**	**107**	**13**
Catered affairs	**100**	**108**	**31**	**106**	**17**
Food on out-of-town trips	**100**	**109**	**25**	**105**	**29**
School lunches	**100**	**102**	**76**	**101**	**67**
Meals as pay	**100**	**102**	**78**	**101**	**60**
ALCOHOLIC BEVERAGES	**100**	**106**	**48**	**102**	**56**
At home	**100**	**103**	**66**	**101**	**67**
Beer and ale	100	103	68	98	92
Whiskey	100	104	65	105	24
Wine	100	107	44	105	32
Other alcoholic beverages	100	98	101	105	27
Away from home	**100**	**110**	**22**	**104**	**39**
Beer and ale	100	110	18	104	39
Wine	100	109	28	102	56
Other alcoholic beverages	100	109	28	104	40
Alcoholic beverages purchased on trips	100	110	20	105	31

Note: Persons of other race include Asians, Native Americans, and Hispanics who did not identify themselves as either white or black. Hispanics may be of any race. (-) means insufficient data.

Race & Hispanic Origin

total spending

(total annual spending on food and alcoholic beverages by race and Hispanic origin of consumer unit reference person, 1994; numbers in thousands)

	total consumer units	race		Hispanic origin	
		white and other	black	non-Hispanic	Hispanic
Number of consumer units	102,210	90,740	11,470	94,479	7,730
Total spending of all cu's	$3,245,231,892	$2,988,515,548	$257,137,557	$3,040,859,523	$204,361,798
Food, total spending	450,799,249	412,114,765	38,882,612	416,067,565	34,753,152
Alcoholic beverages, total spending	28,417,446	26,730,189	1,714,650	26,783,852	1,629,098
FOOD AT HOME	**$277,198,631**	**$249,860,757**	**$27,413,300**	**$251,566,399**	**$25,681,456**
Cereals and bakery products	**43,815,383**	**39,903,822**	**3,933,866**	**40,107,280**	**3,711,096**
Cereals and cereal products	16,531,445	14,757,046	1,777,047	14,771,792	1,765,377
Flour	776,796	638,810	136,952	620,727	157,615
Prepared flour mixes	1,307,266	1,149,676	157,713	1,196,104	111,235
Ready-to-eat and cooked cereals	10,044,177	9,042,241	1,005,001	9,139,898	906,111
Rice	1,577,100	1,360,193	215,521	1,282,080	296,523
Pasta, cornmeal, and other cereal products	2,826,107	2,566,127	261,860	2,532,982	293,895
Bakery products	27,282,915	25,146,776	2,156,819	25,335,489	1,945,718
Bread	7,790,446	7,045,961	746,926	7,097,262	694,541
White bread	3,848,207	3,404,565	443,430	3,493,833	355,194
Bread, other than white	3,942,240	3,641,396	303,496	3,603,429	339,347
Crackers and cookies	6,394,258	5,881,767	516,265	5,969,183	423,527
Cookies	4,391,964	4,011,615	382,295	4,064,487	327,520
Crackers	2,002,294	1,870,151	133,970	1,905,641	96,007
Frozen and refrigerated bakery products	2,203,648	2,035,298	170,215	2,087,041	116,105
Other bakery products	10,894,564	10,182,843	723,413	10,182,002	711,624
Biscuits and rolls	3,675,472	3,455,379	224,009	3,469,269	204,845
Cakes and cupcakes	3,187,930	2,939,976	250,620	2,945,855	242,336
Bread and cracker products	482,431	460,959	22,596	463,892	18,629
Sweetrolls, coffee cakes, doughnuts	2,240,443	2,095,187	147,734	2,067,201	173,461
Pies, tarts, turnovers	1,308,288	1,231,342	78,570	1,235,785	72,430
Meats, poultry, fish, and eggs	**74,863,715**	**64,994,340**	**9,837,246**	**66,941,206**	**7,946,131**
Beef	23,177,140	20,297,631	2,872,891	20,372,507	2,815,498
Ground beef	9,040,475	7,964,250	1,074,739	8,016,543	1,027,858
Roast	4,028,096	3,484,416	541,384	3,618,546	410,154
Chuck roast	1,253,095	1,080,713	171,591	1,133,748	119,506
Round roast	1,516,796	1,350,211	166,544	1,338,767	178,331
Other roast	1,258,205	1,053,491	203,248	1,146,030	112,317
Steak	8,662,298	7,621,253	1,039,297	7,517,694	1,149,451
Round steak	1,635,360	1,435,507	199,922	1,311,369	326,361
Sirloin steak	2,498,012	2,243,093	255,552	2,166,403	332,390
Other steak	4,528,925	3,942,653	583,823	4,038,977	490,623
Other beef	1,446,272	1,227,712	217,586	1,219,724	228,112
Pork	15,918,185	13,423,168	2,478,667	14,378,759	1,542,753
Bacon	2,328,344	1,926,410	398,927	2,131,446	197,502
Pork chops	4,018,897	3,324,714	689,118	3,605,319	415,101

	total consumer units	race		Hispanic origin	
		white and other	black	non-Hispanic	Hispanic
Ham	$3,769,505	$3,392,769	$378,166	$3,439,036	$331,308
Ham, not canned	3,491,494	3,127,808	364,402	3,189,611	302,243
Canned ham	278,011	264,961	13,764	249,425	29,065
Sausage	2,332,432	1,894,651	434,254	2,146,563	185,984
Other pork	3,467,985	2,884,625	578,317	3,056,396	412,782
Other meats	9,602,630	8,594,893	1,008,787	8,722,301	881,761
Frankfurters	1,917,460	1,692,301	224,583	1,728,966	188,767
Lunch meats (cold cuts)	6,711,109	6,070,506	642,779	6,186,485	524,712
Bologna, liverwurst, salami	2,425,443	2,146,001	278,606	2,168,293	257,873
Other lunchmeats	4,285,665	3,924,505	364,173	4,018,192	266,840
Lamb, organ meats and others	974,061	832,086	141,540	806,851	168,282
Lamb and organ meats	955,664	814,845	139,934	792,679	164,263
Mutton, goat and game	18,398	17,241	1,606	15,117	4,097
Poultry	13,959,842	12,076,587	1,876,263	12,569,486	1,394,028
Fresh and frozen chickens	11,027,437	9,426,071	1,593,986	9,776,687	1,255,970
Fresh and frozen whole chicken	3,021,328	2,507,146	510,071	2,623,682	399,641
Fresh and frozen chicken parts	8,006,109	6,918,018	1,084,030	7,153,005	856,329
Other poultry	2,932,405	2,651,423	282,277	2,792,799	138,058
Fish and seafood	9,140,640	7,928,861	1,207,332	8,323,600	818,452
Canned fish and seafood	1,536,216	1,398,303	137,984	1,408,682	127,622
Fresh fish and shellfish	5,239,285	4,405,427	827,561	4,677,655	562,976
Frozen fish and shellfish	2,366,162	2,124,223	241,788	2,237,263	127,854
Eggs	3,066,300	2,672,293	393,077	2,575,498	493,638
Dairy products	**29,530,513**	**27,345,406**	**2,209,925**	**26,900,061**	**2,634,229**
Fresh milk and cream	12,993,957	11,926,866	1,076,115	11,586,905	1,412,271
Fresh milk, all types	12,156,857	11,146,502	1,018,421	10,810,287	1,351,049
Cream	837,100	780,364	57,694	775,673	61,222
Other dairy products	16,536,556	15,418,541	1,133,810	15,314,101	1,221,958
Butter	1,190,747	1,074,362	116,994	1,076,116	114,713
Cheese	8,363,844	7,861,714	512,136	7,702,873	661,611
Ice cream and related products	4,869,284	4,506,148	366,811	4,569,004	299,228
Miscellaneous dairy products	2,111,659	1,976,317	137,984	1,965,163	146,406
Fruits and vegetables	**44,621,820**	**40,395,633**	**4,243,785**	**40,241,440**	**4,391,027**
Fresh fruits	13,595,974	12,477,657	1,127,616	12,178,343	1,422,011
Apples	2,593,068	2,371,944	222,403	2,355,361	237,620
Bananas	3,031,549	2,764,848	268,054	2,657,694	375,910
Oranges	1,672,156	1,484,506	187,305	1,487,099	185,365
Citrus fruits, excl. oranges	1,120,222	1,037,158	84,534	986,361	135,120
Other fresh fruits	5,178,981	4,818,294	365,320	4,691,827	487,995
Fresh vegetables	13,787,107	12,558,416	1,235,893	12,321,951	1,470,169
Potatoes	2,862,902	2,547,072	315,540	2,603,841	259,264
Lettuce	1,776,410	1,652,375	125,023	1,591,026	185,211
Tomatoes	2,147,432	1,971,780	177,441	1,822,500	326,979
Other fresh vegetables	7,001,385	6,387,189	617,889	6,303,639	698,792

	total consumer units	race		Hispanic origin	
		white and other	black	non-Hispanic	Hispanic
Processed fruits	$9,513,707	$8,478,746	$1,036,085	$8,656,166	$859,035
Frozen fruits and fruit juices	1,663,979	1,516,265	148,422	1,528,670	135,352
Frozen orange juice	969,973	882,900	87,287	889,992	80,624
Frozen fruits	163,536	145,184	18,008	153,056	10,281
Frozen fruit juices	530,470	488,181	43,242	486,567	44,448
Canned fruit	1,454,448	1,361,100	95,545	1,369,001	85,494
Dried fruit	602,017	547,162	55,171	562,150	39,810
Fresh fruit juices	1,829,559	1,567,987	259,681	1,643,935	185,443
Canned and bottled fruit juices	3,963,704	3,485,323	477,267	3,551,466	412,937
Processed vegetables	7,724,010	6,880,814	844,077	7,084,980	639,735
Frozen vegetables	2,537,874	2,289,370	249,817	2,398,822	139,063
Canned and dried vegetables and juices	5,186,135	4,591,444	594,261	4,687,103	500,749
Canned beans	1,067,072	932,807	133,855	975,023	92,760
Canned corn	696,050	597,069	98,413	634,899	60,912
Other canned and dried vegetables	2,764,781	2,471,758	293,288	2,470,626	294,745
Frozen vegetable juices	23,508	18,148	5,162	22,675	773
Fresh and canned vegetable juices	634,724	571,662	63,544	582,935	51,482
Other food at home	**84,367,200**	**77,221,555**	**7,188,593**	**77,375,467**	**6,998,974**
Sugar and other sweets	10,757,603	9,759,994	1,002,593	9,859,828	898,535
Candy and chewing gum	6,369,727	5,920,785	454,900	5,920,054	448,727
Sugar	1,871,465	1,558,006	310,608	1,636,376	235,533
Artificial sweeteners	346,492	313,960	33,263	311,781	34,785
Jams, preserves, other sweets	2,169,918	1,967,243	203,822	1,990,673	179,413
Fats and oils	8,100,143	7,293,681	809,323	7,273,938	828,424
Margarine	1,447,294	1,325,711	122,500	1,361,442	85,185
Fats and oils	2,360,029	2,029,854	328,845	1,933,985	428,165
Salad dressings	2,427,488	2,228,574	200,496	2,232,539	195,260
Nondairy cream and imitation milk	670,498	625,199	46,568	633,954	36,408
Peanut butter	1,195,857	1,085,250	110,686	1,112,018	83,484
Miscellaneous foods	36,961,180	33,905,908	3,079,580	33,951,973	3,010,680
Frozen prepared foods	6,760,169	6,342,726	425,537	6,447,247	310,823
Frozen meals	2,190,360	2,064,335	129,038	2,104,047	85,803
Other frozen prepared foods	4,569,809	4,278,391	296,385	4,343,200	225,098
Canned and packaged soups	3,020,306	2,787,533	234,906	2,806,026	213,966
Potato chips, nuts, and other snacks	7,570,695	7,094,961	483,575	7,125,606	442,929
Potato chips and other snacks	5,946,578	5,563,269	389,407	5,607,329	337,646
Nuts	1,624,117	1,531,691	94,054	1,518,278	105,283
Condiments and seasonings	8,150,225	7,381,699	771,702	7,547,927	602,863
Salt, spices and other seasonings	1,972,653	1,678,690	292,829	1,783,764	189,385
Olives, pickles, relishes	1,038,454	970,011	69,623	990,140	48,854
Sauces and gravies	3,723,510	3,406,380	319,210	3,441,870	281,372
Baking needs and misc. products	1,415,609	1,326,619	90,154	1,332,154	83,252
Other canned/packaged prepared foods	11,459,785	10,298,990	1,163,861	10,026,111	1,440,022
Prepared salads	1,121,244	1,043,510	79,602	1,081,785	39,578
Prepared desserts	816,658	774,920	43,127	758,666	57,898

	total consumer units	race		Hispanic origin	
		white and other	black	non-Hispanic	Hispanic
Baby food	$2,873,123	$2,386,462	$482,887	$2,453,620	$421,981
Miscellaneous prepared foods	6,648,761	6,095,006	558,245	5,732,041	920,643
Nonalcoholic beverages	23,803,687	21,676,879	2,139,270	21,742,452	2,063,833
Cola	9,142,685	8,358,061	790,168	8,361,392	782,199
Other carbonated drinks	3,974,947	3,615,989	361,076	3,652,558	322,728
Coffee	4,396,052	4,136,837	264,613	4,052,204	343,830
Roasted coffee	2,977,377	2,808,403	172,738	2,778,627	198,352
Instant and freeze-dried coffee	1,418,675	1,328,434	91,875	1,273,577	145,556
Noncarb. fruit flavored drinks incl. non-frozen lemonade	2,234,311	1,908,262	324,142	1,957,605	276,889
Tea	1,660,913	1,518,080	143,146	1,548,511	112,317
Nonalcoholic beer	67,459	61,703	6,194	68,025	-
Other nonalcoholic beverages	2,327,322	2,077,946	249,931	2,102,158	225,793
Food prepared by cu on out-of-town trips	4,743,566	4,586,000	157,827	4,546,329	197,502
FOOD AWAY FROM HOME	**173,599,597**	**162,254,009**	**11,469,312**	**164,502,111**	**9,071,696**
Meals at restaurants, carry-outs, other	**133,507,724**	**124,065,172**	**9,566,324**	**125,749,659**	**7,732,396**
Lunch	46,174,390	42,498,986	3,708,595	43,197,688	2,970,948
Dinner	66,619,456	62,187,752	4,499,337	63,041,113	3,561,366
Snacks and nonalcoholic beverages	10,396,801	9,761,809	646,449	9,839,988	554,318
Breakfast and brunch	10,318,100	9,616,625	711,943	9,670,870	645,687
Board (including at school)	**5,184,091**	**4,950,774**	**232,612**	**5,112,259**	**70,884**
Catered affairs	**5,732,959**	**5,508,825**	**224,812**	**5,630,948**	**102,423**
Food on out-of-town trips	**21,248,437**	**20,569,851**	**678,909**	**20,609,649**	**638,885**
School lunches	**5,494,810**	**4,967,108**	**527,391**	**5,118,872**	**375,987**
Meals as pay	**2,431,576**	**2,192,278**	**239,264**	**2,280,723**	**151,122**
ALCOHOLIC BEVERAGES	**28,417,446**	**26,730,189**	**1,714,650**	**26,783,852**	**1,629,098**
At home	**16,877,937**	**15,499,299**	**1,389,591**	**15,713,747**	**1,162,283**
Beer and ale	10,188,293	9,323,535	871,491	9,227,764	963,003
Whiskey	1,398,233	1,284,878	114,585	1,354,829	34,862
Wine	3,721,466	3,522,527	203,478	3,598,705	120,975
Other alcoholic beverages	1,568,924	1,368,359	199,922	1,524,891	43,520
Away from home	**11,540,531**	**11,230,890**	**325,060**	**11,070,104**	**466,815**
Beer and ale	3,941,218	3,858,265	90,384	3,781,994	156,764
Wine	1,613,896	1,560,728	56,203	1,521,112	92,528
Other alcoholic beverages	2,857,792	2,762,126	100,707	2,737,057	119,042
Alcoholic beverages purchased on trips	3,128,648	3,050,679	77,767	3,029,942	98,480

Note: Spending for items in a given category may not add to the total for that category because the listing is incomplete. Numbers may not add to total due to rounding. Persons of other race include Asians, Native Americans, and Hispanics who did not identify themselves as either white or black. Hispanics may be of any race. (-) means insufficient data.

Race & Hispanic Origin
market shares

(percent of total annual spending on food accounted for by race and Hispanic origin of consumer unit reference person, 1994)

	total consumer units	race		Hispanic origin	
		white and other	black	non-Hispanic	Hispanic
Share of total consumer units	**100.0%**	**88.8%**	**11.2%**	**92.4%**	**7.6%**
Share of total spending	**100.0**	**92.1**	**7.9**	**93.7**	**6.3**
Share of food spending	**100.0**	**91.4**	**8.6**	**92.3**	**7.7**
Share of alcoholic beverages spending	**100.0**	**94.1**	**6.0**	**94.3**	**5.7**
FOOD AT HOME	**100.0%**	**90.1%**	**9.9%**	**90.8%**	**9.3%**
Cereals and bakery products	**100.0**	**91.1**	**9.0**	**91.5**	**8.5**
Cereals and cereal products	100.0	89.3	10.7	89.4	10.7
Flour	100.0	82.2	17.6	79.9	20.3
Prepared flour mixes	100.0	87.9	12.1	91.5	8.5
Ready-to-eat and cooked cereals	100.0	90.0	10.0	91.0	9.0
Rice	100.0	86.2	13.7	81.3	18.8
Pasta, cornmeal, and other cereal products	100.0	90.8	9.3	89.6	10.4
Bakery products	100.0	92.2	7.9	92.9	7.1
Bread	100.0	90.4	9.6	91.1	8.9
White bread	100.0	88.5	11.5	90.8	9.2
Bread, other than white	100.0	92.4	7.7	91.4	8.6
Crackers and cookies	100.0	92.0	8.1	93.4	6.6
Cookies	100.0	91.3	8.7	92.5	7.5
Crackers	100.0	93.4	6.7	95.2	4.8
Frozen and refrigerated bakery products	100.0	92.4	7.7	94.7	5.3
Other bakery products	100.0	93.5	6.6	93.5	6.5
Biscuits and rolls	100.0	94.0	6.1	94.4	5.6
Cakes and cupcakes	100.0	92.2	7.9	92.4	7.6
Bread and cracker products	100.0	95.5	4.7	96.2	3.9
Sweetrolls, coffee cakes, doughnuts	100.0	93.5	6.6	92.3	7.7
Pies, tarts, turnovers	100.0	94.1	6.0	94.5	5.5
Meats, poultry, fish, and eggs	**100.0**	**86.8**	**13.1**	**89.4**	**10.6**
Beef	100.0	87.6	12.4	87.9	12.1
Ground beef	100.0	88.1	11.9	88.7	11.4
Roast	100.0	86.5	13.4	89.8	10.2
Chuck roast	100.0	86.2	13.7	90.5	9.5
Round roast	100.0	89.0	11.0	88.3	11.8
Other roast	100.0	83.7	16.2	91.1	8.9
Steak	100.0	88.0	12.0	86.8	13.3
Round steak	100.0	87.8	12.2	80.2	20.0
Sirloin steak	100.0	89.8	10.2	86.7	13.3
Other steak	100.0	87.1	12.9	89.2	10.8
Other beef	100.0	84.9	15.0	84.3	15.8
Pork	100.0	84.3	15.6	90.3	9.7
Bacon	100.0	82.7	17.1	91.5	8.5
Pork chops	100.0	82.7	17.1	89.7	10.3

	total consumer units	race white and other	black	Hispanic origin non-Hispanic	Hispanic
Ham	100.0%	90.0%	10.0%	91.2%	8.8%
Ham, not canned	100.0	89.6	10.4	91.4	8.7
Canned ham	100.0	95.3	5.0	89.7	10.5
Sausage	100.0	81.2	18.6	92.0	8.0
Other pork	100.0	83.2	16.7	88.1	11.9
Other meats	100.0	89.5	10.5	90.8	9.2
Frankfurters	100.0	88.3	11.7	90.2	9.8
Lunch meats (cold cuts)	100.0	90.5	9.6	92.2	7.8
Bologna, liverwurst, salami	100.0	88.5	11.5	89.4	10.6
Other lunchmeats	100.0	91.6	8.5	93.8	6.2
Lamb, organ meats and others	100.0	85.4	14.5	82.8	17.3
Lamb and organ meats	100.0	85.3	14.6	82.9	17.2
Mutton, goat and game	100.0	93.7	8.7	82.2	22.3
Poultry	100.0	86.5	13.4	90.0	10.0
Fresh and frozen chickens	100.0	85.5	14.5	88.7	11.4
Fresh and frozen whole chicken	100.0	83.0	16.9	86.8	13.2
Fresh and frozen chicken parts	100.0	86.4	13.5	89.3	10.7
Other poultry	100.0	90.4	9.6	95.2	4.7
Fish and seafood	100.0	86.7	13.2	91.1	9.0
Canned fish and seafood	100.0	91.0	9.0	91.7	8.3
Fresh fish and shellfish	100.0	84.1	15.8	89.3	10.7
Frozen fish and shellfish	100.0	89.8	10.2	94.6	5.4
Eggs	100.0	87.2	12.8	84.0	16.1
Dairy products	**100.0**	**92.6**	**7.5**	**91.1**	**8.9**
Fresh milk and cream	100.0	91.8	8.3	89.2	10.9
Fresh milk, all types	100.0	91.7	8.4	88.9	11.1
Cream	100.0	93.2	6.9	92.7	7.3
Other dairy products	100.0	93.2	6.9	92.6	7.4
Butter	100.0	90.2	9.8	90.4	9.6
Cheese	100.0	94.0	6.1	92.1	7.9
Ice cream and related products	100.0	92.5	7.5	93.8	6.1
Miscellaneous dairy products	100.0	93.6	6.5	93.1	6.9
Fruits and vegetables	**100.0**	**90.5**	**9.5**	**90.2**	**9.8**
Fresh fruits	100.0	91.8	8.3	89.6	10.5
Apples	100.0	91.5	8.6	90.8	9.2
Bananas	100.0	91.2	8.8	87.7	12.4
Oranges	100.0	88.8	11.2	88.9	11.1
Citrus fruits, excl. oranges	100.0	92.6	7.5	88.1	12.1
Other fresh fruits	100.0	93.0	7.1	90.6	9.4
Fresh vegetables	100.0	91.1	9.0	89.4	10.7
Potatoes	100.0	89.0	11.0	91.0	9.1
Lettuce	100.0	93.0	7.0	89.6	10.4
Tomatoes	100.0	91.8	8.3	84.9	15.2
Other fresh vegetables	100.0	91.2	8.8	90.0	10.0

	total consumer units	race		Hispanic origin	
		white and other	black	non-Hispanic	Hispanic
Processed fruits	100.0%	89.1%	10.9%	91.0%	9.0%
Frozen fruits and fruit juices	100.0	91.1	8.9	91.9	8.1
Frozen orange juice	100.0	91.0	9.0	91.8	8.3
Frozen fruits	100.0	88.8	11.0	93.6	6.3
Frozen fruit juices	100.0	92.0	8.2	91.7	8.4
Canned fruit	100.0	93.6	6.6	94.1	5.9
Dried fruit	100.0	90.9	9.2	93.4	6.6
Fresh fruit juices	100.0	85.7	14.2	89.9	10.1
Canned and bottled fruit juices	100.0	87.9	12.0	89.6	10.4
Processed vegetables	100.0	89.1	10.9	91.7	8.3
Frozen vegetables	100.0	90.2	9.8	94.5	5.5
Canned and dried vegetables and juices	100.0	88.5	11.5	90.4	9.7
Canned beans	100.0	87.4	12.5	91.4	8.7
Canned corn	100.0	85.8	14.1	91.2	8.8
Other canned and dried vegetables	100.0	89.4	10.6	89.4	10.7
Frozen vegetable juices	100.0	77.2	22.0	96.5	3.3
Fresh and canned vegetable juices	100.0	90.1	10.0	91.8	8.1
Other food at home	**100.0**	**91.5**	**8.5**	**91.7**	**8.3**
Sugar and other sweets	100.0	90.7	9.3	91.7	8.4
Candy and chewing gum	100.0	93.0	7.1	92.9	7.0
Sugar	100.0	83.3	16.6	87.4	12.6
Artificial sweeteners	100.0	90.6	9.6	90.0	10.0
Jams, preserves, other sweets	100.0	90.7	9.4	91.7	8.3
Fats and oils	100.0	90.0	10.0	89.8	10.2
Margarine	100.0	91.6	8.5	94.1	5.9
Fats and oils	100.0	86.0	13.9	81.9	18.1
Salad dressings	100.0	91.8	8.3	92.0	8.0
Nondairy cream and imitation milk	100.0	93.2	6.9	94.5	5.4
Peanut butter	100.0	90.8	9.3	93.0	7.0
Miscellaneous foods	100.0	91.7	8.3	91.9	8.1
Frozen prepared foods	100.0	93.8	6.3	95.4	4.6
Frozen meals	100.0	94.2	5.9	96.1	3.9
Other frozen prepared foods	100.0	93.6	6.5	95.0	4.9
Canned and packaged soups	100.0	92.3	7.8	92.9	7.1
Potato chips, nuts, and other snacks	100.0	93.7	6.4	94.1	5.9
Potato chips and other snacks	100.0	93.6	6.5	94.3	5.7
Nuts	100.0	94.3	5.8	93.5	6.5
Condiments and seasonings	100.0	90.6	9.5	92.6	7.4
Salt, spices and other seasonings	100.0	85.1	14.8	90.4	9.6
Olives, pickles, relishes	100.0	93.4	6.7	95.3	4.7
Sauces and gravies	100.0	91.5	8.6	92.4	7.6
Baking needs and misc. products	100.0	93.7	6.4	94.1	5.9
Other canned/packaged prepared foods	100.0	89.9	10.2	87.5	12.6
Prepared salads	100.0	93.1	7.1	96.5	3.5
Prepared desserts	100.0	94.9	5.3	92.9	7.1

	total consumer units	race		Hispanic origin	
		white and other	*black*	*non-Hispanic*	*Hispanic*
Baby food	100.0%	83.1%	16.8%	85.4%	14.7%
Miscellaneous prepared foods	100.0	91.7	8.4	86.2	13.8
Nonalcoholic beverages	100.0	91.1	9.0	91.3	8.7
Cola	100.0	91.4	8.6	91.5	8.6
Other carbonated drinks	100.0	91.0	9.1	91.9	8.1
Coffee	100.0	94.1	6.0	92.2	7.8
Roasted coffee	100.0	94.3	5.8	93.3	6.7
Instant and freeze-dried coffee	100.0	93.6	6.5	89.8	10.3
Noncarb. fruit flavored drinks incl. non-frozen lemonade	100.0	85.4	14.5	87.6	12.4
Tea	100.0	91.4	8.6	93.2	6.8
Nonalcoholic beer	100.0	91.5	9.2	100.0	-
Other nonalcoholic beverages	100.0	89.3	10.7	90.3	9.7
Food prepared by cu on out-of-town trips	100.0	96.7	3.3	95.8	4.2
FOOD AWAY FROM HOME	**100.0**	**93.5**	**6.6**	**94.8**	**5.2**
Meals at restaurants, carry-outs, other	**100.0**	**92.9**	**7.2**	**94.2**	**5.8**
Lunch	100.0	92.0	8.0	93.6	6.4
Dinner	100.0	93.3	6.8	94.6	5.3
Snacks and nonalcoholic beverages	100.0	93.9	6.2	94.6	5.3
Breakfast and brunch	100.0	93.2	6.9	93.7	6.3
Board (including at school)	**100.0**	**95.5**	**4.5**	**98.6**	**1.4**
Catered affairs	**100.0**	**96.1**	**3.9**	**98.2**	**1.8**
Food on out-of-town trips	**100.0**	**96.8**	**3.2**	**97.0**	**3.0**
School lunches	**100.0**	**90.4**	**9.6**	**93.2**	**6.8**
Meals as pay	**100.0**	**90.2**	**9.8**	**93.8**	**6.2**
ALCOHOLIC BEVERAGES	**100.0**	**94.1**	**6.0**	**94.3**	**5.7**
At home	**100.0**	**91.8**	**8.2**	**93.1**	**6.9**
Beer and ale	100.0	91.5	8.6	90.6	9.5
Whiskey	100.0	91.9	8.2	96.9	2.5
Wine	100.0	94.7	5.5	96.7	3.3
Other alcoholic beverages	100.0	87.2	12.7	97.2	2.8
Away from home	**100.0**	**97.3**	**2.8**	**95.9**	**4.0**
Beer and ale	100.0	97.9	2.3	96.0	4.0
Wine	100.0	96.7	3.5	94.3	5.7
Other alcoholic beverages	100.0	96.7	3.5	95.8	4.2
Alcoholic beverages purchased on trips	100.0	97.5	2.5	96.8	3.1

Note: Numbers may not add to total due to rounding. Persons of other race include Asians, Native Americans, and Hispanics who did not identify themselves as either white or black. Hispanics may be of any race. (-) means insufficient data.

Chapter 7

Spending by
Education

Food spending varies widely by education. Households headed by college graduates spend heavily on bakery products, fruits and vegetables, condiments, miscellaneous foods, and alcoholic beverages.

They spend about an average amount on dairy products, and relatively little on meat, poultry, fish, and eggs. Households headed by people who did not graduate from high school spend more than average on most meats, sugar, fats and oils, and instant coffee. High school graduates, on the other hand, spend close to the average amount on most food products.

Access to information about diet, health, and nutrition may affect food choices among better-educated households. Knowledge about the relationship between cholesterol and eggs, for example, may account for the 12 percent below-average per capita spending on eggs among college graduates. Concern for fat content may be the reason for their below-average spending on bacon, sausage, and other pork products.

Affluence may also explain some of the spending patterns by education, since the college-educated have higher incomes than those with less education. On a per capita basis, college graduates spend twice as much as the average person on wine consumed at home. Their spending on alcoholic beverages consumed away from home is 76 percent higher than average. And although they may be more nutritionally aware, college graduates spend more than average on potato chips, nuts, and other snacks, as well as sauces, gravies, and condiments. The trade-off diet adopted by many informed, healthful eaters may explain the above-average spending of college graduates on categories like ice cream and butter. These carefully monitored indulgences, balanced by healthy eating on most occasions, is a trend worth watching.

People who did not graduate from high school, typically with low incomes, spend more than average on many less-expensive foods. They spend 13 percent more per capita on white bread, 30 percent more on eggs, 30 percent more on sugar, and 40 percent more on fats and oils.

Households headed by people with some college education spend more than average on only a few items. Their above-average spending on frozen meals, frozen foods, canned and frozen vegetables, canned or packaged prepared foods, and baby food suggests that many of these households have little time to cook from scratch. Indeed, this is the group with the lowest per capita spending on raw ingredients used for cooking or baking—flour, eggs, most cuts of meat, and many fresh vegetables.

Education

average spending

(average annual spending of consumer units on food and alcoholic beverages, by education of consumer unit reference person, 1994)

	total consumer units	not a high school graduate	high school graduate	some college	college graduate
Number of consumer units (in thousands, add 000's)	102,210	21,096	32,148	24,387	24,578
Average number of persons per cu	2.5	2.6	2.6	2.5	2.5
Average before-tax income of cu	$36,838.00	$19,415.00	$32,552.00	$34,436.00	$59,650.00
Average spending of cu, total	31,750.63	19,543.63	28,969.05	31,941.53	45,477.12
Food, average spending	4,410.52	3,393.60	4,120.74	4,549.85	5,448.20
Alcoholic beverages, average spending	278.03	163.16	244.01	276.37	412.17
FOOD AT HOME	**$2,712.05**	**$2,550.26**	**$2,668.16**	**$2,747.73**	**$2,859.14**
Cereals and bakery products	**428.68**	**377.73**	**421.00**	**438.53**	**467.79**
Cereals and cereal products	161.74	146.94	156.48	164.44	176.96
Flour	7.60	12.72	7.73	4.91	6.09
Prepared flour mixes	12.79	12.30	11.97	14.08	12.94
Ready-to-eat and cooked cereals	98.27	78.81	97.28	100.58	112.23
Rice	15.43	16.90	13.74	16.44	15.39
Pasta, cornmeal, and other cereal products	27.65	26.21	25.77	28.43	30.31
Bakery products	266.93	230.79	264.52	274.09	290.83
Bread	76.22	77.35	75.82	72.91	78.99
White bread	37.65	44.31	39.29	33.34	34.66
Bread, other than white	38.57	33.05	36.53	39.57	44.33
Crackers and cookies	62.56	51.41	59.60	66.15	71.30
Cookies	42.97	36.50	41.82	45.28	47.13
Crackers	19.59	14.92	17.77	20.86	24.17
Frozen and refrigerated bakery products	21.56	16.38	21.98	22.01	24.61
Other bakery products	106.59	85.64	107.12	113.02	115.93
Biscuits and rolls	35.96	23.44	34.02	38.29	45.71
Cakes and cupcakes	31.19	25.90	34.55	33.22	29.23
Bread and cracker products	4.72	3.53	4.91	4.49	5.64
Sweetrolls, coffee cakes, doughnuts	21.92	20.54	21.71	23.90	21.34
Pies, tarts, turnovers	12.80	12.23	11.93	13.11	14.01
Meats, poultry, fish, and eggs	**732.45**	**811.82**	**743.98**	**712.29**	**676.65**
Beef	226.76	250.26	234.73	227.56	198.20
Ground beef	88.45	94.66	95.60	92.14	71.44
Roast	39.41	45.19	39.18	38.10	36.50
Chuck roast	12.26	14.52	12.86	11.87	10.16
Round roast	14.84	17.27	15.36	13.68	13.45
Other roast	12.31	13.41	10.96	12.56	12.89
Steak	84.75	92.82	86.44	84.76	76.46
Round steak	16.00	20.01	16.57	17.71	10.60
Sirloin steak	24.44	28.72	23.61	24.68	21.92
Other steak	44.31	44.08	46.26	42.36	43.95
Other beef	14.15	17.59	13.51	12.56	13.80
Pork	155.74	196.80	163.49	146.83	123.24
Bacon	22.78	30.98	21.90	22.87	17.47
Pork chops	39.32	50.49	41.61	36.35	30.80

	total consumer units	not a high school graduate	high school graduate	some college	college graduate
Ham	$36.88	$41.88	$40.69	$32.44	$32.63
Ham, not canned	34.16	38.47	38.47	28.94	30.58
Canned ham	2.72	3.41	2.22	3.50	2.05
Sausage	22.82	29.51	22.95	23.17	17.20
Other pork	33.93	43.93	36.34	31.99	25.14
Other meats	93.95	97.68	100.55	93.27	83.68
Frankfurters	18.76	21.57	20.14	19.90	13.82
Lunch meats (cold cuts)	65.66	64.82	71.87	65.00	59.36
Bologna, liverwurst, salami	23.73	27.32	26.32	23.32	18.19
Other lunchmeats	41.93	37.50	45.54	41.68	41.17
Lamb, organ meats and others	9.53	11.29	8.55	8.36	10.50
Lamb and organ meats	9.35	11.00	8.48	8.36	10.09
Mutton, goat and game	0.18	0.28	0.07	-	0.42
Poultry	136.58	141.52	133.36	131.92	141.18
Fresh and frozen chickens	107.89	114.27	103.11	106.24	110.41
Fresh and frozen whole chicken	29.56	38.14	27.92	24.86	29.45
Fresh and frozen chicken parts	78.33	76.12	75.19	81.39	80.95
Other poultry	28.69	27.26	30.25	25.67	30.77
Fish and seafood	89.43	85.03	82.50	86.52	104.04
Canned fish and seafood	15.03	12.95	14.57	13.24	18.90
Fresh fish and shellfish	51.26	49.87	45.42	50.53	60.13
Frozen fish and shellfish	23.15	22.22	22.51	22.75	25.01
Eggs	30.00	40.53	29.36	26.21	26.32
Dairy products	**288.92**	**253.63**	**287.27**	**304.64**	**303.05**
Fresh milk and cream	127.13	131.05	129.72	130.91	117.36
Fresh milk, all types	118.94	124.57	122.92	120.48	108.31
Cream	8.19	6.48	6.79	10.43	9.05
Other dairy products	161.79	122.57	157.55	173.73	185.69
Butter	11.65	11.20	11.19	11.52	12.68
Cheese	81.83	63.98	81.94	84.85	92.56
Ice cream and related products	47.64	33.14	47.80	53.76	52.75
Miscellaneous dairy products	20.66	14.26	16.62	23.60	27.70
Fruits and vegetables	**436.57**	**407.60**	**399.81**	**427.87**	**511.97**
Fresh fruits	133.02	128.63	119.00	123.38	162.70
Apples	25.37	22.34	23.28	24.23	31.32
Bananas	29.66	32.06	27.13	26.77	33.67
Oranges	16.36	16.27	13.46	15.58	20.70
Citrus fruits, excl. oranges	10.96	10.55	9.65	9.55	14.24
Other fresh fruits	50.67	47.42	45.47	47.25	62.77
Fresh vegetables	134.89	129.58	120.66	128.21	162.71
Potatoes	28.01	31.53	26.68	25.44	29.37
Lettuce	17.38	15.89	16.66	16.13	20.59
Tomatoes	21.01	21.86	20.61	18.91	22.85
Other fresh vegetables	68.50	60.30	56.72	67.73	89.88

	total consumer units	not a high school graduate	high school graduate	some college	college graduate
Processed fruits	$93.08	$80.82	$86.52	$96.06	$107.66
Frozen fruits and fruit juices	16.28	12.48	13.16	18.04	21.32
Frozen orange juice	9.49	7.48	8.19	10.67	11.49
Frozen fruits	1.60	1.07	1.13	1.74	2.44
Frozen fruit juices	5.19	3.93	3.84	5.63	7.39
Canned fruit	14.23	12.25	13.88	14.26	16.17
Dried fruit	5.89	5.05	6.10	5.56	6.62
Fresh fruit juices	17.90	17.46	16.01	16.27	22.08
Canned and bottled fruit juices	38.78	33.58	37.37	41.93	41.47
Processed vegetables	75.57	68.56	73.63	80.21	78.90
Frozen vegetables	24.83	15.43	24.39	27.53	30.03
Canned and dried vegetables and juices	50.74	53.13	49.24	52.68	48.88
Canned beans	10.44	12.62	9.49	10.96	9.44
Canned corn	6.81	7.27	6.32	8.96	5.00
Other canned and dried vegetables	27.05	27.63	27.42	26.67	26.51
Frozen vegetable juices	0.23	0.07	0.22	0.18	0.40
Fresh and canned vegetable juices	6.21	5.55	5.78	5.91	7.53
Other food at home	**825.43**	**699.48**	**816.11**	**864.40**	**899.68**
Sugar and other sweets	105.25	97.25	107.17	106.76	107.62
Candy and chewing gum	62.32	50.34	62.97	64.45	68.70
Sugar	18.31	24.75	19.36	17.19	13.14
Artificial sweeteners	3.39	3.91	3.38	2.82	3.57
Jams, preserves, other sweets	21.23	18.25	21.46	22.30	22.21
Fats and oils	79.25	82.83	81.33	74.86	78.17
Margarine	14.16	13.49	16.50	12.78	13.12
Fats and oils	23.09	33.66	21.66	19.04	20.57
Salad dressings	23.75	18.70	25.41	24.12	25.24
Nondairy cream and imitation milk	6.56	5.73	6.74	6.31	7.23
Peanut butter	11.70	11.24	11.02	12.61	12.01
Miscellaneous foods	361.62	275.70	355.98	390.60	406.86
Frozen prepared foods	66.14	39.05	67.43	77.58	74.46
Frozen meals	21.43	13.42	19.05	28.43	23.79
Other frozen prepared foods	44.71	25.62	48.38	49.15	50.67
Canned and packaged soups	29.55	26.37	28.04		35.27
Potato chips, nuts, and other snacks	74.07	48.09	74.34	76.87	91.04
Potato chips and other snacks	58.18	36.58	58.37	63.08	69.88
Nuts	15.89	11.51	15.97	13.79	21.16
Condiments and seasonings	79.74	63.28	78.84	82.32	91.05
Salt, spices and other seasonings	19.30	17.09	19.40	19.74	20.48
Olives, pickles, relishes	10.16	7.80	11.38	8.50	12.09
Sauces and gravies	36.43	27.39	35.06	40.10	41.54
Baking needs and misc. products	13.85	10.99	13.00	13.98	16.95
Other canned/packaged prepared foods	112.12	98.92	107.33	125.78	115.04
Prepared salads	10.97	5.56	11.33	12.03	13.69
Prepared desserts	7.99	7.04	8.14	8.25	8.28

	total consumer units	not a high school graduate	high school graduate	some college	college graduate
Baby food	$28.11	$21.38	$26.35	$36.61	$27.30
Miscellaneous prepared foods	65.05	64.93	61.51	68.89	65.77
Nonalcoholic beverages	232.89	223.41	235.97	245.50	224.38
Cola	89.45	93.67	93.94	94.73	75.70
Other carbonated drinks	38.89	34.00	42.22	42.44	35.21
Coffee	43.01	45.99	41.02	39.14	46.84
Roasted coffee	29.13	27.79	28.34	27.58	32.59
Instant and freeze-dried coffee	13.88	18.20	12.68	11.56	14.25
Noncarb. fruit flavored drinks incl. non-frozen lemonade	21.86	21.91	20.42	23.31	22.17
Tea	16.25	11.64	16.74	18.18	17.34
Nonalcoholic beer	0.66	0.51	0.24	0.68	1.28
Other nonalcoholic beverages	22.77	15.68	21.39	27.02	25.84
Food prepared by cu on out-of-town trips	46.41	20.30	35.65	46.68	82.64
FOOD AWAY FROM HOME	**1,698.46**	**843.35**	**1,452.57**	**1,802.12**	**2,589.06**
Meals at restaurants, carry-outs, other	**1,306.21**	**713.35**	**1,162.46**	**1,405.41**	**1,842.52**
Lunch	451.76	232.64	400.63	481.30	654.35
Dinner	651.79	350.94	571.29	693.96	940.94
Snacks and nonalcoholic beverages	101.72	60.04	97.63	118.16	123.03
Breakfast and brunch	100.95	69.73	92.91	111.99	124.20
Board (including at school)	**50.72**	**12.48**	**24.01**	**51.34**	**117.84**
Catered affairs	**56.09**	**6.30**	**25.39**	**43.60**	**151.40**
Food on out-of-town trips	**207.89**	**63.73**	**164.85**	**213.42**	**382.44**
School lunches	**53.76**	**34.96**	**56.57**	**57.91**	**62.11**
Meals as pay	**23.79**	**12.51**	**19.30**	**30.45**	**32.75**
ALCOHOLIC BEVERAGES	**278.03**	**163.16**	**244.01**	**276.37**	**412.17**
At home	**165.13**	**131.73**	**154.52**	**155.53**	**212.91**
Beer and ale	99.68	110.18	103.96	91.34	94.38
Whiskey	13.68	3.37	13.50	13.75	21.77
Wine	36.41	10.36	25.18	33.58	72.81
Other alcoholic beverages	15.35	7.82	11.88	16.85	23.94
Away from home	**112.91**	**31.43**	**89.49**	**120.84**	**199.26**
Beer and ale	38.56	11.26	34.41	42.29	61.03
Wine	15.79	5.36	12.52	16.32	27.29
Other alcoholic beverages	27.96	6.97	20.82	29.40	51.42
Alcoholic beverages purchased on trips	30.61	7.84	21.75	32.84	59.52

Note: Expenditures listed for items in a given category may not add to the total for that category because the listing is incomplete. (-) means insufficient data.

Education

indexed spending

(indexed average annual spending of consumer units on food and alcoholic beverages, by education of consumer unit reference person, 1994; index definition: an index of 100 is the average for all consumer units; an index of 132 means that spending by consumer units in the educational group is 32 percent above the average for all consumer units; an index of 68 indicates that spending by consumer units in the educational group is 32 percent below the average for all consumer units)

	total consumer units	not a high school graduate	high school graduate	some college	college graduate
Average spending of cu, total	$31,750.63	$19,543.63	$28,969.05	$31,941.53	$45,477.12
Average spending of cu, index	100	62	91	101	143
Food, spending index	100	77	93	103	124
Alcoholic beverages, spending index	100	59	88	99	148
FOOD AT HOME	**100**	**94**	**98**	**101**	**105**
Cereals and bakery products	**100**	**88**	**98**	**102**	**109**
Cereals and cereal products	100	91	97	102	109
Flour	100	167	102	65	80
Prepared flour mixes	100	96	94	110	101
Ready-to-eat and cooked cereals	100	80	99	102	114
Rice	100	110	89	107	100
Pasta, cornmeal, and other cereal products	100	95	93	103	110
Bakery products	100	86	99	103	109
Bread	100	101	99	96	104
White bread	100	118	104	89	92
Bread, other than white	100	86	95	103	115
Crackers and cookies	100	82	95	106	114
Cookies	100	85	97	105	110
Crackers	100	76	91	106	123
Frozen and refrigerated bakery products	100	76	102	102	114
Other bakery products	100	80	100	106	109
Biscuits and rolls	100	65	95	106	127
Cakes and cupcakes	100	83	111	107	94
Bread and cracker products	100	75	104	95	119
Sweetrolls, coffee cakes, doughnuts	100	94	99	109	97
Pies, tarts, turnovers	100	96	93	102	109
Meats, poultry, fish, and eggs	**100**	**111**	**102**	**97**	**92**
Beef	100	110	104	100	87
Ground beef	100	107	108	104	81
Roast	100	115	99	97	93
Chuck roast	100	118	105	97	83
Round roast	100	116	104	92	91
Other roast	100	109	89	102	105
Steak	100	110	102	100	90
Round steak	100	125	104	111	66
Sirloin steak	100	118	97	101	90
Other steak	100	99	104	96	99
Other beef	100	124	95	89	98
Pork	100	126	105	94	79
Bacon	100	136	96	100	77
Pork chops	100	128	106	92	78

	total consumer units	not a high school graduate	high school graduate	some college	college graduate
Ham	100	114	110	88	88
Ham, not canned	100	113	113	85	90
Canned ham	100	125	82	129	75
Sausage	100	129	101	102	75
Other pork	100	129	107	94	74
Other meats	100	104	107	99	89
Frankfurters	100	115	107	106	74
Lunch meats (cold cuts)	100	99	109	99	90
Bologna, liverwurst, salami	100	115	111	98	77
Other lunchmeats	100	89	109	99	98
Lamb, organ meats and others	100	118	90	88	110
Lamb and organ meats	100	118	91	89	108
Mutton, goat and game	100	156	39	-	233
Poultry	100	104	98	97	103
Fresh and frozen chickens	100	106	96	98	102
Fresh and frozen whole chicken	100	129	94	84	100
Fresh and frozen chicken parts	100	97	96	104	103
Other poultry	100	95	105	89	107
Fish and seafood	100	95	92	97	116
Canned fish and seafood	100	86	97	88	126
Fresh fish and shellfish	100	97	89	99	117
Frozen fish and shellfish	100	96	97	98	108
Eggs	100	135	98	87	88
Dairy products	**100**	**88**	**99**	**105**	**105**
Fresh milk and cream	100	103	102	103	92
Fresh milk, all types	100	105	103	101	91
Cream	100	79	83	127	111
Other dairy products	100	76	97	107	115
Butter	100	96	96	99	109
Cheese	100	78	100	104	113
Ice cream and related products	100	70	100	113	111
Miscellaneous dairy products	100	69	80	114	134
Fruits and vegetables	**100**	**93**	**92**	**98**	**117**
Fresh fruits	100	97	89	93	122
Apples	100	88	92	96	123
Bananas	100	108	91	90	114
Oranges	100	99	82	95	127
Citrus fruits, excl. oranges	100	96	88	87	130
Other fresh fruits	100	94	90	93	124
Fresh vegetables	100	96	89	95	121
Potatoes	100	113	95	91	105
Lettuce	100	91	96	93	118
Tomatoes	100	104	98	90	109
Other fresh vegetables	100	88	83	99	131

	total consumer units	not a high school graduate	high school graduate	some college	college graduate
Processed fruits	100	87	93	103	116
Frozen fruits and fruit juices	100	77	81	111	131
Frozen orange juice	100	79	86	112	121
Frozen fruits	100	67	71	109	153
Frozen fruit juices	100	76	74	108	142
Canned fruit	100	86	98	100	114
Dried fruit	100	86	104	94	112
Fresh fruit juices	100	98	89	91	123
Canned and bottled fruit juices	100	87	96	108	107
Processed vegetables	100	91	97	106	104
Frozen vegetables	100	62	98	111	121
Canned and dried vegetables and juices	100	105	97	104	96
Canned beans	100	121	91	105	90
Canned corn	100	107	93	132	73
Other canned and dried vegetables	100	102	101	99	98
Frozen vegetable juices	100	30	96	78	174
Fresh and canned vegetable juices	100	89	93	95	121
Other food at home	**100**	**85**	**99**	**105**	**109**
Sugar and other sweets	100	92	102	101	102
Candy and chewing gum	100	81	101	103	110
Sugar	100	135	106	94	72
Artificial sweeteners	100	115	100	83	105
Jams, preserves, other sweets	100	86	101	105	
Fats and oils	100	105	103	94	99
Margarine	100	95	117	90	93
Fats and oils	100	146	94	82	89
Salad dressings	100	79	107	102	106
Nondairy cream and imitation milk	100	87	103	96	110
Peanut butter	100	96	94	108	103
Miscellaneous foods	100	76	98	108	113
Frozen prepared foods	100	59	102	117	113
Frozen meals	100	63	89	133	111
Other frozen prepared foods	100	57	108	110	113
Canned and packaged soups	100	89	95	95	119
Potato chips, nuts, and other snacks	100	65	100	104	123
Potato chips and other snacks	100	63	100	108	120
Nuts	100	72	101	87	133
Condiments and seasonings	100	79	99	103	114
Salt, spices and other seasonings	100	89	101	102	106
Olives, pickles, relishes	100	77	112	84	119
Sauces and gravies	100	75	96	110	114
Baking needs and misc. products	100	79	94	101	122
Other canned/packaged prepared foods	100	88	96	112	103
Prepared salads	100	51	103	110	125
Prepared desserts	100	88	102	103	104

	total consumer units	not a high school graduate	high school graduate	some college	college graduate
Baby food	100	76	94	130	97
Miscellaneous prepared foods	100	100	95	106	101
Nonalcoholic beverages	100	96	101	105	96
Cola	100	105	105	106	85
Other carbonated drinks	100	87	109	109	91
Coffee	100	107	95	91	109
Roasted coffee	100	95	97	95	112
Instant and freeze-dried coffee	100	131	91	83	103
Noncarb. fruit flavored drinks incl. non-frozen lemonade	100	100	93	107	101
Tea	100	72	103	112	107
Nonalcoholic beer	100	77	36	103	194
Other nonalcoholic beverages	100	69	94	119	113
Food prepared by cu on out-of-town trips	100	44	77	101	178
FOOD AWAY FROM HOME	**100**	**50**	**86**	**106**	**152**
Meals at restaurants, carry-outs, other	**100**	**55**	**89**	**108**	**141**
Lunch	100	51	89	107	145
Dinner	100	54	88	106	144
Snacks and nonalcoholic beverages	100	59	96	116	121
Breakfast and brunch	100	69	92	111	123
Board (including at school)	**100**	**25**	**47**	**101**	**232**
Catered affairs	**100**	**11**	**45**	**78**	**270**
Food on out-of-town trips	**100**	**31**	**79**	**103**	**184**
School lunches	**100**	**65**	**105**	**108**	**116**
Meals as pay	**100**	**53**	**81**	**128**	**138**
ALCOHOLIC BEVERAGES	**100**	**59**	**88**	**99**	**148**
At home	**100**	**80**	**94**	**94**	**129**
Beer and ale	100	111	104	92	95
Whiskey	100	25	99	101	159
Wine	100	28	69	92	200
Other alcoholic beverages	100	51	77	110	156
Away from home	**100**	**28**	**79**	**107**	**176**
Beer and ale	100	29	89	110	158
Wine	100	34	79	103	173
Other alcoholic beverages	100	25	74	105	184
Alcoholic beverages purchased on trips	100	26	71	107	194

Note: (-) means insufficient data.

Education

average per capita spending

(average annual per capita spending of consumer units on food and alcoholic beverages, by education of consumer unit reference person, 1994; per capita figures are calculated by dividing the average spending of consumer units by the average number of persons per consumer unit)

	total consumer units	not a high school graduate	high school graduate	some college	college graduate
Average number of persons per cu	*2.5*	*2.6*	*2.6*	*2.5*	*2.5*
Per capita spending of cu, total	*$12,700.25*	*$7,516.78*	*$11,141.94*	*$12,776.61*	*$18,190.85*
Food, per capita spending	*1,764.21*	*1,305.23*	*1,584.90*	*1,819.94*	*2,179.28*
Alcoholic beverages, per capita spending	*111.21*	*62.75*	*93.85*	*110.55*	*164.87*
FOOD AT HOME	**$1,084.82**	**$980.87**	**$1,026.22**	**$1,099.09**	**$1,143.66**
Cereals and bakery products	**171.47**	**145.28**	**161.92**	**175.41**	**187.12**
Cereals and cereal products	64.70	56.52	60.18	65.78	70.78
Flour	3.04	4.89	2.97	1.96	2.44
Prepared flour mixes	5.12	4.73	4.60	5.63	5.18
Ready-to-eat and cooked cereals	39.31	30.31	37.42	40.23	44.89
Rice	6.17	6.50	5.28	6.58	6.16
Pasta, cornmeal, and other cereal products	11.06	10.08	9.91	11.37	12.12
Bakery products	106.77	88.77	101.74	109.64	116.33
Bread	30.49	29.75	29.16	29.16	31.60
White bread	15.06	17.04	15.11	13.34	13.86
Bread, other than white	15.43	12.71	14.05	15.83	17.73
Crackers and cookies	25.02	19.77	22.92	26.46	28.52
Cookies	17.19	14.04	16.08	18.11	18.85
Crackers	7.84	5.74	6.83	8.34	9.67
Frozen and refrigerated bakery products	8.62	6.30	8.45	8.80	9.84
Other bakery products	42.64	32.94	41.20	45.21	46.37
Biscuits and rolls	14.38	9.02	13.08	15.32	18.28
Cakes and cupcakes	12.48	9.96	13.29	13.29	11.69
Bread and cracker products	1.89	1.36	1.89	1.80	2.26
Sweetrolls, coffee cakes, doughnuts	8.77	7.90	8.35	9.56	8.54
Pies, tarts, turnovers	5.12	4.70	4.59	5.24	5.60
Meats, poultry, fish, and eggs	**292.98**	**312.24**	**286.15**	**284.92**	**270.66**
Beef	90.70	96.25	90.28	91.02	79.28
Ground beef	35.38	36.41	36.77	36.86	28.58
Roast	15.76	17.38	15.07	15.24	14.60
Chuck roast	4.90	5.58	4.95	4.75	4.06
Round roast	5.94	6.64	5.91	5.47	5.38
Other roast	4.92	5.16	4.22	5.02	5.16
Steak	33.90	35.70	33.25	33.90	30.58
Round steak	6.40	7.70	6.37	7.08	4.24
Sirloin steak	9.78	11.05	9.08	9.87	8.77
Other steak	17.72	16.95	17.79	16.94	17.58
Other beef	5.66	6.77	5.20	5.02	5.52
Pork	62.30	75.69	62.88	58.73	49.30
Bacon	9.11	11.92	8.42	9.15	6.99
Pork chops	15.73	19.42	16.00	14.54	12.32

	total consumer units	not a high school graduate	high school graduate	some college	college graduate
Ham	$14.75	$16.11	$15.65	$12.98	$13.05
Ham, not canned	13.66	14.80	14.80	11.58	12.23
Canned ham	1.09	1.31	0.85	1.40	0.82
Sausage	9.13	11.35	8.83	9.27	6.88
Other pork	13.57	16.90	13.98	12.80	10.06
Other meats	37.58	37.57	38.67	37.31	33.47
Frankfurters	7.50	8.30	7.75	7.96	5.53
Lunch meats (cold cuts)	26.26	24.93	27.64	26.00	23.74
Bologna, liverwurst, salami	9.49	10.51	10.12	9.33	7.28
Other lunchmeats	16.77	14.42	17.52	16.67	16.47
Lamb, organ meats and others	3.81	4.34	3.29	3.34	4.20
Lamb and organ meats	3.74	4.23	3.26	3.34	4.04
Mutton, goat and game	0.07	0.11	0.03	-	0.17
Poultry	54.63	54.43	51.29	52.77	56.47
Fresh and frozen chickens	43.16	43.95	39.66	42.50	44.16
Fresh and frozen whole chicken	11.82	14.67	10.74	9.94	11.78
Fresh and frozen chicken parts	31.33	29.28	28.92	32.56	32.38
Other poultry	11.48	10.48	11.63	10.27	12.31
Fish and seafood	35.77	32.70	31.73	34.61	41.62
Canned fish and seafood	6.01	4.98	5.60	5.30	7.56
Fresh fish and shellfish	20.50	19.18	17.47	20.21	24.05
Frozen fish and shellfish	9.26	8.55	8.66	9.10	10.00
Eggs	12.00	15.59	11.29	10.48	10.53
Dairy products	**115.57**	**97.55**	**110.49**	**121.86**	**121.22**
Fresh milk and cream	50.85	50.40	49.89	52.36	46.94
Fresh milk, all types	47.58	47.91	47.28	48.19	43.32
Cream	3.28	2.49	2.61	4.17	3.62
Other dairy products	64.72	47.14	60.60	69.49	74.28
Butter	4.66	4.31	4.30	4.61	5.07
Cheese	32.73	24.61	31.52	33.94	37.02
Ice cream and related products	19.06	12.75	18.38	21.50	21.10
Miscellaneous dairy products	8.26	5.48	6.39	9.44	11.08
Fruits and vegetables	**174.63**	**156.77**	**153.77**	**171.15**	**204.79**
Fresh fruits	53.21	49.47	45.77	49.35	65.08
Apples	10.15	8.59	8.95	9.69	12.53
Bananas	11.86	12.33	10.43	10.71	13.47
Oranges	6.54	6.26	5.18	6.23	8.28
Citrus fruits, excl. oranges	4.38	4.06	3.71	3.82	5.70
Other fresh fruits	20.27	18.24	17.49	18.90	25.11
Fresh vegetables	53.96	49.84	46.41	51.28	65.08
Potatoes	11.20	12.13	10.26	10.18	11.75
Lettuce	6.95	6.11	6.41	6.45	8.24
Tomatoes	8.40	8.41	7.93	7.56	9.14
Other fresh vegetables	27.40	23.19	21.82	27.09	35.95

	total consumer units	not a high school graduate	high school graduate	some college	college graduate
Processed fruits	$37.23	$31.08	$33.28	$38.42	$43.06
Frozen fruits and fruit juices	6.51	4.80	5.06	7.22	8.53
Frozen orange juice	3.80	2.88	3.15	4.27	4.60
Frozen fruits	0.64	0.41	0.43	0.70	0.98
Frozen fruit juices	2.08	1.51	1.48	2.25	2.96
Canned fruit	5.69	4.71	5.34	5.70	6.47
Dried fruit	2.36	1.94	2.35	2.22	2.65
Fresh fruit juices	7.16	6.72	6.16	6.51	8.83
Canned and bottled fruit juices	15.51	12.92	14.37	16.77	16.59
Processed vegetables	30.23	26.37	28.32	32.08	31.56
Frozen vegetables	9.93	5.93	9.38	11.01	12.01
Canned and dried vegetables and juices	20.30	20.43	18.94	21.07	19.55
Canned beans	4.18	4.85	3.65	4.38	3.78
Canned corn	2.72	2.80	2.43	3.58	2.00
Other canned and dried vegetables	10.82	10.63	10.55	10.67	10.60
Frozen vegetable juices	0.09	0.03	0.08	0.07	0.16
Fresh and canned vegetable juices	2.48	2.13	2.22	2.36	3.01
Other food at home	**330.17**	**269.03**	**313.89**	**345.76**	**359.87**
Sugar and other sweets	42.10	37.40	41.22	42.70	43.05
Candy and chewing gum	24.93	19.36	24.22	25.78	27.48
Sugar	7.32	9.52	7.45	6.88	5.26
Artificial sweeteners	1.36	1.50	1.30	1.13	1.43
Jams, preserves, other sweets	8.49	7.02	8.25	8.92	8.88
Fats and oils	31.70	31.86	31.28	29.94	31.27
Margarine	5.66	5.19	6.35	5.11	5.25
Fats and oils	9.24	12.95	8.33	7.62	8.23
Salad dressings	9.50	7.19	9.77	9.65	10.10
Nondairy cream and imitation milk	2.62	2.20	2.59	2.52	2.89
Peanut butter	4.68	4.32	4.24	5.04	4.80
Miscellaneous foods	144.65	106.04	136.92	156.24	162.74
Frozen prepared foods	26.46	15.02	25.93	31.03	29.78
Frozen meals	8.57	5.16	7.33	11.37	9.52
Other frozen prepared foods	17.88	9.85	18.61	19.66	20.27
Canned and packaged soups	11.82	10.14	10.78	11.22	14.11
Potato chips, nuts, and other snacks	29.63	18.50	28.59	30.75	36.42
Potato chips and other snacks	23.27	14.07	22.45	25.23	27.95
Nuts	6.36	4.43	6.14	5.52	8.46
Condiments and seasonings	31.90	24.34	30.32	32.93	36.42
Salt, spices and other seasonings	7.72	6.57	7.46	7.90	8.19
Olives, pickles, relishes	4.06	3.00	4.38	3.40	4.84
Sauces and gravies	14.57	10.53	13.48	16.04	16.62
Baking needs and misc. products	5.54	4.23	5.00	5.59	6.78
Other canned/packaged prepared foods	44.85	38.05	41.28	50.31	46.02
Prepared salads	4.39	2.14	4.36	4.81	5.48
Prepared desserts	3.20	2.71	3.13	3.30	3.31

	total consumer units	not a high school graduate	high school graduate	some college	college graduate
Baby food	$11.24	$8.22	$10.13	$14.64	$10.92
Miscellaneous prepared foods	26.02	24.97	23.66	27.56	26.31
Nonalcoholic beverages	93.16	85.93	90.76	98.20	89.75
Cola	35.78	36.03	36.13	37.89	30.28
Other carbonated drinks	15.56	13.08	16.24	16.98	14.08
Coffee	17.20	17.69	15.78	15.66	18.74
Roasted coffee	11.65	10.69	10.90	11.03	13.04
Instant and freeze-dried coffee	5.55	7.00	4.88	4.62	5.70
Noncarb. fruit flavored drinks incl. non-frozen lemonade	8.74	8.43	7.85	9.32	8.87
Tea	6.50	4.48	6.44	7.27	6.94
Nonalcoholic beer	0.26	0.20	0.09	0.27	0.51
Other nonalcoholic beverages	9.11	6.03	8.23	10.81	10.34
Food prepared by cu on out-of-town trips	18.56	7.81	13.71	18.67	33.06
FOOD AWAY FROM HOME	**679.38**	**324.37**	**558.68**	**720.85**	**1,035.62**
Meals at restaurants, carry-outs, other	**522.48**	**274.37**	**447.10**	**562.16**	**737.01**
Lunch	180.70	89.48	154.09	192.52	261.74
Dinner	260.72	134.98	219.73	277.58	376.38
Snacks and nonalcoholic beverages	40.69	23.09	37.55	47.26	49.21
Breakfast and brunch	40.38	26.82	35.73	44.80	49.68
Board (including at school)	**20.29**	**4.80**	**9.23**	**20.54**	**47.14**
Catered affairs	**22.44**	**2.42**	**9.77**	**17.44**	**60.56**
Food on out-of-town trips	**83.16**	**24.51**	**63.40**	**85.37**	**152.98**
School lunches	**21.50**	**13.45**	**21.76**	**23.16**	**24.84**
Meals as pay	**9.52**	**4.81**	**7.42**	**12.18**	**13.10**
ALCOHOLIC BEVERAGES	**111.21**	**62.75**	**93.85**	**110.55**	**164.87**
At home	**66.05**	**50.67**	**59.43**	**62.21**	**85.16**
Beer and ale	39.87	42.38	39.98	36.54	37.75
Whiskey	5.47	1.30	5.19	5.50	8.71
Wine	14.56	3.98	9.68	13.43	29.12
Other alcoholic beverages	6.14	3.01	4.57	6.74	9.58
Away from home	**45.16**	**12.09**	**34.42**	**48.34**	**79.70**
Beer and ale	15.42	4.33	13.23	16.92	24.41
Wine	6.32	2.06	4.82	6.53	10.92
Other alcoholic beverages	11.18	2.68	8.01	11.76	20.57
Alcoholic beverages purchased on trips	12.24	3.02	8.37	13.14	23.81

Note: Expenditures listed for items in a given category may not add to the total for that category because the listing is incomplete. (-) means insufficient data.

Education

indexed per capita spending

(indexed average annual per capita spending of consumer units on food and alcoholic beverages, by education of consumer unit reference person, 1994; index definition: an index of 100 is the per capita average for all consumer units; an index of 132 means that per capita spending by consumer units in the educational group is 32 percent above the per capita average for all consumer units; an index of 68 indicates that per capita spending by consumer units in the educational group is 32 percent below the per capita average for all consumer units)

	total consumer units	not a high school graduate	high school graduate	some college	college graduate
Per capita spending of cu, total	*$12,700.25*	*$7,516.78*	*$11,141.94*	*$12,776.61*	*$18,190.85*
Per capita spending of cu, index	*100*	*59*	*88*	*101*	*143*
Food, per capita spending index	*100*	*74*	*90*	*103*	*124*
Alcoholic beverages, per capita spending index	*100*	*56*	*84*	*99*	*148*
FOOD AT HOME	**100**	**90**	**95**	**101**	**105**
Cereals and bakery products	**100**	**85**	**94**	**102**	**109**
Cereals and cereal products	100	87	93	102	109
Flour	100	161	98	65	80
Prepared flour mixes	100	92	90	110	101
Ready-to-eat and cooked cereals	100	77	95	102	114
Rice	100	105	86	107	100
Pasta, cornmeal, and other cereal products	100	91	90	103	110
Bakery products	100	83	95	103	109
Bread	100	98	96	96	104
White bread	100	113	100	89	92
Bread, other than white	100	82	91	103	115
Crackers and cookies	100	79	92	106	114
Cookies	100	82	94	105	110
Crackers	100	73	87	106	123
Frozen and refrigerated bakery products	100	73	98	102	114
Other bakery products	100	77	97	106	109
Biscuits and rolls	100	63	91	106	127
Cakes and cupcakes	100	80	107	107	94
Bread and cracker products	100	72	100	95	119
Sweetrolls, coffee cakes, doughnuts	100	90	95	109	97
Pies, tarts, turnovers	100	92	90	102	109
Meats, poultry, fish, and eggs	**100**	**107**	**98**	**97**	**92**
Beef	100	106	100	100	87
Ground beef	100	103	104	104	81
Roast	100	110	96	97	93
Chuck roast	100	114	101	97	83
Round roast	100	112	100	92	91
Other roast	100	105	86	102	105
Steak	100	105	98	100	90
Round steak	100	120	100	111	66
Sirloin steak	100	113	93	101	90
Other steak	100	96	100	96	99
Other beef	100	120	92	89	98
Pork	100	122	101	94	79
Bacon	100	131	92	100	77
Pork chops	100	123	102	92	78

	total consumer units	not a high school graduate	high school graduate	some college	college graduate
Ham	100	109	106	88	88
Ham, not canned	100	108	108	85	90
Canned ham	100	121	78	129	75
Sausage	100	124	97	102	75
Other pork	100	124	103	94	74
Other meats	100	100	103	99	89
Frankfurters	100	111	103	106	74
Lunch meats (cold cuts)	100	95	105	99	90
Bologna, liverwurst, salami	100	111	107	98	77
Other lunchmeats	100	86	104	99	98
Lamb, organ meats and others	100	114	86	88	110
Lamb and organ meats	100	113	87	89	108
Mutton, goat and game	100	150	37	-	233
Poultry	100	100	94	97	103
Fresh and frozen chickens	100	102	92	98	102
Fresh and frozen whole chicken	100	124	91	84	100
Fresh and frozen chicken parts	100	93	92	104	103
Other poultry	100	91	101	89	107
Fish and seafood	100	91	89	97	116
Canned fish and seafood	100	83	93	88	126
Fresh fish and shellfish	100	94	85	99	117
Frozen fish and shellfish	100	92	93	98	108
Eggs	100	130	94	87	88
Dairy products	**100**	**84**	**96**	**105**	**105**
Fresh milk and cream	100	99	98	103	92
Fresh milk, all types	100	101	99	101	91
Cream	100	76	80	127	111
Other dairy products	100	73	94	107	115
Butter	100	92	92	99	109
Cheese	100	75	96	104	113
Ice cream and related products	100	67	96	113	111
Miscellaneous dairy products	100	66	77	114	134
Fruits and vegetables	**100**	**90**	**88**	**98**	**117**
Fresh fruits	100	93	86	93	122
Apples	100	85	88	96	123
Bananas	100	104	88	90	114
Oranges	100	96	79	95	127
Citrus fruits, excl. oranges	100	93	85	87	130
Other fresh fruits	100	90	86	93	124
Fresh vegetables	100	92	86	95	121
Potatoes	100	108	92	91	105
Lettuce	100	88	92	93	118
Tomatoes	100	100	94	90	109
Other fresh vegetables	100	85	80	99	131

	total consumer units	not a high school graduate	high school graduate	some college	college graduate
Processed fruits	100	83	89	103	116
Frozen fruits and fruit juices	100	74	78	111	131
Frozen orange juice	100	76	83	112	121
Frozen fruits	100	64	68	109	153
Frozen fruit juices	100	73	71	108	142
Canned fruit	100	83	94	100	114
Dried fruit	100	82	100	94	112
Fresh fruit juices	100	94	86	91	123
Canned and bottled fruit juices	100	83	93	108	107
Processed vegetables	100	87	94	106	104
Frozen vegetables	100	60	94	111	121
Canned and dried vegetables and juices	100	101	93	104	96
Canned beans	100	116	87	105	90
Canned corn	100	103	89	132	73
Other canned and dried vegetables	100	98	97	99	98
Frozen vegetable juices	100	29	92	78	174
Fresh and canned vegetable juices	100	86	89	95	121
Other food at home	**100**	**81**	**95**	**105**	**109**
Sugar and other sweets	100	89	98	101	102
Candy and chewing gum	100	78	97	103	110
Sugar	100	130	102	94	72
Artificial sweeteners	100	111	96	83	105
Jams, preserves, other sweets	100	83	97	105	105
Fats and oils	100	100	99	94	99
Margarine	100	92	112	90	93
Fats and oils	100	140	90	82	89
Salad dressings	100	76	103	102	106
Nondairy cream and imitation milk	100	84	99	96	110
Peanut butter	100	92	91	108	103
Miscellaneous foods	100	73	95	108	113
Frozen prepared foods	100	57	98	117	113
Frozen meals	100	60	85	133	111
Other frozen prepared foods	100	55	104	110	113
Canned and packaged soups	100	86	91	95	119
Potato chips, nuts, and other snacks	100	62	97	104	123
Potato chips and other snacks	100	60	96	108	120
Nuts	100	70	97	87	133
Condiments and seasonings	100	76	95	103	114
Salt, spices and other seasonings	100	85	97	102	106
Olives, pickles, relishes	100	74	108	84	119
Sauces and gravies	100	72	93	110	114
Baking needs and misc. products	100	76	90	101	122
Other canned/packaged prepared foods	100	85	92	112	103
Prepared salads	100	49	99	110	125
Prepared desserts	100	85	98	103	104

	total consumer units	not a high school graduate	high school graduate	some college	college graduate
Baby food	100	73	90	130	97
Miscellaneous prepared foods	100	96	91	106	101
Nonalcoholic beverages	100	92	97	105	96
Cola	100	101	101	106	85
Other carbonated drinks	100	84	104	109	91
Coffee	100	103	92	91	109
Roasted coffee	100	92	94	95	112
Instant and freeze-dried coffee	100	126	88	83	103
Noncarb. fruit flavored drinks incl.					
non-frozen lemonade	100	96	90	107	101
Tea	100	69	99	112	107
Nonalcoholic beer	100	74	35	103	194
Other nonalcoholic beverages	100	66	90	119	113
Food prepared by cu on out-of-town trips	100	42	74	101	178
FOOD AWAY FROM HOME	**100**	**48**	**82**	**106**	**152**
Meals at restaurants, carry-outs, other	**100**	**53**	**86**	**108**	**141**
Lunch	100	50	85	107	145
Dinner	100	52	84	106	144
Snacks and nonalcoholic beverages	100	57	92	116	121
Breakfast and brunch	100	66	88	111	123
Board (including at school)	**100**	**24**	**46**	**101**	**232**
Catered affairs	**100**	**11**	**44**	**78**	**270**
Food on out-of-town trips	**100**	**29**	**76**	**103**	**184**
School lunches	**100**	**63**	**101**	**108**	**116**
Meals as pay	**100**	**51**	**78**	**128**	**138**
ALCOHOLIC BEVERAGES	**100**	**56**	**84**	**99**	**148**
At home	**100**	**77**	**90**	**94**	**129**
Beer and ale	100	106	100	92	95
Whiskey	100	24	95	101	159
Wine	100	27	66	92	200
Other alcoholic beverages	100	49	74	110	156
Away from home	**100**	**27**	**76**	**107**	**176**
Beer and ale	100	28	86	110	158
Wine	100	33	76	103	173
Other alcoholic beverages	100	24	72	105	184
Alcoholic beverages purchased on trips	100	25	68	107	194

Note: (-) means insufficient data.

Education

total spending

(total annual spending on food and alcoholic beverages by education of consumer unit reference person, 1994; numbers in thousands)

	total consumer units	not a high school graduate	high school graduate	some college	college graduate
Number of consumer units	**102,210**	**21,096**	**32,148**	**24,387**	**24,578**
Total spending of all cu's	**$3,245,231,892**	**$412,292,418**	**$931,297,019**	**$778,958,092**	**$1,117,736,655**
Food, total spending	**450,799,249**	**71,591,386**	**132,473,550**	**110,957,192**	**133,905,860**
Alcoholic beverages, total spending	**28,417,446**	**3,442,023**	**7,844,433**	**6,739,835**	**10,130,314**
FOOD AT HOME	**$277,198,631**	**$53,800,285**	**$85,776,008**	**$67,008,892**	**$70,271,943**
Cereals and bakery products	**43,815,383**	**7,968,592**	**13,534,308**	**10,694,431**	**11,497,343**
Cereals and cereal products	16,531,445	3,099,846	5,030,519	4,010,198	4,349,323
Flour	776,796	268,341	248,504	119,740	149,680
Prepared flour mixes	1,307,266	259,481	384,812	343,369	318,039
Ready-to-eat and cooked cereals	10,044,177	1,662,576	3,127,357	2,452,844	2,758,389
Rice	1,577,100	356,522	441,714	400,922	378,255
Pasta, cornmeal, and other cereal products	2,826,107	552,926	828,454	693,322	744,959
Bakery products	27,282,915	4,868,746	8,503,789	6,684,233	7,148,020
Bread	7,790,446	1,631,776	2,437,461	1,778,056	1,941,416
White bread	3,848,207	934,764	1,263,095	813,063	851,873
Bread, other than white	3,942,240	697,223	1,174,366	964,994	1,089,543
Crackers and cookies	6,394,258	1,084,545	1,916,021	1,613,200	1,752,411
Cookies	4,391,964	770,004	1,344,429	1,104,243	1,158,361
Crackers	2,002,294	314,752	571,270	508,713	594,050
Frozen and refrigerated bakery products	2,203,648	345,552	706,613	536,758	604,865
Other bakery products	10,894,564	1,806,661	3,443,694	2,756,219	2,849,328
Biscuits and rolls	3,675,472	494,490	1,093,675	933,778	1,123,460
Cakes and cupcakes	3,187,930	546,386	1,110,713	810,136	718,415
Bread and cracker products	482,431	74,469	157,847	109,498	138,620
Sweetrolls, coffee cakes, doughnuts	2,240,443	433,312	697,933	582,849	524,495
Pies, tarts, turnovers	1,308,288	258,004	383,526	319,714	344,338
Meats, poultry, fish, and eggs	**74,863,715**	**17,126,155**	**23,917,469**	**17,370,616**	**16,630,704**
Beef	23,177,140	5,279,485	7,546,100	5,549,506	4,871,360
Ground beef	9,040,475	1,996,947	3,073,349	2,247,018	1,755,852
Roast	4,028,096	953,328	1,259,559	929,145	897,097
Chuck roast	1,253,095	306,314	413,423	289,474	249,712
Round roast	1,516,796	364,328	493,793	333,614	330,574
Other roast	1,258,205	282,897	352,342	306,301	316,810
Steak	8,662,298	1,958,131	2,778,873	2,067,042	1,879,234
Round steak	1,635,360	422,131	532,692	431,894	260,527
Sirloin steak	2,498,012	605,877	759,014	601,871	538,750
Other steak	4,528,925	929,912	1,487,166	1,033,033	1,080,203
Other beef	1,446,272	371,079	434,319	306,301	339,176
Pork	15,918,185	4,151,693	5,255,877	3,580,743	3,028,993
Bacon	2,328,344	653,554	704,041	557,731	429,378
Pork chops	4,018,897	1,065,137	1,337,678	886,467	757,002

	total consumer units	not a high school graduate	high school graduate	some college	college graduate
Ham	$3,769,505	$883,500	$1,308,102	$791,114	$801,980
Ham, not canned	3,491,494	811,563	1,236,734	705,760	751,595
Canned ham	278,011	71,937	71,369	85,355	50,385
Sausage	2,332,432	622,543	737,797	565,047	422,742
Other pork	3,467,985	926,747	1,168,258	780,140	617,891
Other meats	9,602,630	2,060,657	3,232,481	2,274,575	2,056,687
Frankfurters	1,917,460	455,041	647,461	485,301	339,668
Lunch meats (cold cuts)	6,711,109	1,367,443	2,310,477	1,585,155	1,458,950
Bologna, liverwurst, salami	2,425,443	576,343	846,135	568,705	447,074
Other lunchmeats	4,285,665	791,100	1,464,020	1,016,450	1,011,876
Lamb, organ meats and others	974,061	238,174	274,865	203,875	258,069
Lamb and organ meats	955,664	232,056	272,615	203,875	247,992
Mutton, goat and game	18,398	5,907	2,250	-	10,323
Poultry	13,959,842	2,985,506	4,287,257	3,217,133	3,469,922
Fresh and frozen chickens	11,027,437	2,410,640	3,314,780	2,590,875	2,713,657
Fresh and frozen whole chicken	3,021,328	804,601	897,572	606,261	723,822
Fresh and frozen chicken parts	8,006,109	1,605,828	2,417,208	1,984,858	1,989,589
Other poultry	2,932,405	575,077	972,477	626,014	756,265
Fish and seafood	9,140,640	1,793,793	2,652,210	2,109,963	2,557,095
Canned fish and seafood	1,536,216	273,193	468,396	322,884	464,524
Fresh fish and shellfish	5,239,285	1,052,058	1,460,162	1,232,275	1,477,875
Frozen fish and shellfish	2,366,162	468,753	723,651	554,804	614,696
Eggs	3,066,300	855,021	943,865	639,183	646,893
Dairy products	**29,530,513**	**5,350,578**	**9,235,156**	**7,429,256**	**7,448,363**
Fresh milk and cream	12,993,957	2,764,631	4,170,239	3,192,502	2,884,474
Fresh milk, all types	12,156,857	2,627,929	3,951,632	2,938,146	2,662,043
Cream	837,100	136,702	218,285	254,356	222,431
Other dairy products	16,536,556	2,585,737	5,064,917	4,236,754	4,563,889
Butter	1,190,747	236,275	359,736	280,938	311,649
Cheese	8,363,844	1,349,722	2,634,207	2,069,237	2,274,940
Ice cream and related products	4,869,284	699,121	1,536,674	1,311,045	1,296,490
Miscellaneous dairy products	2,111,659	300,829	534,300	575,533	680,811
Fruits and vegetables	**44,621,820**	**8,598,730**	**12,853,092**	**10,434,466**	**12,583,199**
Fresh fruits	13,595,974	2,713,578	3,825,612	3,008,868	3,998,841
Apples	2,593,068	471,285	748,405	590,897	769,783
Bananas	3,031,549	676,338	872,175	652,840	827,541
Oranges	1,672,156	343,232	432,712	379,949	508,765
Citrus fruits, excl. oranges	1,120,222	222,563	310,228	232,896	349,991
Other fresh fruits	5,178,981	1,000,372	1,461,770	1,152,286	1,542,761
Fresh vegetables	13,787,107	2,733,620	3,878,978	3,126,657	3,999,086
Potatoes	2,862,902	665,157	857,709	620,405	721,856
Lettuce	1,776,410	335,215	535,586	393,362	506,061
Tomatoes	2,147,432	461,159	662,570	461,158	561,607
Other fresh vegetables	7,001,385	1,272,089	1,823,435	1,651,732	2,209,071

	total consumer units	not a high school graduate	high school graduate	some college	college graduate
Processed fruits	$9,513,707	$1,704,979	$2,781,445	$2,342,615	$2,646,067
Frozen fruits and fruit juices	1,663,979	263,278	423,068	439,941	524,003
Frozen orange juice	969,973	157,798	263,292	260,209	282,401
Frozen fruits	163,536	22,573	36,327	42,433	59,970
Frozen fruit juices	530,470	82,907	123,448	137,299	181,631
Canned fruit	1,454,448	258,426	446,214	347,759	397,426
Dried fruit	602,017	106,535	196,103	135,592	162,706
Fresh fruit juices	1,829,559	368,336	514,689	396,776	542,682
Canned and bottled fruit juices	3,963,704	708,404	1,201,371	1,022,547	1,019,250
Processed vegetables	7,724,010	1,446,342	2,367,057	1,956,081	1,939,204
Frozen vegetables	2,537,874	325,511	784,090	671,374	738,077
Canned and dried vegetables and juices	5,186,135	1,120,830	1,582,968	1,284,707	1,201,373
Canned beans	1,067,072	266,232	305,085	267,282	232,016
Canned corn	696,050	153,368	203,175	218,508	122,890
Other canned and dried vegetables	2,764,781	582,882	881,498	650,401	651,563
Frozen vegetable juices	23,508	1,477	7,073	4,390	9,831
Fresh and canned vegetable juices	634,724	117,083	185,815	144,127	185,072
Other food at home	**84,367,200**	**14,756,230**	**26,236,304**	**21,080,123**	**22,112,335**
Sugar and other sweets	10,757,603	2,051,586	3,445,301	2,603,556	2,645,084
Candy and chewing gum	6,369,727	1,061,973	2,024,360	1,571,742	1,688,509
Sugar	1,871,465	522,126	622,385	419,213	322,955
Artificial sweeteners	346,492	82,485	108,660	68,771	87,743
Jams, preserves, other sweets	2,169,918	385,002	689,896	543,830	545,877
Fats and oils	8,100,143	1,747,382	2,614,597	1,825,611	1,921,262
Margarine	1,447,294	284,585	530,442	311,666	322,463
Fats and oils	2,360,029	710,091	696,326	464,328	505,569
Salad dressings	2,427,488	394,495	816,881	588,214	620,349
Nondairy cream and imitation milk	670,498	120,880	216,678	153,882	177,699
Peanut butter	1,195,857	237,119	354,271	307,520	295,182
Miscellaneous foods	36,961,180	5,816,167	11,444,045	9,525,562	9,999,805
Frozen prepared foods	6,760,169	823,799	2,167,740	1,891,943	1,830,078
Frozen meals	2,190,360	283,108	612,419	693,322	584,711
Other frozen prepared foods	4,569,809	540,480	1,555,320	1,198,621	1,245,367
Canned and packaged soups	3,020,306	556,302	901,430	683,811	866,866
Potato chips, nuts, and other snacks	7,570,695	1,014,507	2,389,882	1,874,629	2,237,581
Potato chips and other snacks	5,946,578	771,692	1,876,479	1,538,332	1,717,511
Nuts	1,624,117	242,815	513,404	336,297	520,070
Condiments and seasonings	8,150,225	1,334,955	2,534,548	2,007,538	2,237,827
Salt, spices and other seasonings	1,972,653	360,531	623,671	481,399	503,357
Olives, pickles, relishes	1,038,454	164,549	365,844	207,290	297,148
Sauces and gravies	3,723,510	577,819	1,127,109	977,919	1,020,970
Baking needs and misc. products	1,415,609	231,845	417,924	340,930	416,597
Other canned/packaged prepared foods	11,459,785	2,086,816	3,450,445	3,067,397	2,827,453
Prepared salads	1,121,244	117,294	364,237	293,376	336,473
Prepared desserts	816,658	148,516	261,685	201,193	203,506

	total consumer units	not a high school graduate	high school graduate	some college	college graduate
Baby food	$2,873,123	$451,032	$847,100	$892,808	$670,979
Miscellaneous prepared foods	6,648,761	1,369,763	1,977,423	1,680,020	1,616,495
Nonalcoholic beverages	23,803,687	4,713,057	7,585,964	5,987,009	5,514,812
Cola	9,142,685	1,976,062	3,019,983	2,310,181	1,860,555
Other carbonated drinks	3,974,947	717,264	1,357,289	1,034,984	865,391
Coffee	4,396,052	970,205	1,318,711	954,507	1,151,234
Roasted coffee	2,977,377	586,258	911,074	672,593	800,997
Instant and freeze-dried coffee	1,418,675	383,947	407,637	281,914	350,237
Noncarb. fruit flavored drinks incl. non-frozen lemonade	2,234,311	462,213	656,462	568,461	544,894
Tea	1,660,913	245,557	538,158	443,356	426,183
Nonalcoholic beer	67,459	10,759	7,716	16,583	31,460
Other nonalcoholic beverages	2,327,322	330,785	687,646	658,937	635,096
Food prepared by cu on out-of-town trips	4,743,566	428,249	1,146,076	1,138,385	2,031,126
FOOD AWAY FROM HOME	**173,599,597**	**17,791,312**	**46,697,220**	**43,948,300**	**63,633,917**
Meals at restaurants, carry-outs, other	**133,507,724**	**15,048,832**	**37,370,764**	**34,273,734**	**45,285,457**
Lunch	46,174,390	4,907,773	12,879,453	11,737,463	16,082,614
Dinner	66,619,456	7,403,430	18,365,831	16,923,603	23,126,423
Snacks and nonalcoholic beverages	10,396,801	1,266,604	3,138,609	2,881,568	3,023,831
Breakfast and brunch	10,318,100	1,471,024	2,986,871	2,731,100	3,052,588
Board (including at school)	**5,184,091**	**263,278**	**771,873**	**1,252,029**	**2,896,272**
Catered affairs	**5,732,959**	**132,905**	**816,238**	**1,063,273**	**3,721,109**
Food on out-of-town trips	**21,248,437**	**1,344,448**	**5,299,598**	**5,204,674**	**9,399,610**
School lunches	**5,494,810**	**737,516**	**1,818,612**	**1,412,251**	**1,526,540**
Meals as pay	**2,431,576**	**263,911**	**620,456**	**742,584**	**804,930**
ALCOHOLIC BEVERAGES	**28,417,446**	**3,442,023**	**7,844,433**	**6,739,835**	**10,130,314**
At home	**16,877,937**	**2,778,976**	**4,967,509**	**3,792,910**	**5,232,902**
Beer and ale	10,188,293	2,324,357	3,342,106	2,227,509	2,319,672
Whiskey	1,398,233	71,094	433,998	335,321	535,063
Wine	3,721,466	218,555	809,487	818,915	1,789,524
Other alcoholic beverages	1,568,924	164,971	381,918	410,921	588,397
Away from home	**11,540,531**	**663,047**	**2,876,925**	**2,946,925**	**4,897,412**
Beer and ale	3,941,218	237,541	1,106,213	1,031,326	1,499,995
Wine	1,613,896	113,075	402,493	397,996	670,734
Other alcoholic beverages	2,857,792	147,039	669,321	716,978	1,263,801
Alcoholic beverages purchased on trips	3,128,648	165,393	699,219	800,869	1,462,883

Note: Spending for items in a given category may not add to the total for that category because the listing is incomplete. Numbers may not add to total due to rounding. (-) means insufficient data.

Education
market shares

(percent of total annual spending on food accounted for by consumer units by education, 1994)

	total consumer units	not a high school graduate	high school graduate	some college	college graduate
Share of total consumer units	*100.0%*	*20.6%*	*31.5%*	*23.9%*	*24.0%*
Share of total spending	*100.0*	*12.7*	*28.7*	*24.0*	*34.4*
Share of food spending	*100.0*	*15.9*	*29.4*	*24.6*	*29.7*
Share of alcoholic beverages spending	*100.0*	*12.1*	*27.6*	*23.7*	*35.6*
FOOD AT HOME	**100.0%**	**19.4%**	**30.9%**	**24.2%**	**25.4%**
Cereals and bakery products	**100.0**	**18.2**	**30.9**	**24.4**	**26.2**
Cereals and cereal products	100.0	18.8	30.4	24.3	26.3
Flour	100.0	34.5	32.0	15.4	19.3
Prepared flour mixes	100.0	19.8	29.4	26.3	24.3
Ready-to-eat and cooked cereals	100.0	16.6	31.1	24.4	27.5
Rice	100.0	22.6	28.0	25.4	24.0
Pasta, cornmeal, and other cereal products	100.0	19.6	29.3	24.5	26.4
Bakery products	100.0	17.8	31.2	24.5	26.2
Bread	100.0	20.9	31.3	22.8	24.9
White bread	100.0	24.3	32.8	21.1	22.1
Bread, other than white	100.0	17.7	29.8	24.5	27.6
Crackers and cookies	100.0	17.0	30.0	25.2	27.4
Cookies	100.0	17.5	30.6	25.1	26.4
Crackers	100.0	15.7	28.5	25.4	29.7
Frozen and refrigerated bakery products	100.0	15.7	32.1	24.4	27.4
Other bakery products	100.0	16.6	31.6	25.3	26.2
Biscuits and rolls	100.0	13.5	29.8	25.4	30.6
Cakes and cupcakes	100.0	17.1	34.8	25.4	22.5
Bread and cracker products	100.0	15.4	32.7	22.7	28.7
Sweetrolls, coffee cakes, doughnuts	100.0	19.3	31.2	26.0	23.4
Pies, tarts, turnovers	100.0	19.7	29.3	24.4	26.3
Meats, poultry, fish, and eggs	**100.0**	**22.9**	**31.9**	**23.2**	**22.2**
Beef	100.0	22.8	32.6	23.9	21.0
Ground beef	100.0	22.1	34.0	24.9	19.4
Roast	100.0	23.7	31.3	23.1	22.3
Chuck roast	100.0	24.4	33.0	23.1	19.9
Round roast	100.0	24.0	32.6	22.0	21.8
Other roast	100.0	22.5	28.0	24.3	25.2
Steak	100.0	22.6	32.1	23.9	21.7
Round steak	100.0	25.8	32.6	26.4	15.9
Sirloin steak	100.0	24.3	30.4	24.1	21.6
Other steak	100.0	20.5	32.8	22.8	23.9
Other beef	100.0	25.7	30.0	21.2	23.5
Pork	100.0	26.1	33.0	22.5	19.0
Bacon	100.0	28.1	30.2	24.0	18.4
Pork chops	100.0	26.5	33.3	22.1	18.8

	total consumer units	not a high school graduate	high school graduate	some college	college graduate
Ham	100.0%	23.4%	34.7%	21.0%	21.3%
Ham, not canned	100.0	23.2	35.4	20.2	21.5
Canned ham	100.0	25.9	25.7	30.7	18.1
Sausage	100.0	26.7	31.6	24.2	18.1
Other pork	100.0	26.7	33.7	22.5	17.8
Other meats	100.0	21.5	33.7	23.7	21.4
Frankfurters	100.0	23.7	33.8	25.3	17.7
Lunch meats (cold cuts)	100.0	20.4	34.4	23.6	21.7
Bologna, liverwurst, salami	100.0	23.8	34.9	23.4	18.4
Other lunchmeats	100.0	18.5	34.2	23.7	23.6
Lamb, organ meats and others	100.0	24.5	28.2	20.9	26.5
Lamb and organ meats	100.0	24.3	28.5	21.3	25.9
Mutton, goat and game	100.0	32.1	12.2	-	56.1
Poultry	100.0	21.4	30.7	23.0	24.9
Fresh and frozen chickens	100.0	21.9	30.1	23.5	24.6
Fresh and frozen whole chicken	100.0	26.6	29.7	20.1	24.0
Fresh and frozen chicken parts	100.0	20.1	30.2	24.8	24.9
Other poultry	100.0	19.6	33.2	21.3	25.8
Fish and seafood	100.0	19.6	29.0	23.1	28.0
Canned fish and seafood	100.0	17.8	30.5	21.0	30.2
Fresh fish and shellfish	100.0	20.1	27.9	23.5	28.2
Frozen fish and shellfish	100.0	19.8	30.6	23.4	26.0
Eggs	100.0	27.9	30.8	20.8	21.1
Dairy products	**100.0**	**18.1**	**31.3**	**25.2**	**25.2**
Fresh milk and cream	100.0	21.3	32.1	24.6	22.2
Fresh milk, all types	100.0	21.6	32.5	24.2	21.9
Cream	100.0	16.3	26.1	30.4	26.6
Other dairy products	100.0	15.6	30.6	25.6	27.6
Butter	100.0	19.8	30.2	23.6	26.2
Cheese	100.0	16.1	31.5	24.7	27.2
Ice cream and related products	100.0	14.4	31.6	26.9	26.6
Miscellaneous dairy products	100.0	14.2	25.3	27.3	32.2
Fruits and vegetables	**100.0**	**19.3**	**28.8**	**23.4**	**28.2**
Fresh fruits	100.0	20.0	28.1	22.1	29.4
Apples	100.0	18.2	28.9	22.8	29.7
Bananas	100.0	22.3	28.8	21.5	27.3
Oranges	100.0	20.5	25.9	22.7	30.4
Citrus fruits, excl. oranges	100.0	19.9	27.7	20.8	31.2
Other fresh fruits	100.0	19.3	28.2	22.2	29.8
Fresh vegetables	100.0	19.8	28.1	22.7	29.0
Potatoes	100.0	23.2	30.0	21.7	25.2
Lettuce	100.0	18.9	30.1	22.1	28.5
Tomatoes	100.0	21.5	30.9	21.5	26.2
Other fresh vegetables	100.0	18.2	26.0	23.6	31.6

	total consumer units	not a high school graduate	high school graduate	some college	college graduate
Processed fruits	100.0%	17.9%	29.2%	24.6%	27.8%
Frozen fruits and fruit juices	100.0	15.8	25.4	26.4	31.5
Frozen orange juice	100.0	16.3	27.1	26.8	29.1
Frozen fruits	100.0	13.8	22.2	25.9	36.7
Frozen fruit juices	100.0	15.6	23.3	25.9	34.2
Canned fruit	100.0	17.8	30.7	23.9	27.3
Dried fruit	100.0	17.7	32.6	22.5	27.0
Fresh fruit juices	100.0	20.1	28.1	21.7	29.7
Canned and bottled fruit juices	100.0	17.9	30.3	25.8	25.7
Processed vegetables	100.0	18.7	30.6	25.3	25.1
Frozen vegetables	100.0	12.8	30.9	26.5	29.1
Canned and dried vegetables and juices	100.0	21.6	30.5	24.8	23.2
Canned beans	100.0	24.9	28.6	25.0	21.7
Canned corn	100.0	22.0	29.2	31.4	17.7
Other canned and dried vegetables	100.0	21.1	31.9	23.5	23.6
Frozen vegetable juices	100.0	6.3	30.1	18.7	41.8
Fresh and canned vegetable juices	100.0	18.4	29.3	22.7	29.2
Other food at home	**100.0**	**17.5**	**31.1**	**25.0**	**26.2**
Sugar and other sweets	100.0	19.1	32.0	24.2	24.6
Candy and chewing gum	100.0	16.7	31.8	24.7	26.5
Sugar	100.0	27.9	33.3	22.4	17.3
Artificial sweeteners	100.0	23.8	31.4	19.8	25.3
Jams, preserves, other sweets	100.0	17.7	31.8	25.1	25.2
Fats and oils	100.0	21.6	32.3	22.5	23.7
Margarine	100.0	19.7	36.7	21.5	22.3
Fats and oils	100.0	30.1	29.5	19.7	21.4
Salad dressings	100.0	16.3	33.7	24.2	25.6
Nondairy cream and imitation milk	100.0	18.0	32.3	23.0	26.5
Peanut butter	100.0	19.8	29.6	25.7	24.7
Miscellaneous foods	100.0	15.7	31.0	25.8	27.1
Frozen prepared foods	100.0	12.2	32.1	28.0	27.1
Frozen meals	100.0	12.9	28.0	31.7	26.7
Other frozen prepared foods	100.0	11.8	34.0	26.2	27.3
Canned and packaged soups	100.0	18.4	29.8	22.6	28.7
Potato chips, nuts, and other snacks	100.0	13.4	31.6	24.8	29.6
Potato chips and other snacks	100.0	13.0	31.6	25.9	28.9
Nuts	100.0	15.0	31.6	20.7	32.0
Condiments and seasonings	100.0	16.4	31.1	24.6	27.5
Salt, spices and other seasonings	100.0	18.3	31.6	24.4	25.5
Olives, pickles, relishes	100.0	15.8	35.2	20.0	28.6
Sauces and gravies	100.0	15.5	30.3	26.3	27.4
Baking needs and misc. products	100.0	16.4	29.5	24.1	29.4
Other canned/packaged prepared foods	100.0	18.2	30.1	26.8	24.7
Prepared salads	100.0	10.5	32.5	26.2	30.0
Prepared desserts	100.0	18.2	32.0	24.6	24.9

	total consumer units	not a high school graduate	high school graduate	some college	college graduate
Baby food	100.0%	15.7%	29.5%	31.1%	23.4%
Miscellaneous prepared foods	100.0	20.6	29.7	25.3	24.3
Nonalcoholic beverages	100.0	19.8	31.9	25.2	23.2
Cola	100.0	21.6	33.0	25.3	20.4
Other carbonated drinks	100.0	18.0	34.1	26.0	21.8
Coffee	100.0	22.1	30.0	21.7	26.2
Roasted coffee	100.0	19.7	30.6	22.6	26.9
Instant and freeze-dried coffee	100.0	27.1	28.7	19.9	24.7
Noncarb. fruit flavored drinks incl. non-frozen lemonade	100.0	20.7	29.4	25.4	24.4
Tea	100.0	14.8	32.4	26.7	25.7
Nonalcoholic beer	100.0	15.9	11.4	24.6	46.6
Other nonalcoholic beverages	100.0	14.2	29.5	28.3	27.3
Food prepared by cu on out-of-town trips	100.0	9.0	24.2	24.0	42.8
FOOD AWAY FROM HOME	**100.0**	**10.2**	**26.9**	**25.3**	**36.7**
Meals at restaurants, carry-outs, other	**100.0**	**11.3**	**28.0**	**25.7**	**33.9**
Lunch	100.0	10.6	27.9	25.4	34.8
Dinner	100.0	11.1	27.6	25.4	34.7
Snacks and nonalcoholic beverages	100.0	12.2	30.2	27.7	29.1
Breakfast and brunch	100.0	14.3	28.9	26.5	29.6
Board (including at school)	**100.0**	**5.1**	**14.9**	**24.2**	**55.9**
Catered affairs	**100.0**	**2.3**	**14.2**	**18.5**	**64.9**
Food on out-of-town trips	**100.0**	**6.3**	**24.9**	**24.5**	**44.2**
School lunches	**100.0**	**13.4**	**33.1**	**25.7**	**27.8**
Meals as pay	**100.0**	**10.9**	**25.5**	**30.5**	**33.1**
ALCOHOLIC BEVERAGES	**100.0**	**12.1**	**27.6**	**23.7**	**35.6**
At home	**100.0**	**16.5**	**29.4**	**22.5**	**31.0**
Beer and ale	100.0	22.8	32.8	21.9	22.8
Whiskey	100.0	5.1	31.0	24.0	38.3
Wine	100.0	5.9	21.8	22.0	48.1
Other alcoholic beverages	100.0	10.5	24.3	26.2	37.5
Away from home	**100.0**	**5.7**	**24.9**	**25.5**	**42.4**
Beer and ale	100.0	6.0	28.1	26.2	38.1
Wine	100.0	7.0	24.9	24.7	41.6
Other alcoholic beverages	100.0	5.1	23.4	25.1	44.2
Alcoholic beverages purchased on trips	100.0	5.3	22.3	25.6	46.8

Note: Numbers may not add to total due to rounding. (-) means insufficient data.

Chapter 8

Spending by
Number of Earners

For the food industry, there is no more important consumer segment than the two-earner household. Accounting for one-third of all households, dual-earners control 40 percent of spending on food. Two-earner households account for 38 percent of spending on food at home and for 43 percent of spending on food away from home.

The second most important segment of the food market, when analyzing the market by earners in a household, is the multi-person household with a single earner, accounting for 20 percent of spending on food.

Because multi-person households benefit from economies of scale in food purchasing, they spend less on food than single-person households with or without earners—after adjusting for household size. Single-person households in which the householder is employed spend 51 percent more than average on food. Food spending is 21 percent above average for single-person households with no earners. Multi-person households with only one earner spend 13 percent less than average on food, while two-earner households spend about an average amount per capita on both food and alcohol.

Spending statistics by earner status should be examined with care because other factors—especially age and income—may be what shapes spending. Many households without earners are retired couples or elderly widows; some are people dependent on state aid. In each case, food spending will be determined by lifestage as well as financial circumstances.

Multi-person households with no earners (many of them retired couples) spend more than average on many cereals and bakery products, some beef categories, and most pork categories. Their spending on artificial sweeteners; jams, jellies, and other sweets; and fats and oils is also higher than average. Multi-person households with one earner (many of them traditional, single-earner couples) spend an average amount on most foods. The few categories in which they spend more than average include many low- and medium-priced beef products, pork chops, and lamb and organ meats.

Dual-earner households spend more on food away from home than most other households. The only exception is single-person households with one earner, who spend more than twice the average amount per capita on restaurant meals. Dual-earner households spend 6 percent more than average on restaurant meals. In contrast, single-earner, multi-person households spend 33 less per capita eating out.

Number of Earners
average spending

(average annual spending of consumer units on food and alcoholic beverages, by size and number of earners in consumer unit, 1994)

	total consumer units	single person		consumer units with two or more persons			
		no earner	one earner	no earners	one earner	two earners	three+ earners
Number of consumer units							
(in thousands, add 000's)	*102,210*	*11,432*	*17,665*	*10,612*	*19,886*	*33,584*	*9,031*
Average number of persons per cu	*2.5*	*1.0*	*1.0*	*2.5*	*3.0*	*3.1*	*4.3*
Average before-tax income of cu	*$36,838.00*	*$11,403.00*	*$27,485.00*	*$20,239.00*	*$33,505.00*	*$52,191.00*	*$57,726.00*
Average spending of cu, total	*31,750.63*	*14,219.03*	*22,643.85*	*22,887.15*	*31,517.95*	*40,615.64*	*49,044.43*
Food, average spending	*4,410.52*	*2,138.23*	*2,670.12*	*3,881.52*	*4,620.90*	*5,397.54*	*6,863.61*
Alcoholic beverages, average spending	*278.03*	*96.42*	*354.34*	*197.44*	*230.76*	*331.19*	*332.01*
FOOD AT HOME	**$2,712.05**	**$1,527.71**	**$1,297.31**	**$2,690.45**	**$3,201.97**	**$3,164.83**	**$4,131.31**
Cereals and bakery products	**428.68**	**235.70**	**209.56**	**442.55**	**503.74**	**501.16**	**633.61**
Cereals and cereal products	161.74	81.96	74.54	161.90	199.67	187.83	247.45
Flour	7.60	3.82	2.73	7.07	10.14	8.42	13.67
Prepared flour mixes	12.79	9.53	4.79	13.19	14.98	14.94	18.91
Ready-to-eat and cooked cereals	98.27	48.96	45.87	99.96	123.44	113.46	147.11
Rice	15.43	7.27	7.22	15.75	18.39	19.13	20.75
Pasta, cornmeal, and other cereal products	27.65	12.38	13.94	25.95	32.72	31.89	47.01
Bakery products	266.93	153.75	135.02	280.65	304.07	313.33	386.16
Bread	76.22	47.21	39.19	79.80	91.31	87.45	104.86
White bread	37.65	22.73	17.97	38.33	48.25	41.94	54.81
Bread, other than white	38.57	24.48	21.22	41.48	43.06	45.51	50.05
Crackers and cookies	62.56	37.57	29.23	69.38	71.12	73.07	90.76
Cookies	42.97	24.46	18.94	47.30	48.29	50.55	65.91
Crackers	19.59	13.11	10.29	22.08	22.83	22.51	24.85
Frozen and refrigerated bakery products	21.56	9.02	12.34	24.66	24.30	26.28	27.53
Other bakery products	106.59	59.95	54.26	106.81	117.34	126.54	163.01
Biscuits and rolls	35.96	16.60	18.12	33.65	40.05	44.70	54.14
Cakes and cupcakes	31.19	17.13	15.81	32.18	32.10	38.94	44.76
Bread and cracker products	4.72	1.77	2.15	3.68	5.62	5.96	7.86
Sweetrolls, coffee cakes, doughnuts	21.92	14.99	10.64	24.75	24.83	23.66	35.36
Pies, tarts, turnovers	12.80	9.46	7.54	12.55	14.75	13.28	20.88
Meats, poultry, fish, and eggs	**732.45**	**398.68**	**317.04**	**709.13**	**917.45**	**839.89**	**1,164.41**
Beef	226.76	107.97	92.62	202.17	293.17	263.02	379.06
Ground beef	88.45	40.08	38.82	90.21	107.75	104.06	140.11
Roast	39.41	23.63	9.37	33.08	50.29	45.70	75.68
Chuck roast	12.26	8.58	3.15	11.11	16.61	14.66	17.74
Round roast	14.84	9.70	3.48	12.08	18.17	17.03	30.03
Other roast	12.31	5.35	2.73	9.89	15.51	14.01	27.91
Steak	84.75	33.49	40.29	66.89	116.98	98.32	135.24
Round steak	16.00	4.05	4.85	12.77	25.48	18.21	28.05
Sirloin steak	24.44	11.69	10.87	21.41	28.87	28.98	42.23
Other steak	44.31	17.75	24.58	32.71	62.64	51.13	64.97
Other beef	14.15	10.77	4.14	11.98	18.14	14.94	28.03
Pork	155.74	92.05	63.47	167.60	202.92	177.06	220.54
Bacon	22.78	20.12	10.66	24.04	28.79	25.39	26.39
Pork chops	39.32	22.18	14.85	40.02	53.65	43.82	60.09

	total	single person		consumer units with two or more persons			
	consumer units	no earner	one earner	no earners	one earner	two earners	three+ earners
Ham	$36.88	$19.73	$12.54	$49.30	$45.67	$42.45	$51.21
Ham, not canned	34.16	18.14	12.13	42.69	42.27	39.81	48.19
Canned ham	2.72	1.59	0.41	6.62	3.39	2.64	3.03
Sausage	22.82	12.16	12.26	23.77	28.19	27.00	28.54
Other pork	33.93	17.86	13.15	30.46	46.63	38.40	54.30
Other meats	93.95	50.50	37.48	93.61	117.91	107.96	151.71
Frankfurters	18.76	11.03	6.43	17.70	23.00	23.69	25.86
Lunch meats (cold cuts)	65.66	34.44	28.77	65.76	77.31	75.26	111.58
Bologna, liverwurst, salami	23.73	13.37	11.28	23.52	29.86	27.05	35.15
Other lunchmeats	41.93	21.07	17.48	42.24	47.44	48.21	76.44
Lamb, organ meats and others	9.53	5.03	2.28	10.15	17.60	9.01	14.27
Lamb and organ meats	9.35	5.03	2.28	10.15	16.84	8.97	13.87
Mutton, goat and game	0.18	-	-	-	0.76	0.04	0.39
Poultry	136.58	82.29	65.46	126.88	154.14	157.46	229.53
Fresh and frozen chickens	107.89	60.33	50.21	96.29	125.72	124.32	186.51
Fresh and frozen whole chicken	29.56	17.59	10.41	30.56	36.36	33.89	48.70
Fresh and frozen chicken parts	78.33	42.74	39.79	65.73	89.36	90.43	137.81
Other poultry	28.69	21.96	15.26	30.59	28.42	33.14	43.03
Fish and seafood	89.43	46.74	42.96	85.99	114.20	101.69	136.53
Canned fish and seafood	15.03	9.95	9.30	17.18	16.78	16.03	21.94
Fresh fish and shellfish	51.26	26.75	22.30	40.91	68.05	60.14	80.31
Frozen fish and shellfish	23.15	10.04	11.37	27.90	29.37	25.52	34.28
Eggs	30.00	19.15	15.05	32.88	35.11	32.71	47.04
Dairy products	**288.92**	**183.09**	**130.97**	**284.55**	**337.69**	**337.73**	**436.19**
Fresh milk and cream	127.13	83.59	54.35	128.03	152.37	145.25	196.22
Fresh milk, all types	118.94	79.78	51.34	118.68	141.97	135.72	183.77
Cream	8.19	3.81	3.01	9.34	10.40	9.54	12.45
Other dairy products	161.79	99.50	76.62	156.52	185.32	192.48	239.97
Butter	11.65	5.03	5.83	10.71	16.13	12.52	19.31
Cheese	81.83	55.30	38.23	73.35	97.49	95.97	121.08
Ice cream and related products	47.64	23.69	21.48	53.75	49.42	58.78	72.59
Miscellaneous dairy products	20.66	15.48	11.08	18.71	22.28	25.20	27.00
Fruits and vegetables	**436.57**	**303.62**	**219.48**	**441.35**	**516.84**	**489.08**	**640.27**
Fresh fruits	133.02	92.24	68.58	129.39	159.75	148.17	196.60
Apples	25.37	12.30	13.46	22.22	30.50	29.56	40.68
Bananas	29.66	23.12	15.81	33.22	32.60	33.28	40.05
Oranges	16.36	8.29	8.84	14.21	23.90	17.93	22.17
Citrus fruits, excl. oranges	10.96	8.78	5.95	10.94	11.90	12.08	16.77
Other fresh fruits	50.67	39.74	24.53	48.80	60.86	55.32	76.93
Fresh vegetables	134.89	87.92	69.16	125.59	163.90	150.71	207.19
Potatoes	28.01	17.35	12.45	27.55	36.57	30.95	42.56
Lettuce	17.38	11.21	10.24	14.87	19.81	20.02	26.06
Tomatoes	21.01	13.65	10.21	17.74	27.19	23.11	33.53
Other fresh vegetables	68.50	45.71	36.25	65.43	80.32	76.63	105.04

	total consumer units	single person		consumer units with two or more persons			
		no earner	one earner	no earners	one earner	two earners	three+ earners
Processed fruits	$93.08	$72.35	$47.18	$98.00	$105.87	$102.96	$135.45
Frozen fruits and fruit juices	16.28	9.07	8.98	13.34	18.98	19.49	24.50
Frozen orange juice	9.49	6.02	6.72	7.77	11.61	10.59	12.52
Frozen fruits	1.60	1.47	0.29	1.84	1.61	1.98	2.47
Frozen fruit juices	5.19	1.58	1.97	3.73	5.76	6.92	9.50
Canned fruit	14.23	15.07	5.48	21.32	14.25	15.11	18.29
Dried fruit	5.89	5.22	3.00	9.07	6.15	5.07	10.70
Fresh fruit juices	17.90	14.55	12.45	13.84	22.95	17.86	26.62
Canned and bottled fruit juices	38.78	28.43	17.27	40.42	43.53	45.42	55.35
Processed vegetables	75.57	51.11	34.56	88.37	87.33	87.24	101.03
Frozen vegetables	24.83	11.23	12.35	24.70	29.29	29.07	39.66
Canned and dried vegetables and juices	50.74	39.88	22.21	63.67	58.04	58.17	61.37
Canned beans	10.44	9.53	5.04	10.67	12.51	11.72	12.77
Canned corn	6.81	5.95	3.32	6.17	7.87	8.21	7.94
Other canned and dried vegetables	27.05	19.74	10.51	37.73	30.84	30.89	33.32
Frozen vegetable juices	0.23	0.02	0.14	0.09	0.45	0.33	0.05
Fresh and canned vegetable juices	6.21	4.64	3.20	9.02	6.36	7.02	7.29
Other food at home	**825.43**	**406.61**	**420.26**	**812.88**	**926.25**	**996.96**	**1,256.83**
Sugar and other sweets	105.25	56.62	48.87	117.16	118.41	123.85	159.09
Candy and chewing gum	62.32	32.81	30.99	63.59	64.57	76.81	95.29
Sugar	18.31	9.63	6.64	20.78	23.46	19.95	31.14
Artificial sweeteners	3.39	2.52	1.58	6.33	4.63	3.01	3.64
Jams, preserves, other sweets	21.23	11.66	9.66	26.46	25.75	24.09	29.02
Fats and oils	79.25	53.65	33.28	85.13	93.82	89.25	122.57
Margarine	14.16	18.20	5.17	15.47	16.59	14.37	19.18
Fats and oils	23.09	12.97	8.28	27.71	26.84	25.79	39.65
Salad dressings	23.75	11.90	10.05	20.93	28.33	28.30	40.28
Nondairy cream and imitation milk	6.56	4.43	3.57	6.66	8.32	7.27	8.59
Peanut butter	11.70	6.15	6.22	14.35	13.73	13.53	14.87
Miscellaneous foods	361.62	158.46	179.55	345.04	412.77	449.19	535.13
Frozen prepared foods	66.14	34.10	39.85	64.14	72.67	77.37	100.01
Frozen meals	21.43	16.94	18.84	22.58	21.30	21.30	30.36
Other frozen prepared foods	44.71	17.15	21.01	41.55	51.37	56.07	69.65
Canned and packaged soups	29.55	16.42	15.79	33.19	34.12	34.33	40.09
Potato chips, nuts, and other snacks	74.07	25.55	38.18	65.00	82.10	96.54	109.54
Potato chips and other snacks	58.18	17.31	30.02	43.91	64.75	78.31	87.60
Nuts	15.89	8.23	8.16	21.09	17.35	18.23	21.95
Condiments and seasonings	79.74	35.44	39.45	75.71	98.52	94.54	120.27
Salt, spices and other seasonings	19.30	8.82	9.17	20.90	25.41	21.17	29.91
Olives, pickles, relishes	10.16	4.97	4.29	12.14	12.83	11.70	14.26
Sauces and gravies	36.43	14.13	18.71	28.41	45.18	45.14	55.50
Baking needs and misc. products	13.85	7.52	7.28	14.25	15.10	16.54	20.59
Other canned/packaged prepared foods	112.12	46.96	46.27	107.01	125.36	146.41	165.22
Prepared salads	10.97	6.69	6.95	12.01	9.75	13.46	15.35
Prepared desserts	7.99	5.11	3.30	10.18	9.12	9.19	11.04

	total consumer units	single person		consumer units with two or more persons			
		no earner	one earner	no earners	one earner	two earners	three+ earners
Baby food	$28.11	$2.74	$5.41	$27.32	$36.88	$43.41	$29.54
Miscellaneous prepared foods	65.05	32.42	30.62	57.50	69.61	80.34	109.30
Nonalcoholic beverages	232.89	121.56	126.78	222.10	255.19	278.70	358.18
Cola	89.45	32.54	46.40	80.71	91.52	115.49	144.65
Other carbonated drinks	38.89	15.91	18.89	38.89	40.03	50.37	58.30
Coffee	43.01	37.91	24.96	50.81	49.59	46.27	49.68
Roasted coffee	29.13	22.06	17.25	32.68	32.87	33.21	33.68
Instant and freeze-dried coffee	13.88	15.85	7.70	18.13	16.72	13.06	16.00
Noncarb. fruit flavored drinks incl. non-frozen lemonade	21.86	11.60	9.64	19.44	25.96	24.26	41.69
Tea	16.25	8.37	8.78	13.01	18.27	19.54	26.68
Nonalcoholic beer	0.66	1.15	0.27	1.25	0.41	0.82	0.15
Other nonalcoholic beverages	22.77	14.08	17.84	17.99	29.41	21.95	37.04
Food prepared by cu on out-of-town trips	46.41	16.32	31.78	43.45	46.06	55.97	81.87
FOOD AWAY FROM HOME	**1,698.46**	**610.52**	**1,372.81**	**1,191.08**	**1,418.93**	**2,232.71**	**2,732.30**
Meals at restaurants, carry-outs, other	**1,306.21**	**499.58**	**1,096.57**	**956.82**	**1,056.35**	**1,714.50**	**1,974.42**
Lunch	451.76	163.40	375.85	289.36	362.07	597.06	734.19
Dinner	651.79	275.66	541.35	494.20	539.62	847.59	954.21
Snacks and nonalcoholic beverages	101.72	23.38	88.30	50.53	78.38	144.38	160.61
Breakfast and brunch	100.95	37.15	91.07	122.74	76.29	125.47	125.41
Board (including at school)	**50.72**	**14.47**	**42.45**	**13.35**	**31.57**	**66.77**	**139.14**
Catered affairs	**56.09**	**3.16**	**44.08**	**32.97**	**45.24**	**66.45**	**159.14**
Food on out-of-town trips	**207.89**	**91.22**	**151.03**	**177.48**	**203.52**	**269.45**	**283.22**
School lunches	**53.76**	**0.16**	**0.06**	**9.05**	**58.19**	**84.94**	**153.46**
Meals as pay	**23.79**	**1.93**	**38.60**	**1.40**	**24.06**	**30.59**	**22.92**
ALCOHOLIC BEVERAGES	**278.03**	**96.42**	**354.34**	**197.44**	**230.76**	**331.19**	**332.01**
At home	**165.13**	**55.64**	**199.50**	**120.54**	**151.57**	**193.48**	**198.61**
Beer and ale	99.68	35.19	136.68	59.09	81.51	114.30	129.75
Whiskey	13.68	4.93	12.00	25.57	11.23	15.84	10.81
Wine	36.41	11.24	36.53	24.06	42.29	45.57	35.38
Other alcoholic beverages	15.35	4.28	14.29	11.81	16.55	17.78	22.67
Away from home	**112.91**	**40.79**	**154.85**	**76.90**	**79.18**	**137.71**	**133.40**
Beer and ale	38.56	9.50	61.92	24.64	21.36	47.94	42.03
Wine	15.79	5.27	18.81	11.59	11.33	19.87	20.32
Other alcoholic beverages	27.96	9.76	35.26	20.36	20.66	34.73	32.77
Alcoholic beverages purchased on trips	30.61	16.26	38.85	20.31	25.84	35.17	38.29

Note: Expenditures listed for items in a given category may not add to the total for that category because the listing is incomplete. (-) means insufficient data.

Number of Earners
indexed spending

(indexed average annual spending of consumer units on food and alcoholic beverages, by size and number of earners in consumer unit, 1994; index definition: an index of 100 is the average for all consumer units; an index of 132 means that spending by consumer units with that number of earners is 32 percent above the average for all consumer units; an index of 68 indicates that spending by consumer units with that number of earners is 32 percent below the average for all consumer units)

	total consumer units	single person		consumer units with two or more persons			
		no earner	one earner	no earners	one earner	two earners	three+ earners
Average spending of cu, total	$31,750.63	$14,219.03	$22,643.85	$22,887.15	$31,517.95	$40,615.64	$49,044.43
Average spending of cu, index	100	45	71	72	99	128	154
Food, spending index	100	48	61	88	105	122	156
Alcoholic beverages, spending index	100	35	127	71	83	119	119
FOOD AT HOME	100	56	48	99	118	117	152
Cereals and bakery products	100	55	49	103	118	117	148
Cereals and cereal products	100	51	46	100	123	116	153
Flour	100	50	36	93	133	111	180
Prepared flour mixes	100	75	37	103	117	117	148
Ready-to-eat and cooked cereals	100	50	47	102	126	115	150
Rice	100	47	47	102	119	124	134
Pasta, cornmeal, and other cereal products	100	45	50	94	118	115	170
Bakery products	100	58	51	105	114	117	145
Bread	100	62	51	105	120	115	138
White bread	100	60	48	102	128	111	146
Bread, other than white	100	63	55	108	112	118	130
Crackers and cookies	100	60	47	111	114	117	145
Cookies	100	57	44	110	112	118	153
Crackers	100	67	53	113	117	115	127
Frozen and refrigerated bakery products	100	42	57	114	113	122	128
Other bakery products	100	56	51	100	110	119	153
Biscuits and rolls	100	46	50	94	111	124	151
Cakes and cupcakes	100	55	51	103	103	125	144
Bread and cracker products	100	38	46	78	119	126	167
Sweetrolls, coffee cakes, doughnuts	100	68	49	113	113	108	161
Pies, tarts, turnovers	100	74	59	98	115	104	163
Meats, poultry, fish, and eggs	100	54	43	97	125	115	159
Beef	100	48	41	89	129	116	167
Ground beef	100	45	44	102	122	118	158
Roast	100	60	24	84	128	116	192
Chuck roast	100	70	26	91	135	120	145
Round roast	100	65	23	81	122	115	202
Other roast	100	43	22	80	126	114	227
Steak	100	40	48	79	138	116	160
Round steak	100	25	30	80	159	114	175
Sirloin steak	100	48	44	88	118	119	173
Other steak	100	40	55	74	141	115	147
Other beef	100	76	29	85	128	106	198
Pork	100	59	41	108	130	114	142
Bacon	100	88	47	106	126	111	116
Pork chops	100	56	38	102	136	111	153

	total consumer units	single person		consumer units with two or more persons			
		no earner	one earner	no earners	one earner	two earners	three+ earners
Ham	100	53	34	134	124	115	139
Ham, not canned	100	53	36	125	124	117	141
Canned ham	100	58	15	243	125	97	111
Sausage	100	53	54	104	124	118	125
Other pork	100	53	39	90	137	113	160
Other meats	100	54	40	100	126	115	161
Frankfurters	100	59	34	94	123	126	138
Lunch meats (cold cuts)	100	52	44	100	118	115	170
Bologna, liverwurst, salami	100	56	48	99	126	114	148
Other lunchmeats	100	50	42	101	113	115	182
Lamb, organ meats and others	100	53	24	107	185	95	150
Lamb and organ meats	100	54	24	109	180	96	148
Mutton, goat and game	100	-	-	-	422	22	217
Poultry	100	60	48	93	113	115	168
Fresh and frozen chickens	100	56	47	89	117	115	173
Fresh and frozen whole chicken	100	60	35	103	123	115	165
Fresh and frozen chicken parts	100	55	51	84	114	115	176
Other poultry	100	77	53	107	99	116	150
Fish and seafood	100	52	48	96	128	114	153
Canned fish and seafood	100	66	62	114	112	107	146
Fresh fish and shellfish	100	52	44	80	133	117	157
Frozen fish and shellfish	100	43	49	121	127	110	148
Eggs	100	64	50	110	117	109	157
Dairy products	**100**	**63**	**45**	**98**	**117**	**117**	**151**
Fresh milk and cream	100	66	43	101	120	114	154
Fresh milk, all types	100	67	43	100	119	114	155
Cream	100	47	37	114	127	116	152
Other dairy products	100	61	47	97	115	119	148
Butter	100	43	50	92	138	107	166
Cheese	100	68	47	90	119	117	148
Ice cream and related products	100	50	45	113	104	123	152
Miscellaneous dairy products	100	75	54	91	108	122	131
Fruits and vegetables	**100**	**70**	**50**	**101**	**118**	**112**	**147**
Fresh fruits	100	69	52	97	120	111	148
Apples	100	48	53	88	120	117	160
Bananas	100	78	53	112	110	112	135
Oranges	100	51	54	87	146	110	136
Citrus fruits, excl. oranges	100	80	54	100	109	110	153
Other fresh fruits	100	78	48	96	120	109	152
Fresh vegetables	100	65	51	93	122	112	154
Potatoes	100	62	44	98	131	110	152
Lettuce	100	64	59	86	114	115	150
Tomatoes	100	65	49	84	129	110	160
Other fresh vegetables	100	67	53	96	117	112	153

	total consumer units	single person		consumer units with two or more persons			
		no earner	one earner	no earners	one earner	two earners	three+ earners
Processed fruits	100	78	51	105	114	111	146
Frozen fruits and fruit juices	100	56	55	82	117	120	150
Frozen orange juice	100	63	71	82	122	112	132
Frozen fruits	100	92	18	115	101	124	154
Frozen fruit juices	100	30	38	72	111	133	183
Canned fruit	100	106	39	150	100	106	129
Dried fruit	100	89	51	154	104	86	182
Fresh fruit juices	100	81	70	77	128	100	149
Canned and bottled fruit juices	100	73	45	104	112	117	143
Processed vegetables	100	68	46	117	116	115	134
Frozen vegetables	100	45	50	99	118	117	160
Canned and dried vegetables and juices	100	79	44	125	114	115	121
Canned beans	100	91	48	102	120	112	122
Canned corn	100	87	49	91	116	121	117
Other canned and dried vegetables	100	73	39	139	114	114	123
Frozen vegetable juices	100	9	61	39	196	143	22
Fresh and canned vegetable juices	100	75	52	145	102	113	117
Other food at home	**100**	**49**	**51**	**98**	**112**	**121**	**152**
Sugar and other sweets	100	54	46	111	113	118	151
Candy and chewing gum	100	53	50	102	104	123	153
Sugar	100	53	36	113	128	109	170
Artificial sweeteners	100	74	47	187	137	89	107
Jams, preserves, other sweets	100	55	46	125	121	113	137
Fats and oils	100	68	42	107	118	113	155
Margarine	100	129	37	109	117	101	135
Fats and oils	100	56	36	120	116	112	172
Salad dressings	100	50	42	88	119	119	170
Nondairy cream and imitation milk	100	68	54	102	127	111	131
Peanut butter	100	53	53	123	117	116	127
Miscellaneous foods	100	44	50	95	114	124	148
Frozen prepared foods	100	52	60	97	110	117	151
Frozen meals	100	79	88	105	99	99	142
Other frozen prepared foods	100	38	47	93	115	125	156
Canned and packaged soups	100	56	53	112	115	116	136
Potato chips, nuts, and other snacks	100	34	52	88	111	130	148
Potato chips and other snacks	100	30	52	75	111	135	151
Nuts	100	52	51	133	109	115	138
Condiments and seasonings	100	44	49	95	124	119	151
Salt, spices and other seasonings	100	46	48	108	132	110	155
Olives, pickles, relishes	100	49	42	119	126	115	140
Sauces and gravies	100	39	51	78	124	124	152
Baking needs and misc. products	100	54	53	103	109	119	149
Other canned/packaged prepared foods	100	42	41	95	112	131	147
Prepared salads	100	61	63	109	89	123	140
Prepared desserts	100	64	41	127	114	115	138

	total consumer units	single person		consumer units with two or more persons			
		no earner	*one earner*	*no earners*	*one earner*	*two earners*	*three+ earners*
Baby food	100	10	19	97	131	154	105
Miscellaneous prepared foods	100	50	47	88	107	124	168
Nonalcoholic beverages	100	52	54	95	110	120	154
Cola	100	36	52	90	102	129	162
Other carbonated drinks	100	41	49	100	103	130	150
Coffee	100	88	58	118	115	108	116
Roasted coffee	100	76	59	112	113	114	116
Instant and freeze-dried coffee	100	114	55	131	120	94	115
Noncarb. fruit flavored drinks incl.							
non-frozen lemonade	100	53	44	89	119	111	191
Tea	100	52	54	80	112	120	164
Nonalcoholic beer	100	174	41	189	62	124	23
Other nonalcoholic beverages	100	62	78	79	129	96	163
Food prepared by cu on out-of-town trips	100	35	68	94	99	121	176
FOOD AWAY FROM HOME	**100**	**36**	**81**	**70**	**84**	**131**	**161**
Meals at restaurants, carry-outs, other	**100**	**38**	**84**	**73**	**81**	**131**	**151**
Lunch	100	36	83	64	80	132	163
Dinner	100	42	83	76	83	130	146
Snacks and nonalcoholic beverages	100	23	87	50	77	142	158
Breakfast and brunch	100	37	90	122	76	124	124
Board (including at school)	**100**	**29**	**84**	**26**	**62**	**132**	**274**
Catered affairs	**100**	**6**	**79**	**59**	**81**	**118**	**284**
Food on out-of-town trips	**100**	**44**	**73**	**85**	**98**	**130**	**136**
School lunches	**100**	**0**	**0**	**17**	**108**	**158**	**285**
Meals as pay	**100**	**8**	**162**	**6**	**101**	**129**	**96**
ALCOHOLIC BEVERAGES	**100**	**35**	**127**	**71**	**83**	**119**	**119**
At home	**100**	**34**	**121**	**73**	**92**	**117**	**120**
Beer and ale	100	35	137	59	82	115	130
Whiskey	100	36	88	187	82	116	79
Wine	100	31	100	66	116	125	97
Other alcoholic beverages	100	28	93	77	108	116	148
Away from home	**100**	**36**	**137**	**68**	**70**	**122**	**118**
Beer and ale	100	25	161	64	55	124	109
Wine	100	33	119	73	72	126	129
Other alcoholic beverages	100	35	126	73	74	124	117
Alcoholic beverages purchased on trips	100	53	127	66	84	115	125

Note: (-) means insufficient data.

Number of Earners
average per capita spending

(average annual per capita spending of consumer units on food and alcoholic beverages, by size and number of earners in consumer unit, 1994; per capita figures are calculated by dividing the average spending of consumer units by the average number of persons per consumer unit)

	total consumer units	single person no earner	single person one earner	consumer units with two or more persons no earners	consumer units with two or more persons one earner	consumer units with two or more persons two earners	consumer units with two or more persons three+ earners
Average number of persons per cu	2.5	1.0	1.0	2.5	3.0	3.1	4.3
Per capita before-tax income of cu	$14,735.20	$11,403.00	$27,485.00	$8,095.60	$11,168.33	$16,835.81	$13,424.65
Per capita spending of cu, total	12,700.25	14,219.03	22,643.85	9,154.86	10,505.98	13,101.82	11,405.68
Food, per capita spending	1,764.21	2,138.23	2,670.12	1,552.61	1,540.30	1,741.14	1,596.19
Alcoholic beverages, per capita spending	111.21	96.42	354.34	78.98	76.92	106.84	77.21
FOOD AT HOME	**$1,084.82**	**$1,527.71**	**$1,297.31**	**$1,076.18**	**$1,067.32**	**$1,020.91**	**$960.77**
Cereals and bakery products	**171.47**	**235.70**	**209.56**	**177.02**	**167.91**	**161.66**	**147.35**
Cereals and cereal products	64.70	81.96	74.54	64.76	66.56	60.59	57.55
Flour	3.04	3.82	2.73	2.83	3.38	2.72	3.18
Prepared flour mixes	5.12	9.53	4.79	5.28	4.99	4.82	4.40
Ready-to-eat and cooked cereals	39.31	48.96	45.87	39.98	41.15	36.60	34.21
Rice	6.17	7.27	7.22	6.30	6.13	6.17	4.83
Pasta, cornmeal, and other cereal products	11.06	12.38	13.94	10.38	10.91	10.29	10.93
Bakery products	106.77	153.75	135.02	112.26	101.36	101.07	89.80
Bread	30.49	47.21	39.19	31.92	30.44	28.21	24.39
White bread	15.06	22.73	17.97	15.33	16.08	13.53	12.75
Bread, other than white	15.43	24.48	21.22	16.59	14.35	14.68	11.64
Crackers and cookies	25.02	37.57	29.23	27.75	23.71	23.57	21.11
Cookies	17.19	24.46	18.94	18.92	16.10	16.31	15.33
Crackers	7.84	13.11	10.29	8.83	7.61	7.26	5.78
Frozen and refrigerated bakery products	8.62	9.02	12.34	9.86	8.10	8.48	6.40
Other bakery products	42.64	59.95	54.26	42.72	39.11	40.82	37.91
Biscuits and rolls	14.38	16.60	18.12	13.46	13.35	14.42	12.59
Cakes and cupcakes	12.48	17.13	15.81	12.87	10.70	12.56	10.41
Bread and cracker products	1.89	1.77	2.15	1.47	1.87	1.92	1.83
Sweetrolls, coffee cakes, doughnuts	8.77	14.99	10.64	9.90	8.28	7.63	8.22
Pies, tarts, turnovers	5.12	9.46	7.54	5.02	4.92	4.28	4.86
Meats, poultry, fish, and eggs	**292.98**	**398.68**	**317.04**	**283.65**	**305.82**	**270.93**	**270.79**
Beef	90.70	107.97	92.62	80.87	97.72	84.85	88.15
Ground beef	35.38	40.08	38.82	36.08	35.92	33.57	32.58
Roast	15.76	23.63	9.37	13.23	16.76	14.74	17.60
Chuck roast	4.90	8.58	3.15	4.44	5.54	4.73	4.13
Round roast	5.94	9.70	3.48	4.83	6.06	5.49	6.98
Other roast	4.92	5.35	2.73	3.96	5.17	4.52	6.49
Steak	33.90	33.49	40.29	26.76	38.99	31.72	31.45
Round steak	6.40	4.05	4.85	5.11	8.49	5.87	6.52
Sirloin steak	9.78	11.69	10.87	8.56	9.62	9.35	9.82
Other steak	17.72	17.75	24.58	13.08	20.88	16.49	15.11
Other beef	5.66	10.77	4.14	4.79	6.05	4.82	6.52
Pork	62.30	92.05	63.47	67.04	67.64	57.12	51.29
Bacon	9.11	20.12	10.66	9.62	9.60	8.19	6.14
Pork chops	15.73	22.18	14.85	16.01	17.88	14.14	13.97

	total consumer units	single person		consumer units with two or more persons			
		no earner	one earner	no earners	one earner	two earners	three+ earners
Ham	$14.75	$19.73	$12.54	$19.72	$15.22	$13.69	$11.91
Ham, not canned	13.66	18.14	12.13	17.08	14.09	12.84	11.21
Canned ham	1.09	1.59	0.41	2.65	1.13	0.85	0.70
Sausage	9.13	12.16	12.26	9.51	9.40	8.71	6.64
Other pork	13.57	17.86	13.15	12.18	15.54	12.39	12.63
Other meats	37.58	50.50	37.48	37.44	39.30	34.83	35.28
Frankfurters	7.50	11.03	6.43	7.08	7.67	7.64	6.01
Lunch meats (cold cuts)	26.26	34.44	28.77	26.30	25.77	24.28	25.95
Bologna, liverwurst, salami	9.49	13.37	11.28	9.41	9.95	8.73	8.17
Other lunchmeats	16.77	21.07	17.48	16.90	15.81	15.55	17.78
Lamb, organ meats and others	3.81	5.03	2.28	4.06	5.87	2.91	3.32
Lamb and organ meats	3.74	5.03	2.28	4.06	5.61	2.89	3.23
Mutton, goat and game	0.07	-	-	-	0.25	0.01	0.09
Poultry	54.63	82.29	65.46	50.75	51.38	50.79	53.38
Fresh and frozen chickens	43.16	60.33	50.21	38.52	41.91	40.10	43.37
Fresh and frozen whole chicken	11.82	17.59	10.41	12.22	12.12	10.93	11.33
Fresh and frozen chicken parts	31.33	42.74	39.79	26.29	29.79	29.17	32.05
Other poultry	11.48	21.96	15.26	12.24	9.47	10.69	10.01
Fish and seafood	35.77	46.74	42.96	34.40	38.07	32.80	31.75
Canned fish and seafood	6.01	9.95	9.30	6.87	5.59	5.17	5.10
Fresh fish and shellfish	20.50	26.75	22.30	16.36	22.68	19.40	18.68
Frozen fish and shellfish	9.26	10.04	11.37	11.16	9.79	8.23	7.97
Eggs	12.00	19.15	15.05	13.15	11.70	10.55	10.94
Dairy products	**115.57**	**183.09**	**130.97**	**113.82**	**112.56**	**108.95**	**101.44**
Fresh milk and cream	50.85	83.59	54.35	51.21	50.79	46.85	45.63
Fresh milk, all types	47.58	79.78	51.34	47.47	47.32	43.78	42.74
Cream	3.28	3.81	3.01	3.74	3.47	3.08	2.90
Other dairy products	64.72	99.50	76.62	62.61	61.77	62.09	55.81
Butter	4.66	5.03	5.83	4.28	5.38	4.04	4.49
Cheese	32.73	55.30	38.23	29.34	32.50	30.96	28.16
Ice cream and related products	19.06	23.69	21.48	21.50	16.47	18.96	16.88
Miscellaneous dairy products	8.26	15.48	11.08	7.48	7.43	8.13	6.28
Fruits and vegetables	**174.63**	**303.62**	**219.48**	**176.54**	**172.28**	**157.77**	**148.90**
Fresh fruits	53.21	92.24	68.58	51.76	53.25	47.80	45.72
Apples	10.15	12.30	13.46	8.89	10.17	9.54	9.46
Bananas	11.86	23.12	15.81	13.29	10.87	10.74	9.31
Oranges	6.54	8.29	8.84	5.68	7.97	5.78	5.16
Citrus fruits, excl. oranges	4.38	8.78	5.95	4.38	3.97	3.90	3.90
Other fresh fruits	20.27	39.74	24.53	19.52	20.29	17.85	17.89
Fresh vegetables	53.96	87.92	69.16	50.24	54.63	48.62	48.18
Potatoes	11.20	17.35	12.45	11.02	12.19	9.98	9.90
Lettuce	6.95	11.21	10.24	5.95	6.60	6.46	6.06
Tomatoes	8.40	13.65	10.21	7.10	9.06	7.45	7.80
Other fresh vegetables	27.40	45.71	36.25	26.17	26.77	24.72	24.43

	total consumer units	single person		consumer units with two or more persons			
		no earner	one earner	no earners	one earner	two earners	three+ earners
Processed fruits	$37.23	$72.35	$47.18	$39.20	$35.29	$33.21	$31.50
Frozen fruits and fruit juices	6.51	9.07	8.98	5.34	6.33	6.29	5.70
Frozen orange juice	3.80	6.02	6.72	3.11	3.87	3.42	2.91
Frozen fruits	0.64	1.47	0.29	0.74	0.54	0.64	0.57
Frozen fruit juices	2.08	1.58	1.97	1.49	1.92	2.23	2.21
Canned fruit	5.69	15.07	5.48	8.53	4.75	4.87	4.25
Dried fruit	2.36	5.22	3.00	3.63	2.05	1.64	2.49
Fresh fruit juices	7.16	14.55	12.45	5.54	7.65	5.76	6.19
Canned and bottled fruit juices	15.51	28.43	17.27	16.17	14.51	14.65	12.87
Processed vegetables	30.23	51.11	34.56	35.35	29.11	28.14	23.50
Frozen vegetables	9.93	11.23	12.35	9.88	9.76	9.38	9.22
Canned and dried vegetables and juices	20.30	39.88	22.21	25.47	19.35	18.76	14.27
Canned beans	4.18	9.53	5.04	4.27	4.17	3.78	2.97
Canned corn	2.72	5.95	3.32	2.47	2.62	2.65	1.85
Other canned and dried vegetables	10.82	19.74	10.51	15.09	10.28	9.96	7.75
Frozen vegetable juices	0.09	0.02	0.14	0.04	0.15	0.11	0.01
Fresh and canned vegetable juices	2.48	4.64	3.20	3.61	2.12	2.26	1.70
Other food at home	**330.17**	**406.61**	**420.26**	**325.15**	**308.75**	**321.60**	**292.29**
Sugar and other sweets	42.10	56.62	48.87	46.86	39.47	39.95	37.00
Candy and chewing gum	24.93	32.81	30.99	25.44	21.52	24.78	22.16
Sugar	7.32	9.63	6.64	8.31	7.82	6.44	7.24
Artificial sweeteners	1.36	2.52	1.58	2.53	1.54	0.97	0.85
Jams, preserves, other sweets	8.49	11.66	9.66	10.58	8.58	7.77	6.75
Fats and oils	31.70	53.65	33.28	34.05	31.27	28.79	28.50
Margarine	5.66	18.20	5.17	6.19	5.53	4.64	4.46
Fats and oils	9.24	12.97	8.28	11.08	8.95	8.32	9.22
Salad dressings	9.50	11.90	10.05	8.37	9.44	9.13	9.37
Nondairy cream and imitation milk	2.62	4.43	3.57	2.66	2.77	2.35	2.00
Peanut butter	4.68	6.15	6.22	5.74	4.58	4.36	3.46
Miscellaneous foods	144.65	158.46	179.55	138.02	137.59	144.90	124.45
Frozen prepared foods	26.46	34.10	39.85	25.66	24.22	24.96	23.26
Frozen meals	8.57	16.94	18.84	9.03	7.10	6.87	7.06
Other frozen prepared foods	17.88	17.15	21.01	16.62	17.12	18.09	16.20
Canned and packaged soups	11.82	16.42	15.79	13.28	11.37	11.07	9.32
Potato chips, nuts, and other snacks	29.63	25.55	38.18	26.00	27.37	31.14	25.47
Potato chips and other snacks	23.27	17.31	30.02	17.56	21.58	25.26	20.37
Nuts	6.36	8.23	8.16	8.44	5.78	5.88	5.10
Condiments and seasonings	31.90	35.44	39.45	30.28	32.84	30.50	27.97
Salt, spices and other seasonings	7.72	8.82	9.17	8.36	8.47	6.83	6.96
Olives, pickles, relishes	4.06	4.97	4.29	4.86	4.28	3.77	3.32
Sauces and gravies	14.57	14.13	18.71	11.36	15.06	14.56	12.91
Baking needs and misc. products	5.54	7.52	7.28	5.70	5.03	5.34	4.79
Other canned/packaged prepared foods	44.85	46.96	46.27	42.80	41.79	47.23	38.42
Prepared salads	4.39	6.69	6.95	4.80	3.25	4.34	3.57
Prepared desserts	3.20	5.11	3.30	4.07	3.04	2.96	2.57

	total consumer units	single person		consumer units with two or more persons			
		no earner	one earner	no earners	one earner	two earners	three+ earners
Baby food	$11.24	$2.74	$5.41	$10.93	$12.29	$14.00	$6.87
Miscellaneous prepared foods	26.02	32.42	30.62	23.00	23.20	25.92	25.42
Nonalcoholic beverages	93.16	121.56	126.78	88.84	85.06	89.90	83.30
Cola	35.78	32.54	46.40	32.28	30.51	37.25	33.64
Other carbonated drinks	15.56	15.91	18.89	15.56	13.34	16.25	13.56
Coffee	17.20	37.91	24.96	20.32	16.53	14.93	11.55
Roasted coffee	11.65	22.06	17.25	13.07	10.96	10.71	7.83
Instant and freeze-dried coffee	5.55	15.85	7.70	7.25	5.57	4.21	3.72
Noncarb. fruit flavored drinks incl. non-frozen lemonade	8.74	11.60	9.64	7.78	8.65	7.83	9.70
Tea	6.50	8.37	8.78	5.20	6.09	6.30	6.20
Nonalcoholic beer	0.26	1.15	0.27	0.50	0.14	0.26	0.03
Other nonalcoholic beverages	9.11	14.08	17.84	7.20	9.80	7.08	8.61
Food prepared by cu on out-of-town trips	18.56	16.32	31.78	17.38	15.35	18.05	19.04
FOOD AWAY FROM HOME	**679.38**	**610.52**	**1,372.81**	**476.43**	**472.98**	**720.23**	**635.42**
Meals at restaurants, carry-outs, other	**522.48**	**499.58**	**1,096.57**	**382.73**	**352.12**	**553.06**	**459.17**
Lunch	180.70	163.40	375.85	115.74	120.69	192.60	170.74
Dinner	260.72	275.66	541.35	197.68	179.87	273.42	221.91
Snacks and nonalcoholic beverages	40.69	23.38	88.30	20.21	26.13	46.57	37.35
Breakfast and brunch	40.38	37.15	91.07	49.10	25.43	40.47	29.17
Board (including at school)	**20.29**	**14.47**	**42.45**	**5.34**	**10.52**	**21.54**	**32.36**
Catered affairs	**22.44**	**3.16**	**44.08**	**13.19**	**15.08**	**21.44**	**37.01**
Food on out-of-town trips	**83.16**	**91.22**	**151.03**	**70.99**	**67.84**	**86.92**	**65.87**
School lunches	**21.50**	**0.16**	**0.06**	**3.62**	**19.40**	**27.40**	**35.69**
Meals as pay	**9.52**	**1.93**	**38.60**	**0.56**	**8.02**	**9.87**	**5.33**
ALCOHOLIC BEVERAGES	**111.21**	**96.42**	**354.34**	**78.98**	**76.92**	**106.84**	**77.21**
At home	**66.05**	**55.64**	**199.50**	**48.22**	**50.52**	**62.41**	**46.19**
Beer and ale	39.87	35.19	136.68	23.64	27.17	36.87	30.17
Whiskey	5.47	4.93	12.00	10.23	3.74	5.11	2.51
Wine	14.56	11.24	36.53	9.62	14.10	14.70	8.23
Other alcoholic beverages	6.14	4.28	14.29	4.72	5.52	5.74	5.27
Away from home	**45.16**	**40.79**	**154.85**	**30.76**	**26.39**	**44.42**	**31.02**
Beer and ale	15.42	9.50	61.92	9.86	7.12	15.46	9.77
Wine	6.32	5.27	18.81	4.64	3.78	6.41	4.73
Other alcoholic beverages	11.18	9.76	35.26	8.14	6.89	11.20	7.62
Alcoholic beverages purchased on trips	12.24	16.26	38.85	8.12	8.61	11.35	8.90

Note: Expenditures listed for items in a given category may not add to the total for that category because the listing is incomplete. (-) means insufficient data.

Number of Earners
indexed per capita spending

(indexed average annual per capita spending of consumer units on food and alcoholic beverages, by size and number of earners in consumer unit, 1994; index definition: an index of 100 is the per capita average for all consumer units; an index of 132 means that per capita spending by consumer units with that number of earners is 32 percent above the per capita average for all consumer units; an index of 68 indicates that per capita spending by consumer units with that number of earners is 32 percent below the per capita average for all consumer units)

	total consumer units	single person		consumer units with two or more persons			
		no earner	one earner	no earners	one earner	two earners	three+ earners
Per capita spending of cu, total	$12,700.25	$14,219.03	$22,643.85	$9,154.86	$10,505.98	$13,101.82	$11,405.68
Per capita spending of cu, index	100	112	178	72	83	103	90
Food, per capita spending index	100	121	151	88	87	99	90
Alcoholic beverages, per capita spending index	100	87	319	71	69	96	69
FOOD AT HOME	**100**	**141**	**120**	**99**	**98**	**94**	**89**
Cereals and bakery products	**100**	**137**	**122**	**103**	**98**	**94**	**86**
Cereals and cereal products	100	127	115	100	103	94	89
Flour	100	126	90	93	111	89	105
Prepared flour mixes	100	186	94	103	98	94	86
Ready-to-eat and cooked cereals	100	125	117	102	105	93	87
Rice	100	118	117	102	99	100	78
Pasta, cornmeal, and other cereal products	100	112	126	94	99	93	99
Bakery products	100	144	126	105	95	95	84
Bread	100	155	129	105	100	93	80
White bread	100	151	119	102	107	90	85
Bread, other than white	100	159	138	108	93	95	75
Crackers and cookies	100	150	117	111	95	94	84
Cookies	100	142	110	110	94	95	89
Crackers	100	167	131	113	97	93	74
Frozen and refrigerated bakery products	100	105	143	114	94	98	74
Other bakery products	100	141	127	100	92	96	89
Biscuits and rolls	100	115	126	94	93	100	88
Cakes and cupcakes	100	137	127	103	86	101	83
Bread and cracker products	100	94	114	78	99	102	97
Sweetrolls, coffee cakes, doughnuts	100	171	121	113	94	87	94
Pies, tarts, turnovers	100	185	147	98	96	84	95
Meats, poultry, fish, and eggs	**100**	**136**	**108**	**97**	**104**	**92**	**92**
Beef	100	119	102	89	108	94	97
Ground beef	100	113	110	102	102	95	92
Roast	100	150	59	84	106	94	112
Chuck roast	100	175	64	91	113	96	84
Round roast	100	163	59	81	102	93	118
Other roast	100	109	55	80	105	92	132
Steak	100	99	119	79	115	94	93
Round steak	100	63	76	80	133	92	102
Sirloin steak	100	120	111	88	98	96	100
Other steak	100	100	139	74	118	93	85
Other beef	100	190	73	85	107	85	115
Pork	100	148	102	108	109	92	82
Bacon	100	221	117	106	105	90	67
Pork chops	100	141	94	102	114	90	89

	total consumer units	single person		consumer units with two or more persons			
		no earner	one earner	no earners	one earner	two earners	three+ earners
Ham	100	134	85	134	103	93	81
Ham, not canned	100	133	89	125	103	94	82
Canned ham	100	146	38	243	104	78	65
Sausage	100	133	134	104	103	95	73
Other pork	100	132	97	90	115	91	93
Other meats	100	134	100	100	105	93	94
Frankfurters	100	147	86	94	102	102	80
Lunch meats (cold cuts)	100	131	110	100	98	92	99
Bologna, liverwurst, salami	100	141	119	99	105	92	86
Other lunchmeats	100	126	104	101	94	93	106
Lamb, organ meats and others	100	132	60	107	154	76	87
Lamb and organ meats	100	134	61	109	150	77	86
Mutton, goat and game	100	-	-	-	352	18	126
Poultry	100	151	120	93	94	93	98
Fresh and frozen chickens	100	140	116	89	97	93	101
Fresh and frozen whole chicken	100	149	88	103	103	92	96
Fresh and frozen chicken parts	100	136	127	84	95	93	102
Other poultry	100	191	133	107	83	93	87
Fish and seafood	100	131	120	96	106	92	89
Canned fish and seafood	100	166	155	114	93	86	85
Fresh fish and shellfish	100	130	109	80	111	95	91
Frozen fish and shellfish	100	108	123	121	106	89	86
Eggs	100	160	125	110	98	88	91
Dairy products	**100**	**158**	**113**	**98**	**97**	**94**	**88**
Fresh milk and cream	100	164	107	101	100	92	90
Fresh milk, all types	100	168	108	100	99	92	90
Cream	100	116	92	114	106	94	88
Other dairy products	100	154	118	97	95	96	86
Butter	100	108	125	92	115	87	96
Cheese	100	169	117	90	99	95	86
Ice cream and related products	100	124	113	113	86	100	89
Miscellaneous dairy products	100	187	134	91	90	98	76
Fruits and vegetables	**100**	**174**	**126**	**101**	**99**	**90**	**85**
Fresh fruits	100	173	129	97	100	90	86
Apples	100	121	133	88	100	94	93
Bananas	100	195	133	112	92	90	79
Oranges	100	127	135	87	122	88	79
Citrus fruits, excl. oranges	100	200	136	100	90	89	89
Other fresh fruits	100	196	121	96	100	88	88
Fresh vegetables	100	163	128	93	101	90	89
Potatoes	100	155	111	98	109	89	88
Lettuce	100	161	147	86	95	93	87
Tomatoes	100	162	121	84	108	89	93
Other fresh vegetables	100	167	132	96	98	90	89

	total consumer units	single person		consumer units with two or more persons			
		no earner	one earner	no earners	one earner	two earners	three+ earners
Processed fruits	100	194	127	105	95	89	85
Frozen fruits and fruit juices	100	139	138	82	97	97	87
Frozen orange juice	100	159	177	82	102	90	77
Frozen fruits	100	230	45	115	84	100	90
Frozen fruit juices	100	76	95	72	92	108	106
Canned fruit	100	265	96	150	83	86	75
Dried fruit	100	222	127	154	87	69	106
Fresh fruit juices	100	203	174	77	107	80	86
Canned and bottled fruit juices	100	183	111	104	94	94	83
Processed vegetables	100	169	114	117	96	93	78
Frozen vegetables	100	113	124	99	98	94	93
Canned and dried vegetables and juices	100	196	109	125	95	92	70
Canned beans	100	228	121	102	100	91	71
Canned corn	100	218	122	91	96	97	68
Other canned and dried vegetables	100	182	97	139	95	92	72
Frozen vegetable juices	100	22	152	39	163	116	13
Fresh and canned vegetable juices	100	187	129	145	85	91	68
Other food at home	**100**	**123**	**127**	**98**	**94**	**97**	**89**
Sugar and other sweets	100	134	116	111	94	95	88
Candy and chewing gum	100	132	124	102	86	99	89
Sugar	100	131	91	113	107	88	99
Artificial sweeteners	100	186	117	187	114	72	62
Jams, preserves, other sweets	100	137	114	125	101	92	79
Fats and oils	100	169	105	107	99	91	90
Margarine	100	321	91	109	98	82	79
Fats and oils	100	140	90	120	97	90	100
Salad dressings	100	125	106	88	99	96	99
Nondairy cream and imitation milk	100	169	136	102	106	89	76
Peanut butter	100	131	133	123	98	93	74
Miscellaneous foods	100	110	124	95	95	100	86
Frozen prepared foods	100	129	151	97	92	94	88
Frozen meals	100	198	220	105	83	80	82
Other frozen prepared foods	100	96	117	93	96	101	91
Canned and packaged soups	100	139	134	112	96	94	79
Potato chips, nuts, and other snacks	100	86	129	88	92	105	86
Potato chips and other snacks	100	74	129	75	93	109	88
Nuts	100	129	128	133	91	93	80
Condiments and seasonings	100	111	124	95	103	96	88
Salt, spices and other seasonings	100	114	119	108	110	88	90
Olives, pickles, relishes	100	122	106	119	105	93	82
Sauces and gravies	100	97	128	78	103	100	89
Baking needs and misc. products	100	136	131	103	91	96	86
Other canned/packaged prepared foods	100	105	103	95	93	105	86
Prepared salads	100	152	158	109	74	99	81
Prepared desserts	100	160	103	127	95	93	80

	total consumer units	single person		consumer units with two or more persons			
		no earner	one earner	no earners	one earner	two earners	three+ earners
Baby food	100	24	48	97	109	125	61
Miscellaneous prepared foods	100	125	118	88	89	100	98
Nonalcoholic beverages	100	130	136	95	91	97	89
Cola	100	91	130	90	85	104	94
Other carbonated drinks	100	102	121	100	86	104	87
Coffee	100	220	145	118	96	87	67
Roasted coffee	100	189	148	112	94	92	67
Instant and freeze-dried coffee	100	285	139	131	100	76	67
Noncarb. fruit flavored drinks incl. non-frozen lemonade	100	133	110	89	99	89	111
Tea	100	129	135	80	94	97	95
Nonalcoholic beer	100	436	102	189	52	100	13
Other nonalcoholic beverages	100	155	196	79	108	78	95
Food prepared by cu on out-of-town trips	100	88	171	94	83	97	103
FOOD AWAY FROM HOME	**100**	**90**	**202**	**70**	**70**	**106**	**94**
Meals at restaurants, carry-outs, other	**100**	**96**	**210**	**73**	**67**	**106**	**88**
Lunch	100	90	208	64	67	107	94
Dinner	100	106	208	76	69	105	85
Snacks and nonalcoholic beverages	100	57	217	50	64	114	92
Breakfast and brunch	100	92	226	122	63	100	72
Board (including at school)	**100**	**71**	**209**	**26**	**52**	**106**	**159**
Catered affairs	**100**	**14**	**196**	**59**	**67**	**96**	**165**
Food on out-of-town trips	**100**	**110**	**182**	**85**	**82**	**105**	**79**
School lunches	**100**	**1**	**0**	**17**	**90**	**127**	**166**
Meals as pay	**100**	**20**	**406**	**6**	**84**	**104**	**56**
ALCOHOLIC BEVERAGES	**100**	**87**	**319**	**71**	**69**	**96**	**69**
At home	**100**	**84**	**302**	**73**	**76**	**94**	**70**
Beer and ale	100	88	343	59	68	92	76
Whiskey	100	90	219	187	68	93	46
Wine	100	77	251	66	97	101	56
Other alcoholic beverages	100	70	233	77	90	93	86
Away from home	**100**	**90**	**343**	**68**	**58**	**98**	**69**
Beer and ale	100	62	401	64	46	100	63
Wine	100	83	298	73	60	101	75
Other alcoholic beverages	100	87	315	73	62	100	68
Alcoholic beverages purchased on trips	100	133	317	66	70	93	73

Note: (-) means insufficient data.

Number of Earners
total spending

(total annual spending on food and alcoholic beverages by size and number of earners in consumer unit, 1994; numbers in thousands)

	total consumer units	single person		consumer units with two or more persons			
		no earner	one earner	no earners	one earner	two earners	three+ earners
Number of consumer units	102,210	11,432	17,665	10,612	19,886	33,584	9,031
Total spending of all cu's	$3,245,231,892	$162,551,951	$400,003,610	$242,878,436	$626,765,954	$1,364,035,654	$442,920,247
Food, total spending	450,799,249	24,444,245	47,167,670	41,190,690	91,891,217	181,270,983	61,985,262
Alcoholic beverages, total spending	28,417,446	1,102,273	6,259,416	2,095,233	4,588,893	11,122,685	2,998,382
FOOD AT HOME	**$277,198,631**	**$17,464,781**	**$22,916,981**	**$28,551,055**	**$63,674,375**	**$106,287,651**	**$37,309,861**
Cereals and bakery products	**43,815,383**	**2,694,522**	**3,701,877**	**4,696,341**	**10,017,374**	**16,830,957**	**5,722,132**
Cereals and cereal products	16,531,445	936,967	1,316,749	1,718,083	3,970,638	6,308,083	2,234,721
Flour	776,796	43,670	48,225	75,027	201,644	282,777	123,454
Prepared flour mixes	1,307,266	108,947	84,615	139,972	297,892	501,745	170,776
Ready-to-eat and cooked cereals	10,044,177	559,711	810,294	1,060,776	2,454,728	3,810,441	1,328,550
Rice	1,577,100	83,111	127,541	167,139	365,704	642,462	187,393
Pasta, cornmeal, and other cereal products	2,826,107	141,528	246,250	275,381	650,670	1,070,994	424,547
Bakery products	27,282,915	1,757,670	2,385,128	2,978,258	6,046,736	10,522,875	3,487,411
Bread	7,790,446	539,705	692,291	846,838	1,815,791	2,936,921	946,991
White bread	3,848,207	259,849	317,440	406,758	959,500	1,408,513	494,989
Bread, other than white	3,942,240	279,855	374,851	440,186	856,291	1,528,408	452,002
Crackers and cookies	6,394,258	429,500	516,348	736,261	1,414,292	2,453,983	819,654
Cookies	4,391,964	279,627	334,575	501,948	960,295	1,697,671	595,233
Crackers	2,002,294	149,874	181,773	234,313	453,997	755,976	224,420
Frozen and refrigerated bakery products	2,203,648	103,117	217,986	261,692	483,230	882,588	248,623
Other bakery products	10,894,564	685,348	958,503	1,133,468	2,333,423	4,249,719	1,472,143
Biscuits and rolls	3,675,472	189,771	320,090	357,094	796,434	1,501,205	488,938
Cakes and cupcakes	3,187,930	195,830	279,284	341,494	638,341	1,307,761	404,228
Bread and cracker products	482,431	20,235	37,980	39,052	111,759	200,161	70,984
Sweetrolls, coffee cakes, doughnuts	2,240,443	171,366	187,956	262,647	493,769	794,597	319,336
Pies, tarts, turnovers	1,308,288	108,147	133,194	133,181	293,319	445,996	188,567
Meats, poultry, fish, and eggs	**74,863,715**	**4,557,710**	**5,600,512**	**7,525,288**	**18,244,411**	**28,206,866**	**10,515,787**
Beef	23,177,140	1,234,313	1,636,132	2,145,428	5,829,979	8,833,264	3,423,291
Ground beef	9,040,475	458,195	685,755	957,309	2,142,717	3,494,751	1,265,333
Roast	4,028,096	270,138	165,521	351,045	1,000,067	1,534,789	683,466
Chuck roast	1,253,095	98,087	55,645	117,899	330,306	492,341	160,210
Round roast	1,516,796	110,890	61,474	128,193	361,329	571,936	271,201
Other roast	1,258,205	61,161	48,225	104,953	308,432	470,512	252,055
Steak	8,662,298	382,858	711,723	709,837	2,326,264	3,301,979	1,221,352
Round steak	1,635,360	46,300	85,675	135,515	506,695	611,565	253,320
Sirloin steak	2,498,012	133,640	192,019	227,203	574,109	973,264	381,379
Other steak	4,528,925	202,918	434,206	347,119	1,245,659	1,717,150	586,744
Other beef	1,446,272	123,123	73,133	127,132	360,732	501,745	253,139
Pork	15,918,185	1,052,316	1,121,198	1,778,571	4,035,267	5,946,383	1,991,697
Bacon	2,328,344	230,012	188,309	255,112	572,518	852,698	238,328
Pork chops	4,018,897	253,562	262,325	424,692	1,066,884	1,471,651	542,673

	total consumer units	single person		consumer units with two or more persons			
		no earner	one earner	no earners	one earner	two earners	three+ earners
Ham	$3,769,505	$225,553	$221,519	$523,172	$908,194	$1,425,641	$462,478
Ham, not canned	3,491,494	207,376	214,276	453,026	840,581	1,336,979	435,204
Canned ham	278,011	18,177	7,243	70,251	67,414	88,662	27,364
Sausage	2,332,432	139,013	216,573	252,247	560,586	906,768	257,745
Other pork	3,467,985	204,176	232,295	323,242	927,284	1,289,626	490,383
Other meats	9,602,630	577,316	662,084	993,389	2,344,758	3,625,729	1,370,093
Frankfurters	1,917,460	126,095	113,586	187,832	457,378	795,605	233,542
Lunch meats (cold cuts)	6,711,109	393,718	508,222	697,845	1,537,387	2,527,532	1,007,679
Bologna, liverwurst, salami	2,425,443	152,846	199,261	249,594	593,796	908,447	317,440
Other lunchmeats	4,285,665	240,872	308,784	448,251	943,392	1,619,085	690,330
Lamb, organ meats and others	974,061	57,503	40,276	107,712	349,994	302,592	128,872
Lamb and organ meats	955,664	57,503	40,276	107,712	334,880	301,248	125,260
Mutton, goat and game	18,398	-	-	-	-	-	-
Poultry	13,959,842	940,739	1,156,351	1,346,451	3,065,228	5,288,137	2,072,885
Fresh and frozen chickens	11,027,437	689,693	886,960	1,021,829	2,500,068	4,175,163	1,684,372
Fresh and frozen whole chicken	3,021,328	201,089	183,893	324,303	723,055	1,138,162	439,810
Fresh and frozen chicken parts	8,006,109	488,604	702,890	697,527	1,777,013	3,037,001	1,244,562
Other poultry	2,932,405	251,047	269,568	324,621	565,160	1,112,974	388,604
Fish and seafood	9,140,640	534,332	758,888	912,526	2,270,981	3,415,157	1,233,002
Canned fish and seafood	1,536,216	113,748	164,285	182,314	333,687	538,352	198,140
Fresh fish and shellfish	5,239,285	305,806	393,930	434,137	1,353,242	2,019,742	725,280
Frozen fish and shellfish	2,366,162	114,777	200,851	296,075	584,052	857,064	309,583
Eggs	3,066,300	218,923	265,858	348,923	698,197	1,098,533	424,818
Dairy products	**29,530,513**	**2,093,085**	**2,313,585**	**3,019,645**	**6,715,303**	**11,342,324**	**3,939,232**
Fresh milk and cream	12,993,957	955,601	960,093	1,358,654	3,030,030	4,878,076	1,772,063
Fresh milk, all types	12,156,857	912,045	906,921	1,259,432	2,823,215	4,558,020	1,659,627
Cream	837,100	43,556	53,172	99,116	206,814	320,391	112,436
Other dairy products	16,536,556	1,137,484	1,353,492	1,660,990	3,685,274	6,464,248	2,167,169
Butter	1,190,747	57,503	102,987	113,655	320,761	420,472	174,389
Cheese	8,363,844	632,190	675,333	778,390	1,938,686	3,223,056	1,093,473
Ice cream and related products	4,869,284	270,824	379,444	570,395	982,766	1,974,068	655,560
Miscellaneous dairy products	2,111,659	176,967	195,728	198,551	443,060	846,317	243,837
Fruits and vegetables	**44,621,820**	**3,470,984**	**3,877,114**	**4,683,606**	**10,277,880**	**16,425,263**	**5,782,278**
Fresh fruits	13,595,974	1,054,488	1,211,466	1,373,087	3,176,789	4,976,141	1,775,495
Apples	2,593,068	140,614	237,771	235,799	606,523	992,743	367,381
Bananas	3,031,549	264,308	279,284	352,531	648,284	1,117,676	361,692
Oranges	1,672,156	94,771	156,159	150,797	475,275	602,161	200,217
Citrus fruits, excl. oranges	1,120,222	100,373	105,107	116,095	236,643	405,695	151,450
Other fresh fruits	5,178,981	454,308	433,322	517,866	1,210,262	1,857,867	694,755
Fresh vegetables	13,787,107	1,005,101	1,221,711	1,332,761	3,259,315	5,061,445	1,871,133
Potatoes	2,862,902	198,345	219,929	292,361	727,231	1,039,425	384,359
Lettuce	1,776,410	128,153	180,890	157,800	393,942	672,352	235,348
Tomatoes	2,147,432	156,047	180,360	188,257	540,700	776,126	302,809
Other fresh vegetables	7,001,385	522,557	640,356	694,343	1,597,244	2,573,542	948,616

	total consumer units	single person		consumer units with two or more persons			
		no earner	one earner	no earners	one earner	two earners	three+ earners
Processed fruits	$9,513,707	$827,105	$833,435	$1,039,976	$2,105,331	$3,457,809	$1,223,249
Frozen fruits and fruit juices	1,663,979	103,688	158,632	141,564	377,436	654,552	221,260
Frozen orange juice	969,973	68,821	118,709	82,455	230,876	355,655	113,068
Frozen fruits	163,536	16,805	5,123	19,526	32,016	66,496	22,307
Frozen fruit juices	530,470	18,063	34,800	39,583	114,543	232,401	85,795
Canned fruit	1,454,448	172,280	96,804	226,248	283,376	507,454	165,177
Dried fruit	602,017	59,675	52,995	96,251	122,299	170,271	96,632
Fresh fruit juices	1,829,559	166,336	219,929	146,870	456,384	599,810	240,405
Canned and bottled fruit juices	3,963,704	325,012	305,075	428,937	865,638	1,525,385	499,866
Processed vegetables	7,724,010	584,290	610,502	937,782	1,736,644	2,929,868	912,402
Frozen vegetables	2,537,874	128,381	218,163	262,116	582,461	976,287	358,169
Canned and dried vegetables and juices	5,186,135	455,908	392,340	675,666	1,154,183	1,953,581	554,232
Canned beans	1,067,072	108,947	89,032	113,230	248,774	393,604	115,326
Canned corn	696,050	68,020	58,648	65,476	156,503	275,725	71,706
Other canned and dried vegetables	2,764,781	225,668	185,659	400,391	613,284	1,037,410	300,913
Frozen vegetable juices	23,508	229	2,473	955	8,949	11,083	452
Fresh and canned vegetable juices	634,724	53,044	56,528	95,720	126,475	235,760	65,836
Other food at home	**84,367,200**	**4,648,366**	**7,423,893**	**8,626,283**	**18,419,408**	**33,481,905**	**11,350,432**
Sugar and other sweets	10,757,603	647,280	863,289	1,243,302	2,354,701	4,159,378	1,436,742
Candy and chewing gum	6,369,727	375,084	547,438	674,817	1,284,039	2,579,587	860,564
Sugar	1,871,465	110,090	117,296	220,517	466,526	670,001	281,225
Artificial sweeteners	346,492	28,809	27,911	67,174	92,072	101,088	32,873
Jams, preserves, other sweets	2,169,918	133,297	170,644	280,794	512,065	809,039	262,080
Fats and oils	8,100,143	613,327	587,891	903,400	1,865,705	2,997,372	1,106,930
Margarine	1,447,294	208,062	91,328	164,168	329,909	482,602	173,215
Fats and oils	2,360,029	148,273	146,266	294,059	533,740	866,131	358,079
Salad dressings	2,427,488	136,041	177,533	222,109	563,370	950,427	363,769
Nondairy cream and imitation milk	670,498	50,644	63,064	70,676	165,452	244,156	77,576
Peanut butter	1,195,857	70,307	109,876	152,282	273,035	454,392	134,291
Miscellaneous foods	36,961,180	1,811,515	3,171,751	3,661,564	8,208,344	15,085,597	4,832,759
Frozen prepared foods	6,760,169	389,831	703,950	680,654	1,445,116	2,598,394	903,190
Frozen meals	2,190,360	193,658	332,809	239,619	423,572	715,339	274,181
Other frozen prepared foods	4,569,809	196,059	371,142	440,929	1,021,544	1,883,055	629,009
Canned and packaged soups	3,020,306	187,713	278,930	352,212	678,510	1,152,939	362,053
Potato chips, nuts, and other snacks	7,570,695	292,088	674,450	689,780	1,632,641	3,242,199	989,256
Potato chips and other snacks	5,946,578	197,888	530,303	465,973	1,287,619	2,629,963	791,116
Nuts	1,624,117	94,085	144,146	223,807	345,022	612,236	198,230
Condiments and seasonings	8,150,225	405,150	696,884	803,435	1,959,169	3,175,031	1,086,158
Salt, spices and other seasonings	1,972,653	100,830	161,988	221,791	505,303	710,973	270,117
Olives, pickles, relishes	1,038,454	56,817	75,783	128,830	255,137	392,933	128,782
Sauces and gravies	3,723,510	161,534	330,512	301,487	898,449	1,515,982	501,221
Baking needs and misc. products	1,415,609	85,969	128,601	151,221	300,279	555,479	185,948
Other canned/packaged prepared foods	11,459,785	536,847	817,360	1,135,590	2,492,909	4,917,033	1,492,102
Prepared salads	1,121,244	76,480	122,772	127,450	193,889	452,041	138,626
Prepared desserts	816,658	58,418	58,295	108,030	181,360	308,637	99,702

	total consumer units	single person		consumer units with two or more persons			
		no earner	one earner	no earners	one earner	two earners	three+ earners
Baby food	$2,873,123	$31,324	$95,568	$289,920	$733,396	$1,457,881	$266,776
Miscellaneous prepared foods	6,648,761	370,625	540,902	610,190	1,384,264	2,698,139	987,088
Nonalcoholic beverages	23,803,687	1,389,674	2,239,569	2,356,925	5,074,708	9,359,861	3,234,724
Cola	9,142,685	371,997	819,656	856,495	1,819,967	3,878,616	1,306,334
Other carbonated drinks	3,974,947	181,883	333,692	412,701	796,037	1,691,626	526,507
Coffee	4,396,052	433,387	440,918	539,196	986,147	1,553,932	448,660
Roasted coffee	2,977,377	252,190	304,721	346,800	653,653	1,115,325	304,164
Instant and freeze-dried coffee	1,418,675	181,197	136,021	192,396	332,494	438,607	144,496
Noncarb. fruit flavored drinks incl. non-frozen lemonade	2,234,311	132,611	170,291	206,297	516,241	814,748	376,502
Tea	1,660,913	95,686	155,099	138,062	363,317	656,231	240,947
Nonalcoholic beer	67,459	13,147	4,770	13,265	8,153	27,539	1,355
Other nonalcoholic beverages	2,327,322	160,963	315,144	190,910	584,847	737,169	334,508
Food prepared by cu on out-of-town trips	4,743,566	186,570	561,394	461,091	915,949	1,879,696	739,368
FOOD AWAY FROM HOME	**173,599,597**	**6,979,465**	**24,250,689**	**12,639,741**	**28,216,842**	**74,983,333**	**24,675,401**
Meals at restaurants, carry-outs, other	**133,507,724**	**5,711,199**	**19,370,909**	**10,153,774**	**21,006,576**	**57,579,768**	**17,830,987**
Lunch	46,174,390	1,867,989	6,639,390	3,070,688	7,200,124	20,051,663	6,630,470
Dinner	66,619,456	3,151,345	9,562,948	5,244,450	10,730,883	28,465,463	8,617,471
Snacks and nonalcoholic beverages	10,396,801	267,280	1,559,820	536,224	1,558,665	4,848,858	1,450,469
Breakfast and brunch	10,318,100	424,699	1,608,752	1,302,517	1,517,103	4,213,784	1,132,578
Board (including at school)	**5,184,091**	**165,421**	**749,879**	**141,670**	**627,801**	**2,242,404**	**1,256,573**
Catered affairs	**5,732,959**	**36,125**	**778,673**	**349,878**	**899,643**	**2,231,657**	**1,437,193**
Food on out-of-town trips	**21,248,437**	**1,042,827**	**2,667,945**	**1,883,418**	**4,047,199**	**9,049,209**	**2,557,760**
School lunches	**5,494,810**	**1,829**	**1,060**	**96,039**	**1,157,166**	**2,852,625**	**1,385,897**
Meals as pay	**2,431,576**	**22,064**	**681,869**	**14,857**	**478,457**	**1,027,335**	**206,991**
ALCOHOLIC BEVERAGES	**28,417,446**	**1,102,273**	**6,259,416**	**2,095,233**	**4,588,893**	**11,122,685**	**2,998,382**
At home	**16,877,937**	**636,076**	**3,524,168**	**1,279,170**	**3,014,121**	**6,497,832**	**1,793,647**
Beer and ale	10,188,293	402,292	2,414,452	627,063	1,620,908	3,838,651	1,171,772
Whiskey	1,398,233	56,360	211,980	271,349	223,320	531,971	97,625
Wine	3,721,466	128,496	645,302	255,325	840,979	1,530,423	319,517
Other alcoholic beverages	1,568,924	48,929	252,433	125,328	329,113	597,124	204,733
Away from home	**11,540,531**	**466,311**	**2,735,425**	**816,063**	**1,574,573**	**4,624,853**	**1,204,735**
Beer and ale	3,941,218	108,604	1,093,817	261,480	424,765	1,610,017	379,573
Wine	1,613,896	60,247	332,279	122,993	225,308	667,314	183,510
Other alcoholic beverages	2,857,792	111,576	622,868	216,060	410,845	1,166,372	295,946
Alcoholic beverages purchased on trips	3,128,648	185,884	686,285	215,530	513,854	1,181,149	345,797

Note: Spending for items in a given category may not add to the total for that category because the listing is incomplete. Numbers may not add to total due to rounding. (-) means insufficient data.

Number of Earners
market shares

(percent of total annual spending on food accounted for by consumer units of specified size and number of earners, 1994)

	total consumer units	single person		consumer units with two or more persons			
		no earner	one earner	no earners	one earner	two earners	three+ earners
Share of total consumer units	*100.0%*	*11.2%*	*17.3%*	*10.4%*	*19.5%*	*32.9%*	*8.8%*
Share of total spending	*100.0*	*5.0*	*12.3*	*7.5*	*19.3*	*42.0*	*13.6*
Share of food spending	*100.0*	*5.4*	*10.5*	*9.1*	*20.4*	*40.2*	*13.8*
Share of alcoholic beverages spending	*100.0*	*3.9*	*22.0*	*7.4*	*16.1*	*39.1*	*10.6*
FOOD AT HOME	**100.0%**	**6.3%**	**8.3%**	**10.3%**	**23.0%**	**38.3%**	**13.5%**
Cereals and bakery products	**100.0**	**6.1**	**8.4**	**10.7**	**22.9**	**38.4**	**13.1**
Cereals and cereal products	100.0	5.7	8.0	10.4	24.0	38.2	13.5
Flour	100.0	5.6	6.2	9.7	26.0	36.4	15.9
Prepared flour mixes	100.0	8.3	6.5	10.7	22.8	38.4	13.1
Ready-to-eat and cooked cereals	100.0	5.6	8.1	10.6	24.4	37.9	13.2
Rice	100.0	5.3	8.1	10.6	23.2	40.7	11.9
Pasta, cornmeal, and other cereal products	100.0	5.0	8.7	9.7	23.0	37.9	15.0
Bakery products	100.0	6.4	8.7	10.9	22.2	38.6	12.8
Bread	100.0	6.9	8.9	10.9	23.3	37.7	12.2
White bread	100.0	6.8	8.2	10.6	24.9	36.6	12.9
Bread, other than white	100.0	7.1	9.5	11.2	21.7	38.8	11.5
Crackers and cookies	100.0	6.7	8.1	11.5	22.1	38.4	12.8
Cookies	100.0	6.4	7.6	11.4	21.9	38.7	13.6
Crackers	100.0	7.5	9.1	11.7	22.7	37.8	11.2
Frozen and refrigerated bakery products	100.0	4.7	9.9	11.9	21.9	40.1	11.3
Other bakery products	100.0	6.3	8.8	10.4	21.4	39.0	13.5
Biscuits and rolls	100.0	5.2	8.7	9.7	21.7	40.8	13.3
Cakes and cupcakes	100.0	6.1	8.8	10.7	20.0	41.0	12.7
Bread and cracker products	100.0	4.2	7.9	8.1	23.2	41.5	14.7
Sweetrolls, coffee cakes, doughnuts	100.0	7.6	8.4	11.7	22.0	35.5	14.3
Pies, tarts, turnovers	100.0	8.3	10.2	10.2	22.4	34.1	14.4
Meats, poultry, fish, and eggs	**100.0**	**6.1**	**7.5**	**10.1**	**24.4**	**37.7**	**14.0**
Beef	100.0	5.3	7.1	9.3	25.2	38.1	14.8
Ground beef	100.0	5.1	7.6	10.6	23.7	38.7	14.0
Roast	100.0	6.7	4.1	8.7	24.8	38.1	17.0
Chuck roast	100.0	7.8	4.4	9.4	26.4	39.3	12.8
Round roast	100.0	7.3	4.1	8.5	23.8	37.7	17.9
Other roast	100.0	4.9	3.8	8.3	24.5	37.4	20.0
Steak	100.0	4.4	8.2	8.2	26.9	38.1	14.1
Round steak	100.0	2.8	5.2	8.3	31.0	37.4	15.5
Sirloin steak	100.0	5.3	7.7	9.1	23.0	39.0	15.3
Other steak	100.0	4.5	9.6	7.7	27.5	37.9	13.0
Other beef	100.0	8.5	5.1	8.8	24.9	34.7	17.5
Pork	100.0	6.6	7.0	11.2	25.4	37.4	12.5
Bacon	100.0	9.9	8.1	11.0	24.6	36.6	10.2
Pork chops	100.0	6.3	6.5	10.6	26.5	36.6	13.5

	total consumer units	single person		consumer units with two or more persons			
		no earner	one earner	no earners	one earner	two earners	three+ earners
Ham	100.0%	6.0%	5.9%	13.9%	24.1%	37.8%	12.3%
Ham, not canned	100.0	5.9	6.1	13.0	24.1	38.3	12.5
Canned ham	100.0	6.5	2.6	25.3	24.2	31.9	9.8
Sausage	100.0	6.0	9.3	10.8	24.0	38.9	11.1
Other pork	100.0	5.9	6.7	9.3	26.7	37.2	14.1
Other meats	100.0	6.0	6.9	10.3	24.4	37.8	14.3
Frankfurters	100.0	6.6	5.9	9.8	23.9	41.5	12.2
Lunch meats (cold cuts)	100.0	5.9	7.6	10.4	22.9	37.7	15.0
Bologna, liverwurst, salami	100.0	6.3	8.2	10.3	24.5	37.5	13.1
Other lunchmeats	100.0	5.6	7.2	10.5	22.0	37.8	16.1
Lamb, organ meats and others	100.0	5.9	4.1	11.1	35.9	31.1	13.2
Lamb and organ meats	100.0	6.0	4.2	11.3	35.0	31.5	13.1
Mutton, goat and game	100.0	-	-	-	-	-	-
Poultry	100.0	6.7	8.3	9.6	22.0	37.9	14.8
Fresh and frozen chickens	100.0	6.3	8.0	9.3	22.7	37.9	15.3
Fresh and frozen whole chicken	100.0	6.7	6.1	10.7	23.9	37.7	14.6
Fresh and frozen chicken parts	100.0	6.1	8.8	8.7	22.2	37.9	15.5
Other poultry	100.0	8.6	9.2	11.1	19.3	38.0	13.3
Fish and seafood	100.0	5.8	8.3	10.0	24.8	37.4	13.5
Canned fish and seafood	100.0	7.4	10.7	11.9	21.7	35.0	12.9
Fresh fish and shellfish	100.0	5.8	7.5	8.3	25.8	38.5	13.8
Frozen fish and shellfish	100.0	4.9	8.5	12.5	24.7	36.2	13.1
Eggs	100.0	7.1	8.7	11.4	22.8	35.8	13.9
Dairy products	**100.0**	**7.1**	**7.8**	**10.2**	**22.7**	**38.4**	**13.3**
Fresh milk and cream	100.0	7.4	7.4	10.5	23.3	37.5	13.6
Fresh milk, all types	100.0	7.5	7.5	10.4	23.2	37.5	13.7
Cream	100.0	5.2	6.4	11.8	24.7	38.3	13.4
Other dairy products	100.0	6.9	8.2	10.0	22.3	39.1	13.1
Butter	100.0	4.8	8.6	9.5	26.9	35.3	14.6
Cheese	100.0	7.6	8.1	9.3	23.2	38.5	13.1
Ice cream and related products	100.0	5.6	7.8	11.7	20.2	40.5	13.5
Miscellaneous dairy products	100.0	8.4	9.3	9.4	21.0	40.1	11.5
Fruits and vegetables	**100.0**	**7.8**	**8.7**	**10.5**	**23.0**	**36.8**	**13.0**
Fresh fruits	100.0	7.8	8.9	10.1	23.4	36.6	13.1
Apples	100.0	5.4	9.2	9.1	23.4	38.3	14.2
Bananas	100.0	8.7	9.2	11.6	21.4	36.9	11.9
Oranges	100.0	5.7	9.3	9.0	28.4	36.0	12.0
Citrus fruits, excl. oranges	100.0	9.0	9.4	10.4	21.1	36.2	13.5
Other fresh fruits	100.0	8.8	8.4	10.0	23.4	35.9	13.4
Fresh vegetables	100.0	7.3	8.9	9.7	23.6	36.7	13.6
Potatoes	100.0	6.9	7.7	10.2	25.4	36.3	13.4
Lettuce	100.0	7.2	10.2	8.9	22.2	37.8	13.2
Tomatoes	100.0	7.3	8.4	8.8	25.2	36.1	14.1
Other fresh vegetables	100.0	7.5	9.1	9.9	22.8	36.8	13.5

	total consumer units	single person		consumer units with two or more persons			
		no earner	one earner	no earners	one earner	two earners	three+ earners
Processed fruits	100.0%	8.7%	8.8%	10.9%	22.1%	36.3%	12.9%
Frozen fruits and fruit juices	100.0	6.2	9.5	8.5	22.7	39.3	13.3
Frozen orange juice	100.0	7.1	12.2	8.5	23.8	36.7	11.7
Frozen fruits	100.0	10.3	3.1	11.9	19.6	40.7	13.6
Frozen fruit juices	100.0	3.4	6.6	7.5	21.6	43.8	16.2
Canned fruit	100.0	11.8	6.7	15.6	19.5	34.9	11.4
Dried fruit	100.0	9.9	8.8	16.0	20.3	28.3	16.1
Fresh fruit juices	100.0	9.1	12.0	8.0	24.9	32.8	13.1
Canned and bottled fruit juices	100.0	8.2	7.7	10.8	21.8	38.5	12.6
Processed vegetables	100.0	7.6	7.9	12.1	22.5	37.9	11.8
Frozen vegetables	100.0	5.1	8.6	10.3	23.0	38.5	14.1
Canned and dried vegetables and juices	100.0	8.8	7.6	13.0	22.3	37.7	10.7
Canned beans	100.0	10.2	8.3	10.6	23.3	36.9	10.8
Canned corn	100.0	9.8	8.4	9.4	22.5	39.6	10.3
Other canned and dried vegetables	100.0	8.2	6.7	14.5	22.2	37.5	10.9
Frozen vegetable juices	100.0	1.0	10.5	4.1	38.1	47.1	1.9
Fresh and canned vegetable juices	100.0	8.4	8.9	15.1	19.9	37.1	10.4
Other food at home	**100.0**	**5.5**	**8.8**	**10.2**	**21.8**	**39.7**	**13.5**
Sugar and other sweets	100.0	6.0	8.0	11.6	21.9	38.7	13.4
Candy and chewing gum	100.0	5.9	8.6	10.6	20.2	40.5	13.5
Sugar	100.0	5.9	6.3	11.8	24.9	35.8	15.0
Artificial sweeteners	100.0	8.3	8.1	19.4	26.6	29.2	9.5
Jams, preserves, other sweets	100.0	6.1	7.9	12.9	23.6	37.3	12.1
Fats and oils	100.0	7.6	7.3	11.2	23.0	37.0	13.7
Margarine	100.0	14.4	6.3	11.3	22.8	33.3	12.0
Fats and oils	100.0	6.3	6.2	12.5	22.6	36.7	15.2
Salad dressings	100.0	5.6	7.3	9.1	23.2	39.2	15.0
Nondairy cream and imitation milk	100.0	7.6	9.4	10.5	24.7	36.4	11.6
Peanut butter	100.0	5.9	9.2	12.7	22.8	38.0	11.2
Miscellaneous foods	100.0	4.9	8.6	9.9	22.2	40.8	13.1
Frozen prepared foods	100.0	5.8	10.4	10.1	21.4	38.4	13.4
Frozen meals	100.0	8.8	15.2	10.9	19.3	32.7	12.5
Other frozen prepared foods	100.0	4.3	8.1	9.6	22.4	41.2	13.8
Canned and packaged soups	100.0	6.2	9.2	11.7	22.5	38.2	12.0
Potato chips, nuts, and other snacks	100.0	3.9	8.9	9.1	21.6	42.8	13.1
Potato chips and other snacks	100.0	3.3	8.9	7.8	21.7	44.2	13.3
Nuts	100.0	5.8	8.9	13.8	21.2	37.7	12.2
Condiments and seasonings	100.0	5.0	8.6	9.9	24.0	39.0	13.3
Salt, spices and other seasonings	100.0	5.1	8.2	11.2	25.6	36.0	13.7
Olives, pickles, relishes	100.0	5.5	7.3	12.4	24.6	37.8	12.4
Sauces and gravies	100.0	4.3	8.9	8.1	24.1	40.7	13.5
Baking needs and misc. products	100.0	6.1	9.1	10.7	21.2	39.2	13.1
Other canned/packaged prepared foods	100.0	4.7	7.1	9.9	21.8	42.9	13.0
Prepared salads	100.0	6.8	10.9	11.4	17.3	40.3	12.4
Prepared desserts	100.0	7.2	7.1	13.2	22.2	37.8	12.2

	total consumer units	single person		consumer units with two or more persons			
		no earner	one earner	no earners	one earner	two earners	three+ earners
Baby food	100.0%	1.1%	3.3%	10.1%	25.5%	50.7%	9.3%
Miscellaneous prepared foods	100.0	5.6	8.1	9.2	20.8	40.6	14.8
Nonalcoholic beverages	100.0	5.8	9.4	9.9	21.3	39.3	13.6
Cola	100.0	4.1	9.0	9.4	19.9	42.4	14.3
Other carbonated drinks	100.0	4.6	8.4	10.4	20.0	42.6	13.2
Coffee	100.0	9.9	10.0	12.3	22.4	35.3	10.2
Roasted coffee	100.0	8.5	10.2	11.6	22.0	37.5	10.2
Instant and freeze-dried coffee	100.0	12.8	9.6	13.6	23.4	30.9	10.2
Noncarb. fruit flavored drinks incl. non-frozen lemonade	100.0	5.9	7.6	9.2	23.1	36.5	16.9
Tea	100.0	5.8	9.3	8.3	21.9	39.5	14.5
Nonalcoholic beer	100.0	19.5	7.1	19.7	12.1	40.8	2.0
Other nonalcoholic beverages	100.0	6.9	13.5	8.2	25.1	31.7	14.4
Food prepared by cu on out-of-town trips	100.0	3.9	11.8	9.7	19.3	39.6	15.6
FOOD AWAY FROM HOME	**100.0**	**4.0**	**14.0**	**7.3**	**16.3**	**43.2**	**14.2**
Meals at restaurants, carry-outs, other	**100.0**	**4.3**	**14.5**	**7.6**	**15.7**	**43.1**	**13.4**
Lunch	100.0	4.0	14.4	6.7	15.6	43.4	14.4
Dinner	100.0	4.7	14.4	7.9	16.1	42.7	12.9
Snacks and nonalcoholic beverages	100.0	2.6	15.0	5.2	15.0	46.6	14.0
Breakfast and brunch	100.0	4.1	15.6	12.6	14.7	40.8	11.0
Board (including at school)	**100.0**	**3.2**	**14.5**	**2.7**	**12.1**	**43.3**	**24.2**
Catered affairs	**100.0**	**0.6**	**13.6**	**6.1**	**15.7**	**38.9**	**25.1**
Food on out-of-town trips	**100.0**	**4.9**	**12.6**	**8.9**	**19.0**	**42.6**	**12.0**
School lunches	**100.0**	**0.0**	**0.0**	**1.7**	**21.1**	**51.9**	**25.2**
Meals as pay	**100.0**	**0.9**	**28.0**	**0.6**	**19.7**	**42.2**	**8.5**
ALCOHOLIC BEVERAGES	**100.0**	**3.9**	**22.0**	**7.4**	**16.1**	**39.1**	**10.6**
At home	**100.0**	**3.8**	**20.9**	**7.6**	**17.9**	**38.5**	**10.6**
Beer and ale	100.0	3.9	23.7	6.2	15.9	37.7	11.5
Whiskey	100.0	4.0	15.2	19.4	16.0	38.0	7.0
Wine	100.0	3.5	17.3	6.9	22.6	41.1	8.6
Other alcoholic beverages	100.0	3.1	16.1	8.0	21.0	38.1	13.0
Away from home	**100.0**	**4.0**	**23.7**	**7.1**	**13.6**	**40.1**	**10.4**
Beer and ale	100.0	2.8	27.8	6.6	10.8	40.9	9.6
Wine	100.0	3.7	20.6	7.6	14.0	41.3	11.4
Other alcoholic beverages	100.0	3.9	21.8	7.6	14.4	40.8	10.4
Alcoholic beverages purchased on trips	100.0	5.9	21.9	6.9	16.4	37.8	11.1

Note: Numbers may not add to total due to rounding. (-) means insufficient data.

Chapter 9

Spending by

Occupation

The average household headed by a wage and salary worker spent $4,770 on food in 1994, but those headed by managers and professionals spent much more—$5,704.

After adjusting for household size, households headed by managers and professionals spend 24 percent more than average on food. Per capita food spending is 6 percent higher for the self-employed and 13 percent higher for households headed by retirees.

On a per capita basis, households headed by managers and professionals spend 31 percent more than the average household on biscuits and rolls, 16 percent more on cheese, 18 percent more on oranges, 36 percent more on frozen fruit juices, and 25 percent more on potato chips and other snacks. They spend 55 percent more on food away from home, including 72 percent more on food while on out-of-town trips. This group spends 85 percent more than average on wine consumed at home. Managers and professionals control 33 percent of spending on food away from home, although they account for just 20 percent of households.

The self-employed account for only 6 percent of households, but they spend more than average on most categories of food. In particular, their per capita spending on food for out-of-town trips is 34 percent above average. They spend 23 percent more than average on wine consumed at home and 19 percent more on alcoholic beverages purchased on trips.

Retirees are above-average spenders on food, but they are a smaller share of the food market than are managers and professionals. While 18 percent of households are headed by retirees, this group accounts for only 14 percent of food spending. In most categories, the retiree share of the market is less than 20 percent. Notable exceptions include canned ham (29 percent), canned and dried fruit (26 and 25 percent, respectively), artificial sweeteners (28 percent), margarine (26 percent), instant and freeze-dried coffee (26 percent), nonalcoholic beer (41 percent), and whiskey consumed at home (25 percent).

Occupation
average spending

(average annual spending of consumer units on food and alcoholic beverages, by occupation of consumer unit reference person, 1994)

	total consumer units	wage and salary workers		self employed	retired
		total	managers and professionals		
Number of consumer units (in thousands, add 000's)	102,210	66,675	20,700	6,343	18,387
Average number of persons per cu	2.5	2.7	2.6	2.8	1.7
Average before-tax income of cu	$36,838.00	$43,045.00	$60,456.00	$51,731.00	$20,476.00
Average spending of cu, total	31,750.63	35,521.17	47,245.75	40,734.73	22,097.85
Food, average spending	4,410.52	4,770.09	5,704.34	5,246.24	3,396.50
Alcoholic beverages, average spending	278.03	322.88	386.02	287.29	183.54
FOOD AT HOME	**$2,712.05**	**$2,797.05**	**$2,973.89**	**$3,191.96**	**$2,312.92**
Cereals and bakery products	**428.68**	**439.52**	**500.23**	**512.42**	**379.75**
Cereals and cereal products	161.74	167.99	188.45	187.63	132.16
Flour	7.60	7.70	7.11	8.64	5.72
Prepared flour mixes	12.79	12.98	14.49	14.61	12.82
Ready-to-eat and cooked cereals	98.27	102.14	118.54	108.80	83.96
Rice	15.43	15.70	15.82	22.03	9.44
Pasta, cornmeal, and other cereal products	27.65	29.46	32.50	33.54	20.22
Bakery products	266.93	271.53	311.78	324.79	247.60
Bread	76.22	76.02	77.40	93.31	72.14
White bread	37.65	37.45	35.36	42.45	33.04
Bread, other than white	38.57	38.56	42.04	50.86	39.10
Crackers and cookies	62.56	62.27	74.42	82.56	58.49
Cookies	42.97	42.40	50.96	58.01	39.68
Crackers	19.59	19.87	23.46	24.55	18.81
Frozen and refrigerated bakery products	21.56	23.30	28.26	21.22	18.29
Other bakery products	106.59	109.95	131.69	127.70	98.67
Biscuits and rolls	35.96	37.73	49.11	43.08	30.83
Cakes and cupcakes	31.19	32.42	34.94	38.63	27.25
Bread and cracker products	4.72	5.14	6.27	6.30	2.91
Sweetrolls, coffee cakes, doughnuts	21.92	21.65	26.42	24.62	25.48
Pies, tarts, turnovers	12.80	13.00	14.95	15.08	12.20
Meats, poultry, fish, and eggs	**732.45**	**755.93**	**721.14**	**841.42**	**581.22**
Beef	226.76	239.24	209.68	239.98	167.09
Ground beef	88.45	93.32	79.01	92.37	66.28
Roast	39.41	40.95	32.46	39.99	32.36
Chuck roast	12.26	12.19	9.65	12.76	11.20
Round roast	14.84	15.31	11.28	16.32	12.64
Other roast	12.31	13.45	11.54	10.92	8.51
Steak	84.75	90.12	83.27	96.95	56.25
Round steak	16.00	17.00	12.75	19.89	8.76
Sirloin steak	24.44	25.65	24.43	26.09	19.71
Other steak	44.31	47.46	46.10	50.96	27.77
Other beef	14.15	14.85	14.93	10.68	12.20
Pork	155.74	157.39	139.90	171.94	133.45
Bacon	22.78	21.86	18.99	25.70	24.07
Pork chops	39.32	40.90	37.83	42.25	26.50

	total consumer units	wage and salary workers		self employed	retired
		total	managers and professionals		
Ham	$36.88	$35.77	$33.19	$45.59	$38.72
Ham, not canned	34.16	33.72	31.66	40.52	34.28
Canned ham	2.72	2.05	1.53	5.07	4.45
Sausage	22.82	23.65	20.33	18.29	17.65
Other pork	33.93	35.21	29.56	40.11	26.51
Other meats	93.95	95.84	94.75	118.02	85.97
Frankfurters	18.76	18.99	16.51	24.82	16.22
Lunch meats (cold cuts)	65.66	67.79	66.50	79.31	60.87
Bologna, liverwurst, salami	23.73	24.03	19.78	28.78	22.41
Other lunchmeats	41.93	43.76	46.72	50.53	38.46
Lamb, organ meats and others	9.53	9.06	11.74	13.89	8.87
Lamb and organ meats	9.35	8.86	11.74	13.89	8.87
Mutton, goat and game	0.18	0.20	-	-	-
Poultry	136.58	141.91	148.53	163.34	99.92
Fresh and frozen chickens	107.89	112.45	116.23	138.49	75.23
Fresh and frozen whole chicken	29.56	28.82	28.50	44.84	21.31
Fresh and frozen chicken parts	78.33	83.63	87.73	93.66	53.92
Other poultry	28.69	29.47	32.30	24.84	24.69
Fish and seafood	89.43	91.50	102.05	113.32	67.94
Canned fish and seafood	15.03	15.18	17.67	17.42	13.51
Fresh fish and shellfish	51.26	52.55	58.07	63.33	34.52
Frozen fish and shellfish	23.15	23.77	26.31	32.57	19.91
Eggs	30.00	30.04	26.23	34.82	26.84
Dairy products	**288.92**	**295.11**	**320.84**	**332.72**	**264.00**
Fresh milk and cream	127.13	129.25	130.04	136.22	116.13
Fresh milk, all types	118.94	121.14	120.28	126.82	107.32
Cream	8.19	8.11	9.76	9.40	8.81
Other dairy products	161.79	165.86	190.80	196.50	147.86
Butter	11.65	12.27	11.78	12.88	8.52
Cheese	81.83	84.73	98.67	89.57	75.97
Ice cream and related products	47.64	48.20	53.43	63.33	45.36
Miscellaneous dairy products	20.66	20.67	26.92	30.73	18.02
Fruits and vegetables	**436.57**	**438.50**	**482.18**	**526.17**	**417.55**
Fresh fruits	133.02	133.98	150.49	172.90	127.76
Apples	25.37	26.81	31.01	35.83	18.69
Bananas	29.66	28.83	29.78	38.17	30.71
Oranges	16.36	17.70	20.11	19.49	12.13
Citrus fruits, excl. oranges	10.96	10.51	12.67	15.20	11.85
Other fresh fruits	50.67	50.13	56.92	64.21	54.38
Fresh vegetables	134.89	137.02	149.40	154.99	121.45
Potatoes	28.01	28.33	29.24	27.98	26.20
Lettuce	17.38	18.11	19.66	21.13	14.61
Tomatoes	21.01	21.48	21.06	23.52	18.49
Other fresh vegetables	68.50	69.11	79.44	82.36	62.14

	total consumer units	wage and salary workers		self employed	retired
		total	managers and professionals		
Processed fruits	$93.08	$92.05	$102.50	$119.37	$94.47
Frozen fruits and fruit juices	16.28	16.75	19.68	26.24	13.66
Frozen orange juice	9.49	9.78	11.06	12.85	8.49
Frozen fruits	1.60	1.24	1.30	4.92	1.95
Frozen fruit juices	5.19	5.73	7.32	8.47	3.22
Canned fruit	14.23	12.93	13.96	16.38	20.59
Dried fruit	5.89	5.29	6.26	7.51	8.27
Fresh fruit juices	17.90	18.02	20.22	20.58	16.55
Canned and bottled fruit juices	38.78	39.06	42.38	48.66	35.39
Processed vegetables	75.57	75.45	79.80	78.90	73.87
Frozen vegetables	24.83	25.97	31.35	27.61	21.58
Canned and dried vegetables and juices	50.74	49.48	48.44	51.29	52.29
Canned beans	10.44	10.20	9.15	11.37	10.26
Canned corn	6.81	7.05	6.16	6.40	5.75
Other canned and dried vegetables	27.05	25.74	25.67	27.89	28.74
Frozen vegetable juices	0.23	0.26	0.43	0.33	0.07
Fresh and canned vegetable juices	6.21	6.24	7.03	5.30	7.47
Other food at home	**825.43**	**868.00**	**949.49**	**979.23**	**670.41**
Sugar and other sweets	105.25	107.29	117.14	124.74	97.15
Candy and chewing gum	62.32	66.41	76.68	69.40	52.86
Sugar	18.31	17.84	15.43	23.32	15.45
Artificial sweeteners	3.39	2.78	2.85	4.65	5.27
Jams, preserves, other sweets	21.23	20.26	22.18	27.37	23.56
Fats and oils	79.25	78.08	80.68	93.69	77.88
Margarine	14.16	12.33	12.64	16.76	20.66
Fats and oils	23.09	22.42	21.24	26.54	20.52
Salad dressings	23.75	25.31	26.06	27.20	19.41
Nondairy cream and imitation milk	6.56	6.60	7.94	6.17	6.60
Peanut butter	11.70	11.42	12.80	17.02	10.70
Miscellaneous foods	361.62	388.22	430.04	417.69	271.06
Frozen prepared foods	66.14	70.39	80.69	76.41	56.73
Frozen meals	21.43	21.84	26.80	24.66	22.95
Other frozen prepared foods	44.71	48.54	53.89	51.75	33.77
Canned and packaged soups	29.55	30.03	35.93	31.57	27.12
Potato chips, nuts, and other snacks	74.07	82.07	96.25	89.78	53.12
Potato chips and other snacks	58.18	66.39	74.56	71.33	35.19
Nuts	15.89	15.68	21.69	18.46	17.93
Condiments and seasonings	79.74	83.09	93.16	106.22	59.28
Salt, spices and other seasonings	19.30	19.39	19.09	25.71	15.87
Olives, pickles, relishes	10.16	10.33	11.39	13.74	9.39
Sauces and gravies	36.43	39.54	45.40	45.21	22.86
Baking needs and misc. products	13.85	13.84	17.28	21.56	11.16
Other canned/packaged prepared foods	112.12	122.63	124.01	113.70	74.82
Prepared salads	10.97	11.49	14.45	12.34	11.07
Prepared desserts	7.99	7.76	8.53	8.99	9.66

	total consumer units	wage and salary workers		self employed	retired
		total	managers and professionals		
Baby food	$28.11	$31.68	$31.67	$32.88	$7.15
Miscellaneous prepared foods	65.05	71.71	69.37	59.50	46.95
Nonalcoholic beverages	232.89	244.56	250.46	269.02	186.53
Cola	89.45	98.29	87.57	103.91	56.34
Other carbonated drinks	38.89	40.89	43.28	44.62	28.47
Coffee	43.01	39.72	45.68	50.34	50.33
Roasted coffee	29.13	28.19	33.10	33.48	30.44
Instant and freeze-dried coffee	13.88	11.53	12.58	16.86	19.89
Noncarb. fruit flavored drinks incl. non-frozen lemonade	21.86	23.73	24.01	24.43	15.30
Tea	16.25	17.41	19.96	21.28	13.39
Nonalcoholic beer	0.66	0.60	1.31	-	1.49
Other nonalcoholic beverages	22.77	23.92	28.65	24.45	21.21
Food prepared by cu on out-of-town trips	46.41	49.84	71.17	74.10	37.79
FOOD AWAY FROM HOME	**1,698.46**	**1,973.04**	**2,730.45**	**2,054.28**	**1,083.58**
Meals at restaurants, carry-outs, other	**1,306.21**	**1,510.20**	**1,982.17**	**1,513.94**	**856.25**
Lunch	451.76	530.90	708.05	539.24	265.85
Dinner	651.79	744.20	997.16	754.42	457.22
Snacks and nonalcoholic beverages	101.72	125.89	147.86	107.25	42.08
Breakfast and brunch	100.95	109.20	129.11	113.03	91.09
Board (including at school)	**50.72**	**64.05**	**117.15**	**75.62**	**9.01**
Catered affairs	**56.09**	**72.94**	**138.99**	**48.38**	**26.57**
Food on out-of-town trips	**207.89**	**224.51**	**371.61**	**311.41**	**182.82**
School lunches	**53.76**	**69.86**	**78.25**	**69.24**	**6.58**
Meals as pay	**23.79**	**31.49**	**42.28**	**35.69**	**2.36**
ALCOHOLIC BEVERAGES	**278.03**	**322.88**	**386.02**	**287.29**	**183.54**
At home	**165.13**	**189.11**	**203.32**	**171.95**	**107.00**
Beer and ale	99.68	117.39	93.76	100.24	55.46
Whiskey	13.68	14.41	15.60	4.53	19.01
Wine	36.41	41.83	70.01	50.21	20.63
Other alcoholic beverages	15.35	15.48	23.94	16.97	11.89
Away from home	**112.91**	**133.77**	**182.70**	**115.34**	**76.54**
Beer and ale	38.56	47.77	57.22	32.00	21.13
Wine	15.79	18.43	25.06	16.62	11.38
Other alcoholic beverages	27.96	33.12	46.39	26.00	19.69
Alcoholic beverages purchased on trips	30.61	34.44	54.04	40.72	24.33

Note: Expenditures listed for items in a given category may not add to the total for that category because the listing is incomplete. (-) means insufficient data.

Occupation

indexed spending

(indexed average annual spending of consumer units on food and alcoholic beverages, by occupation of consumer unit reference person, 1994; index definition: an index of 100 is the average for all consumer units; an index of 132 means that spending by consumer units in the occupational group is 32 percent above the average for all consumer units; an index of 68 indicates that spending by the occupational group is 32 percent below the average for all consumer units)

	total consumer units	wage and salary workers		self employed	retired
		total	managers and professionals		
Average spending of cu, total	$31,750.63	$35,521.17	$47,245.75	$40,734.73	$22,097.85
Average spending of cu, index	100	112	149	128	70
Food, spending index	100	108	129	119	77
Alcoholic beverages, spending index	100	116	139	103	66
FOOD AT HOME	**100**	**103**	**110**	**118**	**85**
Cereals and bakery products	**100**	**103**	**117**	**120**	**89**
Cereals and cereal products	100	104	117	116	82
Flour	100	101	94	114	75
Prepared flour mixes	100	101	113	114	100
Ready-to-eat and cooked cereals	100	104	121	111	85
Rice	100	102	103	143	61
Pasta, cornmeal, and other cereal products	100	107	118	121	73
Bakery products	100	102	117	122	93
Bread	100	100	102	122	95
White bread	100	99	94	113	88
Bread, other than white	100	100	109	132	101
Crackers and cookies	100	100	119	132	93
Cookies	100	99	119	135	92
Crackers	100	101	120	125	96
Frozen and refrigerated bakery products	100	108	131	98	85
Other bakery products	100	103	124	120	93
Biscuits and rolls	100	105	137	120	86
Cakes and cupcakes	100	104	112	124	87
Bread and cracker products	100	109	133	133	62
Sweetrolls, coffee cakes, doughnuts	100	99	121	112	116
Pies, tarts, turnovers	100	102	117	118	95
Meats, poultry, fish, and eggs	**100**	**103**	**98**	**115**	**79**
Beef	100	106	92	106	74
Ground beef	100	106	89	104	75
Roast	100	104	82	101	82
Chuck roast	100	99	79	104	91
Round roast	100	103	76	110	85
Other roast	100	109	94	89	69
Steak	100	106	98	114	66
Round steak	100	106	80	124	55
Sirloin steak	100	105	100	107	81
Other steak	100	107	104	115	63
Other beef	100	105	106	75	86
Pork	100	101	90	110	86
Bacon	100	96	83	113	106
Pork chops	100	104	96	107	67

	total consumer units	wage and salary workers		self employed	retired
		total	managers and professionals		
Ham	100	97	90	124	105
Ham, not canned	100	99	93	119	100
Canned ham	100	75	56	186	164
Sausage	100	104	89	80	77
Other pork	100	104	87	118	78
Other meats	100	102	101	126	92
Frankfurters	100	101	88	132	86
Lunch meats (cold cuts)	100	103	101	121	93
Bologna, liverwurst, salami	100	101	83	121	94
Other lunchmeats	100	104	111	121	92
Lamb, organ meats and others	100	95	123	146	93
Lamb and organ meats	100	95	126	149	95
Mutton, goat and game	100	111	-	-	-
Poultry	100	104	109	120	73
Fresh and frozen chickens	100	104	108	128	70
Fresh and frozen whole chicken	100	97	96	152	72
Fresh and frozen chicken parts	100	107	112	120	69
Other poultry	100	103	113	87	86
Fish and seafood	100	102	114	127	76
Canned fish and seafood	100	101	118	116	90
Fresh fish and shellfish	100	103	113	124	67
Frozen fish and shellfish	100	103	114	141	86
Eggs	100	100	87	116	89
Dairy products	**100**	**102**	**111**	**115**	**91**
Fresh milk and cream	100	102	102	107	91
Fresh milk, all types	100	102	101	107	90
Cream	100	99	119	115	108
Other dairy products	100	103	118	121	91
Butter	100	105	101	111	73
Cheese	100	104	121	109	93
Ice cream and related products	100	101	112	133	95
Miscellaneous dairy products	100	100	130	149	87
Fruits and vegetables	**100**	**100**	**110**	**121**	**96**
Fresh fruits	100	101	113	130	96
Apples	100	106	122	141	74
Bananas	100	97	100	129	104
Oranges	100	108	123	119	74
Citrus fruits, excl. oranges	100	96	116	139	108
Other fresh fruits	100	99	112	127	107
Fresh vegetables	100	102	111	115	90
Potatoes	100	101	104	100	94
Lettuce	100	104	113	122	84
Tomatoes	100	102	100	112	88
Other fresh vegetables	100	101	116	120	91

	total consumer units	wage and salary workers		self employed	retired
		total	managers and professionals		
Processed fruits	100	99	110	128	101
Frozen fruits and fruit juices	100	103	121	161	84
Frozen orange juice	100	103	117	135	89
Frozen fruits	100	78	81	308	122
Frozen fruit juices	100	110	141	163	62
Canned fruit	100	91	98	115	145
Dried fruit	100	90	106	128	140
Fresh fruit juices	100	101	113	115	92
Canned and bottled fruit juices	100	101	109	125	91
Processed vegetables	100		106	104	98
Frozen vegetables	100	105	126	111	87
Canned and dried vegetables and juices	100	98	95	101	103
Canned beans	100	98	88	109	98
Canned corn	100	104	90	94	84
Other canned and dried vegetables	100	95	95	103	106
Frozen vegetable juices	100	113	187	143	30
Fresh and canned vegetable juices	100	100	113	85	120
Other food at home	**100**	**105**	**115**	**119**	**81**
Sugar and other sweets	100	102	111	119	92
Candy and chewing gum	100	107	123	111	85
Sugar	100	97	84	127	84
Artificial sweeteners	100	82	84	137	155
Jams, preserves, other sweets	100	95	104	129	111
Fats and oils	100	99	102	118	98
Margarine	100	87	89	118	146
Fats and oils	100	97	92	115	89
Salad dressings	100	107	110	115	82
Nondairy cream and imitation milk	100	101	121	94	101
Peanut butter	100	98	109	145	91
Miscellaneous foods	100	107	119	116	75
Frozen prepared foods	100	106	122	116	86
Frozen meals	100	102	125	115	107
Other frozen prepared foods	100	109	121	116	76
Canned and packaged soups	100	102	122	107	92
Potato chips, nuts, and other snacks	100	111	130	121	72
Potato chips and other snacks	100	114	128	123	60
Nuts	100	99	137	116	113
Condiments and seasonings	100	104	117	133	74
Salt, spices and other seasonings	100	100	99	133	82
Olives, pickles, relishes	100	102	112	135	92
Sauces and gravies	100	109	125	124	63
Baking needs and misc. products	100	100	125	156	81
Other canned/packaged prepared foods	100	109	111	101	67
Prepared salads	100	105	132	112	101
Prepared desserts	100	97	107	113	121

	total consumer units	wage and salary workers		self employed	retired
		total	managers and professionals		
Baby food	100	113	113	117	25
Miscellaneous prepared foods	100	110	107	91	72
Nonalcoholic beverages	100	105	108	116	80
Cola	100	110	98	116	63
Other carbonated drinks	100	105	111	115	73
Coffee	100	92	106	117	117
Roasted coffee	100	97	114	115	104
Instant and freeze-dried coffee	100	83	91	121	143
Noncarb. fruit flavored drinks incl. non-frozen lemonade	100	109	110	112	70
Tea	100	107	123	131	82
Nonalcoholic beer	100	91	198	-	226
Other nonalcoholic beverages	100	105	126	107	93
Food prepared by cu on out-of-town trips	100	107	153	160	81
FOOD AWAY FROM HOME	**100**	**116**	**161**	**121**	**64**
Meals at restaurants, carry-outs, other	**100**	**116**	**152**	**116**	**66**
Lunch	100	118	157	119	59
Dinner	100	114	153	116	70
Snacks and nonalcoholic beverages	100	124	145	105	41
Breakfast and brunch	100	108	128	112	90
Board (including at school)	**100**	**126**	**231**	**149**	**18**
Catered affairs	**100**	**130**	**248**	**86**	**47**
Food on out-of-town trips	**100**	**108**	**179**	**150**	**88**
School lunches	**100**	**130**	**146**	**129**	**12**
Meals as pay	**100**	**132**	**178**	**150**	**10**
ALCOHOLIC BEVERAGES	**100**	**116**	**139**	**103**	**66**
At home	**100**	**115**	**123**	**104**	**65**
Beer and ale	100	118	94	101	56
Whiskey	100	105	114	33	139
Wine	100	115	192	138	57
Other alcoholic beverages	100	101	156	111	77
Away from home	**100**	**118**	**162**	**102**	**68**
Beer and ale	100	124	148	83	55
Wine	100	117	159	105	72
Other alcoholic beverages	100	118	166	93	70
Alcoholic beverages purchased on trips	100	113	177	133	79

Note: (-) means insufficient data.

Occupation

average per capita spending

(average annual per capita spending of consumer units on food and alcoholic beverages, by occupation of consumer unit reference person, 1994; per capita figures are calculated by dividing the average spending of consumer units by the average number of persons per consumer unit)

	total consumer units	wage and salary workers total	managers and professionals	self employed	retired
Average number of persons per cu	2.5	2.7	2.6	2.8	1.7
Per capita before-tax income of cu	$14,735.20	$15,942.59	$23,252.31	$18,475.36	$12,044.71
Per capita spending of cu, total	12,700.25	13,155.99	18,171.44	14,548.12	12,998.74
Food, per capita spending	1,764.21	1,766.70	2,193.98	1,873.66	1,997.94
Alcoholic beverages, per capita spending	111.21	119.59	148.47	102.60	107.96
FOOD AT HOME	**$1,084.82**	**$1,035.94**	**$1,143.80**	**$1,139.99**	**$1,360.54**
Cereals and bakery products	**171.47**	**162.79**	**192.40**	**183.01**	**223.38**
Cereals and cereal products	64.70	62.22	72.48	67.01	77.74
Flour	3.04	2.85	2.73	3.09	3.36
Prepared flour mixes	5.12	4.81	5.57	5.22	7.54
Ready-to-eat and cooked cereals	39.31	37.83	45.59	38.86	49.39
Rice	6.17	5.81	6.08	7.87	5.55
Pasta, cornmeal, and other cereal products	11.06	10.91	12.50	11.98	11.89
Bakery products	106.77	100.57	119.92	116.00	145.65
Bread	30.49	28.16	29.77	33.33	42.44
White bread	15.06	13.87	13.60	15.16	19.44
Bread, other than white	15.43	14.28	16.17	18.16	23.00
Crackers and cookies	25.02	23.06	28.62	29.49	34.41
Cookies	17.19	15.70	19.60	20.72	23.34
Crackers	7.84	7.36	9.02	8.77	11.06
Frozen and refrigerated bakery products	8.62	8.63	10.87	7.58	10.76
Other bakery products	42.64	40.72	50.65	45.61	58.04
Biscuits and rolls	14.38	13.97	18.89	15.39	18.14
Cakes and cupcakes	12.48	12.01	13.44	13.80	16.03
Bread and cracker products	1.89	1.90	2.41	2.25	1.71
Sweetrolls, coffee cakes, doughnuts	8.77	8.02	10.16	8.79	14.99
Pies, tarts, turnovers	5.12	4.81	5.75	5.39	7.18
Meats, poultry, fish, and eggs	**292.98**	**279.97**	**277.36**	**300.51**	**341.89**
Beef	90.70	88.61	80.65	85.71	98.29
Ground beef	35.38	34.56	30.39	32.99	38.99
Roast	15.76	15.17	12.48	14.28	19.04
Chuck roast	4.90	4.51	3.71	4.56	6.59
Round roast	5.94	5.67	4.34	5.83	7.44
Other roast	4.92	4.98	4.44	3.90	5.01
Steak	33.90	33.38	32.03	34.63	33.09
Round steak	6.40	6.30	4.90	7.10	5.15
Sirloin steak	9.78	9.50	9.40	9.32	11.59
Other steak	17.72	17.58	17.73	18.20	16.34
Other beef	5.66	5.50	5.74	3.81	7.18
Pork	62.30	58.29	53.81	61.41	78.50
Bacon	9.11	8.10	7.30	9.18	14.16
Pork chops	15.73	15.15	14.55	15.09	15.59

	total consumer units	wage and salary workers		self employed	retired
		total	managers and professionals		
Ham	$14.75	$13.25	$12.77	$16.28	$22.78
Ham, not canned	13.66	12.49	12.18	14.47	20.16
Canned ham	1.09	0.76	0.59	1.81	2.62
Sausage	9.13	8.76	7.82	6.53	10.38
Other pork	13.57	13.04	11.37	14.33	15.59
Other meats	37.58	35.50	36.44	42.15	50.57
Frankfurters	7.50	7.03	6.35	8.86	9.54
Lunch meats (cold cuts)	26.26	25.11	25.58	28.33	35.81
Bologna, liverwurst, salami	9.49	8.90	7.61	10.28	13.18
Other lunchmeats	16.77	16.21	17.97	18.05	22.62
Lamb, organ meats and others	3.81	3.36	4.52	4.96	5.22
Lamb and organ meats	3.74	3.28	4.52	4.96	5.22
Mutton, goat and game	0.07	0.07	-	-	-
Poultry	54.63	52.56	57.13	58.34	58.78
Fresh and frozen chickens	43.16	41.65	44.70	49.46	44.25
Fresh and frozen whole chicken	11.82	10.67	10.96	16.01	12.54
Fresh and frozen chicken parts	31.33	30.97	33.74	33.45	31.72
Other poultry	11.48	10.91	12.42	8.87	14.52
Fish and seafood	35.77	33.89	39.25	40.47	39.96
Canned fish and seafood	6.01	5.62	6.80	6.22	7.95
Fresh fish and shellfish	20.50	19.46	22.33	22.62	20.31
Frozen fish and shellfish	9.26	8.80	10.12	11.63	11.71
Eggs	12.00	11.13	10.09	12.44	15.79
Dairy products	**115.57**	**109.30**	**123.40**	**118.83**	**155.29**
Fresh milk and cream	50.85	47.87	50.02	48.65	68.31
Fresh milk, all types	47.58	44.87	46.26	45.29	63.13
Cream	3.28	3.00	3.75	3.36	5.18
Other dairy products	64.72	61.43	73.38	70.18	86.98
Butter	4.66	4.54	4.53	4.60	5.01
Cheese	32.73	31.38	37.95	31.99	44.69
Ice cream and related products	19.06	17.85	20.55	22.62	26.68
Miscellaneous dairy products	8.26	7.66	10.35	10.98	10.60
Fruits and vegetables	**174.63**	**162.41**	**185.45**	**187.92**	**245.62**
Fresh fruits	53.21	49.62	57.88	61.75	75.15
Apples	10.15	9.93	11.93	12.80	10.99
Bananas	11.86	10.68	11.45	13.63	18.06
Oranges	6.54	6.56	7.73	6.96	7.14
Citrus fruits, excl. oranges	4.38	3.89	4.87	5.43	6.97
Other fresh fruits	20.27	18.57	21.89	22.93	31.99
Fresh vegetables	53.96	50.75	57.46	55.35	71.44
Potatoes	11.20	10.49	11.25	9.99	15.41
Lettuce	6.95	6.71	7.56	7.55	8.59
Tomatoes	8.40	7.96	8.10	8.40	10.88
Other fresh vegetables	27.40	25.60	30.55	29.41	36.55

	total consumer units	wage and salary workers		self employed	retired
		total	managers and professionals		
Processed fruits	$37.23	$34.09	$39.42	$42.63	$55.57
Frozen fruits and fruit juices	6.51	6.20	7.57	9.37	8.04
Frozen orange juice	3.80	3.62	4.25	4.59	4.99
Frozen fruits	0.64	0.46	0.50	1.76	1.15
Frozen fruit juices	2.08	2.12	2.82	3.03	1.89
Canned fruit	5.69	4.79	5.37	5.85	12.11
Dried fruit	2.36	1.96	2.41	2.68	4.86
Fresh fruit juices	7.16	6.67	7.78	7.35	9.74
Canned and bottled fruit juices	15.51	14.47	16.30	17.38	20.82
Processed vegetables	30.23	27.94	30.69	28.18	43.45
Frozen vegetables	9.93	9.62	12.06	9.86	12.69
Canned and dried vegetables and juices	20.30	18.33	18.63	18.32	30.76
Canned beans	4.18	3.78	3.52	4.06	6.04
Canned corn	2.72	2.61	2.37	2.29	3.38
Other canned and dried vegetables	10.82	9.53	9.87	9.96	16.91
Frozen vegetable juices	0.09	0.10	0.17	0.12	0.04
Fresh and canned vegetable juices	2.48	2.31	2.70	1.89	4.39
Other food at home	**330.17**	**321.48**	**365.19**	**349.73**	**394.36**
Sugar and other sweets	42.10	39.74	45.05	44.55	57.15
Candy and chewing gum	24.93	24.60	29.49	24.79	31.09
Sugar	7.32	6.61	5.93	8.33	9.09
Artificial sweeteners	1.36	1.03	1.10	1.66	3.10
Jams, preserves, other sweets	8.49	7.50	8.53	9.78	13.86
Fats and oils	31.70	28.92	31.03	33.46	45.81
Margarine	5.66	4.57	4.86	5.99	12.15
Fats and oils	9.24	8.30	8.17	9.48	12.07
Salad dressings	9.50	9.37	10.02	9.71	11.42
Nondairy cream and imitation milk	2.62	2.44	3.05	2.20	3.88
Peanut butter	4.68	4.23	4.92	6.08	6.29
Miscellaneous foods	144.65	143.79	165.40	149.18	159.45
Frozen prepared foods	26.46	26.07	31.03	27.29	33.37
Frozen meals	8.57	8.09	10.31	8.81	13.50
Other frozen prepared foods	17.88	17.98	20.73	18.48	19.86
Canned and packaged soups	11.82	11.12	13.82	11.28	15.95
Potato chips, nuts, and other snacks	29.63	30.40	37.02	32.06	31.25
Potato chips and other snacks	23.27	24.59	28.68	25.48	20.70
Nuts	6.36	5.81	8.34	6.59	10.55
Condiments and seasonings	31.90	30.77	35.83	37.94	34.87
Salt, spices and other seasonings	7.72	7.18	7.34	9.18	9.34
Olives, pickles, relishes	4.06	3.83	4.38	4.91	5.52
Sauces and gravies	14.57	14.64	17.46	16.15	13.45
Baking needs and misc. products	5.54	5.13	6.65	7.70	6.56
Other canned/packaged prepared foods	44.85	45.42	47.70	40.61	44.01
Prepared salads	4.39	4.26	5.56	4.41	6.51
Prepared desserts	3.20	2.87	3.28	3.21	5.68

	total consumer units	wage and salary workers		self employed	retired
		total	managers and professionals		
Baby food	$11.24	$11.73	$12.18	$11.74	$4.21
Miscellaneous prepared foods	26.02	26.56	26.68	21.25	27.62
Nonalcoholic beverages	93.16	90.58	96.33	96.08	109.72
Cola	35.78	36.40	33.68	37.11	33.14
Other carbonated drinks	15.56	15.14	16.65	15.94	16.75
Coffee	17.20	14.71	17.57	17.98	29.61
Roasted coffee	11.65	10.44	12.73	11.96	17.91
Instant and freeze-dried coffee	5.55	4.27	4.84	6.02	11.70
Noncarb. fruit flavored drinks incl. non-frozen lemonade	8.74	8.79	9.23	8.73	9.00
Tea	6.50	6.45	7.68	7.60	7.88
Nonalcoholic beer	0.26	0.22	0.50	-	0.88
Other nonalcoholic beverages	9.11	8.86	11.02	8.73	12.48
Food prepared by cu on out-of-town trips	18.56	18.46	27.37	26.46	22.23
FOOD AWAY FROM HOME	**679.38**	**730.76**	**1,050.17**	**733.67**	**637.40**
Meals at restaurants, carry-outs, other	**522.48**	**559.33**	**762.37**	**540.69**	**503.68**
Lunch	180.70	196.63	272.33	192.59	156.38
Dinner	260.72	275.63	383.52	269.44	268.95
Snacks and nonalcoholic beverages	40.69	46.63	56.87	38.30	24.75
Breakfast and brunch	40.38	40.44	49.66	40.37	53.58
Board (including at school)	**20.29**	**23.72**	**45.06**	**27.01**	**5.30**
Catered affairs	**22.44**	**27.01**	**53.46**	**17.28**	**15.63**
Food on out-of-town trips	**83.16**	**83.15**	**142.93**	**111.22**	**107.54**
School lunches	**21.50**	**25.87**	**30.10**	**24.73**	**3.87**
Meals as pay	**9.52**	**11.66**	**16.26**	**12.75**	**1.39**
ALCOHOLIC BEVERAGES	**111.21**	**119.59**	**148.47**	**102.60**	**107.96**
At home	**66.05**	**70.04**	**78.20**	**61.41**	**62.94**
Beer and ale	39.87	43.48	36.06	35.80	32.62
Whiskey	5.47	5.34	6.00	1.62	11.18
Wine	14.56	15.49	26.93	17.93	12.14
Other alcoholic beverages	6.14	5.73	9.21	6.06	6.99
Away from home	**45.16**	**49.54**	**70.27**	**41.19**	**45.02**
Beer and ale	15.42	17.69	22.01	11.43	12.43
Wine	6.32	6.83	9.64	5.94	6.69
Other alcoholic beverages	11.18	12.27	17.84	9.29	11.58
Alcoholic beverages purchased on trips	12.24	12.76	20.78	14.54	14.31

Note: Expenditures listed for items in a given category may not add to the total for that category because the listing is incomplete. (-) means insufficient data.

Occupation

indexed per capita spending

(indexed average annual per capita spending of consumer units on food and alcoholic beverages, by occupation of consumer unit reference person, 1994; index definition: an index of 100 is the per capita average for all consumer units; an index of 132 means that per capita spending by consumer units in the occupational group is 32 percent above the per capita average for all consumer units; an index of 68 indicates that per capita spending by consumer units in the occupational group is 32 percent below the per capita average for all consumer units)

	total consumer units	wage and salary workers		self employed	retired
		total	managers and professionals		
Per capita spending of cu, total	$12,700.25	$13,155.99	$18,171.44	$14,548.12	$12,998.74
Per capita spending of cu, index	100	104	143	115	102
Food, per capita spending index	100	100	124	106	113
Alcoholic beverages, per capita spending index	100	108	134	92	97
FOOD AT HOME	**100**	**95**	**105**	**105**	**125**
Cereals and bakery products	**100**	**95**	**112**	**107**	**130**
Cereals and cereal products	100	96	112	104	120
Flour	100	94	90	102	111
Prepared flour mixes	100	94	109	102	147
Ready-to-eat and cooked cereals	100	96	116	99	126
Rice	100	94	99	127	90
Pasta, cornmeal, and other cereal products	100	99	113	108	108
Bakery products	100	94	112	109	136
Bread	100	92	98	109	139
White bread	100	92	90	101	129
Bread, other than white	100	93	105	118	149
Crackers and cookies	100	92	114	118	137
Cookies	100	91	114	121	136
Crackers	100	94	115	112	141
Frozen and refrigerated bakery products	100	100	126	88	125
Other bakery products	100	96	119	107	136
Biscuits and rolls	100	97	131	107	126
Cakes and cupcakes	100	96	108	111	128
Bread and cracker products	100	101	128	119	91
Sweetrolls, coffee cakes, doughnuts	100	91	116	100	171
Pies, tarts, turnovers	100	94	112	105	140
Meats, poultry, fish, and eggs	**100**	**96**	**95**	**103**	**117**
Beef	100	98	89	94	108
Ground beef	100	98	86	93	110
Roast	100	96	79	91	121
Chuck roast	100	92	76	93	134
Round roast	100	96	73	98	125
Other roast	100	101	90	79	102
Steak	100	98	94	102	98
Round steak	100	98	77	111	81
Sirloin steak	100	97	96	95	119
Other steak	100	99	100	103	92
Other beef	100	97	101	67	127
Pork	100	94	86	99	126
Bacon	100	89	80	101	155
Pork chops	100	96	93	96	99

	total consumer units	wage and salary workers		self employed	retired
		total	managers and professionals		
Ham	100	90	87	110	154
Ham, not canned	100	91	89	106	148
Canned ham	100	70	54	166	241
Sausage	100	96	86	72	114
Other pork	100	96	84	106	115
Other meats	100	94	97	112	135
Frankfurters	100	94	85	118	127
Lunch meats (cold cuts)	100	96	97	108	136
Bologna, liverwurst, salami	100	94	80	108	139
Other lunchmeats	100	97	107	108	135
Lamb, organ meats and others	100	88	118	130	137
Lamb and organ meats	100	88	121	133	140
Mutton, goat and game	100	103	-	-	-
Poultry	100	96	105	107	108
Fresh and frozen chickens	100	97	104	115	103
Fresh and frozen whole chicken	100	90	93	135	106
Fresh and frozen chicken parts	100	99	108	107	101
Other poultry	100	95	108	77	127
Fish and seafood	100	95	110	113	112
Canned fish and seafood	100	94	113	103	132
Fresh fish and shellfish	100	95	109	110	99
Frozen fish and shellfish	100	95	109	126	126
Eggs	100	93	84	104	132
Dairy products	**100**	**95**	**107**	**103**	**134**
Fresh milk and cream	100	94	98	96	134
Fresh milk, all types	100	94	97	95	133
Cream	100	92	115	102	158
Other dairy products	100	95	113	108	134
Butter	100	98	97	99	108
Cheese	100	96	116	98	137
Ice cream and related products	100	94	108	119	140
Miscellaneous dairy products	100	93	125	133	128
Fruits and vegetables	**100**	**93**	**106**	**108**	**141**
Fresh fruits	100	93	109	116	141
Apples	100	98	118	126	108
Bananas	100	90	97	115	152
Oranges	100	100	118	106	109
Citrus fruits, excl. oranges	100	89	111	124	159
Other fresh fruits	100	92	108	113	158
Fresh vegetables	100	94	106	103	132
Potatoes	100	94	100	89	138
Lettuce	100	96	109	109	124
Tomatoes	100	95	96	100	129
Other fresh vegetables	100	93	112	107	133

	total consumer units	wage and salary workers		self employed	retired
		total	managers and professionals		
Processed fruits	100	92	106	115	149
Frozen fruits and fruit juices	100	95	116	144	123
Frozen orange juice	100	95	112	121	132
Frozen fruits	100	72	78	275	179
Frozen fruit juices	100	102	136	146	91
Canned fruit	100	84	94	103	213
Dried fruit	100	83	102	114	206
Fresh fruit juices	100	93	109	103	136
Canned and bottled fruit juices	100	93	105	112	134
Processed vegetables	100	92	102	93	144
Frozen vegetables	100	97	121	99	128
Canned and dried vegetables and juices	100	90	92	90	152
Canned beans	100	90	84	97	145
Canned corn	100	96	87	84	124
Other canned and dried vegetables	100	88	91	92	156
Frozen vegetable juices	100	105	180	128	45
Fresh and canned vegetable juices	100	93	109	76	177
Other food at home	**100**	**97**	**111**	**106**	**119**
Sugar and other sweets	100	94	107	106	136
Candy and chewing gum	100	99	118	99	125
Sugar	100	90	81	114	124
Artificial sweeteners	100	76	81	122	229
Jams, preserves, other sweets	100	88	100	115	163
Fats and oils	100	91	98	106	145
Margarine	100	81	86	106	215
Fats and oils	100	90	88	103	131
Salad dressings	100	99	106	102	120
Nondairy cream and imitation milk	100	93	116	84	148
Peanut butter	100	90	105	130	134
Miscellaneous foods	100	99	114	103	110
Frozen prepared foods	100	99	117	103	126
Frozen meals	100	94	120	103	157
Other frozen prepared foods	100	101	116	103	111
Canned and packaged soups	100	94	117	95	135
Potato chips, nuts, and other snacks	100	103	125	108	105
Potato chips and other snacks	100	106	123	109	89
Nuts	100	91	131	104	166
Condiments and seasonings	100	96	112	119	109
Salt, spices and other seasonings	100	93	95	119	121
Olives, pickles, relishes	100	94	108	121	136
Sauces and gravies	100	100	120	111	92
Baking needs and misc. products	100	93	120	139	118
Other canned/packaged prepared foods	100	101	106	91	98
Prepared salads	100	97	127	100	148
Prepared desserts	100	90	103	100	178

	total consumer units	wage and salary workers		self employed	retired
		total	managers and professionals		
Baby food	100	104	108	104	37
Miscellaneous prepared foods	100	102	103	82	106
Nonalcoholic beverages	100	97	103	103	118
Cola	100	102	94	104	93
Other carbonated drinks	100	97	107	102	108
Coffee	100	86	102	105	172
Roasted coffee	100	90	109	103	154
Instant and freeze-dried coffee	100	77	87	108	211
Noncarb. fruit flavored drinks incl.					
non-frozen lemonade	100	101	106	100	103
Tea	100	99	118	117	121
Nonalcoholic beer	100	84	191	-	332
Other nonalcoholic beverages	100	97	121	96	137
Food prepared by cu on out-of-town trips	100	99	147	143	120
FOOD AWAY FROM HOME	**100**	**108**	**155**	**108**	**94**
Meals at restaurants, carry-outs, other	**100**	**107**	**146**	**103**	**96**
Lunch	100	109	151	107	87
Dinner	100	106	147	103	103
Snacks and nonalcoholic beverages	100	115	140	94	61
Breakfast and brunch	100	100	123	100	133
Board (including at school)	**100**	**117**	**222**	**133**	**26**
Catered affairs	**100**	**120**	**238**	**77**	**70**
Food on out-of-town trips	**100**	**100**	**172**	**134**	**129**
School lunches	**100**	**120**	**140**	**115**	**18**
Meals as pay	**100**	**123**	**171**	**134**	**15**
ALCOHOLIC BEVERAGES	**100**	**108**	**134**	**92**	**97**
At home	**100**	**106**	**118**	**93**	**95**
Beer and ale	100	109	90	90	82
Whiskey	100	98	110	30	204
Wine	100	106	185	123	83
Other alcoholic beverages	100	93	150	99	114
Away from home	**100**	**110**	**156**	**91**	**100**
Beer and ale	100	115	143	74	81
Wine	100	108	153	94	106
Other alcoholic beverages	100	110	160	83	104
Alcoholic beverages purchased on trips	100	104	170	119	117

Note: (-) means insufficient data.

(total annual spending on food and alcoholic beverages by occupational groups, 1994; numbers in thousands)

	total consumer units	wage and salary workers		self employed	retired
		total	managers and professionals		
Number of consumer units	102,210	66,675	20,700	6,343	18,387
Total spending of all cu's	$3,245,231,892	$2,368,374,010	$977,987,025	$258,380,392	$406,313,168
Food, total spending	450,799,249	318,045,751	118,079,838	33,276,900	62,451,446
Alcoholic beverages, total spending	28,417,446	21,528,024	7,990,614	1,822,280	3,374,750
FOOD AT HOME	**$277,198,631**	**$186,493,309**	**$61,559,523**	**$20,246,602**	**$42,527,660**
Cereals and bakery products	**43,815,383**	**29,304,996**	**10,354,761**	**3,250,280**	**6,982,463**
Cereals and cereal products	16,531,445	11,200,733	3,900,915	1,190,137	2,430,026
Flour	776,796	513,398	147,177	54,804	105,174
Prepared flour mixes	1,307,266	865,442	299,943	92,671	235,721
Ready-to-eat and cooked cereals	10,044,177	6,810,185	2,453,778	690,118	1,543,773
Rice	1,577,100	1,046,798	327,474	139,736	173,573
Pasta, cornmeal, and other cereal products	2,826,107	1,964,246	672,750	212,744	371,785
Bakery products	27,282,915	18,104,263	6,453,846	2,060,143	4,552,621
Bread	7,790,446	5,068,634	1,602,180	591,865	1,326,438
White bread	3,848,207	2,496,979	731,952	269,260	607,506
Bread, other than white	3,942,240	2,570,988	870,228	322,605	718,932
Crackers and cookies	6,394,258	4,151,852	1,540,494	523,678	1,075,456
Cookies	4,391,964	2,827,020	1,054,872	367,957	729,596
Crackers	2,002,294	1,324,832	485,622	155,721	345,859
Frozen and refrigerated bakery products	2,203,648	1,553,528	584,982	134,598	336,298
Other bakery products	10,894,564	7,330,916	2,725,983	810,001	1,814,245
Biscuits and rolls	3,675,472	2,515,648	1,016,577	273,256	566,871
Cakes and cupcakes	3,187,930	2,161,604	723,258	245,030	501,046
Bread and cracker products	482,431	342,710	129,789	39,961	53,506
Sweetrolls, coffee cakes, doughnuts	2,240,443	1,443,514	546,894	156,165	468,501
Pies, tarts, turnovers	1,308,288	866,775	309,465	95,652	224,321
Meats, poultry, fish, and eggs	**74,863,715**	**50,401,633**	**14,927,598**	**5,337,127**	**10,686,892**
Beef	23,177,140	15,951,327	4,340,376	1,522,193	3,072,284
Ground beef	9,040,475	6,222,111	1,635,507	585,903	1,218,690
Roast	4,028,096	2,730,341	671,922	253,657	595,003
Chuck roast	1,253,095	812,768	199,755	80,937	205,934
Round roast	1,516,796	1,020,794	233,496	103,518	232,412
Other roast	1,258,205	896,779	238,878	69,266	156,473
Steak	8,662,298	6,008,751	1,723,689	614,954	1,034,269
Round steak	1,635,360	1,133,475	263,925	126,162	161,070
Sirloin steak	2,498,012	1,710,214	505,701	165,489	362,408
Other steak	4,528,925	3,164,396	954,270	323,239	510,607
Other beef	1,446,272	990,124	309,051	67,743	224,321
Pork	15,918,185	10,493,978	2,895,930	1,090,615	2,453,745
Bacon	2,328,344	1,457,516	393,093	163,015	442,575
Pork chops	4,018,897	2,727,008	783,081	267,992	487,256

	total consumer units	wage and salary workers		self employed	retired
		total	managers and professionals		
Ham	$3,769,505	$2,384,965	$687,033	$289,177	$711,945
Ham, not canned	3,491,494	2,248,281	655,362	257,018	630,306
Canned ham	278,011	136,684	31,671	32,159	81,822
Sausage	2,332,432	1,576,864	420,831	116,013	324,531
Other pork	3,467,985	2,347,627	611,892	254,418	487,439
Other meats	9,602,630	6,390,132	1,961,325	748,601	1,580,730
Frankfurters	1,917,460	1,266,158	341,757	157,433	298,237
Lunch meats (cold cuts)	6,711,109	4,519,898	1,376,550	503,063	1,119,217
Bologna, liverwurst, salami	2,425,443	1,602,200	409,446	182,552	412,053
Other lunchmeats	4,285,665	2,917,698	967,104	320,512	707,164
Lamb, organ meats and others	974,061	604,076	243,018	88,104	163,093
Lamb and organ meats	955,664	590,741	243,018	88,104	163,093
Mutton, goat and game	18,398	13,335	-	-	-
Poultry	13,959,842	9,461,849	3,074,571	1,036,066	1,837,229
Fresh and frozen chickens	11,027,437	7,497,604	2,405,961	878,442	1,383,254
Fresh and frozen whole chicken	3,021,328	1,921,574	589,950	284,420	391,827
Fresh and frozen chicken parts	8,006,109	5,576,030	1,816,011	594,085	991,427
Other poultry	2,932,405	1,964,912	668,610	157,560	453,975
Fish and seafood	9,140,640	6,100,763	2,112,435	718,789	1,249,213
Canned fish and seafood	1,536,216	1,012,127	365,769	110,495	248,408
Fresh fish and shellfish	5,239,285	3,503,771	1,202,049	401,702	634,719
Frozen fish and shellfish	2,366,162	1,584,865	544,617	206,592	366,085
Eggs	3,066,300	2,002,917	542,961	220,863	493,507
Dairy products	**29,530,513**	**19,676,459**	**6,641,388**	**2,110,443**	**4,854,168**
Fresh milk and cream	12,993,957	8,617,744	2,691,828	864,043	2,135,282
Fresh milk, all types	12,156,857	8,077,010	2,489,796	804,419	1,973,293
Cream	837,100	540,734	202,032	59,624	161,989
Other dairy products	16,536,556	11,058,716	3,949,560	1,246,400	2,718,702
Butter	1,190,747	818,102	243,846	81,698	156,657
Cheese	8,363,844	5,649,373	2,042,469	568,143	1,396,860
Ice cream and related products	4,869,284	3,213,735	1,106,001	401,702	834,034
Miscellaneous dairy products	2,111,659	1,378,172	557,244	194,920	331,334
Fruits and vegetables	**44,621,820**	**29,236,988**	**9,981,126**	**3,337,496**	**7,677,492**
Fresh fruits	13,595,974	8,933,117	3,115,143	1,096,705	2,349,123
Apples	2,593,068	1,787,557	641,907	227,270	343,653
Bananas	3,031,549	1,922,240	616,446	242,112	564,665
Oranges	1,672,156	1,180,148	416,277	123,625	223,034
Citrus fruits, excl. oranges	1,120,222	700,754	262,269	96,414	217,886
Other fresh fruits	5,178,981	3,342,418	1,178,244	407,284	999,885
Fresh vegetables	13,787,107	9,135,809	3,092,580	983,102	2,233,101
Potatoes	2,862,902	1,888,903	605,268	177,477	481,739
Lettuce	1,776,410	1,207,484	406,962	134,028	268,634
Tomatoes	2,147,432	1,432,179	435,942	149,187	339,976
Other fresh vegetables	7,001,385	4,607,909	1,644,408	522,409	1,142,568

	total consumer units	wage and salary workers		self employed	retired
		total	managers and professionals		
Processed fruits	$9,513,707	$6,137,434	$2,121,750	$757,164	$1,737,020
Frozen fruits and fruit juices	1,663,979	1,116,806	407,376	166,440	251,166
Frozen orange juice	969,973	652,082	228,942	81,508	156,106
Frozen fruits	163,536	82,677	26,910	31,208	35,855
Frozen fruit juices	530,470	382,048	151,524	53,725	59,206
Canned fruit	1,454,448	862,108	288,972	103,898	378,588
Dried fruit	602,017	352,711	129,582	47,636	152,060
Fresh fruit juices	1,829,559	1,201,484	418,554	130,539	304,305
Canned and bottled fruit juices	3,963,704	2,604,326	877,266	308,650	650,716
Processed vegetables	7,724,010	5,030,629	1,651,860	500,463	1,358,248
Frozen vegetables	2,537,874	1,731,550	648,945	175,130	396,791
Canned and dried vegetables and juices	5,186,135	3,299,079	1,002,708	325,332	961,456
Canned beans	1,067,072	680,085	189,405	72,120	188,651
Canned corn	696,050	470,059	127,512	40,595	105,725
Other canned and dried vegetables	2,764,781	1,716,215	531,369	176,906	528,442
Frozen vegetable juices	23,508	17,336	8,901	2,093	1,287
Fresh and canned vegetable juices	634,724	416,052	145,521	33,618	137,351
Other food at home	**84,367,200**	**57,873,900**	**19,654,443**	**6,211,256**	**12,326,829**
Sugar and other sweets	10,757,603	7,153,561	2,424,798	791,226	1,786,297
Candy and chewing gum	6,369,727	4,427,887	1,587,276	440,204	971,937
Sugar	1,871,465	1,189,482	319,401	147,919	284,079
Artificial sweeteners	346,492	185,357	58,995	29,495	96,899
Jams, preserves, other sweets	2,169,918	1,350,836	459,126	173,608	433,198
Fats and oils	8,100,143	5,205,984	1,670,076	594,276	1,431,980
Margarine	1,447,294	822,103	261,648	106,309	379,875
Fats and oils	2,360,029	1,494,854	439,668	168,343	377,301
Salad dressings	2,427,488	1,687,544	539,442	172,530	356,892
Nondairy cream and imitation milk	670,498	440,055	164,358	39,136	121,354
Peanut butter	1,195,857	761,429	264,960	107,958	196,741
Miscellaneous foods	36,961,180	25,884,569	8,901,828	2,649,408	4,983,980
Frozen prepared foods	6,760,169	4,693,253	1,670,283	484,669	1,043,095
Frozen meals	2,190,360	1,456,182	554,760	156,418	421,982
Other frozen prepared foods	4,569,809	3,236,405	1,115,523	328,250	620,929
Canned and packaged soups	3,020,306	2,002,250	743,751	200,249	498,655
Potato chips, nuts, and other snacks	7,570,695	5,472,017	1,992,375	569,475	976,717
Potato chips and other snacks	5,946,578	4,426,553	1,543,392	452,446	647,039
Nuts	1,624,117	1,045,464	448,983	117,092	329,679
Condiments and seasonings	8,150,225	5,540,026	1,928,412	673,753	1,089,981
Salt, spices and other seasonings	1,972,653	1,292,828	395,163	163,079	291,802
Olives, pickles, relishes	1,038,454	688,753	235,773	87,153	172,654
Sauces and gravies	3,723,510	2,636,330	939,780	286,767	420,327
Baking needs and misc. products	1,415,609	922,782	357,696	136,755	205,199
Other canned/packaged prepared foods	11,459,785	8,176,355	2,567,007	721,199	1,375,715
Prepared salads	1,121,244	766,096	299,115	78,273	203,544
Prepared desserts	816,658	517,398	176,571	57,024	177,618

	total consumer units	wage and salary workers		self employed	retired
		total	managers and professionals		
Baby food	$2,873,123	$2,112,264	$655,569	$208,558	$131,467
Miscellaneous prepared foods	6,648,761	4,781,264	1,435,959	377,409	863,270
Nonalcoholic beverages	23,803,687	16,306,038	5,184,522	1,706,394	3,429,727
Cola	9,142,685	6,553,486	1,812,699	659,101	1,035,924
Other carbonated drinks	3,974,947	2,726,341	895,896	283,025	523,478
Coffee	4,396,052	2,648,331	945,576	319,307	925,418
Roasted coffee	2,977,377	1,879,568	685,170	212,364	559,700
Instant and freeze-dried coffee	1,418,675	768,763	260,406	106,943	365,717
Noncarb. fruit flavored drinks incl. non-frozen lemonade	2,234,311	1,582,198	497,007	154,959	281,321
Tea	1,660,913	1,160,812	413,172	134,979	246,202
Nonalcoholic beer	67,459	40,005	27,117	-	27,397
Other nonalcoholic beverages	2,327,322	1,594,866	593,055	155,086	389,988
Food prepared by cu on out-of-town trips	4,743,566	3,323,082	1,473,219	470,016	694,845
FOOD AWAY FROM HOME	**173,599,597**	**131,552,442**	**56,520,315**	**13,030,298**	**19,923,785**
Meals at restaurants, carry-outs, other	**133,507,724**	**100,692,585**	**41,030,919**	**9,602,921**	**15,743,869**
Lunch	46,174,390	35,397,758	14,656,635	3,420,399	4,888,184
Dinner	66,619,456	49,619,535	20,641,212	4,785,286	8,406,904
Snacks and nonalcoholic beverages	10,396,801	8,393,716	3,060,702	680,287	773,725
Breakfast and brunch	10,318,100	7,280,910	2,672,577	716,949	1,674,872
Board (including at school)	**5,184,091**	**4,270,534**	**2,425,005**	**479,658**	**165,667**
Catered affairs	**5,732,959**	**4,863,275**	**2,877,093**	**306,874**	**488,543**
Food on out-of-town trips	**21,248,437**	**14,969,204**	**7,692,327**	**1,975,274**	**3,361,511**
School lunches	**5,494,810**	**4,657,916**	**1,619,775**	**439,189**	**120,986**
Meals as pay	**2,431,576**	**2,099,596**	**875,196**	**226,382**	**43,393**
ALCOHOLIC BEVERAGES	**28,417,446**	**21,528,024**	**7,990,614**	**1,822,280**	**3,374,750**
At home	**16,877,937**	**12,608,909**	**4,208,724**	**1,090,679**	**1,967,409**
Beer and ale	10,188,293	7,826,978	1,940,832	635,822	1,019,743
Whiskey	1,398,233	960,787	322,920	28,734	349,537
Wine	3,721,466	2,789,015	1,449,207	318,482	379,324
Other alcoholic beverages	1,568,924	1,032,129	495,558	107,641	218,621
Away from home	**11,540,531**	**8,919,115**	**3,781,890**	**731,602**	**1,407,341**
Beer and ale	3,941,218	3,185,065	1,184,454	202,976	388,517
Wine	1,613,896	1,228,820	518,742	105,421	209,244
Other alcoholic beverages	2,857,792	2,208,276	960,273	164,918	362,040
Alcoholic beverages purchased on trips	3,128,648	2,296,287	1,118,628	258,287	447,356

Note: Spending for items in a given category may not add to the total for that category because the listing is incomplete. Numbers will not add to total because not all occupations are shown. (-) means insufficient data.

Occupation
market shares

(percent of total annual spending on food accounted for by occupational groups, 1994)

	total consumer units	wage and salary workers total	wage and salary workers managers and professionals	self employed	retired
Share of total consumer units	100.0%	65.2%	20.3%	6.2%	18.0%
Share of total spending	100.0	73.0	30.1	8.0	12.5
Share of food spending	100.0	70.6	26.2	7.4	13.9
Share of alcoholic beverages spending	100.0	75.8	28.1	6.4	11.9
FOOD AT HOME	100.0%	67.3%	22.2%	7.3%	15.3%
Cereals and bakery products	100.0	66.9	23.6	7.4	15.9
Cereals and cereal products	100.0	67.8	23.6	7.2	14.7
Flour	100.0	66.1	18.9	7.1	13.5
Prepared flour mixes	100.0	66.2	22.9	7.1	18.0
Ready-to-eat and cooked cereals	100.0	67.8	24.4	6.9	15.4
Rice	100.0	66.4	20.8	8.9	11.0
Pasta, cornmeal, and other cereal products	100.0	69.5	23.8	7.5	13.2
Bakery products	100.0	66.4	23.7	7.6	16.7
Bread	100.0	65.1	20.6	7.6	17.0
White bread	100.0	64.9	19.0	7.0	15.8
Bread, other than white	100.0	65.2	22.1	8.2	18.2
Crackers and cookies	100.0	64.9	24.1	8.2	16.8
Cookies	100.0	64.4	24.0	8.4	16.6
Crackers	100.0	66.2	24.3	7.8	17.3
Frozen and refrigerated bakery products	100.0	70.5	26.5	6.1	15.3
Other bakery products	100.0	67.3	25.0	7.4	16.7
Biscuits and rolls	100.0	68.4	27.7	7.4	15.4
Cakes and cupcakes	100.0	67.8	22.7	7.7	15.7
Bread and cracker products	100.0	71.0	26.9	8.3	11.1
Sweetrolls, coffee cakes, doughnuts	100.0	64.4	24.4	7.0	20.9
Pies, tarts, turnovers	100.0	66.3	23.7	7.3	17.1
Meats, poultry, fish, and eggs	100.0	67.3	19.9	7.1	14.3
Beef	100.0	68.8	18.7	6.6	13.3
Ground beef	100.0	68.8	18.1	6.5	13.5
Roast	100.0	67.8	16.7	6.3	14.8
Chuck roast	100.0	64.9	15.9	6.5	16.4
Round roast	100.0	67.3	15.4	6.8	15.3
Other roast	100.0	71.3	19.0	5.5	12.4
Steak	100.0	69.4	19.9	7.1	11.9
Round steak	100.0	69.3	16.1	7.7	9.8
Sirloin steak	100.0	68.5	20.2	6.6	14.5
Other steak	100.0	69.9	21.1	7.1	11.3
Other beef	100.0	68.5	21.4	4.7	15.5
Pork	100.0	65.9	18.2	6.9	15.4
Bacon	100.0	62.6	16.9	7.0	19.0
Pork chops	100.0	67.9	19.5	6.7	12.1

	total consumer units	wage and salary workers		self employed	retired
		total	managers and professionals		
Ham	100.0%	63.3%	18.2%	7.7%	18.9%
Ham, not canned	100.0	64.4	18.8	7.4	18.1
Canned ham	100.0	49.2	11.4	11.6	29.4
Sausage	100.0	67.6	18.0	5.0	13.9
Other pork	100.0	67.7	17.6	7.3	14.1
Other meats	100.0	66.5	20.4	7.8	16.5
Frankfurters	100.0	66.0	17.8	8.2	15.6
Lunch meats (cold cuts)	100.0	67.3	20.5	7.5	16.7
Bologna, liverwurst, salami	100.0	66.1	16.9	7.5	17.0
Other lunchmeats	100.0	68.1	22.6	7.5	16.5
Lamb, organ meats and others	100.0	62.0	24.9	9.0	16.7
Lamb and organ meats	100.0	61.8	25.4	9.2	17.1
Mutton, goat and game	100.0	72.5	-	-	-
Poultry	100.0	67.8	22.0	7.4	13.2
Fresh and frozen chickens	100.0	68.0	21.8	8.0	12.5
Fresh and frozen whole chicken	100.0	63.6	19.5	9.4	13.0
Fresh and frozen chicken parts	100.0	69.6	22.7	7.4	12.4
Other poultry	100.0	67.0	22.8	5.4	15.5
Fish and seafood	100.0	66.7	23.1	7.9	13.7
Canned fish and seafood	100.0	65.9	23.8	7.2	16.2
Fresh fish and shellfish	100.0	66.9	22.9	7.7	12.1
Frozen fish and shellfish	100.0	67.0	23.0	8.7	15.5
Eggs	100.0	65.3	17.7	7.2	16.1
Dairy products	**100.0**	**66.6**	**22.5**	**7.1**	**16.4**
Fresh milk and cream	100.0	66.3	20.7	6.6	16.4
Fresh milk, all types	100.0	66.4	20.5	6.6	16.2
Cream	100.0	64.6	24.1	7.1	19.4
Other dairy products	100.0	66.9	23.9	7.5	16.4
Butter	100.0	68.7	20.5	6.9	13.2
Cheese	100.0	67.5	24.4	6.8	16.7
Ice cream and related products	100.0	66.0	22.7	8.2	17.1
Miscellaneous dairy products	100.0	65.3	26.4	9.2	15.7
Fruits and vegetables	**100.0**	**65.5**	**22.4**	**7.5**	**17.2**
Fresh fruits	100.0	65.7	22.9	8.1	17.3
Apples	100.0	68.9	24.8	8.8	13.3
Bananas	100.0	63.4	20.3	8.0	18.6
Oranges	100.0	70.6	24.9	7.4	13.3
Citrus fruits, excl. oranges	100.0	62.6	23.4	8.6	19.5
Other fresh fruits	100.0	64.5	22.8	7.9	19.3
Fresh vegetables	100.0	66.3	22.4	7.1	16.2
Potatoes	100.0	66.0	21.1	6.2	16.8
Lettuce	100.0	68.0	22.9	7.5	15.1
Tomatoes	100.0	66.7	20.3	6.9	15.8
Other fresh vegetables	100.0	65.8	23.5	7.5	16.3

	total consumer units	wage and salary workers		self employed	retired
		total	managers and professionals		
Processed fruits	100.0%	64.5%	22.3%	8.0%	18.3%
Frozen fruits and fruit juices	100.0	67.1	24.5	10.0	15.1
Frozen orange juice	100.0	67.2	23.6	8.4	16.1
Frozen fruits	100.0	50.6	16.5	19.1	21.9
Frozen fruit juices	100.0	72.0	28.6	10.1	11.2
Canned fruit	100.0	59.3	19.9	7.1	26.0
Dried fruit	100.0	58.6	21.5	7.9	25.3
Fresh fruit juices	100.0	65.7	22.9	7.1	16.6
Canned and bottled fruit juices	100.0	65.7	22.1	7.8	16.4
Processed vegetables	100.0	65.1	21.4	6.5	17.6
Frozen vegetables	100.0	68.2	25.6	6.9	15.6
Canned and dried vegetables and juices	100.0	63.6	19.3	6.3	18.5
Canned beans	100.0	63.7	17.7	6.8	17.7
Canned corn	100.0	67.5	18.3	5.8	15.2
Other canned and dried vegetables	100.0	62.1	19.2	6.4	19.1
Frozen vegetable juices	100.0	73.7	37.9	8.9	5.5
Fresh and canned vegetable juices	100.0	65.5	22.9	5.3	21.6
Other food at home	**100.0**	**68.6**	**23.3**	**7.4**	**14.6**
Sugar and other sweets	100.0	66.5	22.5	7.4	16.6
Candy and chewing gum	100.0	69.5	24.9	6.9	15.3
Sugar	100.0	63.6	17.1	7.9	15.2
Artificial sweeteners	100.0	53.5	17.0	8.5	28.0
Jams, preserves, other sweets	100.0	62.3	21.2	8.0	20.0
Fats and oils	100.0	64.3	20.6	7.3	17.7
Margarine	100.0	56.8	18.1	7.3	26.2
Fats and oils	100.0	63.3	18.6	7.1	16.0
Salad dressings	100.0	69.5	22.2	7.1	14.7
Nondairy cream and imitation milk	100.0	65.6	24.5	5.8	18.1
Peanut butter	100.0	63.7	22.2	9.0	16.5
Miscellaneous foods	100.0	70.0	24.1	7.2	13.5
Frozen prepared foods	100.0	69.4	24.7	7.2	15.4
Frozen meals	100.0	66.5	25.3	7.1	19.3
Other frozen prepared foods	100.0	70.8	24.4	7.2	13.6
Canned and packaged soups	100.0	66.3	24.6	6.6	16.5
Potato chips, nuts, and other snacks	100.0	72.3	26.3	7.5	12.9
Potato chips and other snacks	100.0	74.4	26.0	7.6	10.9
Nuts	100.0	64.4	27.6	7.2	20.3
Condiments and seasonings	100.0	68.0	23.7	8.3	13.4
Salt, spices and other seasonings	100.0	65.5	20.0	8.3	14.8
Olives, pickles, relishes	100.0	66.3	22.7	8.4	16.6
Sauces and gravies	100.0	70.8	25.2	7.7	11.3
Baking needs and misc. products	100.0	65.2	25.3	9.7	14.5
Other canned/packaged prepared foods	100.0	71.3	22.4	6.3	12.0
Prepared salads	100.0	68.3	26.7	7.0	18.2
Prepared desserts	100.0	63.4	21.6	7.0	21.7

	total consumer units	wage and salary workers		self employed	retired
		total	managers and professionals		
Baby food	100.0%	73.5%	22.8%	7.3%	4.6%
Miscellaneous prepared foods	100.0	71.9	21.6	5.7	13.0
Nonalcoholic beverages	100.0	68.5	21.8	7.2	14.4
Cola	100.0	71.7	19.8	7.2	11.3
Other carbonated drinks	100.0	68.6	22.5	7.1	13.2
Coffee	100.0	60.2	21.5	7.3	21.1
Roasted coffee	100.0	63.1	23.0	7.1	18.8
Instant and freeze-dried coffee	100.0	54.2	18.4	7.5	25.8
Noncarb. fruit flavored drinks incl. non-frozen lemonade	100.0	70.8	22.2	6.9	12.6
Tea	100.0	69.9	24.9	8.1	14.8
Nonalcoholic beer	100.0	59.3	40.2	-	40.6
Other nonalcoholic beverages	100.0	68.5	25.5	6.7	16.8
Food prepared by cu on out-of-town trips	100.0	70.1	31.1	9.9	14.6
FOOD AWAY FROM HOME	**100.0**	**75.8**	**32.6**	**7.5**	**11.5**
Meals at restaurants, carry-outs, other	**100.0**	**75.4**	**30.7**	**7.2**	**11.8**
Lunch	100.0	76.7	31.7	7.4	10.6
Dinner	100.0	74.5	31.0	7.2	12.6
Snacks and nonalcoholic beverages	100.0	80.7	29.4	6.5	7.4
Breakfast and brunch	100.0	70.6	25.9	6.9	16.2
Board (including at school)	**100.0**	**82.4**	**46.8**	**9.3**	**3.2**
Catered affairs	**100.0**	**84.8**	**50.2**	**5.4**	**8.5**
Food on out-of-town trips	**100.0**	**70.4**	**36.2**	**9.3**	**15.8**
School lunches	**100.0**	**84.8**	**29.5**	**8.0**	**2.2**
Meals as pay	**100.0**	**86.3**	**36.0**	**9.3**	**1.8**
ALCOHOLIC BEVERAGES	**100.0**	**75.8**	**28.1**	**6.4**	**11.9**
At home	**100.0**	**74.7**	**24.9**	**6.5**	**11.7**
Beer and ale	100.0	76.8	19.0	6.2	10.0
Whiskey	100.0	68.7	23.1	2.1	25.0
Wine	100.0	74.9	38.9	8.6	10.2
Other alcoholic beverages	100.0	65.8	31.6	6.9	13.9
Away from home	**100.0**	**77.3**	**32.8**	**6.3**	**12.2**
Beer and ale	100.0	80.8	30.1	5.2	9.9
Wine	100.0	76.1	32.1	6.5	13.0
Other alcoholic beverages	100.0	77.3	33.6	5.8	12.7
Alcoholic beverages purchased on trips	100.0	73.4	35.8	8.3	14.3

Note: Numbers will not add to total because not all occupations are shown. (-) means insufficient data.

Appendix

History and Description of the Consumer Expenditure Survey

History

The Consumer Expenditure Survey (CEX) is an ongoing study of the day-to-day spending of American households. In taking the survey, government interviewers collect spending data on products and services as well as the amount and sources of household income, changes in saving and debt, and demographic and economic characteristics of household members. Data collection for the CEX is done by the Bureau of the Census, under contract with the Bureau of Labor Statistics (BLS). The BLS is responsible for analysis and publication of the survey.

Expenditure surveys are not new. Since the late 19th century, they have been conducted about every ten years by the federal government. Although the results have been used for a variety of purposes, their primary application is to track consumer prices. Beginning in 1980, the CEX became a continuous survey with annual publication of the data (with a lag-time between data collection and data publication of about two years.) The survey is still used to update prices for the market basket of products and services used in calculating the Consumer Price Index.

Description

The CEX is actually two surveys: an interview survey and a diary survey. In the interview portion of the survey, respondents are asked to report their expenditures for the previous three-month period each quarter for five consecutive quarters. The purchase of big-ticket items such as houses, cars, and major appliances, or recurring expenses such as insurance premiums, utility payments, and rent are recorded by the interview survey. About 95 percent of all expenditures are covered by the interview component.

Expenditures on small, frequently purchased items are recorded during a two-week period for the diary survey. These detailed records include expenses for food and beverages at home and in eating places, and other items such as tobacco, housekeeping supplies, non-prescription drugs, and personal-care products and services. The diary survey is intended to capture expenditures that respondents are likely to forget or recall incorrectly over longer periods of time.

Data Collection and Processing

Two separate nationally representative samples are used for the interview and diary surveys. For the interview survey, about 5,000 consumer units are interviewed on a rotating panel basis each quarter for five consecutive quarters. Another 5,000 consumer units keep weekly diaries of spending for two consecutive weeks. The 10,000 diaries accumulated in a survey year are the basis for the diary survey. Data collection is carried out in 101 areas of the country.

The data are reviewed, audited, and cleaned up by the BLS, and then weighted to reflect the number and characteristics of all U.S. consumer units. CEX data are available from the BLS in the form of news releases, bulletins, analytical papers, public-use tapes, and diskettes. Technical supplements such as standard error tables are also available.

As with any sample survey, the CEX is subject to two major types of error. Non-sampling error occurs when respondents misinterpret questions or interviewers are inconsistent. Respondents may forget items, recall expenses incorrectly, or deliberately give wrong answers. A respondent may remember what he or she spent on a big grocery shopping trip but forget the items picked up at a local convenience store. Most surveys of alcohol consumption or spending on alcohol suffer from this type of underreporting, for example. Non-sampling error can also be caused by mistakes during the various stages of data processing and refinement.

Sampling error occurs when a sample does not accurately represent the population it is supposed to represent. This kind of error is present in every sample-based survey and is minimized by using a proper sampling procedure. As previously mentioned, standard error tables that document the extent of sampling error in the CEX are available from the BLS.

Although the CEX is the best source of information about the spending behavior of American households, it should be treated with caution because of the above factors. Comparisons with consumption data from other sources show that CEX data tend to underestimate expenditures except for rent, fuel, telephone service, furniture, transportation, and personal care services. Nevertheless, the data do reveal important patterns of spending by demographic segment that can be used by businesses to better market their products and services.

Sampling Unit: The Consumer Unit

The CEX uses "consumer units" as its sampling unit instead of households, which are used by the Census Bureau. The term "household" is used throughout this book for convenience, although they are not exactly the same. There may, for example, be more than one consumer unit in a household.

Consumer units are defined by the BLS as either: 1) members of a household who are related by blood, marriage, adoption, or other legal arrangements; 2) a person living alone or sharing a household with others or living as a roomer in a private home or lodging house or in permanent living quarters in a hotel or motel, but who is financially independent; or 3) two persons or more living together who pool their income to make joint expenditure decisions. The BLS defines financial independence in terms of "the three major expenses categories: housing, food, and other living expenses. To be considered financially independent, at least two of the three major expense categories have to be provided by the respondent."

The Census Bureau uses households as its sampling unit in the decennial census and in the monthly Current Population Survey. The Census Bureau's household "consists of all persons who occupy a housing unit. A house, an apartment or other groups of rooms, or a single room is regarded as a housing unit when it is occupied or intended for occupancy as separate living quarters; that is, when the occupants do not live and eat with any other persons in the structure and there is direct access from the outside or through a common hall."

The definition goes on to specify that "a household includes the related family members and all the unrelated persons, if any, such as lodgers, foster children, wards, or employees who share the housing unit. A person living alone in a housing unit or a group of unrelated persons sharing a housing unit as partners is also counted as a household. The count of households excludes group quarters."

Because there can be more than one consumer unit in a household, consumer units outnumber households by several million. Most of the excess consumer units are headed by young adults, under age 25. Because a significant proportion of households headed by people under age 25 contain more than one consumer unit, the average spending of households headed by people under age 25 is significantly greater than the average spending of consumer units headed by young adults.

Glossary

The following definitions are taken from the Consumer Expenditure Survey. For more information, call the Consumer Expenditure Survey specialists at the Bureau of Labor Statistics, telephone (202) 606-6900.

adjusted for inflation Income or a change in income that has been adjusted for the rise in the cost of living, or the consumer price index (CPI-U-X1). In the income tables in this book, income for years prior to 1993 are adjusted using the CPI-U-X1 and expressed in 1993 dollars.

central cities The largest city in a metropolitan area is called the central city. The balance of the metropolitan area outside the central city is regarded as the "suburbs."

consumer unit For convenience, consumer units are sometimes called households in this book, although consumer units are somewhat different from the Census Bureau's households. Consumer units are all related members of a household, or financially independent members of a household. A household may include more than one consumer unit.

dual-earner couples A married couple in which both the householder and the householder's spouse are in the labor force. Also called two-income couples.

earnings One type of income. *See also* income.

employed All civilians who did any work as a paid employee or farmer/self-employed worker, or who worked 15 hours or more as an unpaid farm worker or in a family-owned business during the reference period. All those who have jobs but who are temporarily absent from their jobs due to illness, bad weather, vacation, labor management disputes, or personal reasons are considered employed.

expenditure The transaction cost including excise and sales taxes of goods and services acquired during the survey period. The full cost of each purchase is recorded even though full payment may not have been made at the date of purchase. Expenditure estimates include money spent on gifts for others.

family A group of two or more people (one of whom is the householder) related by birth, marriage, or adoption and living together in the same household.

family household A household maintained by a householder who lives with one or more people related to him or her by blood, marriage, or adoption.

female/male householder A woman or man who maintains a household without a spouse present. May head family or nonfamily households.

full-time, year-round Fifty or more weeks of full-time employment during the previous calendar year.

geographic regions The four major regions and nine census divisions of the United States are grouped as shown below:
Northeast:
—New England: Connecticut, Maine, Massachusetts, New Hampshire, Rhode Island, and Vermont
—Middle Atlantic: New Jersey, New York, and Pennsylvania
Midwest:
—East North Central: Illinois, Indiana, Michigan, Ohio, and Wisconsin
—West North Central: Iowa, Kansas, Minnesota, Missouri, Nebraska, North Dakota, and South Dakota
South:
—East South Central: Alabama, Kentucky, Mississippi, and Tennessee
—South Atlantic: Delaware, District of Columbia, Florida, Georgia, Maryland, North Carolina, South Carolina, Virginia, and West Virginia
West:
—Mountain: Arizona, Colorado, Idaho, Montana, Nevada, New Mexico, Utah, and Wyoming
—Pacific: Alaska, California, Hawaii, Oregon, and Washington
—West South Central: Arkansas, Louisiana, Oklahoma, and Texas

Hispanic Persons or householders who identify their origin as Mexican, Puerto Rican, Central or South American, or some other Hispanic origin. Unless otherwise noted, persons of Hispanic origin may be of any race. In other words, there are black Hispanics, white Hispanics, and Asian Hispanics.

home workers Workers who perform work in their own homes for which they are compensated by an employer or through self-employment earnings.

household All the persons who occupy a housing unit. A household includes the related family members and all the unrelated persons, if any, such as lodgers, foster children, wards, or employees who share the housing unit. A person living alone is counted as a household. A group of unrelated people who share a housing unit as roommates or unmarried partners is also counted as a household. Households do not include group quarters such as college dormitories, prisons, or nursing homes.

household, race/ethnicity of Households are categorized according to the race or ethnicity of the householder only.

householder The householder is the person (or one of the persons) in whose name the housing unit is owned or rented or, if there is no such person, any adult member. With married couples, the householder may be either the husband or wife. The householder is the reference person for the household.

householder, age of The age of the householder is used to categorize households into age groups such as those used in this book. Married couples, for example, are classified according to the age of either the husband or wife, depending on which one identified him or herself as the householder.

income Money received in the preceding calendar year by each person aged 15 or older from each of the following sources: (1) earnings from longest job (or self-employment); (2) earnings from jobs other than longest job; (3) unemployment compensation; (4) workers' compensation; (5) Social Security; (6) Supplemental Security Income; (7) public assistance; (8) veterans' payments; (9) survivor benefits; (10) disability benefits; (11) retirement pensions; (12) interest; (13) dividends; (14) rents and royalties or estates and trusts; (15) educational assistance; (16) alimony; (17) child support; (18) financial assistance from outside the household, and other periodic income. Income is reported in several ways in this book. Household income is the combined income of all household members. Income of persons is all income accruing to a person from all sources. Earnings is the amount of money a person received from his or her job.

income fifths or quintiles Where the total number of households or persons are divided into fifths based on household or personal income. One-fifth of households or persons fall into the lowest income quintile, one-fifth into the second income quintile, and so on. This is a useful way to compare the characteristics of low-, middle-, and high-income households.

job tenure The length of time a person has been employed continuously by the same employer.

labor force The labor force tables in this book are based on the civilian labor force, which includes all employed or unemployed civilians.

labor force participation rate The percent of the population in the labor force. Labor force participation rates in this book are based on the civilian labor force and civilian population. Labor force participation rates are also shown for sex–age groups and other special populations such as mothers of children of a given age.

married couples with or without children under age 18 Refers to married couples with or without children under age 18 living in the same household. Couples without children under age 18 may be parents of grown children who live elsewhere or childless couples.

median The amount that divides the population or households into two equal halves; one below and one above the median. Medians can be calculated for income, age, and many other characteristics.

median income The amount that divides the income distribution into two equal groups, half having incomes above the median, half having incomes below the median. The medians for households or families are based on all households or families. The medians for persons are based on all persons aged 15 or older with income.

metropolitan area An area qualifies for recognition as a metropolitan area if (1) it includes a city of at least 50,000 population, or (2) it includes a Census Bureau-defined urbanized area of at least 50,000 with a total metropolitan population of at least 100,000 (75,000 in New England). In addition to the county containing the main city or urbanized area, a metropolitan area may include other counties having strong commuting ties to the central county.

nonfamily household A household maintained by a householder who lives alone or who lives with people to whom he or she is not related.

nonfamily householder A householder who lives alone or with nonrelatives only.

nonmetropolitan area Counties that are not classified as metropolitan areas.

occupation Occupational classification is based on the kind of work a person did at his or her job during the previous calendar year. For persons who changed jobs during the year, the data refer to the occupation of the job held the longest during that year.

occupational tenure The length of time a person has been employed in the same occupation, regardless of who they are employed by.

outside central city The portion of a metropolitan county or counties that falls outside of the central city or cities; generally regarded as the suburbs.

own children Sons, daughters, stepchildren, and adopted children of the householder, including never-married children living away from home in college dormitories.

part-time or full-time employment Part-time is less than 35 hours of work per week in a majority of the weeks worked during the year. Full-time is 35 or more hours of work per week during a majority of the weeks worked.

percent change The change (either positive or negative) in a measure that is expressed as a proportion of the starting measure. When median income changes from $20,000 to $25,000, for example, this is a 25 percent increase.

percentage point change The change (either positive or negative) in a value that is already expressed as a percentage. When a labor force participation rate changes from 70 percent to 75 percent, for example, this is a 5 percentage point increase.

poverty level The official income threshold below which families and persons are classified as living in poverty. The threshold rises each year with inflation and varies depending on family size and age of householder. In 1993, the poverty threshold for one person under age 65 was $7,518. The threshold for a family of four was $14,763.

proportion or share The value of a part expressed as a percentage of the whole. If there are a total of 4 million people and 3 million are white, then the white proportion is 75 percent.

race Race is self-reported and usually appears in three categories in this book: white, black, or Asian. A household is assigned the race of the householder.

rounding Percentages are rounded to the nearest tenth of a percent; therefore, the percentages in a distribution do not always add exactly to 100.0 percent. The totals, however, are always shown as 100.0. Moreover, individual figures are rounded to the nearest thousand without being adjusted to group totals, which are independently rounded; percentages are based on the unrounded numbers.

self employment A person is categorized as self-employed in this book if he or she was self-employed in the job held longest during the reference period. Persons who report self-employment from a second job are excluded, but those who report wage and salary income from a second job are included. Unpaid workers in family businesses are excluded. Self-employment statistics in this book include only nonagricultural workers and exclude people who work for themselves in an incorporated business.

suburbs See outside central city.

sex ratio The number of men per 100 women.

tenure A housing unit is "owner occupied" if the owner lives in the unit, even if it is mortgaged or not fully paid for. A cooperative or condominium unit is "owner occupied" only if the owner lives in it. All other occupied units are classified as "renter occupied."

unemployed Unemployed persons are those who, during the survey period, had no employment but were available and looking for work. Those who were laid off from their jobs and were waiting to be recalled are also classified as unemployed.

Index

About the Author

Marcia Mogelonsky is a consumer trend writer, speaker and consultant. An award-winning journalist, she is the author of *Everybody Eats: Supermarket Consumers in the 1990s* (American Demographics Books, 1995 and 1996). She has also ghost-written and edited more than a dozen books, including general titles on demographics and business management and texts on the retail food and restaurant industries. Dr. Mogelonsky is a contributing editor to *American Demographics* magazine, which features her monthly column on shopping trends and purchase patterns. The subjects she covers range from running shoes, greeting cards and beer to toys, the Internet and batteries. Her work has also appeared in numerous trade and consumer publications, including *National Business Employment Weekly*, *Wall Street Journal (College Edition)*, *The Food Channel*, *Confectioner*, *Truck Accessory News*, *Ad Hoc*, *The Numbers News*, *Marketing Tools*, *Magazine Retailer* (contributing editor), *The Dallas Morning News*, *The Packer*, and *Modern Woman*.

Dr. Mogelonsky has been an active participant in ideation and new product development sessions for Frigidaire Appliances, Whirlpool Appliances, Eastman Kodak Company, Thomas J. Lipton, M&M/Mars, and other corporations. She has consulted for a number of clients, including HealthFocus, Market Segment Research, *Eating Well* magazine, Innovation Focus, the Food Marketing Institute, and Frito Lay, providing expertise on demographic and lifestyle trends. She was the keynote speaker at the National Broiler Council's 1996 marketing seminar and has been a featured speaker at the American Meat Institute's International Conference, ACNielsen's Food Marketing Institute presentation series and the Empire State Food and Agricultural Leadership Institute. She has also addressed marketing divisions at a number of corporations, including Ocean Spray and Unilever.

Dr. Mogelonsky has a B.A. from McGill University and a Ph.D. from Cornell University. She currently lives in Ithaca, New York, with her husband and two children.

Target American Consumers
with these highly acclaimed books by
demographic and industry experts

Who We Are

The Official Guide to
the American Marketplace, 2nd ed.

An in-depth look at the trends that define who we are as consumers—our education, health, incomes, occupations, living arrangements, racial and ethnic makeup, spending patterns, and wealth.
(ISBN 0-9628092-4-1; Jan. 1995)   **$79.95**

The Official Guide to
Racial & Ethnic Diversity

An in-depth guide to the demographics and spending patterns of Asians, blacks, Hispanics, Native Americans, and whites, including ethnic groups among Asians and Hispanics.
(ISBN 1-885070-03-9; April 1996)   **$89.95**

How We Differ by Age

The Official Guide to
the Generations

by Susan Mitchell

The demographics and spending patterns of adult consumers—Generation X, born 1965-76; the Baby Boom, born 1946-64; the Swing Generation, born 1933-45; and the World War II Generation, born before 1933.
(ISBN 0-9628092-8-4; May 1995)   **$69.95**

Wise Up to Teens
Insights Into Marketing & Advertising to Teenagers

by Peter Zollo

A ground-breaking book that gives you an in-depth look at teen lifestyles and values, where teens get their money, how and why they spend it, and proven, hands-on techniques that you can use to research and advertise to teens.
(ISBN 0-9628092-9-2;Oct. 1995)
                                                    $34.95

How We Live
THE MID-YOUTH MARKET

by Cheryl Russell

The author, a nationally recognized expert on the baby boom, examines the demographics and spending patterns of that generation,

which spends more than any other age group.
(ISBN 1-885070-06-3; Oct. 1996)   **$69.95**

How Much We Earn

The Official Guide to
American Incomes

(Selected as a Best Reference Source by Library Journal)

A storehouse of information on income trends, household and personal income, discretionary income, household income projections, spending and wealth data, and poverty trends.
(ISBN 1-885070-00-4; Nov. 1996)   **$89.95**

What We Spend It On

The Official Guide to
Household Spending, 3rd ed.

(formerly Consumer Power: How Americans Spend Their Money)

Who buys? What do they buy? How much do they spend? Here are detailed spending data on almost 1,000 products, broken out by scores of demographic variables.
(ISBN 1-885070-01-2; Oct. 1995)   **$89.95**

Who's Buying
FOOD & DRINK

by Marcia Mogelonsky

The source of data on who spends how much on food and alcohol consumed at home and away from home—the variables include age, income, household type, region, race and Hispanic origin, education, number of earners in household, and occupation.
(ISBN 1-885070-0407; Oct. 1996)   **$69.95**

Who's Buying
FOR THE HOME

by Alison Stein Wellner

Who spends how much on products and services for the home—the variables are the same as for *Who's Buying Food & Drink*, and the subjects include maintenance and repairs, utilities, fuels, public services, household services and supplies, furniture, and appliances.
(ISBN 1-885070-05-5; Oct. 1996)   **$89.95**

Kresge Business
Administration Library
Stacks
HC110.C6 M72
Mogelonsky, Marcia K